· PEOPLE, PLANS, AND POLICIES ·

D0906034

THE COLUMBIA HISTORY OF URBAN LIFE
KENNETH T. JACKSON, GENERAL EDITOR

· HERBERT J. GANS ·

PEOPLE, PLANS, AND POLICIES

Essays on Poverty, Racism, and Other National Urban Problems

COLUMBIA UNIVERSITY PRESS
RUSSELL SAGE FOUNDATION

NEW YORK

COLUMBIA UNIVERSITY PRESS
NEW YORK CHICHESTER, WEST SUSSEX

Copyright © 1993 Herbert J. Gans
Copyright © 1991 Herbert J. Gans
Library of Congress Cataloging-in-Publication Data

Gans, Herbert J.
People, plans, and policies : essays on poverty, racism, and other
national urban problems / Herbert J. Gans.
p. cm. — (Columbia history of urban life)
Includes bibliographical references and index.
ISBN 0-231-07402-6
ISBN 0-231-07403-4 (pbk.)
1. City planning—United States. 2. United States—Social policy.
3. Urban poor—United States. 4. United States—Race relations.
I. Title. II. Series.
HT167.G36 1991
307.76′0973—dc20   90-23224
                                                              CIP

Printed in the United States of America
c 10 9 8 7 6 5 4 3 2 1
p 10 9 8 7 6 5 4 3 2 1

This book is dedicated to the memory of three colleagues:
Paul Davidoff, the planner and lawyer;
Michael Harrington, the political leader and author;
and Robert Lekachman, the economist and writer.
Over the years, I worked, discussed, and at times
disagreed with them—but I always learned from them.
I miss them all!

· C O N T E N T S ·

· P R E F A C E ·

THIS IS A book of essays about how to think about national problems —often wrongly thought to be only urban—for example, poverty and racism or racial inequality. It is also about planning and public policy for dealing with these problems.

When I entered city planning in 1950, I was struck by how much it was, as I wrote in the preface of *People and Plans* (1968), "dedicated to a set of narrowly architectural goals and to land use and design programs for realizing them." As a result, about half of the book was devoted to essays about, and often critical of, city planning practice. Even before that collection was published, however, I had learned to understand that America's major urban problems were poverty, joblessness, the scarcity of decent jobs (well-paying, reasonably secure, and not dead-end ones), racism, and other kinds of inequality. These were really far more serious and wide-ranging urban problems than the land-use-related ones the city planners of the time were dealing with, for their effects touched nearly everyone, non-poor as well as poor people. Consequently, the majority of essays in this book are devoted to these problems, which is reflected in the subtitle.

The title is also related to my changed concerns. During the 1960s I became involved, along with a number of other social scientists, in a variety of antipoverty research and planning projects, in the course of which we began to talk and write about social policy. I discovered that thinking about social policy allowed me to analyze critical issues without always having to pay attention to the land use implications.

Policy is a broader term than social policy, and in this book, I use it in the broadest possible sense, to cover not only what sociologists think of as social policy but also what the economists call economic policy and the political scientists—and politicians—describe as public policy. Policy is narrower than planning, however, for plans, including city and national varieties, are *sets* of interrelated policies. Dealing only with policies may be a little more manageable, but I also write about sets of policies, and their interrelations, because limiting the discussion to individual policies is too narrow. Planning may be a liberal term that is unpopular in conservative times, but even conservative government officials and politicians plan, whatever their rhetoric to the contrary.

The book's organization still resembles that of its predecessor, *People and Plans.* Thus, the first three parts are mainly concerned with city and city planning issues. The last two, and considerably longer, parts are about various issues of poverty and race. (My ending the book with them does not prevent readers from reading them first, or from reading only them.) Actually, the book's five divisions are not hard and fast, for problems of race and poverty are now so intertwined with other urban and national issues that they appear in the first three parts of the book as well.

Everyone of the previously published essays in this book has been rewritten not only substantively but, where necessary, to bring the language up to date. In the oldest essays, I have gotten rid of sexist he's and his's, and have replaced Negro with black. I thought long and hard about using African-American instead, but it is a term that seems to me to emphasize an ethnic heritage, and thus to deemphasize, if not intentionally, the racial issues inherent in the term black. All other changes made in the original versions of the essays are described in a footnote at the beginning of each.

The introductions to the five parts of the book—all newly written— explain how the individual essays came to be written and for which audiences, but some general remarks on what the essays have in common, i.e., the ideas about which I feel most urgent, are in order here. These number five.

First, I believe that planning and social policy must and can be *rational,* rationality being achieved when the plans or policies can be proved to implement the goals that are being sought. (I do not believe that goals can be rational, or rationally selected, however. They must reflect values about which people differ—and about which they therefore have to argue so as to persuade one another or achieve a viable compromise.)

Second, planning and policy are usually carried out in the bureaucracies of government, be they local or federal, and bureaucracies tend to act from a *top-down* perspective, if only because bureaucracies are often located near the top of the social hierarchy or have connections to those who are near the top. Effective planning and policy should also be *bottoms-up,* or street level, however, done by professionals as well as citizens, so that the final products address themselves to the conditions under which most people live—and to the fact that we all live in a democracy.

Planners and policy designers (my term to cover policy researchers, analysts, and policymakers) must also be *user oriented*, attentive to the goals, preferences, and values of the people for and with whom they are making plans or policies. At the same time, they have to think about which users are to be attended to in what order of priority, even if that decision is usually a political one into which planners and policy designers have only partial input. (The concept of user orientation I learned from Martin Meyerson, as I did a number of other concepts and ideas in this volume.)

Third, and really a corollary of the previous point, planners, policy designers, and professionals in general do not monopolize wisdom about goals and values, and should not feel that they do. Not only is diversity valuable, but all people are entitled to live in any way they choose, unless that way can be proven to be destructive to them and others. Planners and policy designers ought to help give their citizen-clients the opportunities, resources, and freedom to choose what they want to do whenever possible. I favor democracy in all spheres of life, cultural, economic, and social, as well as political, for I do not believe anyone has the definitive conception of the purposes of individual and social life.

Fourth, planners and policy designers are one part technician and one part citizen, and while their primary duty is to carry out their professional work, they also have the right to state what *they* think ought to be done. At work, they are servants of the community and the nation (as well as of the relevant elected representatives), but not all politicians always represent the citizenry, and planners and policy designers are also always citizens too.

Fifth but also first, genuine democracy in America cannot be achieved without much greater economic, political, and social equality—and this requires a concerted attack on poverty, segregation, and other forms of inequality. Poverty is partly responsible for the segregation that marks so much of American life, although segregation also helps keep too many blacks in poverty. Both are also major causes of the plight of the cities, and of the low quality of life in too many other parts of America, from affluent neighborhoods to slums.

While the essays express my ideas, they also reflect my occupational role. I write basically as a researcher and teacher who is interested in the work of planning and policy agencies but does not participate in their everyday activities. As a result, I have generally looked at agency programs from a broader perspective than is available to the practitioner on the front lines. Concurrently, however, that perspective is also less responsive to the assigned tasks, typical restraints, and frequent crises that mark agency life. Thus, my policy ideas and proposals may sometimes appear to be impractical and naive.

This impracticality is in part intentional. As a sociologist, I realize the limitations under which planners and policy designers work, and more often than not, I understand why they act as they do when I disapprove of their actions. Sociological analysis does not justify these actions; it only explains why they occur. But as a planner, I have not hesitated to evaluate such actions, although as often as possible less from my own point of view than from that of the people being planned for. And as a policy-oriented sociologist, I realize that institutions, bureaucratic and otherwise, can best be changed when they are given funds to change and when they are confronted with political pressure.

Academics have no funds and can generate little political pressure, however; they cannot call on a power base of interest groups or a constituency of voters able to influence elected representatives. If academics have political skills, they can become activists and politicians, as they sometimes do; otherwise they can become advisers to and advocates for groups they support or they can advise professionals and elected officials in the government.

Whatever political pressure they can exert in behalf of their ideas and their principal leverage in all these roles comes from their expertise, and, if they are researchers, from their data and findings. They must use these levers to their fullest advantage, for whatever power they have resides in their ideas, concepts, data, analysis, critiques, and policy proposals, and without them they are no different from other citizens.

Academics who are not directly on or near the agency firing line have a special responsibility, I believe: they must not hesitate to suggest policies that are currently impractical or politically unfeasible. Precisely because they are not on the firing line, they have an obligation to look away from the mainstream and toward the future. Society changes constantly and the future cannot be predicted; therefore an idea that at first seems impractical or is favored by only a minority may later become practical and accepted as the conventional wisdom.

Meanwhile the academic must make sure that the idea survives until its time has come, when social and political arrangements are in the proper conjunction for it to be implemented.

Since this happy turn of events cannot be predicted, the academic's best strategy is to fight for his or her ideas and to keep fighting, sometimes even in the hope that mere repetition will eventually make the idea politically acceptable. True, social change is rarely the result of the repetition of ideas, but an academic's political repertoire is limited. However impractical the ideas put forth by this academic, they are rarely either utopian or radical. Although utopian writings are often stimulating and sometimes useful, they are too often peopled by human beings with superhuman characters, economies with unlimited resources, and polities with near-total consensus. Radical writings have roughly similar pros and cons. I frequently share the radical impatience with the sparsity and slowness of change, admire radical perseverance, and welcome the moral pressure radicals put on liberals—as long as these radicals believe in democracy. In the end, I work on the basis of a faith, often uneasy, that bit by bit, a more egalitarian and democratic America can be created—and that planning and social policy can help.

Thus, this book is very much the work of a liberal and one who sees no need to apologize for proposing, among other things, a modern version of the New Deal. Those who believe that such ideas, like liberalism itself, are obsolescent because they do not accord with an imagined zeitgeist have no special data or insight about either the present or the future; they are merely conservatives unwilling to admit where they stand!

ACKNOWLEDGMENTS

THIS BOOK came into being because Luna Carne-Ross suggested it, and because she urged me to decide by myself what should be included. I am grateful to her for both those good ideas, as well to all those colleagues who have over the years suggested I do a new *People and Plans*. I am also grateful to the Russell Sage Foundation, and its president Eric Wanner, for a Visiting Scholarship for the 1989–1990 academic year. It allowed me, among other things, to write the last chapter—which was also a part of my foundation project—and finish the editing and rewriting work that I had begun much earlier. Vivian Kaufman of the foundation helped to back up my still-primitive word-processing skills by typing drafts of some of the chapters.

· I N T R O D U C T I O N ·
TO THE PAPERBACK EDITION

I WILL NOT pretend that a new preface can properly update this book. Nonetheless, with some exceptions to be spelled out below, America's cities and suburbs as well as its problems of race and poverty remain at this writing in August 1993 as they were in late summer 1990, when I made the last changes in the book.

The main exception is the economy. For while selected economic indicators suggest a recent upturn in some sectors, the economic downturn that has affected the parts of America about which I was mainly writing in the last two parts of the book has become worse. The country may be in a long-term depression, particularly for its workers, for some observers now suggest that future economic growth may take place without significant job increases among the college educated as well as the unskilled.

Even when America's economy is in poor health, residential mobility never stops entirely; people as well as firms are still moving away from the city to either the suburbs I write about in Part Two of the book or sometimes to the countryside where life is cheaper and wages are lower. At the same time, many cities themselves continue to grow, particularly those, such as New York and Los Angeles, which offer jobs to immigrants. America's streets are not paved with gold, but in such cities immigrants can earn enough money, even through below-minimum-wage jobs in the off-the-books economy, to enable them to subsist here and to send some money back home to help their families survive.

In 1992 it looked as if Edge City was going to replace surburbia, at least as the regnant buzzword for the latest suburban growth trends. In fact, Edge City, a fancy name for new commercial-industrial nodes or CONS in outer suburbia, was always partly hype and some of the CONS went under during the economic downturn. Whatever the latest buzzword, and suburbia was itself one in the 1950s, America remains the suburbanizing country it has been since the 19th century; the surburban house—or an ever larger one on an ever larger piece of ground—remains a major building block of the American Dream. Likewise, many manufacturing and service firms find life more pleasant in the suburbs.

To be sure, the suburbs have changed since they first began to grow significantly after World War I. Moreover, the spread of shopping malls to some cities indicates that either cities are themselves suburbanizing or, more likely, the physical differences between the suburbs and the typical low-density American city have been exaggerated. In any case, poverty, not being spatial, grows in the same way in cities and suburbs. The jobless, the homeless, and those who must raise families on insufficient welfare payments suffer equally on both sides of the city limits.

Still, suburbs continue to beckon not only because they continue to offer the optimum mixture of minimal density and maximal "lifestyle," but also because they now supply most of the better jobs in the country. In addition, lily-white or mostly white middle class suburbs can still keep out people of lower status and of darker skin, as well as most homelessness and street crime. Then too, suburbs provide _new_ space, both for people and for industry. America has almost always expanded into new space, rather than modernized the old, the limited examples of gentrification notwithstanding.

The book already dwelt so heavily on America's poverty and racism that adding more would be repetitive. Incidentally, it has to be poverty _and_ racism because one hope of the 1980s, that racism would decline if poverty could be conquered, seems to have temporarily ended. Still, I continue to believe that a truly effective attack on poverty would help to reduce racism—one of my themes in the articles of part 5.

However, the chance of an effective attack on poverty currently seems dim. For illustration, one need only compare the governmental failure to help the people of South Central Los Angeles after the 1992 riot and the speed with which the same government rushed aid to victims of the 1993 flooding of the Mississippi river.

One of the newest political obstacles to a proper attack on poverty is its increasing conception as a racial problem, as a failure distinctive to blacks and some Hispanics, who, as I note in the final chapter, can then be dismissed as an underclass which is morally undeserving of help.

The identification of race (in its special definition as black and Hispanic) and poverty has increased for at least three reasons. One is the invidious comparison of poor blacks and Hispanics with recent immigrants, the latter sometimes being romanticized because they are seen as willing to take the worst and poorest-paid jobs, although in actual fact most have no choice in the matter. Meanwhile, native-born Americans—including the children of recent immigrants—are thought lazy for not taking such jobs, even though they have almost never taken immigrants' jobs in the past.

A second reason for the identification of race and poverty is the fact that when and where economic good times created economic growth, the new jobs and higher incomes went first and foremost to whites, thus enabling more and more to move out of poverty. Once racial minorities bear the brunt of poverty, it can then be viewed as a racial problem.

A third reason is that the white poverty that has newly developed since the depression of the late 1980s is still emerging and relatively invisible. The official poverty rates did rise sharply in recent years, but the long-term effects of the lower 60 percent of the population losing income during the Reagan-Bush era have not yet played themselves out. In addition, the already mentioned continuing decline of jobs is not yet apparent in the official unemployment rate because of the way *unemployment* is officially defined and counted. As I note in the book, the *actual* unemployment rate is probably nearly double the *official*.

The American infatuation with new technology has not yet made it possible to determine how many jobs have been and in the future will be lost to the computer, even if it has also been responsible for creating new jobs. However, in 1993 the major problem is the extreme weakness of whatever economic recovery that has taken place. Even if firms regain some or all of their economic health, many now hire few new full-time workers. Instead, they put their present employees on overtime or, if they must have additional hands, they hire "contingent" or part-time temps, who receive low hourly wages and no health insurance, pension, or other benefits. Furthermore, some companies are now planning to reduce their labor force in order to increase their profit margins. Thus, until the present nervousness about the future ends, it will be marked by "jobless economic growth."

Most of these trends are also taking place in Europe, which suggests that they are part of the latest stage of advanced capitalism. Western European workers are still protected by their welfare state. Generally speaking, part-time workers have access to all the benefits for which full-time workers are eligible and health services remain an entitlement for all. Still, the job decline is now found almost everywhere in Europe, sapping both private economies and the resources of the welfare state.

Chapters 15 and 16 of the book, which propose a labor intensive economy and discuss dealing with joblessness through work sharing, are becoming ever more timely. But then so is Chapter 14, which argues that if America's job picture is gloomy, poor youngsters without unusual academic talent will have little incentive to obtain a decent education (something not so easy to do in the first place in the low quality schools many attend). The always available jobs in the drug industry and the escapist temptations of "the streets" are often more inviting than the classrooms, even of a good school.

When candidate Clinton campaigned for the Presidency in 1992, the need to create new jobs was one of his most urgent themes. It was also a theme that seemed to appeal to many prospective voters. But Bill Clinton was elected by a small margin, and in 1993 a coalition of Republicans, Perotists, and conservative Democrats chose to give first priority instead to reduction of the deficit. In fact, some treated that deficit as the latest monster and the successor to Communism that has to be destroyed if America is to survive. Whether Americans really want a new monster to destroy is not clear at this writing, but other factors may also be at play.

For one thing, President Clinton made enough mistakes in his first months in office to lose some of his initial political capital. Partly as a result, his campaign rhetoric about job creation was replaced by the conventional rhetoric about job training, which is cheaper and less threatening to existing economic arrangements. However, Americans still seem to have faith in the job potential of further training, even if no Administration official can prove that graduating every jobless worker from college would thereby create new jobs for them.

In addition, Clinton's failings may have further strengthened already strong American suspicions of politicians' promises and, perhaps more important, the country's mistrust of what government can actually accomplish. Perhaps Americans have even been convinced by the business lobbies to prefer the low-taxes-reduced-services solution which Republicans have always advocated and which in 1993 was also proposed to destroy the Deficit Monster.

Neither the suspicion nor the mistrust are new: ordinary citizens are always less impressed by what government can actually deliver than by elected and appointed officials, social scientists, and liberals. These popular reactions, which also reflect a desire for minimal taxes so as to maximize disposable income, fit what I called America's "defensive individualism" in my 1988 book *Middle American Individualism*.

Concurrently, the opposition to the conservatism, both of the business lobbies and of defensive individualism, is weaker than it has been in a long time. The unions have been decimated by the changes in the economy, their own rigidities, and the anti-union policies of both the Reagan-Bush administration and the corporate union busters. The poor have never participated much in politics since the polity ignores them anyway. The unemployed, whose gripes often reflect the same radical economic ideas found among the poor, still tend to drop out of the polity once they lose their jobs. Meanwhile the political significance of the rioting, nihilism, and self-destruction of the angrier poor is missed or ignored by better-off Americans and their elected representatives.

Liberal activists have become rarer in part because funds to support them have shrunk, since some of the liberal "fatcats" now favor economically more conservative solutions. At the same time, liberal writers and thinkers have become quieter, but then there is less call for their ideas. This is one of the great victories of the Republicans, for during the era in which they were dominant, they created a cadre of ideologically-driven right-wing social scientists and intellectuals. Even now, that cadre's highly vocal presence helps to keep liberals out of the media. For example, the so-called liberal position on media op-ed pages and television panels is usually occupied instead by a moderate Democrat. Still, generalizations about the political culture are risky for it can change quickly. In 1932, America was in many ways more conservative and business-dominated than the America of 1993, but look at what happened in 1933.

One question I should have asked in the book itself but did not and can now ask only briefly is: where are the planners and architects while the problems of poverty, race, and the economy are getting worse? What I wrote about the social failings of architects in the book's first chapter remains as true as ever. They, like planners and other professionals who manipulate space, have not yet learned that the built environment is more important to them than to the lives of the rest of the population. This theme, which dominates Part One of the book, also helps to answer why the spatial professions do not pay enough attention to the economy, the polity and the larger society.

Still, even non-physical planning has never been significantly concerned with economic and social planning, which is a major point of Part Three of the book. Virtually all of the experts who were active in the New Deal and, again, in the Great Society came from professions other than planning—as do most of those now writing about what to do about the economy. The absence of planners ought to in fact be a loss because they are supposedly trained to think about the future and to be broader-minded, at least in some respects, than representatives of other policy-oriented social sciences.

Economists, for example, can be maddeningly narrow. Too many confuse the real economy with their beloved neoclassical economic model.

Equally important, they frequently value efficiency and profit as the only truly proper economic goals—but these goals also turn workers from clients of planning into a commodity called labor and turn planning into a process favoring elites. The other social sciences also have theoretical or disciplinary blinders and sometimes equate the country with its elites.

Economic decline and its attendant political difficulties cannot be halted by experts, of course, but even a broadly based public policy requires the right analyses. What's needed is a combination of thinkers and doers who can blend expertise with a street-level empathy of how societies can resolve their economic and other problems both effectively and democratically. If such a blend exists, it surely deserves to be called planning.

· PEOPLE, PLANS, AND POLICIES ·

ENVIRONMENT
AND
BEHAVIOR

· I N T R O D U C T I O N ·

WHEN I FIRST came into planning in 1950, its focus was almost entirely architectural or "physical": planners devoted themselves to master plans that rearranged the physical environment of the community by separating "residential" land uses from "commercial" and "industrial" uses; by advocating a variety of quasi-educational public facilities, such as libraries, playgrounds, community centers, all in large numbers; and by enveloping the array of ordered land uses and properly placed facilities with a network of transportation facilities. The result would be a well-planned community, efficient in moving people and goods and in attracting taxes to the city coffers, beautiful so that people would have pride in their cities, and emotionally satisfying so that they could enjoy the good life.

As a sociologist, I had been taught to study people in terms of the groups and social structures in which they lived, the behavior patterns to which they resorted on a recurring basis, and the values that helped to support these patterns—and none of these concepts seemed to pay the same amount of attention to land uses, public facilities, or expressways. This could indicate the deficiencies of sociological concepts, of course, but when I studied people in communities, they were mainly concerned with job satisfaction and security, adequate incomes, good health, a happy family —or single—life, good friends, pleasant neighbors who were helpful when help was needed, and if they were home owners, space, status, low taxes, and rising property values.

Consequently, I found myself in constant disagreement with the planners' basic assumption that the physical environment, man-made or natural, played a major role in people's lives and that rearranging this environment was the most urgent priority for social action to achieve the good life. I was skeptical about the importance of such burning planning issues as whether strip-shopping (a series of stores on "Main Street") was inferior to the shopping center with adequate off-street parking, and whether zoning ordinances should classify row houses with apartments or with single-family dwellings.

Moreover, even when the planners' concerns *were* relevant to most people's most urgent concerns, they were too often framed in terms that met the planners' professional goals, but excluded the concerns of their citizen-clients. Planners tended to design town centers that gave people a fine view of historic landmarks, but they failed to provide for the kinds of stores that serve the less affluent shopper; they drew blueprints in which houses were clustered around a public open space, but deprived home

3

owners of their own backyards; and they advocated single-family housing at low densities without doing anything for the many people who could afford only a tenement or for those who preferred high-density living even if they could afford something else. In other places or at other times, they promoted high-rise housing even though nearly everyone wanted low-rise units.

Today, planning has changed in many ways, notably in the big cities, and physical planning has become more sophisticated, less class biased, and less influential. At the same time, however, urban design, a term that did not exist when I was a practicing planner, has become very important. Oversimplifying a little, urban design is often physical planning done by architects, and it is virtually always more exciting and flashier than that of the old-fashioned master planners. I suppose that this is why some cities like it, for cities are "growth machines," as Harvey Molotch has put it, and if they can sell excitement and flashiness, they may grow more and more quickly, as well as faster than the cities with which they must compete.

Urban design is also more oriented around individual buildings or groups of them than master planning and thus is useful for selling the glitzy new suburban mini-downtowns that ironically enough are being called "urban villages"—a term I once used to describe the ethnic working-class enclave of Boston's West Enders. Last but not least, urban design is important in and to architecture schools, for it enables architects and planners to work together, although sometimes architects may decide that they can plan by themselves and cut planning faculties back.

The importance of architecture and my doubts about what too many architects are doing, either when they do urban design or design buildings, explains why part 1 of this book begins with an essay about them. I first gave another version of it as a talk in the late 1960s, in response to a group of young left-wing architects who had asked me to speak on how architectural design could contribute to "the revolution," and my answer, that they should instead be designing homes and workplaces, etc., that are user oriented, did not go over very well. Others have made my points before and after me, but they never received much publicity until the mid-1980s, when Prince Charles of England made them once more—only to neutralize the effect of his good ideas by some unwarranted criticism of modern and postmodern (oh, how I hate that word) architecture for not being classical.

The remaining essays are reprinted from *People and Plans*. The first, chapter 2, raises an issue implicit in the planners' schemes to rearrange the physical environment, for it suggests that the traditional planning distinction between the natural and the built forms of the physical environment is invalid. Most natural environments are altered for human use, even if only by giving them names or attaching access roads. Moreover, whether natural or built, perhaps a more significant fact for planning is how that environment is perceived and defined, or constructed (to use the current sociological jargon) by the people who occupy it or use it some other way. Thus no proper planning can or should be done until what I call the effective environment is known—and if the planner wants to be user oriented, until he or she understands how various types of people want to use it and will actually use it.

A similar theme underlies chapter 3, a review of Jane Jacobs' *Death and Life of Great American Cities,* which I have reprinted because that book remains very influential in professional and lay planning thought. Furthermore, in her so often insightful volume, Ms. Jacobs had fallen prey to the same fallacies as the planners she was attacking. She, too, had a recipe for how people ought to live in the physical environment, and like the planners, she felt that the good life could be achieved through physical environmental planning. She rejected only the vision of the community advocated by the professional planners and wanted to retain the eighteenth- and nineteenth-century land-use patterns, site plans, and house types of New York's Greenwich Village or Boston's North End.

Planners and architects have as much right as anyone else to promote their conception of the ideal physical environment and the ideal good life. They should do it in books, like Ms. Jacobs, however, rather than in plans or designs made in or for government, or even for private agencies whose plans cannot become real until they are approved by the government. True, citizens usually get a chance to review and to protest, but often the citizens who need to protest most are not consulted until it is too late. In fact, the citizens who will actually occupy and use the buildings and spaces that eventually result are too rarely involved, which is one reason why the plans are still too rarely user-oriented.

Needless to say, there is more to planning than pleasing users, and sometimes planning is good precisely because the citizenry is unhappy with it. But that does not justify planning that seeks to improve people's lives without evidence that they need improving, or to demand improvements that they cannot afford.

· O N E ·

TOWARD A HUMAN ARCHITECTURE: A SOCIOLOGIST'S VIEW OF THE PROFESSION

E VER SINCE THEY came on the American scene, professions have generally sought, among other things, to be of public service. They have wanted to serve by improving society through the application of their distinctive expertise—sometimes whether or not the improvements were actually wanted or needed by the society, and whether or not the expertise was actually relevant to these wants or needs. In other words, the professions have sought to do good as they defined good, in ways that also increased the power, status, and income of their members through a benevolent "professional imperialism" which has not always been benevolent for the ultimate recipients of professional services.

In addition, the professions have worked mainly for the approval and respect of their peers and colleagues; only secondarily have they been concerned with their clients' own wants or needs. Partly as a result, they have looked for clients who accepted peer values and practices, which meant, whenever possible, clients of similar socioeconomic status. Finally, in their educational programs, the professions have tried to train students

Reprinted, with some revisions and updating, from *Professionals and Urban Form,* edited by J. Blau, M. LaGory, and J. Pipkin by permission of the State University of New York Press. © 1984 State University of New York Press.

to "advance" the profession, that is, to be original, innovative, and prestigious (by peer standards), although in actual fact, many of the students have wound up in fairly prosaic jobs with little opportunity to be innovative.

During the 1960s, the traditional goals and structures of the professions came under strong criticism from students and young practitioners. Although they also wanted to improve society through the use of their professional expertise, they defined improvement as drastic if not revolutionary change—often toward a more egalitarian society—and they rejected the traditional professional alliance with the elite. In almost all professions, young people wanted to work less for peers and high-status clients and more for the poor. (In those professions that deal with individual clients on a case-by-case basis, they wanted to undertake class actions that would benefit large numbers of people at the same time.) In the process they also rejected traditional professional methods, so that, for example, radical sociologists gave up detached research, social workers moved from case work to community organization, and doctors and lawyers eschewed the commercial relationship with patients and clients. A few professionals gave up professional methods altogether, resorting to various forms of political action that they hoped would produce a more democratic and egalitarian society.[1]

THE SITUATION IN ARCHITECTURE

VIRTURALLY ALL of these observations apply to architecture as well. Traditionally, architects have wanted to improve society through better building, whether or not this actually improved society in a way that society wanted to be improved. They have been designed for their peers and have pursued originality, so that too often architects cared more how a building would look in the architectural journals than how it would work in actual use; and they have gravitated to high-income clients because they were most likely to let architects do their own thing.[2]

But architecture is also distinctive in at least two ways. First, professional imperialism has perhaps been greater, or at least more visible, in architecture than in other professions, partly because some architects felt that their role was to express the contemporary culture or the philosophy of their society through their buildings. Others saw themselves as social reconstructionists, who would build or rebuild social relationships—and thus, people's lives—through physically or otherside innovative plans and buildings. Indeed, some acted out what I call "the Fountainhead syndrome," the urge to remake society through building that obsessed the hero of the Ayn Rand novel.

Second, architecture's professional expertise involves taste and style, that is, aesthetics—and more so than most other professions. As a result, architecture has been caught up, if not always intentionally, in the long-standing debate over the merits of high culture and popular culture. The most celebrated architects, and the architectural elite generally, are on the side of high culture, although they may not be aware of it, for they share its disdain for popular culture, and with it, for popular or vernacular building. Like other high-culture artists, they venerate folk art and folk building —as soon as the folk drop it—but they despise commercially produced products, whether television programs made in Hollywood or buildings designed by or for commercial builders. High culture is, however, a minority culture that attracts only a tiny—but affluent and well-educated— sector of society.[3] As a result, architects play only a minor role in America's residential design, and most housing is designed by builders who respond to the aesthetics of the dominant popular cultures.

To be sure, other professions also supply only a minor portion of the product or service over which they claim expertise, and because of similar cultural conflicts. Medical aid is probably still administered more often by druggists and relatives than doctors, just as most counseling is done by ministers, relatives, and friends rather than by social workers or psychiatrists. Similarly, professional sociologists supply only a small amount of the total sociology produced in our society. Many Americans sometimes read professional sociologists who have also become popular, such as Robert Bellah and his co-authors of *Habits of the Heart*. Far more look at the "pop sociology" written by journalists who do a little social research, and probably most if not all resort to the vital but virtually invisible "lay" sociology that people develop on their own in order to deal with society. In all cases, there are some differences between the professional and nonprofessional service, but some of these are differences of style. Doctors often treat patients as collections of diseases rather than people; and like sociologists and social workers, they supply their services in a technical language that puts off their patients and clients.

Of course, the minor role that architects play in American building is also a function of cost; few people can afford a custom-built house, or a Park Avenue medical specialist. Sometimes builders have rejected architects for the same reason; thus, when William Levitt began to make plans for his third Levittown in the mid-1950s, he called in two internationally famous architects to design new prototypes for him, only to find that their designs would cost around $100,000 to build. He was then selling houses (with land) at $11,500 to $14,500.[4]

During the 1960s, young architects questioned the traditional ways of their profession in much the same way as young people in other professions. They rejected the elite architecture that built only for affluent clients and criticized the emphasis on aesthetics and social reconstruction through architectural methods. Some gave up the idea of designing and building altogether, becoming planners and political activists instead. Indeed, young architects seem to have played a proportionately larger role in the radical movements of the 1960s than young members of other professions, attesting perhaps to their own version of the Fountainhead syndrome.

Today, the ideas and plans of the 1960s are less visible, even if they have not entirely disappeared. However, the economic crises of the 1970s, the Reaganite type of affluence of the 1980s, and the new design opportunities generated by new foreign monies, new technologies, and "postmodernism" have encouraged many architects, like other professionals, to go or go back to work to the kinds of clients and the ways of doing architecture that were taken for granted before the 1960s.

ARCHITECTURE IN THE 1990s

MANY OF the criticisms of architecture that emerged in the 1960s continue to be valid, in spirit if not always in letter. Still, times have changed in the last thirty years, and I want to consider what architecture should and can do in the years to come.

To begin with, it is wrong to think of architecture or any other profession in the singular, for no profession can or ought to be homogeneous. In a heterogeneous society, there should be many architectures, and sociologies. Even so, architects should concern themselves mainly with the design and construction of buildings, for that is their distinctive expertise. (This means they should not ordinarily try to be planners, a point to which I will return.) Also, architects should continue to be innovative whenever possible, but the greatest opportunity for innovation, as I will note in more detail below, is in designing buildings for the people who use them.

Furthermore, while some architects should continue to work for, and by, the standards of high culture, more architectural effort ought to be devoted to popular culture, because its aesthetic standards are as valid as those of high culture. As long as taste is determined largely by amount of education and income, different socioeconomic levels are entitled to have different standards of beauty and good design, and to have these standards put into practice. Until all Americans have an opportunity to obtain the education and income prerequisite to high culture, architects should be working for and in all cultures. This, as I understand Denise Scott Brown and Robert Venturi, is one of the points they want to make, although they are also engaged in using popular culture to develop their own high-culture form, much as high-culture composers incorporate rock and jazz into their works.

Understanding and accepting the standards of popular culture may also be in the economic self-interest of architects, for it would enable them to play a larger role in commercial building: a rational strategy in an era when other clients are scarce. Competing with commercial builders is easier said than done, however, for, consciously or not, commercial builders have developed a much better sense of what rank-and-file clients, particularly home buyers, want than have architects. Whatever their other motives, builders do not look down their aesthetic noses at such clients. The varieties of Eastern U.S. neo-Colonial and Southwestern U.S. neo-Spanish design that have dominated residential building for many years may not meet the standards of high culture but they have been popular for a long time, and their popularity cannot therefore be ascribed simply to the aesthetic ignorance or pathology of builders and home buyers.

To be sure, commercial builders will rarely employ the innovative designers who are held in highest regard by the profession, at least not until they can prove their willingness to work within popular styles. At the same time, the predicted energy shortages of the future may provide a new opportunity for architects, for if energy really becomes scarcer and more expensive, American building of all kinds will have to change, and designers who can come up with energy-saving solutions that are also popular in style will find themselves extremely busy. But such solutions cannot involve resettling people in a new version of the post-Miesian high-rise apartment building; instead, architects must find better ways of saving the single-family house and adapting the town-house or garden-apartment–type condominium.

A major distinguishing characteristic of high-culture architecture has been its self-conscious attempt to make philosophical and symbolic statements, but this is overdone. Buildings have many functions, utilitarian and others, and they can also serve as vehicles for statements, but not at the expense of their other functions. Architects are generally not accomplished philosophers in the first place; the statements they want to make are often half-baked or clichéd even when the architecture itself is good. Moreover, it is plainly impossible to capture the ethos of a society or an era in a single statement. Modern societies are too diverse and eras of too short duration, but there are also better media for the pursuit of philosophy than buildings.

Much the same observation applies to the making of symbolic statements, except when a building's major function is to be symbolic. Symbols are perhaps easier to integrate into design without neglecting other functions than philosophical statements, but even so, their importance has been overrated. In addition, the symbol makers tend to favor high-culture symbols and styles and to forget that the rest of the population may have different symbols. For example, many public buildings follow the dictates of high cultures, even though most of the public, which pays for the buildings, does not share these dictates, expressing its feelings in the satirical names that are attached to such buildings. People might feel differently about architects if at least some public buildings expressed popular symbols and styles.

The Fountainhead syndrome has also been primarily associated with high-culture architecture, although even designers of otherwise conventional residential subdivisions have wanted to redo people's friendship choices, and to encourage their identification with the community through design and site planning. But whether the urge is to reconstruct the entire society or merely neighborhood sociability, architects cannot, and should not, try to play social engineer with architectural methods. In the last several decades many studies have been made on the impact of buildings, building types, and site plans on social relationships, other behavior patterns, and attitudes, and most of the research indicates that sites and buildings have very complex, but usually not intensive or long-lasting effects on people's behavior and attitudes—and in any case far fewer than what architects and planners believe.[5] Whether buildings are judged to be "good design" and win architectural prizes makes no difference, and even when effects have been intended by the architects of such buildings, they do not necessarily materialize—or very different effects are found.[6]

The Fountainhead syndrome is misplaced. Society cannot be remade through architecture, and architects cannot solve problems of poverty, mental illness, or marital discord through better design. Nor can they shape friendship choices, civic participation, community identity, and social cohesion through site planning. Their designs can make people's lives a little more comfortable or uncomfortable, but human behavior, and social as well as political relationships, are shaped by so many causal factors that rarely is any single factor of crucial importance. Even more rarely is architectural design or site planning that single factor. One so-called physical factor that may have some social and emotional effects is the amount of space, although recent studies of density suggest that high density does not by itself generate pathology.[7] People who live in crowded conditions almost always suffer from other, more serious problems, notably poverty, and while lack of space may cause considerable discomfort, even architects cannot do much about it. Space is not a physical factor that architects can manipulate through design, but an economic factor which depends on the income of those purchasing or renting space.

Social reconstruction through design is also undemocratic, for architects are not political representatives, and are neither chosen by, nor accountable to, an electorate or other constituency. Thus, architects have no right to decide that people should be friendlier with their neighbors, that they ought to identify with their community—and that they should, therefore, use public open space rather than their own backyards.

Finally, architecture should deemphasize aesthetics, or at least give less priority to the aesthetic functions of buildings, treating them less as works of art or pieces of sculpture. How buildings look from the outside and to the outsider is far less important than how they feel to their users. They ought to be beautiful, but their elevations, and their aesthetic functions generally, should not be the tails that wag the dogs.

HUMAN ARCHITECTURE

ABOVE ALL, architecture should be human. The term is merely a label, and one that has sometimes been used to indulge in polemics against tall buildings, but I mean by it that buildings should be designed for the people who use them.[8] Architecture should be *user-oriented,* to employ yet another label. Specifically, buildings should be humanly functional, comfortable, and beautiful—and when all three objectives cannot be met, they should be met in that order of priority. I use the term *functional* here in the literal sense: a building ought to perform the functions for which it is intended. A building should work as a mechanical system, of course, but more important, it ought to facilitate, or at least not get in the way of, the important and recurring tasks, and the social, political, and economic relationships that go on within it. By comfortable, I mean that a building ought to be convenient and pleasant for its occupants, although not all buildings can be comfortable. Some, I suppose, have to be awe-inspiring, and I doubt whether any designer can make a prison comfortable for its involuntary occupants, at least until penology is humanized. A beautiful building is one that satisfies the aesthetic standards of its users.

Functionality, as I conceive it, is particularly relevant to a human architecture, for it calls attention to the fact that the building ought to work for the often prosaic and mundane needs of people that are sometimes forgotten because the architect is emphasizing symbols or aesthetic goals. Above all, perhaps, functionality has to do with the allocation of the scarcest resource with which the architect works, space, so that major activities and relationships can be satisfied effectively. For example, in a house for young families, functionality has to do with so locating the kitchen that mothers can watch their children playing outside; in an apartment, providing play space for them when they cannot go outside but will not stay in their own rooms—as they rarely do. It means designing bedrooms for teenagers so that they can entertain their friends with high-decibel records but without deafening their elders, and finding ways to give both age groups visual and aural privacy. In an office building, functionality means finding a design that will provide enough—and comfortable—space for all the various users, from keypunch operators and factory workers to managers and executives, as well as janitors. In short, human architecture is understanding how people actually use the buildings they live and work in, and then finding design solutions for these uses.

User-oriented architecture is simpler to propose than to design.[9] For one thing, user orientation has implications for a building's functions, for the users should, in one way or another, have a role in determining the intended functions. Second, most buildings have diverse sets of users, and the issue of which users ought to determine the building's functions and its design, and in what order of priority, is a complex one. Occasionally, buildings can be designed to satisfy all users, but more often, they cannot, and then the priority issue becomes a political issue. Whether a house should be designed first and foremost for adults or children, or an office building for executives or for secretaries is at bottom a question of power, and normally adults and executives will end up with more and better space. Architects cannot by themselves reallocate power, or even find solutions to power struggles. Ideally, they should be spokespersons for users in their discussions with a client, and make sure that those of lesser power do not automatically wind up with lower priority. More pragmatically, they should encourage discussions among clients and users as to how the building is to be designed, indicating that priority determinations are political ones. At the least, they should remind clients not to ignore users.

Clearly, buildings should not be designed simply for clients, and all other things being equal, first priority should be given to those users who make the most intensive or extensive use of a building. But all other things are not always equal; thus, a firm that can flourish only by attracting customers must obviously assign high priority to them. Building users who serve these customers would probably agree, since their paychecks depend on satisfying customers; even so, if these users are consulted, their wants will at least be put on the agenda. One complicating factor is that architects are usually hired and paid by clients, not by users, and must battle for the authority to consider the latter. In a competitive situation, those who do so may be at a disadvantage, for an architect who argues that office buildings should provide comfortable work space for secretaries as well as executives may obtain fewer commissions than one who pays maximum attention to executives. The experienced user-oriented architect can, however, argue that secretarial productivity and turnover are affected by pleasant working conditions and that these conditions can sometimes be made more pleasant through design. Admittedly, design has its limits; for no architect can design a building in which everyone, executives *and* clerks, can have window offices. Nevertheless, addressing itself to users, and to the problems this raises, is what makes architecture human.

One of the simplest ways of making working—and living—conditions pleasant is to reinvent the openable window. Although it is understandable why this window disappeared originally, the days of low energy costs are over, and so is the belief that technology can conquer any trick nature can play upon us. To be sure, the sealed glass box was and is cheaper and it enhances architects' ability to achieve sculptural and other effects with their buildings.

Still, for the human beings inside, such buildings are anything but user-friendly. In most of them, heating and cooling systems cannot be adapted quickly enough when summer weather suddenly appears for a few days in March, or if winter returns for a while in June. Moreover, when cold and flu epidemics strike, these systems circulate people's bacteria and viruses along with the in-house air, making sure that more people get sick than would otherwise be the case. Above all, no heating or cooling system is perfectly designed, and the building's occupants suffer whenever it breaks down. Even the architects' intended visual effects are lost when people are forced—and able—to install shades to protect themselves against the burning sun.

When future historians write the architectural history of our era, they will puzzle over the fuss pundits and critics made about modern and postmodern elevations and wonder why no one commented about the inhumanity of working or residing in tightly sealed glass boxes. They may also criticize us for not rebelling against the tortures that the various designers and manufacturers of these boxes imposed upon us.

A second issue in user-oriented design concerns the determination of user needs and wants. Need is an unfortunate concept, for too often it is projected onto users, and turns out to be what other people think users should need or want. I would emphasize user wants, and when not all wants are achievable, user choices among alternatives. Even wants are not easily determined, for while it may be simple to get people to say what they want, the user-oriented architect must also consider how people actually want to use, and do use, buildings, once they are inside them. Since no one can predict what people will do in a building they have not yet occupied, architects need to know, in considerable depth and detail, how people use different types of buildings—and building components—in the mechanical, social, and emotional senses of use. Architects should, in fact, be constant observers of how people use buildings; their own, those of other architects, and those of commercial builders. They should understand how use patterns are enhanced and hindered by various design solutions; and they should be talking with users to find out what they like and dislike about their present buildings and what should be changed in the future.

Observing use patterns and ascertaining user wants for the future is only part of the assignment, for architects must synthesize these two kinds of data, and this, too, is complicated. No synthesis can totally rely on use patterns, or else architects will only be perpetuating the status quo. On the other hand, the synthesis cannot rely too heavily on verbally expressed wants for the future, since even the most observant users cannot always express what they want, and even when they can, talk is cheap, and what people say they want may ultimately not be as important as how they have acted in the past. Finally, no synthesis is complete without the architectural input, combining the data with design ideas. One of the challenges of a human architecture is to develop and perfect this synthesis, through experience, research, and professional discussion and education.

TALKING TO THE USERS: THE ROLE OF SOCIAL RESEARCH

WHEN I suggest that architects must talk with users, I do not necessarily mean this literally, for in many cases the dialogue may be carried on by researchers, and besides, there is no single formula for everyone. Some architects are user-oriented by inclination; they have an intuitive sense of how people use buildings, the ability to observe that use, and the willingness (and time) to do some observing and interviewing before going to the drawing board. Other architects are most at home at the drawing board or with the calculator, and lack the skill and patience to talk with others.[10]

Whatever the architect's own inclination, ideally, users should do their own talking, and should help to determine the program and design of their own buildings. One 1960s idea that has deservedly survived is user participation in architectural and planning decisions. In a literal sense, such participation is often impractical, for even talking with the family of a client for a private house takes a good deal of time and energy; and no one can hold a dialogue with the eventual occupants of a subdivision or office building. Sometimes it is possible to talk with a sample of surrogates, people who are similar to eventual occupants, but often the dialogue will in fact have to be research: studies by social scientists, especially sociologists and psychologists, which provide architects with data on user behavior and user wants.

There have been a number of attempts at teamwork between architects and social scientists, and some have been successful.[11] I am also well aware, however, that often they have not worked out. Architects have claimed, and rightly so, that the social scientists have different interests, being more concerned with innovations in theory than with improved architecture; they have also complained, again correctly, that social scientists often lack the knowledge and the inclination to work with architects. Social scientists, they say, cannot adapt to architectural deadlines, and cannot communicate in jargon-free English. Most important, they are unable to come up with findings specific enough to be useful for design solutions, or are unwilling to make firm generalizations when their findings are ambiguous. Social scientists are equally unhappy with architects, charging—and often rightly so—that architects are unable or unwilling to use research findings. The complaints of both professions boil down to the charge that the other is unsuited to the teamwork task, suggesting that both must make changes in their methods of operation before effective teamwork can take place.

If social scientists are too often marching to theoretical rather than architectural drummers, architects are frequently at fault for asking the wrong questions. For one thing, some still want to be social reconstructionists and reject social science findings which indicate that an architectural solution is irrelevant. Having once done a study of a low-income ethnic neighborhood, I am sometimes asked by architects how one designs buildings and neighborhoods that respond to the distinctive culture of low-income people or of an ethnic group, but this is a good example of the wrong question. The fundamental, or at least most urgent, user patterns do not vary by class or ethnicity; that is, different income and ethnic groups do not use dwelling units all that differently. They all need living rooms, bedrooms, kitchens, and so on, and they all put these rooms to roughly the same use. True, low-income people have traditionally socialized informally and in the kitchen, while high-income people entertain more formally and in the living room, but such class differences are few, and in most cases too insignificant to affect design.

The main distinction between the rich and the poor is in their ability to pay for space, and the main problem of the latter is to get enough space. Of course, poor people virtually never get new housing and they cannot hire architects, but when architects design projects for low-income people, they should worry less about designing for the distinctive characteristics of low-income social life and more about how to design functional, comfortable, and beautiful architecture when space is at a minimum. In addition, they should use their professional expertise and status to fight against low-income housing projects that try to cram their occupants into an unreasonably small amount of space. Together with researchers, they ought to determine the space requirements of low-income families, so they can develop proper space standards for the poor. I suspect that these standards will require as much space as for affluent families, thus casting doubt on the desirability of special (and, especially tiny or "transitory") housing units for the poor. Instead, housing will need to meet a universal threshold of space, with rent supplements for those to poor to afford the minimum.

As for use patterns in low-income or ethnic neighborhoods, these are not so rigid or permanent that they require special designs; in fact, such designs sometimes ask people to continue behavior patterns which they would just as soon give up. For example, among some low-income groups street life is not a choice but a necessity, born of lack of space in the dwelling; it would disappear if apartments were large enough. Among some ethnic groups, street life exists because of immigrants' cultural restrictions against inviting people other than relatives into the house, but these restrictions are not being maintained by today's third-and fourth-generation ethnics. More important, there are few people or cultural patterns that cannot —and do not—adapt themselves to available space and design. My observations suggest that in first- and second-generation Italian neighborhoods in American cities, social life was much the same whether people lived in tenements, row houses, or single-family houses; whether in all-Italian or mixed neighborhoods; and whether the streets were wide or narrow, traffic laden or empty.

The cooperation between architects and social scientists is still beginning, and early failures do not invalidate the possibility of a joint effort. Such an effort requires at least three separate tasks. One is the development of a basic research compendium of user behavior and wants for different types of buildings. Although considerable new research will be required to discover the fundamental generalizations about user behavior, the task is not as huge as it might appear. There are many uniformities in the way people use houses, offices, factories, and the like, with relatively little variation either by demographic characteristics or region. Also, people's wants are more similar than commonly thought; what differs mainly is their financial and other ability to satisfy them.

The needed research compendium is already beginning to exist, thanks in part to the emergence of the sociology and psychology of design, sometimes called environmental sociology and psychology. To be sure, much of the research is still preliminary, of narrow scope, and overly concerned with theoretical, conceptual, and methodological issues. In part, architects, and architecture as a profession, have only themselves to blame, for they have so far remained quiet about their research needs and have left the agendas entirely to the social scientists. If architects would become interested in user research and exert some influence on those who fund such research, they might obtain more usable data.

But this also awaits a second task, the recruitment and training of architects who are sufficiently sympathetic to, and familiar with, the social sciences, and with the use of social science data in architecture to initiate research—at least to the extent of identifying architecturally inclined social scientists who will write the actual grant proposals and do the research. And this in turn must go hand in hand with a third task, the recruitment and training of social scientists who are interested in working with architects.

All three tasks require funds, people, and the development of new research organizations, teaching bodies, and curriculums in order to develop an effective interdisciplinary relationship, in which architects with some training in the social sciences, and social scientists with some training in architecture can develop a common language and research methods that contribute to the common objective.

The basic research compendium should consist of specific studies, the broader generalizations drawn from them, and translations, by architects, into broad and general user-oriented design guidelines.[12] These cannot

always solve the specific design problems encountered by individual architects, however, and will have to be supplemented either by special studies
or by social science consultants who can adapt compendium findings to
specific design problems for architects who lack the time or money to do
new research. It is to be hoped that the compendium can be updated and
elaborated continuously with results of these studies or consultancies, and
more important, by followup studies of user behavior and user satisfactions
once buildings have been occupied.

ARCHITECTURE AND PLANNING

IN THE early 1950s, when I worked as a city planner in public and private
planning agencies, many of my colleagues were architects, for in those days
trained planners were fewer than today, and many architects thought that
their professional training entitled them to be planners as well. Times have
changed considerably since then, at least in America; architects can no
longer become planners just by taking a few planning courses, any more
than planners can also be architects by dipping into the architectural curriculum. Planning is rapidly shedding the remainder of its architectural origins
and becoming an applied social science, although it is still unclear whether
it will be an independent discipline, or one dominated by public administration, or by one of its equivalents in business or engineering.

At the same time, however, physical planning will continue to exist,
because some of the issues with which planners deal, and some of the
decisions on which they advise, have physical consequences and require
design solutions. In some places, and on some campuses, urban design,
often under architectural auspices, has replaced physical planning, but even
so, the social and political questions with which physical planners have to
grapple, particularly in the big cities, still have to be dealt with, whether by
the urban designer or someone else. If in the future urban designers take
over the physical planning function, which is a possibility, urban design may
wind up splitting off from architecture, especially the kind devoted to
individual buildings. As scarcities of energy and money increase, and as
public expectations for the efficiency and effectiveness of public agencies
rise, no one can be expert in both architecture and urban design, and the
era in which the architect could function as a generalist who can also plan
will finally end.

ARCHITECTURE AND SOCIAL CHANGE

DURING THE 1960s, some architects went into planning because they thought that the latter profession, having a large scope, would be more able to bring about drastic social change. They were disappointed, for while architecture cannot do very much to change society, nor can planning, embedded as it is in growth-dominated municipal politics. Indeed, it seems fair to say that most professions can do little to bring about social change, at least in a radical direction, for their employers or clients tend to represent the business elite.

Radical social change comes about largely because of the interplay of macroeconomic and political forces over which no one group or stratum has very much control. More modest social change, on the other hand, is often the result of deliberate political activities, and architects, like all other professionals, can be politically active, either as professionals or as citizens. They can lobby, demonstrate, or run for elective office; they can also try to persuade their firms and professional organizations to lobby for changes they consider desirable.

As the 1960s activists discovered, however, there is not likely to be a revolution, especially one led by architects. The opposition to social change, especially in an egalitarian direction, remains strong, and since few architects are politicians, and even those who are rarely have a sizable political base from which to operate, most architects will have to exert political influence through their expertise. As experts, they can play advocate and technical adviser roles in community organizations involved in building, or in fighting urban renewal or other programs to reduce the supply of inexpensive housing. They can also lobby for more research and action to reduce the cost of housing and housing maintenance.

Still, the main costs of housing are the price of land and money, which architects cannot affect, either as experts or as activists. If these prices are to be brought down, architects must join with other professionals and with citizen groups to undertake joint political action for the elimination and land speculation, and for the transformation of the housing industry into some form of public utility, so that all housing, except for the very rich, becomes a governmental responsibility, as it already is in many countries all over the world. But political action along these lines requires considerably more expertise in the economics and politics of housing, and of urban development and politics generally, than architects usually have.

SOME EDUCATIONAL IMPLICATIONS

MOST OF the educational implications of my proposals for the future role of architecture are self-evident, and I shall only summarize them briefly. First, architectural schools should devote themselves to the training of architects, sending those students who want to be planners to planning schools, but they should also work with planning schools to develop urban design curriculums that properly train architects to deal with, or at least understand, those urban design decisions that cannot be based solely on architectural expertise.

In addition, schools should train students in what I call human architecture, encouraging in them an empathic understanding of—and curiosity about—how people use buildings, and teaching them how to apply a user orientation to architectural programming and design. Architectural students ought to have sufficient training and practice in observational and interviewing techniques to develop the habit of and skills for informal observation of user behavior. (Although architects need not do systematic social science research, it would help if some know how to use it.) More important, architecture students need courses that will supply them with findings and ideas on how people use buildings, and how these findings can be applied. Such courses will have to be taught by social scientists who have themselves been taught to address architects, or by architects who have learned how to use design-relevant social research.

Furthermore, architectural schools should provide more courses on the economics and politics of building, housing, and related subjects. Architects must be knowledgeable not only in cost estimation, but also in the macroeconomics of housing (and other building), especially in an economy in which only a minuscule proportion of the population can now afford to buy a new house. Similarly, architects must understand the politics of housing and building so they can be familiar with the political context within which they work; and they ought to take a course on the political structure of their own profession, and on strategies of architectural and social change.

Finally, architects could also use more training in the aesthetics of culture so they can understand why so many Americans like neocolonial design and can create architecture that is beautiful by popular standards.

CONCLUSION

MY PROPOSALS probably sound revisionist to architectural activists who want to expand the horizons of their profession to encompass planning, and reactionary to those who want to transform architecture into a handmaiden for a future revolution. My proposals may also be unrealistic, for as sociological studies of the professions have shown, most professions are imperialistic and seek to enlarge their roles and increase their power so they can be the leader of the team—and of an ever larger team.

The human architecture I consider desirable is not new; essentially, what I am arguing for is only a variant of the now almost extinct idea that form should follow function, and buildings should be designed from the inside out, rather than from the outside in. In its brief life-span, the idea that form should follow function received more lip-service than drawing-board activity, however, and even when it was applied, it overemphasized a narrowly mechanistic conception of function. Human architecture must design for human functions; it has nothing to do with Bauhaus asceticism, letting the plumbing hang out, the restoration of ornamentation, postmodernism, or whatever other design innovations are introduced in the future to enable architects to be original or compete for clients who demand originality. Rather, human architecture requires attention to the users as social and psychological beings, and design solutions that allow them to live as they want to live—and in buildings they enjoy being in and consider beautiful. Human architecture may not be published in today's architectural journals, but if offers enough design and other challenges to involve several generations of practitioners, researchers, students, and teachers in an innovative, creative, and socially useful professional endeavor.

THE POTENTIAL
ENVIRONMENT
AND THE
EFFECTIVE
ENVIRONMENT

M ANY CITY PLANNERS and architects believe that the physical environment, natural and built, directly affects human behavior. Conversely,
social scientists suggest that social structure, especially the economy and
the polity, and culture are the crucial variables in behavior—and that these
also determine what people and societies do to the physical environment.
For example, in planning and housing thought, substandard housing is bad
for poor people's physical and mental health, and should be replaced by
newer housing or be rehabilitated and modernized. Social scientists interested in housing are likely to point out that physical and mental health are
first and foremost a function of people's income level, for poverty means
poor diets, lack of routine medical care, and a greater risk of depression,
alcoholism, and the like. The quality of housing plays a smaller part, and
the research data on the bad effects of substandard housing remains incon-
clusive. Accordingly, policy-oriented social scientists would recommend
better paying jobs, income subsidies, and adequate welfare payments for
those who cannot work; recommendations for housing improvements are
of lesser priority. In fact, poor people are often less concerned with the

---

Reprinted from *People and Plans* but greatly revised for this volume.

quality of their housing than with how much the rent cuts into their meager budgets.

Planners and social scientists make different recommendations in part because they play different roles in society, but the diversity of their ideas can shed some light on the solution of a significant planning issue. The city planner's role in the community and his or her ability to change the community revolve largely around the manipulation of buildings and land uses, while the policy-oriented social scientist has no such occupational restrictions. He or she can recommend changes in the economy, social structure, and to a lesser extent culture—and frequently, the two occupations talk past each other. This essay attempts to formulate a frame of reference that begins to make room for the ideas of both planners and social scientists.

The basic conception to be argued here is: The physical environment is relevant to behavior insofar as this environment affects the social system and culture of the people involved or as it is taken up into their social system. Between the physical environment and empirically observable human behavior, there exist a social system and a set of cultural norms through and with which people define and evaluate portions of the physical environment relevant to their lives and structure the way they will use (and react to) this environment in their daily lives.

The several parts of the environment with which planners work vary in the extent to which they are subject to human influence or manipulation. The physical environment is, as already noted, defined as the sum of the natural and built environments. The natural environment in turn contains parts which cannot be influenced or manipulated, and others which can be. The built environment is by definition manipulable.

The nonmanipulable part of the natural environment can have a direct effect on human behavior, as in an earthquake. Human beings cannot stop or otherwise manipulate earthquakes, but they can develop some protection against their effects. In addition, some of the damage of the earthquake depends on the buildings people are in at the time, and that is a function of their roles and positions in the social structure, for example, where they live and work, and what quality housing they can afford. Moreover, the activities that follow an earthquake, from panic to rebuilding, have little to do with the original natural event, because post-disaster behavior is shaped by the society in which it takes place. Some portions of the nonmanipulable natural environment are less directly relevant to human behavior, such as occurrences within the depths of the earth. Since these help cause earthquakes, we pay for experts who track them, but neither what happens in the depths of the earth nor the experts are paid much attention until there is another earthquake.

Most planning activity deals with the manipulable natural and the built environments. Because planners manipulate nature and buildings, their planning is generally called physical, but physical planning is as much the product of social decisions and cultural values as of designs and blueprints. A park may be a natural or built environment, or a mix of both, but the choices and arrangements of flora, fauna, walkways, and park facilities are based on social, cultural, and even political and economic conceptions about the features of a desirable park.

Consequently, it is at least as important to decide which cultures will be reflected in the planner's (or landscape architect's) scheme as what kinds of material objects will be used for the park. The planner may make decisions that reflect his or her professional judgments, which are usually based on his or her professional culture, and which may also pay some attention to the cultures of the people for whom the park is intended. Alternatively, planners can base their decisions entirely on professional judgments, but if there is conflict between these judgments and the values of the intended users, the plan may not be adopted—or, if adopted, it may result in a park that will not be used as much as it could have been. Or the plan may be altered informally by people as they make use of the park. Most likely, in the end one or another compromise will be struck between planner and user values.

Planners too rarely see the social aspects of the built environment. For example, they assume that the mixture of natural and built environmental features that go into the making of a park will provide the pleasure, aesthetic satisfaction, and perhaps exercise that are associated with park use. I would argue, however, that it is not the park alone but the functions and meanings that the park has for the people who choose to use it or not use it that are crucial for what happens to the park.

The park proposed by the planner is only a *potential* environment; the social positions and cultures of the people who will use it determine to what extent the park becomes an *effective* environment. Without the park, the emotional and aesthetic benefits predicated by the planner cannot be made available, but without use of the park by the people for whom it is planned, these benefits cannot be achieved either. (Presumably the visual presence of the park and its addition to light and air benefit even the nonuser; then the planner must decide whether the park is the best functional alternative for increasing visual pleasure and the supply of light and air, and whether the benefits to be gained are worth the costs involved.)

I have used the term *potential* environment because most physical environments are only potential with respect to how they affect people. For example, wildernesses are potential environments if they are inaccessible to people, because then they can have no effect on people's activities, although they may improve the air quality for those living near such areas. When access roads or canals are built, then wildernesses can be used, becoming effective environments for those who use or intend to use them. To put it another way, the potential environment is necessary, but does not become sufficient as a part of people's lives until they transform it into an effective environment. Planning itself may be seen as an early stage in the transformation of the potential environment into an effective one.

With respect to its influence on behavior, therefore, the manipulable environment or elements of it are a potential environment, and its perception and conception is the effective environment. The effective environment may thus be defined as *that version of the potential environment that is perceived, conceived—and created by users.* In one way, I am only restating the truism that an objective environment must be perceived subjectively before it affects behavior. However, the planners' conception of the park is no more objective than that of the users'; each focuses on elements of the environment relevant to them. The planner sees what I call the potential environment; the user is concerned with the effective environment.

The planner sees especially those parts of the potential environment that are:

1. Amenable to his or her manipulation, that is, those over which he or she has professional control.
2. Related to his or her training. Planners are concerned with the technical aspects of the potential environment, whether or not these are relevant to its use.
3. Visible to his or her perspective, which is basically that of the surveyor or spectator, and sometimes the professional tourist. Planners see an environment as it appears on the map or the blueprint; they look it over again in initial phases of construction and when it is completed. But unless the environment is planned for the neighborhood in which the planner lives, he or she sees it only fleetingly and does not use it. While he or she may have ideas on how it ought to be used, the planner does not see it as do the people who live with it.

The planner's perspective can be compared to the very different perspective of the West Enders I once studied in Boston. Most of the planning

reports described the area as a neighborhood of five-story tenement buildings in narrow streets, without sufficient sun and air, and characterized by
insufficient parking, garbage-strewn alleys, and high delinquency statistics.
The people who lived in it saw something entirely different: cheap, spacious
apartments, a neighborhood full of friends and family, and freedom from
attack by delinquents (who did their troublemaking outside the West End).
They noticed and complained about the lack of parking, but I was never
sure if they even saw the garbage-strewn alleys—and the vacated buildings
on them—since they were able to avoid them in their own activities.

The tenements built in the West End at the beginning of the twentieth
century were an ingenious example of that period's speculative builder
architecture designed to fit the demands of the law, the housing market,
and the profit motive, but they did deprive the first and second floors of
light and air. Air can be supplied by fans and air conditioners, but sunlight
cannot be substituted for. Even so, I doubt that these apartments were the
danger to health that planners have suggested. Many of the people who
inhabited them, all except the shut-ins perhaps, may have gotten sufficient
sunlight because they spent much time in the open, at work, at play, and in
street-corner socializing. (It would be interesting to discover whether they
spent more time outside than do the professionals whose values with
respect to light and air inside the house are reflected in housing standards.)

I do not mean to attack housing standards. However, if such standards
give people an effective choice between very cheap apartments with too
little sunlight and even moderately-priced apartments with sunlight, it can
easily be understood why poor people would choose the former.

These observations suggest that it is time to stop asking whether or not
"better" housing as such improves the living conditions of its tenants and to
inquire instead: what aspects of such housing have what impact on these
tenants, within the context of their lives and the choices open to them? For
example, most planners and housers would agree that moving people from
walk-up tenement apartments to single-family dwellings would be beneficial, but housing, like everything else, must be viewed within the context
of choices available to people. If the single-family house is located far from
job opportunities, it will not be beneficial to people who suffer from job
insecurity. They should be living where they are centrally located with
respect to job opportunities and mass-transit facilities. If such housing is
more expensive than what people had before, its advantages may be offset
by deprivations resulting from new budgetary pressures. Or if such housing
isolates people from a friendly social environment, it is not better for those

who depend on such an environment more than for "better" housing. Similarly, if planners locate a park in an overcrowded neighborhood without solving the housing problem in that area, the park may be interpreted by the neighborhood not as an improvement, but as an indication of the city's lack of interest in what its residents perceive as their real needs.

This is not an argument against better housing or more parks, but a reminder that the facilities planned must be better in terms of the frames of reference of both the planner and the users. In the terminology used previously, the planner's main tool is not the potential environment, but that environment as it would be defined in its effective form. There are, however, three important qualifications to the primacy of effective over potential environment.

First, there may be potential environmental conditions that will affect all aspects of the effective environment. For example, the biologist Jack Calhoun has argued that among rats, a certain level of density will result in such overcrowding as to paralyze their social system and result in depression, conflict, and eventual destruction of the rat population. In this instance, high density may well be an absolute environmental factor that operates regardless of the nature of the effective environment.

Calhoun and others have taken the findings of animal research to suggest that such absolute factors also control human behavior. Before one can agree with this argument, however, it is necessary to determine whether the findings of research on animals are transferable to human beings; whether higher densities will also have destructive effects on people. I doubt that such findings are always or even often transferable, because the relationship of rats to their environment is different from that of people to theirs. Rats and other animals make direct use of the natural environment; it provides them with food and shelter, and they can manipulate it only minimally. Human beings do not make such direct use of the natural environment; they manipulate nature and add or superimpose a built environment—as well as the functions and meanings that I have called the effective environment.

When people crowd a given space, they can adapt that space by building high-rise buildings, in which they may live at low floor densities if they can afford to do so, as on Park Avenue. Or, as in many third world societies, they may develop patterns that eschew privacy, enabling a large family to live together in a small space. Indeed, some cultures place such high value on sociability and on living in social proximity that they become anxious at low densities. For example, many of the West Enders I studied enjoyed living among their peers in five-story tenements and some were frightened by the low densities they saw in "the country," by which they meant the suburbs. They could live satisfactorily at densities that would have been anxiety provoking to middle-class people, whose individualistic cultural norms apply as much to residential densities as to economic arrangements.

Conversely, Calhoun's findings apply very much to people when they live in the same relationship to their environment as do animals: for example, farmers, hunters, fishermen—and city dwellers looking for a parking space. When a tribe of hunters or a group of farmers live in an area without sufficient fauna or flora to provide food, the members of such groups will starve, turn against one another, or unite to conquer the lands of another group so that they can obtain the needed food supply.

Until they are able to obtain that food supply, they may show the same social and emotional pathological reactions that Calhoun noticed among the rats he studied. Similarly, when parking spaces are insufficient, automobile owners will fight for the limited supply, and on a cold rainy day, sometimes like rats.

Until the findings of research among rats are tested systematically among people, it is wrong to argue that high density is always undesirable. Even so, some types of density may be bad for people as universally as for animals. Room overcrowding which forces even people from sociable cultures to live so closely together that they cannot avoid one another when their cultural norms demand privacy—for example, during sexual intercourse—is likely to have detrimental consequences. Similarly, structural overcrowding that leads to a breakdown of basic utilities such as plumbing facilities is undesirable for all people, regardless of their cultural norms for privacy and sociability.

A second qualification to the primacy of the effective environment is that parts of the potential environment may remain hidden; they may not be perceived by people and thus cannot become a part of the effective environment. For example, if the gasoline fumes exhausted by vehicles are shown to breed lung cancer, people living on major traffic routes who see nothing wrong with where they live because they have become used to breathing these fumes should be told that they are in danger of becoming ill with lung cancer. If they want to leave, they should be helped with all possible relocation aids, including new housing; if they do not want to leave once they have been informed of their other choices, including access to housing elsewhere, planners have done their duty. Still, ideally, people should not be forced to have to consider such choices, for residential areas should be far enough away from major highways to eliminate the danger of lung cancer or other diseases. If mass transit is not feasible, as it often is not, one can also hope that the electric or solar-powered car and truck will soon be perfected.

Third, what I have called a potential environment could always set off changes in the effective environment, if it were only tried. Thus, public recreation officials have often argued that if the right playground were provided for a neighborhood, the children would use it, even if they can be shown not to make much use of playgrounds at the present time. Similarly, architects opposed to suburban "sprawl" claim that people would accept high-rise housing if it were only built so that they could try it. Neither logic nor empirical inquiry enables us to determine the validity of this argument. The future cannot be predicted, and while one might argue that fundamental change, in housing type preferences, for example, occurs only rarely, such change does take place. Moreover, our present knowledge is never so complete that we can say with all assurance that a proposed innovation would not in fact fit needs, for there might be hidden needs that do not come into view in even the best research.

Since innovation is itself a value, especially among professionals, such proposals deserve testing. The problem arises only when the proposed innovation is so costly compared to the promised benefits that the community with limited resources cannot risk the luxury of failure. Under those conditions, it seems to me that the burden of proof falls on those who claim that the proposed playground or high-rise project will be accepted. Research can provide a little aid in this situation, for innovations are constantly being introduced in our society and others. These can be studied to determine under what conditions what kinds of innovation are adopted and which are rejected; and perhaps such data exist for high-rise housing in societies in which people who have a choice prefer to live at low densities.

This statement of the relationship of physical environment and human behavior does not deny the assumption that the former influences the latter. It only attempts to insert between these two concepts the idea of the effective environment, so that the argument about whether or not the physical environment affects human behavior can be replaced by the more fruitful question of when, how, how much, and with what consequences such effects occur—which are the kinds of questions that social scientists are apt to raise. If planners recognize that the potential and effective environments can never be alike, they may also become aware of the fact that they are inserting their own values into the process of transforming a potential environment into an effective environment. Moreover, even if they still lack the power to deal with the poverty of those who live in substandard housing, they may understand how poor people see and deal with the physical and social worlds in which they live. At that point, their plans may also begin to be helpful to the poor—and more generally, to all the people who are intended to use the results of the planners' work.

· T H R E E ·

URBAN VITALITY
AND THE
FALLACY OF
PHYSICAL
DETERMINISM

O NE OF THE basic themes in the ongoing critique of American society
has been the replacement (or destruction) of tradition by modernity,
and the critique has been especially bitter when modernity was mass-
produced. During the 1950s, the critique centered on the ravages produced
by pathological or vulgar mass culture and conformity-ridden cookie-cutter
suburbia—suburbia often being symbolized by mass-produced new towns
like Levittown. In the 1960s, new targets of criticism emerged. Mass
culture was replaced by equally dangerous television, and suburbia, by the
new city. Specifically, the critics objected to the appearance of inhumane
city buildings designed by "modern" architects and the concurrent destruction of smaller and older city structures and areas. The critics attacked
primarily big new office blocks and high-rise residential apartment projects,
and although these may not have been mass produced, the architecture
often looked sufficiently alike or uninspired to evoke the usual critical
hostility to mass production.

Many of the initial ideas behind the new urban critique have come from
the writings of Jane Jacobs, an associate editor of *Architectural Forum.*

Reprinted from *People and Plans* with minor changes, and with the addition of a postscript.
The original essay was published in *Commentary* in February 1962.

Now she has put her ideas into a book which seems destined to spearhead the attack, just as another book by an editor of another Luce magazine—William H. Whyte's *The Organization Man*—spearheaded the attack on suburbia. *The Death and Life of Great American Cities* is a thoughtful and imaginative tract on behalf of the traditional city, an analysis of the principles that make it desirable, an attack on the city planner—whom Ms. Jacobs takes to be the agent of its transformation—and a program of new planning principles that she believes will create vital cities and vital neighborhoods.

The vital neighborhood—and vitality is Jane Jacobs' central aim—should be diverse in its use of land and in the people who inhabit it. Every district should be a mixture of residences, business, and industry; of old buildings and new; of young people and old; of rich and poor. Ms. Jacobs argues that people want diversity, and in neighborhoods where it exists, they strike roots and participate in community life, thus generating vitality. When diversity is lacking, when neighborhoods are scourged by what she calls the great blight of dullness, residents who are free to leave do so and are replaced by the poverty-stricken, who have no other choice, and the areas soon turn into slums.

According to Ms. Jacobs, the most important component of vitality is an abundant street life. Neighborhoods that are designed to encourage people to use the streets, or to watch what goes on in them, make desirable quarters for residence, work, and play. Moreover, where there is street life, there is little crime, for the people on the street and in the buildings which overlook it watch and protect each other, thus discouraging criminal acts more efficiently than police patrols.

The abundance of street life, Ms. Jacobs argues, is brought about by planning principles which are diametrically opposed to those practiced by orthodox city planners. First, a district must have several functions, so that its buildings and streets are used at all times of the day and do not (like Wall Street) stand empty in off-hours. The area should be built up densely with structures close to the street and low enough in number of stories to encourage both street life and street watching. Blocks should be short, for corners invite stores, and these bring people out into the streets for shopping and socializing. Sidewalks should be wide enough for pavement socials and children's play; streets should be narrow enough to prevent intensive and high-speed automobile traffic, for the automobile frightens away pedestrians. Small parks and playgrounds are desirable, but large open spaces—especially those intended only for decoration and not for use

—not only deaden a district by separating people from one another but also invite criminals. Buildings should be both old and new, expensive and cheap, for low rents invite diversity in the form of new industries, shops, and artists' studios.

Neighborhoods which are designed on the basis of these principles— and which provide Ms. Jacobs with concrete evidence for her argument— are areas like New York's Greenwich Village and San Francisco's Telegraph Hill (where residences of all types, prices, and ages mix with small business, industry, and cultural facilities) and low-income ethnic quarters like Boston's North End and Chicago's Back-of-the-Yards district.

The new forms of city building, Ms. Jacobs says, discourage street life and create only dullness. High-rise apartment buildings, whether in public housing or private luxury flats, are standardized, architecturally undistinguished, and institutional in appearance if not operation. They house homogeneous populations, segregating people by income, race, and often even age and isolating them in purely residential quarters. Elevators, and the separation of the building from the street by a moat of useless open space, frustrate maternal supervision of children, thus keeping children off the street. Often there are no real streets at all, because prime access is by car. Nor is there any reason for people to use the streets, for instead of large numbers of small stores fronting on a street, there are shopping centers containing a small number of large stores—usually chains—each of which has a monopoly in its line. The small merchant, who watches the street and provides a center for neighborhood communication and social life, is absent here. In such projects, the residents have no place to meet each other, and there is no spontaneous neighborhood life. As a result, people have no feeling for their neighbors and no identification with the area. In luxury buildings, doormen watch the empty streets and discourage the criminal visitor, but in public housing projects, there are no doormen, and the interior streets and elevators invite rape, theft, and vandalism. Areas like this are blighted by dullness from the start and are destined to become slums before their time.

The major responsibility for the new forms of city building Ms. Jacobs places on the city planner and on two theories of city form: Ebenezer Howard's low-density Garden City and Le Corbusier's high-rise apartment complex, the Radiant City. Planners are artists who want to restructure life by principles applicable only to art. By putting these principles into action, they are methodically destroying the features that produce vitality. Planning theories have also influenced the policymakers, and especially realtors, bankers, and other sources of mortgage funds. As a result, they refuse to lend money to older but still vital areas which are trying to rehabilitate themselves, thus encouraging further deterioration of the structures until they are ripe for slum clearance, redevelopment with projects—and inevitable dullness.

Anyone who have ever wandered through New York's Greenwich Village or Boston's North End is bound to respond to Ms. Jacobs' conception of a vital city. Her analysis of the mechanics of street life, and of the ways in which people use buildings, streets, and vacant spaces in such areas, is eye-opening. The principles of neighborhood planning which derive from her observations—she is herself a resident of Greenwich Village—are far more closely attuned to how people actually live than are those of orthodox city planning. It would be easy to succumb to the charm of the neighborhoods she describes and to read her book only as a persuasive appeal for their retention. But since Ms. Jacobs is out to reform all of city planning, it is necessary to examine her central ideas more closely.

Her argument is built on three fundamental assumptions: that people desire diversity; that diversity is ultimately what makes cities live and that the lack of it makes them die; and that buildings, streets, and the planning principles on which they are based shape human behavior. The first two of these assumptions are not entirely supported by the facts of the areas she describes. The last assumption, which she shares with the planners whom she attacks, might be called the *physical fallacy,* and it leads her to ignore the social, cultural, and economic factors that contribute to vitality or dullness. It also blinds her to less visible kinds of neighborhood vitality and to the true causes of the city's problems.

Ethnic neighborhoods like the North End, or the Italian and Irish sections of Greenwich Village, are not diverse, but quite homogeneous in population as well as in building type. The street life of these areas stems not so much from their physical character as from the working-class culture of their inhabitants. In this culture, the home is reserved for the family, so that much social life takes place outdoors. Also, children are not kept indoors as frequently as in the middle class, and since they are less closely supervised in their play, they too wind up in the streets.

If such districts are near the downtown area, they may attract intellectuals, artists, and Bohemian types, who also tend to spend a good deal of time outside their apartments, contributing further to the street life. The street life, the small stores that traditionally serve ethnic groups and other cultural minorities, and the area's exotic flavor then draw visitors and tourists, whose presence helps to make the district even livelier. The resulting blend of unusual cultures makes for a highly visible kind of vitality. It helps if the district is old and basically European in architecture, but traditional-looking frontages can be superimposed by today's clever builder.

In other working-class neighborhoods, especially those far away from the downtown area, street life is also abundant, but the people and the stores are neither ethnic nor esoteric. In middle-class neighborhoods, there is no street life, for social activities take place inside the home, children play less often on the sidewalks, and the street is used only for transportation. Such neighborhoods look dull, notably to the visitor, and therefore they seem to be less vital than their ethnic and Bohemian counterparts. But visibility is not the only measure of vitality, and areas that are uninteresting to the visitor may be quite vital to the people who live in them.

This possibility must also be considered for the new luxury and middle-class housing projects. Since they are largely occupied by childless middle-class people, they look even duller than other areas, just as their newness makes them seem more standardized to the visitor than older areas in which the initial homogeneity of buildings has been altered by conversion or just covered by the accretions of dirt and age. It is clear that we need to learn how residents live in such projects before we can be sure of the validity of Ms. Jacobs' charges.

In proposing that cities be planned to stimulate an abundant street life, Ms. Jacobs not only overestimates the power of planning in shaping behavior but in effect demands that middle-class people adopt working-class styles of family life, child rearing and sociability. The truth is that the new forms of residential building—in suburb as well as city—are not products of orthodox planning theory, but expressions of the middle-class culture which guides the housing market and which planners also serve. Often the planners serve it too loyally, and they ignore the needs of a working-class population. Thus, Jane Jacobs' criticism is most relevant to the planning of public housing projects, for its middle-class designers have made no provision for the street life that some of its tenants probably want.

But middle-class people, especially those raising children, do not want working-class—or even Bohemian—neighborhoods. They do not want the visible vitality of a North End, but rather the quiet and the privacy obtainable in low-density neighborhoods and elevator apartment houses. Not all of their social life involves neighbors, and their friends may be scattered all over the metropolitan area, as are the commercial and recreational facilities which they frequent. For this, they want a car, expressways, and all the freedom of movement that expressways create when properly planned. Middle-class people tend to value status over convenience, and thus they reject neighborhoods in which residence and business are mixed—or in which there is any real diversity in population. Having no love for walking or for riding public transit, they have brought shopping centers into being. Nor does their life-style leave much room for the small merchant. Since their tastes are no longer ethnic but not yet esoteric, they prefer the supermarket to the small store, for it does provide more choice—if only among prosaic items—and its wider aisles facilitate gossip with neighbors.

One can quarrel with some of these tastes, but the fact is that the areas about which Ms. Jacobs writes were built for a style of life which is out of fashion with the large majority of Americans who are free to choose their place of residence. The North End and Chicago's Back-of-the-Yards district are not holding their young people, who tend to move to the suburbs as soon as they have children to raise. Even in Europe, the old working-class districts invariably empty out when prosperity reaches the blue-collar workers.

Middle-class visitors do not see these cultural changes. Nor do they see that the houses in these traditional districts are often hard to maintain, that parking is often impossible, that noise and dirt are ever present, that some of the neighbors watch too much, and that not all the shopkeepers are kind. Because the traditional districts are so different from his or her own neighborhood, and because he or she is a visitor, he or she sees only their charm and excitement. Visitors are therefore most understandably reluctant to see them disappear.

But for the planning of cities, the visitor's wishes are less important than the inhabitant's. One cannot design all neighborhoods for a traditional style of life if only a few people want to live this way. Nevertheless, areas like the North End and Greenwich Village are worth saving. They provide low-rent housing for people with low incomes; they give pleasure to visitors and may even attract tourists; and they are appealing reminders of our European heritage and our preautomobile past. The city would be a poorer place without them.

Even so, the future of the American city is not going to be determined by the life or death of the North Ends and the Greenwich Villages. The real problems lie elsewhere. Ms. Jacobs' concentration on these areas diverts her from properly analyzing the more fundamental problems, even while she makes some highly pertinent comments. This can be best illustrated by examining her discussion of slums and her proposals for urban renewal.

As noted earlier, she argues that slums are caused ultimately by lack of diversity. Homogeneous and dull areas are deserted by residents who have the resources to go elsewhere and are replaced by people who have no other choice and who, for reasons of poverty and racial discrimination, are forced to live in overcrowded conditions. She suggests that if these areas could be made more diverse, the initial occupants might not leave, and owners would then be able to rehabilitate the buildings.

This analysis is too simple. People leave such areas, not to seek diversity, but to practice new life-styles, and additional diversity would not persuade them to stay. It is true that some areas occupied by nonmobile ethnic groups, notably the North End and Back-of-the-Yards, hold their residents longer than other areas. It is also true that these areas are not slums; they are low-rent districts, and Ms. Jacobs is right in insisting on the distinction. Slums (she calls them perpetual slums) are areas in which housing and other facilities are physically and socially harmful to the inhabitants and to the larger community, primarily because of overcrowding. Low-rent areas (which she calls unslumming slums) may look equally dilapidated to the casual observer—and planners sometimes base their decisions only on casual observation—but they are not overcrowded and they are not harmful. Ms. Jacobs criticizes urban renewal—and rightly so—for confusing such areas with real slums and clearing them needlessly with grievous hurt to their inhabitants. She proposes that they can be rehabilitated by providing home and tenement owners with easier access to mortgage funds and by planning for greater diversity. This proposal has merit, although landlords probably would not undertake as much rehabilitation as she envisages unless the area were attracting middle-class people with quasi-Bohemian tastes, as in the case of Greenwich Village and Philadelphia's West Rittenhouse Square district.

But such neighborhoods—and purely working-class ones like the North End—are numerically unimportant in most cities. It is also no coincidence that they are occupied almost exclusively by whites. Their improvement cannot solve the problem of the real slums. These slums are caused not by dullness—they are often similar in plan and architecture to low-rent areas—but by the overcrowding of already old buildings by poverty-stricken and otherwise deprived peoples, who have no other place to go. To be sure, such people usually move into areas being deserted by their previous residents, but even when the older residents are not leaving, the same thing can happen. Chicago's Hyde Park district was not being deserted by its middle-class residents, but portions of it became a slum because the "Black Belt" to the north simply could not accommodate any more inmigrants.

Once an area becomes an overcrowded slum, rehabilitating the structures is no solution. The crucial step in rehabilitation is the uncrowding of the buildings. But slum structures are owned by absentee landlords who have no incentive to rehabilitate because they reap immense profits from overcrowding. Even if they were willing to convert rooming houses back to apartments, most of the slum dwellers who would then have to move would not be able to do so. They cannot afford to pay the rentals demanded for an apartment, and when they are nonwhite, other districts of the city are unwilling to accept them even if there are vacant apartments, which is rarely the case.

The slums cannot be emptied unless and until there is more low-cost housing elsewhere. Private enterprise cannot afford to build such housing. The traditional solution has been to rely on public housing, but thanks to the opposition of the real-estate industry and the private builders, it was never supplied in large enough amounts. Even then, it had to be located in the slums, because other city districts were unwilling to give over vacant or industrial land. In order to minimize clearance, public housing has had to resort to elevator buildings, and in order to protect itself from the surrounding slums, it has constructed fenced-in projects. In order to satisfy its powerful opponents that it was not wasting tax money on ne'er-do-wells, it has had to impose institutional restrictions on its hapless occupants, and in order to avoid competition with the private housing market, it has been forced to expel tenants whose income rises above a certain level.

Ms. Jacobs suggests that the government stop building public housing and instead subsidize builders to make their units available to low-income tenants. This is a useful suggestion, and one that has been proposed by planners and public housing advocates before. But earlier attempts to scatter low-income housing in other ways have been rejected by the recipient neighborhoods. Ms. Jacobs' scheme has more merit than some earlier ones, but I doubt whether middle-class areas in the city and suburbs will make room for the large number of nonwhite poor who need to be taken out of overcrowded slums.

The sad fact is that until we abolish poverty and discrimination—or until the middle class becomes tolerant of poor nonwhite neighbors—the government is probably going to have to build more low-income ghettos.

Unfortunately, Ms. Jacobs' anger with the planners is so intense that she blames them for the sins of private enterprise and the middle class, and she is eager to return functions to private enterprise that it has shown itself unable and unwilling to perform. She also forgets that private enterprise—acting through the well-heeled builder and realtor lobby in Washington—is responsible for some of the more obnoxious features of the urban-renewal laws and for hamstringing public housing in the ways I have indicated. Her blanket indictment of planners detracts from the persuasiveness of her other proposals and antagonizes people who might agree with her on many points. More important, it is likely to win her the support of those who profit from the status quo, of the nostalgic who want to bring back the city and the society of the eighteenth and nineteenth centuries, and of the ultra-right-wing groups who oppose planning—and all government action—whether good or bad.

Orthodox city planning deserves considerable criticism for its antiurban bias, for giving higher priority to buildings, plans, and design concepts than to the needs of people, and for trying to transform ways of living before even examining how people live or want to live. But not all the planners think this way—actually, much of the theory Ms. Jacobs rejects was developed by architects and architecturally trained planners—and some of her ideas have in fact been set forth by planners themselves.

No one, it is true, has stated these ideas as forcefully as she or integrated them into an overall approach before. The neighborhoods with which she is most concerned cannot serve as models for future planning, but the way in which she has observed them, the insights she has derived, and the principles she has inferred from her observations can be and ought to be adapted for use in planning cities and suburbs in the future. Her book is a path-breaking achievement, and because it is so often right, I am all the more disappointed by the fact that it is also so often wrong.

· P O S T S C R I P T ·

JANE JACOBS' *The Death and Life of Great American Cities* is now thirty years old (it was published in 1961), and it is not difficult to guess why it is still popular and influential. Whether intentionally or not, she has turned out to be quite prescient; for the urban way of life she associated with Greenwich Village and which she in effect preached in the book has itself become popular and spread far beyond the Village and the handful of other neighborhoods she mentioned in the book.

To be sure, she was describing both an essentially white ethnic working-class style of life and an upper-middle-class one, and what has become popular is the upper-middle-class variant. While young urban professionals existed when she wrote (she herself as well as this author having been in that category themselves once), their numbers were far fewer and their disposable income considerably less before the rise of the urban professional service industries. (Indeed, in the early 1960s they were not important enough to be noticed by the mass media and to be called yuppies.)

When she wrote the book, gentrification had already been in existence on a small scale as well, though the term had not yet been invented, but it too flourished after the book became famous and influential—so much so that Jane Jacobs has sometimes been unjustly held responsible for the arrival of gentrification.

The Death and Life of Great American Cities also remains popular because Ms. Jacobs' antigovernment, antibureaucracy and antiprofessional perspective and her faith in private enterprise's ability to do better in restoring cities to life became widespread as well, although as part of a right-wing politics which I doubt that she then shared or now shares.

Furthermore, the book continues to be popular and important because of her persuasive call for more urban vitality. This is something that is always lacking in big cities, where change has to be funneled through a bureaucratic system so as to prevent the return of autocratic decision making, as typified by Robert Moses. In addition, and perhaps even more important, she spoke for vitality on a small scale, without the gigantistic growth that has created another kind of vitality in many urban downtowns. Indeed, in many respects she represented an antigrowth position, but one that did not automatically include stasis.

Jane Jacobs was not completely prescient and it would be unfair to expect her to be, especially because urban economies have changed so drastically in the last thirty years. I have already noted that the urban life-style she sought has developed mainly in the upper-middle class, and the street life that accompanies it is around mainly on weekends. Then, too, she did not notice that the mixed-class neighborhoods she thought desirable did not long stay that way. Even when the gentrifiers want diversity, the poor people in the areas into which they move are quickly forced out by rising rents. Besides, most gentrifiers actually only like poor or working-class people who can pay enough rent so that their buildings do not look slummy, who share some of the middle-class life-styles, or who keep discordant behavior strictly invisible.

Moreover, she could not have realized the extent to which the developers of high-rise housing would still be in business, including in gentrified areas, if only because the demand for housing in such areas far exceeded the supply of small old houses that could be gentrified. The small stores she favors came into being, and continue to do so, but again, they are followed by supermarkets and department stores—although some of the latter are collections of small stores, or boutiques as they are now called, under one roof.

Finally, Ms. Jacobs' faith in private enterprise was not justified, for most of the developers of high-rise housing built the same standard buildings they have always built, except that they look even more out of scale next to six-story tenements and old town houses. More significant, private enterprise never did anything for the poor once government, as far back as the second Nixon administration, virtually shut down public-housing construction and other housing programs for the poor. Ms. Jacobs should have known better than to expect more from private enterprise, for it has been unable and unwilling to build for the poor since the start of the twentieth century. Conversely, Ms. Jacobs' idea of mixing private and subsidized units was implemented as the so-called eighty–twenty plan, which has produced some additions to the low-income housing supply for poor or moderate-income people. The major actors in the low-income housing market have been the nonprofit groups, but for all practical purposes, they did not exist when Ms. Jacobs was writing.

Although the major flaws in the book can be traced to Ms. Jacobs' physical determinism, she has also been a closer analyst of everyday city life than most other people, including planners and urban sociologists. *Death and Life of Great American Cities* reflects the findings of a gifted urban observer who lived where she was studying, and the book shows it still. Yet perhaps the primary long-run effect of the book has been its own vitality, and the interest it created in cities and city living, especially among students and other young people. That interest seems to be here to stay for a while, even if many of the "yuppies," present and future, will still move out to the suburbs when they "settle down" and have children.

UNDERSTANDING
CITIES
AND
SUBURBS

· I N T R O D U C T I O N ·

PART 1 OF this book consists of essays that dealt largely with the human uses of small environments, from houses and blocks to streets and neighborhoods. Now I shift to the larger canvas of cities, and therefore to different issues as well.

Although the essays that follow are no longer concerned so much with making the immediate environment user oriented or user-friendly, some of them still stress that people's ties to the physical environment have been exaggerated. Indeed, Chapter 4, which I wrote while analyzing my data from my study of suburban Levittown, concludes with the point that people's lives are not determined by whether they live in cities or suburbs, or by their relationship to the built environment generally. Rather, I pointed out that which side of the city limits people live on is much less important for understanding their behavior than their socioeconomic level and life-cycle position—i.e., their jobs, incomes, schooling, and ages, and what these imply about their position in the society. (Like most other males writing in 1962, I paid insufficient attention to gender, or to the role of race, but that was mainly because the essay focused so much on the relationship between social structure and the physical environment.)

The essay is also a critique of Louis Wirth's classic, and once definitive, conception of the city, written twenty-five years after Wirth's 1938 article, when the suburban exodus was in full swing. Still, I also suggested that my essay was as time bound as Wirth's and now that my original article is nearly thirty years old, I have updated it as well with a brief postscript.

Chapter 5 is in some respects a sequel to chapter 4, because it looks again at cities and suburbs, and also nearly thirty years after chapter 4 was written. However, its main theme is a comparison of the two dominant schools of urban sociology, neo-ecology and neo-Marxism, and how they explain what has been going on in American cities and suburbs. Since I rarely agree with either, I also offer my own explanations for various aspects of the urban and suburban experience since World War II.

When I wrote the first version of the essay, a small group of neo-ecologists had gained some attention in Washington, both in the Carter and the Reagan administrations, and that had me worried. I was not entirely happy with the neo-Marxists either, however. While their coming into the field revived American urban sociology and gave it a needed emphasis on the relationship between economic and political power, they failed to see other aspects of what was happening to both cities and suburbs.

I had originally sought to end the essay with a liberal conclusion, a description of a liberal urban sociology in fact, but I could not find a way of connecting liberalism qua political ideology with an empirical approach to the study of cities. Also, a list of liberal urban policy issues on which further research was needed would have been trite, since most of the policy issues discussed by urban sociologists have been liberal for a long time. Besides, my thinking was running much more along populist lines, and so I concluded chapter 5 with some observations on user-oriented sociology, the major users I had in mind being the working- and lower-middle-class Americans often called Middle Americans, about whom I had just finished a book.

Nonetheless, if neo-ecology, which is basically on the right of the ideological spectrum and neo-Marxism, which is on the left, continue to dominate urban sociology, an attempt to develop a liberal urban sociology is worthwhile. However, many of America's neo-Marxists are turning into left-liberals, or social democrats, in their policy thinking already and may actually end up developing the needed liberal urban sociology.

Chapter 6, which I gave at a conference of historians of ancient cities, takes off in some ways from chapter 4. That chapter questioned the conventional distinctions between city and suburb; this essay tries to figure out how one can compare a set of settlements over time which are all called cities, but which otherwise are quite diverse.

The essay has no direct policy-relevance, and was not meant to have any. Instead, I was starting to look at the social role of concepts and names, something that is analytically relevant because American cities are changing in function and structure so that adjectives have to be added to describe them properly. For example, we talk of central, inner, and outer cities and are inventing a bewildering variety of new terms to describe the now-urbanizing suburbs. (Nearly twenty years later I undertook a second examination of a concept and name, and this one, of the underclass, does have policy relevance, and is the final chapter of this book.)

The last essay in this section is also policy relevant. It is a critical review of Robert Caro's exhaustive study of Robert Moses, and I include it here because of a recent trend to treat Robert Moses and his planning methods more kindly than I think they deserve. I am also including it because it puts Moses into the social and political context that made his successes possible. By calling attention to other men (women were not considered for such jobs then) in other cities who built in much the same way as Robert Moses did, if on a smaller scale, I sought to emphasize the conditions that produced all these men, and to deflate the image of Moses as the Master Builder.

At the same time, I wanted to demonstrate that a sociological analysis of

Moses and the people whom he served explained more of the recent history of American cities than an analysis that centered on the individual as Great Man. If Moses was a hero to many, and is becoming a hero again —a point I discuss in the brief postscript—then I also want to add, in paraphrase, Berthold Brecht's classic point in *Galileo* that sorry is the city that needs a hero.

URBANISM AND SUBURBANISM AS WAYS OF LIFE: A REEVALUATION OF DEFINITIONS

THE CONTEMPORARY SOCIOLOGICAL conception of cities and of urban life is based largely on the work of the Chicago School and its summary statement in Louis Wirth's essay "Urbanism as a Way of Life."[1] In that paper, Wirth developed a "minimum sociological definition of the city" as "a relatively large, dense and permanent settlement of socially heterogeneous individuals." From these prerequisites, he then deduced the major outlines of the urban way of life. As he saw it, number, density, and heterogeneity created a social structure in which primary-group relationships were inevitably replaced by secondary contacts that were impersonal, segmental, superficial, transitory, and often predatory in nature. As a result, the city dweller became anonymous, isolated, secular, relativistic, rational, and sophisticated. In order to function in an urban society, he or she was forced to combine with others to organize corporations, voluntary associations, representative forms of government, and the impersonal mass media of communications. These replaced the primary groups and the integrated way of life found in rural and other preindustrial settlements.

Wirth's paper has become a classic in urban sociology, and most texts have followed his definition and description faithfully.[2] In recent years,

---

Reprinted from *People and Plans*. I have added a postscript.

however, a considerable number of studies and essays have questioned his formulations.[3] In addition, a number of changes have taken place in cities since the article was published in 1938, notably the exodus of white residents to low- and medium-priced houses in the suburbs and the decentralization of industry. The evidence from these studies and the changes in American cities suggest that Wirth's statement must be revised.

There is yet another and more important reason for such a revision. Despite its title and intent, Wirth's paper deals with urban-industrial society, rather than with the city. This is evident from his approach. Like other urban sociologists, Wirth based his analysis on a comparison of settlement types, but unlike his colleagues, who pursued urban-rural comparisons, Wirth contrasted the city to the folk society. Thus, he compared settlement types of preindustrial and industrial society. This allowed him to include in his theory of urbanism the entire range of modern institutions which are not found in the folk society, even though many such groups (for example, voluntary associations) are by no means exclusively urban. Moreover, Wirth's conception of the city dweller as depersonalized, atomized, and susceptible to mass movements suggests that his paper is based on, and contributes to, the theory of the mass society.

Many of Wirth's conclusions may be relevant to the understanding of ways of life in modern society. However, since the theory argues that all of society is now urban, his analysis does not distinguish ways of life in the city from those in other settlements within modern society. In Wirth's time, the comparison of urban and preurban settlement types was still fruitful, but today, the primary task for urban (or community) sociology seems to me to be the analysis of the similarities and differences between contemporary settlement types.

This paper is an attempt at such an analysis; it limits itself to distinguishing ways of life in the modern city and the modern suburb. A reanalysis of Wirth's conclusions from this perspective suggests that his characterization of the urban way of life applies only—and not too accurately—to the residents of the inner city. The remaining city dwellers, as well as most suburbanites, pursue a different way of life which I shall call "quasi-primary." This proposition raises some doubt about the mutual exclusiveness of the concepts of city and suburb and leads to a yet broader question: whether settlement concepts and other ecological concepts are useful for explaining ways of life.

THE INNER CITY

WIRTH ARGUED that number, density, and heterogeneity had two social consequences which explain the major features of urban life. On the one hand, the crowding of diverse types of people into a small area led to the segregation of homogeneous types of people into separate neighborhoods. On the other hand, the lack of physical distance between city dwellers resulted in social contact between them, which broke down existing social and cultural patterns and encouraged assimilation as well as acculturation— the melting-pot effect. Wirth implied that the melting-pot effect was far more powerful than the tendency toward segregation and concluded that, sooner or later, the pressures engendered by the dominant social, economic, and political institutions of the city would destroy the remaining pockets of primary-group relationships. Eventually, the social system of the city would resemble Tönnies' *Gesellschaft*—a way of life which Wirth considered undesirable.

Because Wirth had come to see the city as the prototype of mass society, and because he examined the city from the distant vantage point of the folk society—from the wrong end of the telescope, so to speak—his view of urban life is not surprising. In addition, Wirth found support for his theory in the empirical work of his Chicago colleagues. As Greer and Kube[4] and Wilensky[5] have pointed out, the Chicago sociologists conducted their most intensive studies in the inner city.[6] At that time, it consisted mainly of slums recently invaded by new waves of European immigrants and rooming-house and skid-row districts, as well as the habitat of Bohemians and well-to-do "Gold Coast" apartment dwellers. Wirth himself studied the Maxwell Street Ghetto, a poor inner-city Jewish neighborhood then being dispersed by the acculturation and mobility of its inhabitants.[7] Some of the characteristics of urbanism which Wirth stressed in his essay abounded in these areas.

Wirth's diagnosis of the city as *Gesellschaft* must be questioned on three counts. First, the conclusions derived from a study of the inner city cannot be generalized to the entire urban area. Second, there is as yet not enough evidence to prove—or, admittedly, to deny—that number, density, and heterogeneity result in the social consequences which Wirth proposed. Finally, even if the causal relationship could be verified, it can be shown that a significant proportion of the city's inhabitants were, and are, isolated from these consequences by social structures and cultural patterns which they either brought to the city or developed by living in it. Wirth conceived the urban population as consisting of heterogeneous individuals, torn from past social systems, unable to develop new ones, and therefore prey to social anarchy in the city. While it is true that a not insignificant proportion of the inner-city population was, and still is, made up of unattached individuals,[8] Wirth's formulation ignores the fact that this population consists mainly of relatively homogeneous groups, with social and cultural moorings that shield it fairly effectively from the suggested consequences of number, density, and heterogeneity. This applies even more to the residents of the outer city, who constitute a majority of the total city population.

The social and cultural moorings of the inner-city population are best described by a brief analysis of the five major types of inner-city residents. These are: 1. the "cosmopolites"; 2. the unmarried or childless; 3. the "ethnic villagers"; 4. the "deprived"; and 5. the "trapped" and downward-mobile.

The "cosmopolites" include students, artists, writers, musicians, and entertainers, as well as other intellectuals and professionals. They live in the city in order to be near the special "cultural" facilities that can be located only near the center of the city. Many cosmopolites are unmarried or childless. Others rear children in the city, especially if they have the income to afford the aid of servants and governesses. The less affluent ones may move to the suburbs to raise their children, continuing to live as cosmopolites under considerable handicaps, especially in the lower-middle-class suburbs. Many of the very rich and powerful are also cosmopolites, although they are likely to have at least two residences, one of which is suburban or exurban.

The unmarried or childless must be divided into two subtypes, depending on the permanence or transience of their status. The temporarily unmarried or childless live in the inner city for only a limited time. Young adults may team up to rent an apartment away from their parents and close to job or entertainment opportunities. When they marry, they may move first to an apartment in a transient neighborhood, but if they can afford to do so, they leave for the outer city or the suburbs with the arrival of the first or second child. The permanently unmarried may stay in the inner city for the remainder of their lives, their housing depending on their income.

The "ethnic villagers" are ethnic groups which are found in such inner-city neighborhoods as New York's Lower East Side, living in some ways as they did when they were peasants in European or Puerto Rican villages.[9] Although they reside in the city, they isolate themselves from significant contact with most city facilities, aside from workplaces. Their way of life differs sharply from Wirth's urbanism in its emphasis on kinship and the primary group, the lack of anonymity and secondary-group contacts, the weakness of formal organizations, and the suspicion of anything and anyone outside their neighborhood.

The first two types live in the inner city by choice; the third is there partly because of necessity, partly because of tradition. The final two types are in the inner city because they have no other choice. One is the "deprived" population: the emotionally disturbed or otherwise handicapped; broken families; and, most important, the poor-white and especially the nonwhite population. These urban dwellers must take the dilapidated housing and blighted neighborhoods to which the housing market relegates them, although among them are some for whom the slum is a hiding place or a temporary stopover to save money for a house in the outer city or the suburbs.[10]

The "trapped" are the people who stay behind when a neighborhood is invaded by nonresidential land uses or lower-status immigrants, because they cannot afford to move or are otherwise bound to their present location.[11] The "downward-mobiles" are a related type; they may have started life in a higher class position, but have been forced down in the socioeconomic hierarchy and in the quality of their accommodations. Many of them are old people, living out their existence on small pensions.

These five types may all live in dense and heterogeneous surroundings; yet they have such diverse ways of life that it is hard to see how density and heterogeneity could exert a common influence. Moreover, all but the last two types are isolated or detached from their neighborhood and thus from the social consequences that Wirth described.

When people who live together have social ties based on criteria other than mere common occupancy, they can set up social barriers, regardless of the physical closeness or the heterogeneity of their neighbors. The ethnic villagers are the best illustration. While a number of ethnic groups are usually found living together in the same neighborhood, they are able to isolate themselves from one another through a variety of social devices. Wirth himself recognized this when he wrote that "two groups can occupy a given area without losing their separate identity because each side is permitted to live its own inner life and each somehow fears or idealizes the other."[12] Although it is true that the children in these areas were often oblivious of the social barriers set up by their parents, at least until adolescence, it is doubtful whether their acculturation can be traced to the melting-pot effect as much as to the pervasive influence of the American culture that flowed into these areas from the outside.[13]

The cosmopolites, the unmarried, and the childless are *detached* from neighborhood life. The cosmopolites possess a distinct subculture which causes them to be uninterested in all but the most superficial contacts with their neighbors, somewhat like the ethnic villagers. The unmarried and childless—who may also be cosmopolites—are detached from the neighborhood because of their life-cycle stage, which frees them from the routine family responsibilities that entail some relationship to the local area. In their choice of residence, the two types are therefore not always concerned about their neighbors or the availability and quality of local community facilities. Even the well-to-do can choose expensive apartments in or near poor neighborhoods, because if they have children, these are sent to special schools and summer camps which effectively isolate them from neighbors. In addition, the childless and unmarried are often transient. Therefore, they tend to live in areas marked by high population turnover, where their own mobility and that of their neighbors creates a universal detachment from the neighborhood. [14]

The deprived and the trapped do seem to be affected by some of the consequences of number, density, and heterogeneity. The deprived population suffers considerably from overcrowding, but this is a consequence of low income, racial discrimination, and other handicaps and cannot be considered an inevitable result of the ecological makeup of the city. [15] Because the deprived have no residential choice, they are also forced to live amid neighbors not of their own choosing, with ways of life different and even contradictory to their own. If familial defenses against the neighborhood climate are weak, as may happen among single-parent families and downward-mobile people, parents may lose their children to the culture of "the street." The trapped are the unhappy people who remain behind when their more advantaged neighbors move on; they must endure the heterogeneity which results from neighborhood change.

Wirth's description of the urban way of life fits best the transient areas of the inner city. Such areas are typically heterogeneous in population, partly because they are inhabited by transient types who do not require homogeneous neighbors or by deprived people who have no choice or may themselves be quite mobile. Under conditions of transience and heterogeneity, people interact only in terms of the segmental roles necessary for obtaining local services. Their social relationships may thus display anonymity, impersonality, and superficiality. [16]

The social features of Wirth's concept of urbanism seem, therefore, to be a result of residential instability, rather than of number, density, or heterogeneity. In fact, heterogeneity is itself an effect of residential instability, resulting when the influx of transients causes landlords and realtors to stop acting as gatekeepers—that is, wardens of neighborhood homo-geneity.[17] Residential instability is found in all types of settlements, and presumably its social consequences are everywhere similar. These consequences cannot, therefore, be identified with the ways of life of the city.

THE OUTER CITY AND THE SUBURBS

THE SECOND effect which Wirth ascribed to number, density, and hetero-geneity was the segregation of homogeneous people into distinct neighborhoods[18] on the basis of "place and nature of work, income, racial and ethnic characteristics, social status, custom, habit, taste, preference and prejudice."[19] This description fits the residential districts of the *outer city*.[20] Although these districts contain the majority of the city's inhabitants, Wirth went into little detail about them. He made it clear, however, that the sociopsychological aspects of urbanism were prevalent there as well.[21]

Because existing neighborhood studies deal primarily with the exotic sections of the inner city, very little is known about the more typical residential neighborhoods of the outer city. However, it is evident that the way of life in these areas bears little resemblance to Wirth's urbanism. Both the studies which question Wirth's formulation and my own observa-tions suggest that the common element in the ways of life of these neigh-borhoods is best described as *quasi-primary*. I use this term to characterize relationships between neighbors. Whatever the intensity or frequency of these relationships, the interaction is more intimate than a secondary con-tact, but more guarded than a primary one.[22]

There are actually few secondary relationships, because of the isolation of residential neighborhoods from economic institutions and workplaces. Even shopkeepers, store managers, and other local functionaries who live in the area are treated as acquaintances or friends, unless they are of a vastly different social status or are forced by their corporate employers to treat their customers as economic units.[23] Voluntary associations attract only a minority of the population. Moreover, much of the organizational activity is of a sociable nature, and it is often difficult to accomplish the association's "business" because of the members' preference for sociability. Thus, it would appear that interactions in organizations, or between neigh-bors generally, do not fit the secondary-relationship model of urban life. As anyone who has lived in these neighborhoods knows, there is little anonym-ity, impersonality, or privacy.[24] In fact, American cities have sometimes been described as collections of small towns.[25] There is some truth to this description, especially if the city is compared to the actual small town, rather than to the romantic construct of antiurban critics.[26]

Postwar suburbia represents the most contemporary version of the quasi-primary way of life. Owing to increases in real income and the encouragement of homeownership provided by the F.H.A., families in the lower middle class and upper working class can now live in modern single-family homes in low-density subdivisions, an opportunity previously available only to the upper and upper-middle classes.[27]

The popular literature of the 1950s described the new suburbs as communities in which conformity, homogeneity, and other-direction are unusually rampant.[28] The implication is that the move from city to suburb initiates a new way of life which causes considerable behavior and personality change in previous urbanites. My research in Levittown, New Jersey, suggests, however, that the move from the city to this predominantly lower-middle-class suburb does not result in any major behavioral changes for most people. Moreover, the changes which do occur reflect the move from the social isolation of a transient city or suburban apartment building to the quasi-primary life of a neighborhood of single-family homes. Also, many of the people whose life has changed report that the changes were intended. They existed as aspirations before the move or as reasons for it. In other words, the suburb itself creates few changes in ways of life.[29]

A COMPARISON OF CITY AND SUBURB

IF OUTER-URBAN and suburban areas are similar in that the way of life in both is quasi-primary, and if urban residents who move out to the suburbs do not undergo any significant changes in behavior, it is fair to argue that the differences in ways of life between the two types of settlements have been overestimated. Yet the fact remains that a variety of physical and demographic differences exist between the city and the suburb. However, upon closer examination, many of these differences turn out to be either spurious or of little significance for the way of life of the inhabitants.[30]

The differences between the residential areas of cities and suburbs which have been cited most frequently are:

1. Suburbs are more likely to be dormitories.
2. They are further away from the work and play facilities of the central business districts.
3. They are newer and more modern than city residential areas and are

designed for the automobile rather than for pedestrian and mass-transit forms of movement.

4. They are built up with single-family rather than multifamily structures and are therefore less dense.
5. Their populations are more homogeneous.
6. Their populations differ demographically: they are younger; more of them are married; they have higher incomes; and they hold proportionately more white-collar jobs. [31]

Most urban neighborhoods are as much dormitories as the suburbs. Only in a few older inner-city areas are factories and offices still located in the middle of residential blocks, and even here many of the employees do not live in the neighborhood.

The fact that the suburbs are farther from the central business district is often true only in terms of distance, not travel time. Moreover, most people make relatively little use of downtown facilities, other than workplaces. [32] Many downtown stores seem to hold their greatest attraction for the upper-middle class; [33] the same is probably true of typically urban entertainment facilities. Teenagers and young adults may take their dates to first-run movie theaters, but the museums, concert halls, and lecture rooms attract mainly upper-middle-class ticket buyers, many of them suburban. [34]

The suburban reliance on the train and the automobile has given rise to an imaginative folklore about the consequences of commuting on alcohol consumption, sex life, and parental duties. Many of these conclusions are, however, drawn from selected high-income suburbs and exurbs and reflect job tensions in such hectic occupations as advertising and show business more than the effects of residence. [35] It is true that the upper-middle-class housewife must become a chauffeur in order to expose her children to the proper educational facilities, but such differences as walking to the corner drugstore and driving to its suburban equivalent seem to me of little emotional, social, or cultural import. [36] In addition, the continuing shrinkage in the number of mass-transit users suggests that even in the city many younger people are now living a wholly auto-based way of life.

The fact that suburbs are smaller is primarily a function of political boundaries drawn long before the communities were suburban. This affects the kinds of political issues which develop and provides somewhat greater opportunity for citizen participation. Even so, in the suburbs as in the city, the minority who participate routinely are the professional politicians, the economically concerned businesspeople, lawyers, and salespeople, and the ideologically motivated middle- and upper-middle-class people with better than average education.

The social consequences of differences in density and house type also seem overrated. Single-family houses in quiet streets facilitate the supervision of children; this is one reason why middle-class parents who want to keep an eye on their children move to the suburbs. House type also has some effects on relationships between neighbors, insofar as there are more opportunities for visual contact between adjacent homeowners than between people on different floors of an apartment house. However, if occupants' characteristics are also held constant, the differences in actual social contact are less marked. Homogeneity of residents turns out to be more important than proximity as a determinant of sociability. If the population is heterogeneous, there is little social contact between neighbors, either on apartment-house floors or in single-family-house blocks; if people are homogeneous, there is likely to be considerable social contact in both house types. One need only contrast the apartment house located in a transient, heterogeneous neighborhood and exactly the same structure in a neighborhood occupied by a single ethnic group. The former is a lonely, anonymous building; the latter, a bustling microsociety. I have observed similar patterns in suburban areas: on blocks where people are homogeneous, they socialize; where they are heterogeneous, they do little more than exchange polite greetings.[37]

Suburbs are usually described as being more homogeneous in house type than the city, but if they are compared to the outer city, the differences are small. Most inhabitants of the outer city, other than well-to-do homeowners, live on blocks of uniform structures as well; for example, the endless streets of row houses in Philadelphia and Baltimore or of two-story duplexes and six-flat apartment houses in Chicago. They differ from the new suburbs only in that they were erected through more primitive methods of mass production. Suburbs are, of course, more predominantly areas of owner-occupied single homes, though in the outer districts of most American cities homeownership is also extremely high.

Demographically, suburbs as a whole are clearly more homogeneous than cities as a whole, though probably not more so than outer cities. However, people do not live in cities or suburbs as a whole, but in specific neighborhoods. An analysis of ways of life would require a determination of the degree of population homogeneity within the boundaries of areas defined as neighborhoods by residents' social contacts. Such an analysis would no doubt indicate that many neighborhoods in the city as well as the suburbs are homogeneous. Neighborhood homogeneity is actually a result of factors having little or nothing to do with the house type, density, or location of the area relative to the city limits. Brand new neighborhoods are more homogeneous than older ones, because they have not yet experienced resident turnover, which frequently results in population heterogeneity. Neighborhoods of low- and medium-priced housing are usually less homogeneous than those with expensive dwellings because they attract families who have reached the peak of occupational and residential mobility, as well as young families who are just starting their climb and will eventually move to neighborhoods of higher status. The latter, being accessible only to high-income people, are therefore more homogeneous with respect to other resident characteristics as well. Moreover, such areas have the economic and political power to slow down or prevent invasion.

The demographic differences between cities and suburbs cannot be questioned, especially since the suburbs have attracted a large number of middle-class child-rearing families. The differences are, however, much reduced if suburbs are compared only to the outer city. In addition, a detailed comparison of suburban and outer-city residential areas would show that neighborhoods with the same kinds of people can be found in the city as well as the suburbs. Once again, the age of the area and the cost of housing are more important determinants of demographic characteristics than the location of the area with respect to the city limits.

CHARACTERISTICS, SOCIAL ORGANIZATION, AND ECOLOGY

THE PRECEDING sections of the paper may be summarized in three propositions:

1. As concerns ways of life, the inner city must be distinguished from the outer city and the suburbs; and the latter two exhibit a way of life bearing little resemblance to Wirth's urbanism.
2. Even in the inner city, ways of life resemble Wirth's description only to a limited extent. Moreover, economic condition, cultural characteristics, life-cycle stage, and residential instability explain ways of life more satisfactorily than number, density, or heterogeneity.
3. Physical and other differences between city and suburb are often spurious or without much meaning for ways of life.

These propositions suggest that the concepts "urban" and "suburban" are neither mutually exclusive nor especially relevant for understanding ways of life. They—and number, density, and heterogeneity as well—are ecological concepts which describe human adaptation to the environment. However, they are not sufficient to explain social phenomena, because these phenomena cannot be understood solely as the consequences of ecological processes. Therefore, other explanations must be considered.

Ecological explanations of social life are most applicable if the subjects under study lack the ability to *make choices,* be they plants, animals, or human beings. Thus, if there is a housing shortage, people will live almost anywhere, and under extreme conditions of no choice, as in a disaster, married and single, old and young, middle and working class, stable and transient will be found side by side in whatever accommodations are available. At that time, their ways of life represent an almost direct adaptation to the environment. If the supply of housing and of neighborhoods is such that alternatives are available, however, people will make choices, and if the housing market is responsive, they can even make and satisfy explicit *demands.*

Choices and demands do not develop independently or at random; they are functions of the roles people play in the social system. These can best be understood in terms of the *characteristics* of the people involved; that is, characteristics can be used as indices to choices and demands made in the roles that constitute ways of life. Although many characteristics affect the choices and demands people make with respect to housing and neighborhoods, the most important ones seem to be *class*—in all its economic, social, and cultural ramifications—and *life-cycle stage.*[38] If people have an opportunity to choose, these two characteristics will go far in explaining the kinds of housing and neighborhood they will occupy and the ways of life they will try to establish within them.

Many of the previous assertions about ways of life in cities and suburbs can be analyzed in terms of class and life-cycle characteristics. Thus, in the inner city, the unmarried and childless live as they do, detached from neighborhood, because of their life-cycle stage; the cosmopolites, because of a combination of life-cycle stage and a distinctive but class-based subculture. The way of life of the deprived and trapped can be explained by low socioeconomic level and related handicaps. The quasi-primary way of life is associated with the family stage of the life cycle and the norms of child-rearing and parental role found in the upper working class, the lower-middle class, and the noncosmopolite portions of the upper-middle and upper classes.

The attributes of the so-called suburban way of life can also be understood largely in terms of these characteristics. The postwar suburbia is nothing more than a highly visible showcase for the ways of life of young, upper-working-class and lower-middle-class people. Ktsanes and Reissman have aptly described it as "new homes for old values."[39] Much of the descriptive and critical writing about suburbia assumes that as long as the new suburbanites lived in the city, they behaved like upper-middle-class cosmopolites and that suburban living has mysteriously transformed them.[40] The critics fail to see that the behavior and personality patterns ascribed to suburbia are in reality those of class and age.[41] These patterns could have been found among the new suburbanites when they still lived in the city and could now be observed among their peers who still reside there—if the latter were as visible to critics and researchers as are the suburbanites.

Needless to say, the concept of "characteristics" cannot explain all aspects of ways of life, among either urban or suburban residents. Some aspects must be explained by concepts of social organization that are independent of characteristics. For example, some features of the quasi-primary way of life are independent of class and age, because they evolve from the roles and situations created by joint and adjacent occupancy of land and dwellings. Likewise, residential instability is a universal process which has a number of invariate consequences. In each case, however, the way in which people react varies with their characteristics. So it is with ecological processes. Thus, there are undoubtedly differences between ways of life in urban and suburban settlements which remain after behavior patterns based on residents' characteristics have been analyzed and which must therefore be attributed to features of the settlement.[42]

Characteristics do not explain the causes of behavior, however; rather, they are clues to socially created and culturally defined roles, choices, and demands. A causal analysis must trace them to the larger social, economic, and political systems which determine the situations in which roles are played and the cultural content of choices and demands, as well as the opportunities for their achievement.[43] These systems determine income distributions, educational and occupational opportunities, and, in turn, fertility patterns and child-rearing methods, as well as the entire range of consumer behavior. Thus, a complete analysis of the way of life of the deprived residents of the inner city cannot stop at indicating the influence of low income, lack of education, or family instability. These must be related to such conditions as the urban economy's "need" for low-wage workers and the housing-market practices which restrict residential choice. The urban economy is in turn shaped by national economic and social systems, as well as by local and regional ecological processes. Some phenomena can be explained exclusively by reference to these ecological processes. However, it must also be recognized that as human beings have gained greater control over the natural environment, they have been able to free themselves from many of the determining and limiting effects of that environment. Thus, changes in local transportation technology, the ability of industries to be footloose, and the relative affluence of American society have given ever-larger numbers of people increasing amounts of residential choice. The greater the amount of choice available, the more important the concept of characteristics becomes in understanding behavior.

Consequently, the study of ways of life in communities must begin with an analysis of characteristics. If characteristics are dealt with first and held constant, we may be able to discover which behavior patterns can be attributed to features of the settlement and its natural environment.[44] Only then will it be possible to discover to what extent city and suburb are independent—rather than dependent or intervening—variables in the explanation of ways of life.

This kind of analysis might help to reconcile the ecological point of view with the behavioral and cultural one and possibly put an end to the conflict between conceptual positions which insist on one explanation or the other.[45] Both explanations have some relevance, and future research and theory must clarify the role of each in the analysis of ways of life in various types of settlement.[46] Another important rationale for this approach is its usefulness for applied sociology; for example, city planning. Planners can recommend changes in the spatial and physical arrangements of the city. Frequently, they seek to achieve social goals or to change social conditions through physical solutions, having been attracted to ecological explanations because these relate behavior to phenomena which they can affect. For example, many planners tend to agree with Wirth's formulations because they stress number and density, over which the planner has some control. If the undesirable social conditions of the inner city could be traced to these two factors, the planner could propose large-scale clearance projects which would reduce the size of the urban population and lower residential densities. Experience with public housing projects has, however, made it apparent that low densities, new buildings, or modern site plans do not eliminate antisocial or self-destructive behavior. The analysis of characteristics will call attention to the fact that this behavior is lodged in the deprivations of low socioeconomic status and racial discrimination and that it can be changed only through the removal of these deprivations. Conversely, if such an analysis suggests residues of behavior that can be attributed to ecological processes or physical aspects of housing and neighborhoods, the planner can recommend physical changes that can really affect behavior.

A REEVALUATION OF DEFINITIONS

THE ARGUMENT presented here has implications for the sociological definition of the city. Such a definition relates ways of life to environmental features of the city qua settlement type. But if ways of life do not coincide with settlement types, and if these ways are functions of class and life-cycle stage rather than of the ecological attributes of the settlement, a sociological definition of the city cannot be formulated.[47] Concepts such as "city" and "suburb" allow us to distinguish settlement types from each other physically and demographically, but the ecological processes and conditions which they synthesize have no direct or invariate consequences for ways of life. The sociologist cannot, therefore, speak of an urban or suburban way of life.

CONCLUSION

MANY OF the descriptive statements made here are as time bound as Wirth's.[48] In the 1940s Wirth concluded that some form of urbanism would eventually predominate in all settlement types. He was, however, writing during a time of immigrant acculturation and at the end of a serious depression, an era of minimal choice. Today, it is apparent that high-density, heterogeneous surroundings are for most people a temporary place of residence; other than for the Park Avenue or Greenwich Village cosmopolites, they are a result of necessity, rather than choice. As soon as they can afford to do so, most Americans head for the single-family house and the quasi-primary way of life of the low-density neighborhood, in the outer city or the suburbs.[49]

Changes in the national economy and in government housing policy can affect many of the variables that make up housing supply and demand. For example, urban sprawl may eventually outdistance the ability of present and proposed transportation systems to move workers into the city; further industrial decentralization can forestall it and alter the entire relationship between work and residence. The expansion of urban-renewal activities can perhaps lure a significant number of cosmopolites back from the suburbs, while a drastic change in renewal policy might begin to ameliorate the housing conditions of the deprived population. A serious depression could once again make America a nation of doubled-up tenants.

These events will affect housing supply and residential choice; they will frustrate, but not suppress, demands for the quasi-primary way of life. However, changes in the national economy, society, and culture can affect people's characteristics—family size, educational level, and various other concomitants of life-cycle stage and class. These in turn will stimulate changes in demands and choices. The rising number of college graduates, for example, is likely to increase the cosmopolite ranks. This might in turn create a new set of city dwellers, although it will probably do no more than encourage the development of cosmopolite facilities in some suburban areas.

The current revival of interest in urban sociology and in community studies, as well as the sociologist's increasing curiosity about city planning, suggests that data may soon be available to formulate a more adequate theory of the relationship between settlements and the ways of life within them. The speculations presented in this essay are intended to raise questions; they can be answered only by more systematic data collection and theorizing.

· P O S T S C R I P T ·

WHEN I reread this essay again after many years, I was struck by how much the first sentence remains largely true. While no single school, including the ecological school, is now dominant in urban sociology, Louis Wirth's "Urbanism as a Way of Life" remains the most often cited article and probably the most often read one as well. It still supplies the simplest and seemingly most accurate definition of the city, and a rationale, not to mention an outline, for studying urban sociology—all the research and writing questioning Wirth's ideas notwithstanding. In fact, although over half of all Americans now live in the suburbs, urban sociology courses remain resolutely urban, although often because they deal with the urban sociology of the poor and the minorities who remain stuck in the city. Whatever the merit of that approach (which I use myself), we still do not have a sociology of the suburbs or even a respectable sociological literature on suburbia.

I pointed out in my article, originally published in 1962, that it was as time bound as Wirth's, and I was by and large right. Even though I seem to have predicted the yuppies in my penultimate paragraph, I did not consider the possibility that someday suburbia would be the majority form of residence, and that it would then be inhabited by people of all ages and households of all types, rather than mainly young families with young children. I did mention the decentralization of industry, but did not think that it might one day become a flood. Now, about two-thirds or more of those living in the suburbs also work there, and even fewer than a third need to come to the city's central business district, except perhaps for high culture, since museums and concert halls have by and large not decentralized (yet). Professional sports teams have, however, even if they are still called by the name of the city nearest to where they play.

I should also have thought about the possibility that when the suburbs became more popular, the mainly urban essayists and intellectuals who criticized them—and by implication their middle-American residents—for undue conformity, homogeneity, and other sociocultural diseases would have to end the suburban critique. This they did, shortly after I published this article, but they found new targets with which to continue the cultural class war. Such targets are always available, however, beginning and still ending with television viewing and television programming.

Having understimated the extent of the suburban move, I also failed to consider the likelihood of a city inhabited increasingly by the very rich and the poor. Nor did I consider that black ghettos would also be found in what I called the outer city, even if they are ghettos of the black working class and lower middle class more than of the black poor, and are thus not altogether different than when they were inhabited by the white working and lower middle classes. It did not even occur to me that housing might one day become expensive, so that most American home buyers could no longer afford either a new or a secondhand single-family house, that suburbia would be filling up with row houses and condominiums—and that the major housing problem of the poor was the inability to pay high rents, which was one cause of the tragic increase in homelessness exacted by the Reagan administration on the poor, the cities, and even many suburbs.

Actually, my prediction of the yuppies was partly luck, for while I expected more young people to come into the inner city after college, some having done so already in the 1950s, I did not expect the large number who came and for whom old neighborhoods near the central business district and elsewhere were gentrified. They have come largely because of the dramatic increase in *professional* service employment in the central business districts of many cities, although because they spend so much time on the streets and in expensive "boutiques," their visibility is greater than their actual number. Moreover, that number could decline sharply in the 1990s, not only because when they marry and have children many move to the suburbs, but also because if the boom times in professional service employment end, their number—and visibility—will shrink quickly and considerably.

I could list other ways in which the 1962 article was time bound; for example, it paid no more attention than Wirth's article to the various political battles—about race, or class, or just property values—that take place in cities and suburbs, and thus could not consider that as all resources became scarcer, these battles would increase in number and intensity. Still, in its basic conception, the article remains accurate as I write this postscript in the spring of 1990. The basic differences are not between city and suburb, but between the inner city and the rest of the metropolitan area, and the major reasons are more or less as I stated them.

Even the five types of inner city residents can still be found, if not solely in the inner city, in the poorer parts of the outer city as well. I should have begun my list of types with those who are in the city by necessity, especially the poor; also, some of my labels seem a bit archaic now, notably because the people who are in the city mainly because of its high culture facilities—and whom I called cosmopolites—have been joined by the aforementioned yuppies. The ethnic villages are now largely *barrios* or Southeast Asian areas, because the white ethnic villages left over from the European immigration are mainly in the outer city and to a lesser extent in the suburbs. (In New York, Bensonhurst, Canarsie, and Howard Beach are among the best known at the start of the 1990s, though unfortunately for tragic reasons.)

Most of the inner city ethnic enclaves were either displaced by an enlarged central business district, were gentrified, or became slums for a later wave of immigrants. Thus, a part of New York's Jewish Lower East Side became a middle-class Jewish area, another is being gentrified for young people, and the rest of it became Loisada, which is the "Puerto Ricanization" of the old neighborhood name. Likewise, New York's Little Italy has become part of the rapidly growing Chinatown, although so far many of the retail stores remain Italian; they are restaurants, food stores and giftshops for the Italians who come back for a visit from the suburbs. Meanwhile, the Chinese immigration has been so large that most Chinese now live in Queens. the prototypical outer city borough.

From here on in, writing about the cities will be even more time bound, because as I note in the next chapter, America is part of the world economy now, and what economic changes will affect it, and its cities, will vary and be unpredictable. This may lengthen the life of Wirth's classic article even further, because it transcends economic conditions and thus provides a seemingly timeless definition of the city that is never totally inaccurate. It may even become a bit more accurate as, in growing metropolitan areas, areas we now call suburbs become larger in population, higher in density, and more diverse in population.

· F I V E ·

AMERICAN URBAN THEORIES AND URBAN AREAS: *OBSERVATIONS ON CONTEMPORARY ECOLOGICAL, MARXIST, AND OTHER PARADIGMS*

THIS PAPER ATTEMPTS to understand what is going on not only in American urban sociology, but also in American cities—a generic term used to cover central cities, suburbs, and metropolitan areas. I offer some observations about the two paradigms that dominate urban sociology at this writing (spring 1990) but from a perspective that sees similarities as much as differences, and that finds good and bad in both. The paper ends with some ideas about alternative paradigms, although I am less interested in what should be happening in urban sociology than in national, and national urban, policies and politics.

Obviously, the two paradigms are ecology and Marxism. Since I am writing about today's urban sociologists, however, and since their work differs in a variety of ways from classical Chicago School ecology and classical Marxism, the paradigms are more accurately called neo-ecology and neo-Marxism. Perhaps they should also be described by that old-fashioned term "schools," if only to emphasize that they are constructions of reality, and of goals, by particular people in particular social positions and

---

An earlier version of this paper appeared in Ivan Szeleny, ed., *Cities in Recession* (London: Sage Publications, 1984). The present version is not only longer but I have revised and updated it (except for the bibliography) as well.

places. Still, even the term "school" does not indicate that major and minor differences in concepts, methods, and values exist in each group. I shall not, however, consider these differences, but shall discuss the two paradigms in such general terms that I treat them as ideal types.

As a result, I will sometimes be unfair to some writers in both schools, although that unfairness is somewhat mitigated by my not discussing individual works or citing individual authors in the text. I must emphasize that what I say about neo-ecology and neo-Marxism does not necessarily apply to any individuals, including those cited in or left out of the bibliography. This disclaimer is necessary because my descriptions of the two paradigms are ideal types, which cannot properly be associated with any individual author. While these types are sometimes oversimplified, my intent is not to be unfair but to offer broad generalizations. I realize that a comparative analysis of the two paradigms is, from some Marxist perspectives, logically impossible, but I will be unfair to the extent of rejecting Marxist claims that Marxism is a perfect and therefore closed system. I will be unfair also in ignoring some other paradigms that deal with cities, but my analysis is limited to those that seem to me to be dominant at this time.

THE TWO PARADIGMS

THE NEO-MARXISTS are mainly located in and write about the older, economically and demographically declining central cities. They seek the explanation for this decline in the development of late or advanced corporate capitalism, and in the relationship between capitalism and the state. Although there seems to be considerable agreement about the whys of capitalist behavior, which focuses on the concept of capital accumulation, there is disagreement about the relationship between capitalism and the state. Whether they are doing national or urban research, neo-Marxist scholars disagree among themselves about the extent to which governments seek to maximize capital accumulation directly, aim to aid the accumulators, divert the short-term accumulation process in order to maintain social peace, or focus mainly on enhancing conditions for long-term accumulation.

Classical and human ecology appear to be virtually dormant now, or have become overshadowed by what I call neo-ecology. Just as neo-Marxists became prominent, outside purely Marxist circles, in connection with the fiscal crises of the early 1970s, so the neo-ecologists have become visible partly as a result of the economic boom in sectors of the Sun Belt, and partly because of the conservative political and intellectual backlash of the 1970s and 1980s. Indeed, the most active sociological contributors to neo-ecology come from Sun Belt universities. That is not coincidental, for many Sun Belt universities have been growing and hiring. Also, neo-ecologists generally celebrate the Sun Belt booms. A second set of neo-ecologists includes conservative and neoconservative social scientists and essayists who write in the same vein but may not even know that they are taking neo-ecological perspectives. Both types of neo-ecologists write as much about the suburbs and nonmetropolitan areas as about central cities, and their posture toward the latter is almost always quite critical.

Neo-ecologists diverge more from classical ecology than neo-Marxists from classical Marxism. The Chicago School explained urban growth largely by a mixture of Darwinian (and, to ecologists, "natural") forces such as population movements and technological progress. Although neo-ecologists still discuss innovation in transportation and communication technology—with insufficient curiosity about the economic agents and conditions that bring them about—they now also devote a good deal of attention to capital accumulation and the state, even if they do not use these terms. Instead, they discuss the reasons for corporate location decisions and their search for favorable business climates, i.e., places where wages, taxes, unions, and public services are minimal. If one ignores differences in terms and values, some similarities with neo-Marxist analysis become apparent.

Differences remain, of course, and they are large, but they are greatest in the area of values. Neo-Marxists are, needless to say, critical of capitalism, but many rarely discuss policy other than to suggest—often by implication—the replacement of capitalism by socialism. Neo-ecologists, on the other hand, are very enthusiastic about capitalism, and suggest, sometimes explicitly, that the economic decline of the older Northeast and Midwest cities could be halted by a reduction of government intervention and regulation. However, the implicit social Darwinism of classical ecology, which assumed that any deliberate government action that interfered with private economic activities was unnatural, is gone, and today's neo-ecologists often make explicit policy recommendations. These tend, as just noted, to propose greater freedom for private enterprise, although some neo-ecologists believe that the government should retrain the employable poor of the Northeast and Midwest and help them move to areas of economic growth, after which the welfare agencies in these cities can be closed up and private enterprise can do the rest.

Among the similarities between the two schools, two are most important. First, both schools treat cities mainly as economic units, and examine economic change in which the large corporation is the primary actor. As a result, urban sociology currently appears to be turning into a kind of institutional economics, with emphasis on the spatial and other effects of national and international economic development on cities, and to a lesser extent other settlement types. Second, the analysis is frequently shaped by the analyst's economic and political ideology. As a result, urban sociology is now sometimes as much a critical or favorable commentary on the national political economy as it is an empirical or theoretical analysis, with enough local and spatial data to make it urban as well.

The rest of the paper elaborates and sometimes evaluates these observations.

THE LIMITS OF URBAN ECONOMICS

INSOFAR AS both neo-ecological and neo-Marxist commentaries about the national political economy are also empirical and policy-oriented analyses of cities, they are about urban sociology, or urban economics, or both. Moreover, contemporary urban sociology's economic emphasis has properly focused attention on the extent to which cities are economic entities, or, more correctly, are dominated by their economic institutions. Although classical ecologists studied the competition for land and location, they ignored the extent to which they were actually analyzing the activities of urban economic institutions. As a result they lacked interest in, or failed to deal with, economic institutions not centrally involved with land and location.

Shortly after the establishment of the Chicago School, American sociologists who were neither ecologists nor even urban sociologists started to undertake community studies; and what began in Middletown and Yankee City led, after World War II, to studies in poor and working-class central city neighborhoods, working- and middle-class suburbs and also factories and their surroundings. These studies shattered the ecologists' monopoly in the United States and the identification of the field with land and location. Still, it remained for the neo-Marxists to define urban sociology as being concerned overtly with economic phenomena, and to look not only at urban but also at national and multinational economic institutions in the process. Thus, they were able to focus quickly and directly on what strikes me as the major problem of the old central cities: the drastic loss of firms and jobs, and all the economic, political, social, and other consequences of this loss.

Still, a purely economic analysis has disadvantages as well; for, as I have already suggested, it becomes difficult to put boundaries on the analysis, which moves quickly from urban to national and world levels. What American firms do in Taiwan's low-wage factories is directly related to the fate of American cities, but once the analysis turns to the world economy, it is sometimes difficult to return to the American city. Equally important, such an economic analysis can quickly become overly general, so that it no longer deals with actual cities, but with an ideal type or stereotype. Then, the diversity among and inside American cities is too easily forgotten.

Most important, and despite the assumptions made in both paradigms, cities are not really economic units. In fact, they are not units of any kind, except insofar as political boundaries turn central cities, and suburbs, into individual administrative-political units in a limited sense. Nor are cities economic systems. There is no urban economy sui generis, except in comparison with an ideal-type agricultural economy—but actual agricultural economies also differ. Interdependencies and linkages among a city's—and even a central city's—economic institutions are numerous, but describing the aggregate of such institutions as a unit or system is an analytic exaggeration. (That system also becomes a policy nightmare, for it implies that policymakers can, in theory, control or cope with the economy of a specific central city.) Any central city with a fairly diversified set of economic institutions can therefore experience both boom and bust concurrently. For example, black unemployment in booming cities is sometimes higher than in declining ones.

Furthermore, in a period in which the world economy increasingly shapes the fate of individual national economies, it is not even clear whether booms and busts will ever have any significant duration again. In the 1960s and 1970s Boston was in most respects a declining city and Houston a boomtown, but by the 1980s, Boston was benefiting from a partially Pentagon-inspired demand for the products of various "high tech" industries while Houston was suffering badly from the sharp decline in world oil prices. In early 1990, the Houston economy is on the upswing again while Boston is in deep trouble, and ten years from now, the economic conditions of the two cities could be quite different again.

Holistic metaphors apply even less to metropolitan areas, which also are not economic units or systems. Nor are they regions, if only because the catchment or market or service areas of individual economic institutions vary, and some are literally national or international. I suppose that, on heuristic grounds, a region can be constructed out of the catchment area boundaries shared by a majority or plurality of major firms, but it remains an analytic construct that cannot easily be translated into a policy concept. The Tennessee Valley is an economic region because so many of its activities are linked to those of the Tennessee Valley Authority, but metropolitan areas are rarely dominated by a single agency, or by a watershed, to the same extent. Single-industry areas of the country, like some of the oil-producing areas, could perhaps be described as regions, but such areas are increasingly atypical. Likewise, single-industry cities may be considered economic units, but they are also becoming scarce.

Ultimately, central cities and suburbs make analytic sense only in relation to each other and their city limits. Operationally, they are administrative-political units within boundaries established long ago for reasons, and in locations, that are often irrelevant today. That city limits and boundaries exist is not irrelevant, since they indicate where the powers of government begin and end. Insofar as taxes, public services, and other economically relevant local governmental actions can change at and vary with the boundaries, political units have some influence on economic institutions, particularly if taxes or public services are important in their operations.

The concept of metropolitan area, on the other hand, is mainly statistical, fitting the convenience of the U.S. Bureau of the Census as well as the political need to respect historical county boundaries and, I suppose, the least-effort principle of looking at counties adjacent to central cities. Economic comparisons of metropolitan areas are thus basically comparisons of Census categories, falling prey to yet other ecological fallacies.

More confusing still is a conceptual innovation of the 1970s, nonmetropolitan growth. Urban and suburban boundaries at least demarcate different settlements and settlement types, but nonmetropolitan growth can take a number of forms, all quite different. These include, among others: overspill from adjacent suburbs, i.e., growth just across the metropolitan area boundary; retirement colonies; subdivisions of footloose young families seeking a more rural ambience or outdoor recreation or both; and, probably most important, locations of individual and linked firms taking advantage of low wages, taxes, and land costs, with accompanying subdivisions that spring up to house the workers. The result is then a modern version of a small industrial town.

SOCIOLOGY VERSUS ECONOMICS

THE FRAMERS and users of economic paradigms cannot be blamed for Census concepts and categories, but they can be taken to task for paying insufficient attention to the actual social consequences of economic phenomena, and to social phenomena that have no direct relation either to land use or to advanced capitalism. Among other things, central cities, suburbs, etc., supply shelter, networks, neighborhoods, and a variety of support institutions for families, whatever the family type—and the fact that dwelling units and communities are fundamentally shelters for the family is often lost in the economic models of both neo-ecologists and neo-Marxists.

While urban sociology should not recapitulate or swallow other fields of sociology, there must be room in a proper urban paradigm for the familial-social side of human settlements. I do not argue here for a new wave of urban-suburban comparisons, since past ones measured class differences more than anything else; or for a new concern with the effects of density, the effects themselves appearing to be small once the ability to afford space is factored out. Issues of size and critical mass remain important to understanding communities, however, and so does population heterogeneity— not to differentiate central cities and suburbs, but as a variable that helps to explain relationships and conflicts in all settlements. Struggles over issues of race, religion, ethnicity, and culture that may have little to do with the economy take place in American communities so that class, in the Marxist, Weberian, or Warnerian sense, is sometimes only a side issue.

Indeed, basic patterns of residential, neighborhood, and community behavior can occasionally be unrelated, or only little related, to economic phenomena. For example, these patterns differ surprisingly little between economically vital and declining communities, even though economic conditions crucially affect other aspects of people's lives. Sometimes the lack of difference is the result of an overly narrow notion of residential behavior; on the other hand, it may also reflect the separation of work and community that has existed since the rise of capitalism, according to Marxism—or to the time when workers, blue- and white-collar, were affluent enough to move their community life out from under the eyes of their employers.

Americans have always tried to maintain a sharp separation between job and home, work and family; often the former remains mainly a funding source for the latter. Undoubtedly, more people obtain satisfaction from their work (if not their workplace) today than in earlier periods of industrialization, and for some of them, particularly "workalcoholics" who are more dedicated to work than home, the community is little more than a dormitory. Nonetheless, their number remains small. This is not to say that the job and its pressures, as well as the income it pays, do not affect people's home or community lives, but to suggest once more, in a somewhat different way, that family and community stand in a very complicated relationship to economy and work. Even so, the relationship may be less complex than in preindustrial times, when peasants spent most of their time working, and when for them, but even more so for landless laborers, the community was an extension of their work relationships and of their powerlessness to affect these. Furthermore, many of the peasants and laborers lived not in communities but in what would today be called company housing.

The way people carry on their lives, in workplaces and in residential communities, has generally been left to urban and industrial ethnography, of which there has always been too little. In addition, ethnography is usually not connected to urban theory. Admittedly, community studies are usually so broad and intensely empirical that they are not useful for testing theories, and besides, no single theory can deal with the sociological riches mined by a good community study. But the gulf between community studies and urban sociology may also reflect the fact the neither economic nor spatial phenomena occupy as vital a role in people's community lives as they do in urban paradigms.

For example, neither paradigm is well equipped to deal with the latest installment of the widespread American search for lower residential density, the previously discussed nonmetropolitan growth. Neo-ecologists have emphasized the footlooseness of both firms and people, but there is no satisfactory explanation yet of why people's footlooseness takes the form it currently does, other than the search for good weather and recreation opportunity—and, of course, the availability of "nonmetropolitan" jobs. Are people looking mainly for cheaper land and housing or for lower density per se, or are they trying once again to find a modern version of an old rural idyll? Or are they merely attempting to put greater distance between themselves and so-called urban problems, such as poverty, racial minorities, high crime, traffic congestion, and the like? Are they hoping to get away from strangers, or from the family circles and networks that followed metropolitan area residents from central city to suburb? Is the move a renewed search for *Gemeinschaft,* or conversely, a further attempt for yet more complete privacy, a maximal escape from organized society?

These questions are all empirical and could be answered by researchers, except that they do not easily fit into either the neo-ecological or the neo-Marxist ideological preoccupations. For neo-ecology, nonmetropolitan residential growth is an application and endorsement of laissez-faire economics. Young mobile couples are viewed as acting somewhat like businesses: they look for communities with lower prices and taxes, both to save money and to escape public services that produce needless government intervention in their lives. In neo-ecological thought, the nonmetropolitan people are either frontier individuals who want to do without public services, or capitalists eager to satisfy their service needs in the marketplace. These hypotheses could be tested empirically but they may also be ahistorical, for new communities of young people often begin with minimal public services, but over time either choice or necessity leads to the reinvention of the public services that already exist elsewhere.

For neo-Marxists, nonmetropolitan residential mobility is ideologically even more jarring, for it conflicts with the prescription that people should want to use public services, shunning private or market solutions, and that all other things being equal, they should therefore prefer higher density to lower density. Accordantly, workers should choose public housing over the owned house, apartments over the single-family house, and the public park over the private backyard. When workers fail to behave in this manner, their choices must be explained away or criticized, by blaming either capitalists or the workers themselves. Capitalists are blamed for inventing suburbia in order to disperse militant workers or to defuse their revolutionary impulses by tempting them with home ownership of single-family houses. Workers themselves are blamed for false consciousness, for commodity fetishism, or for listening to the seductive voices of greedy suburban builders and commercial mass culture.

The Marxist nervousness about low-density housing is a by-product of its rejection of individualism. A paradigm that argues that the community should always transcend the individual (or household) should also prefer public to private goods, particularly when public goods are more likely to be available to, or cheaper for, workers than private goods which must be bought in the market. Such an argument may not even be persuasive in today's Europe, but it is particularly out of place in America, not only because it gets in the way of understanding settlement patterns and worker behavior, but also because it is likely to alienate workers. Whatever the virtues of European public housing, most American workers who can afford to choose select the nonurban single-family house and the status of home ownership. Even those who cannot afford to make such a choice are not always eager to live in public housing, although they may do so until they can afford their choice, or because they want to devote more of their income to their children's education. Perhaps more workers would have more physically decent housing if all were required to live in public housing, but few would support such a requirement. To argue that American workers, and the working class generally, are being seduced by commercial mass culture is patronizing when not insulting, for such an argument implies that workers are irrational, or are unable to choose properly, and are too stupid to preserve peasant folk culture or adopt urban high culture.

Conversely, neo-ecologists have blind spots in understanding why some people *must* live in public housing. Moreover, while neo-ecologists appreciate American individualism, they overestimate the American fondness for private enterprise. Although the faith that private enterprise can restore old levels of economic growth remains strong, popular thought is much less optimistic than neo-ecology. Besides, polls have shown that even people who call themselves conservatives favor government intervention in the economy to save or create jobs. In any case population movement to nonmetropolitan areas should not be interpreted as a popular endorsement of Republican party economics. Such an interpretation is, like the neo-Marxist faith in working-class preference for public housing, a projection of ideology on analysis.

Actually, both paradigms have difficulties in dealing with cultural values and preferences. Neo-ecology and neo-Marxism are alike in being descendants of deterministic theories, and while both now leave some room for voluntarism and the ability of people to make choices, the two paradigms also seem more comfortable with choice-making behavior that is economically or politically rational, i.e., self-interested, than with the culturally or socially rational phenomena that ethnographers rediscover regularly. Admittedly, neo-ecologists are more sensitive to the dominant American culture than are neo-Marxists, partly because they approve of it, and perhaps because they are mainly sociologists rather than economists. Ethnographers, on the other hand, sometimes have difficulty in seeing the economic structures that the two paradigms properly locate at the center of their views of empirical reality.

THE CORPORATION AND THE CITY

BECAUSE OF their economic approach, both paradigms in effect "star" the large American national and multinational corporation, making it a major actor not only in the economy but also in the society and polity. This is all to the good, particularly since the corporation is still underemphasized in the rest of sociology, and since economic sociology and institutional economics remain marginal fields in their respective disciplines. Obviously, the two paradigms do not agree about the role of the corporation; neo-ecology views it as an institution that is buffeted by other forces even as it wields power of its own, while neo-Marxism considers it as much more powerful and a frequent instigator of the forces posited by neo-ecologists.

Unfortunately, the disagreement is hard to deal with because corporations do not often open themselves to empirical study, so that many of their structures and actions must be inferred from visible but not necessarily reliable or valid indicators. Most likely, however, both paradigms overestimate the economic rationality and bureaucratic efficiency of large corporations, as well as their ability to devote themselves only and completely to the pursuit of profit or capital accumulation.

Since corporations are large organizations, they are subject to internal differentiation and all the conflicts of goals, interests, and activities that follow. Corporate management appears torn between long- and short-term profit as well as between profit and security, i.e., control over the firm's market share and a stability of relations with competitors. In addition, there are differences of interest between top and middle managements and within and between other sectors of the work force, some of which are at times as intense as those between management and labor. Furthermore, large corporations are also subject to the internal power struggles, communication blocs, inefficiencies, etc., that are often thought to exist only in government bureaucracies. Moreover, capital-intensive corporations differ from labor-intensive ones, and conglomerates vary from traditional corporations and privately held firms.

These and other functional and structural variations among corporations affect not only their economic behavior and location decisions but also their activities in and impact on the community once the location decision is made. For example, local firms are often more involved in "civic" activities than are absentee-owned firms. In addition, whether a firm draws its workers mainly from the primary, secondary, or subterranean labor market, and whether or not it sells to (and therefore seeks the goodwill of) consumers will affect a firm's civic as well as less visible political activities. In some cities unions still play a distinctive role; in others, corporate labor forces are dominated by powerful ethnic groups which then establish linkages with ethnic group representatives elsewhere, notably in government.

I do not want to overemphasize the noneconomic functions and activities of the American corporation, or to suggest that community ties are as important to it as profit. Still, it would be wrong to base analyses of the corporate role in cities on either left or right stereotypes of corporations or of their top managers.

CAPITALISM AND THE STATE

THE FOREGOING notwithstanding, in recent years neo-Marxist urbanists seem to have paid greater attention to the relationships between the corporations and the state than to the corporations themselves. This pattern may reflect the state's more active role in the economy in the last few decades, and its greater accessibility to scholars. I would also argue, however, that the American scholarly preoccupation with the state reflects the fact that it is a European concept and that inherent analytic and policy problems are created when it is applied to the U.S. scene. In effect, the scholarly concern with the state reflects an attempt to Americanize the concept.

In a country with a highly centralized national government, in which local and regional bodies are of minor importance and in which nationally organized political parties have relatively stable, loyal, and ideologically consistent and predictable constituencies, the state is not only a relevant concept but one that lends itself to fairly easy operationalization for empirical research. This is not the case in the United States, however. It is a continental country, with major regional and supraregional economic and other differences of interest. It is also a country in which local and state governments are constitutionally and politically of considerable importance. Not only does the federal government have less control over the country than does any European government over its country and people (at least until European unity arrives in 1992), but the federal government is further weakened by the separation of powers and the checks-and-balances mechanisms built into it originally—precisely to minimize central governmental power. If one adds the continuing weakness of political parties and the immense influence of lobbies and pressure groups, it is difficult to determine how and where to find the state in Washington, D.C., other than with respect to foreign policy.

While it can be argued that since the beginnings of the New Deal in 1933, if not before, the White House has attempted to create a European-type state, it has not been fully successful except in wartime. In many respects, the federal government is actually more competitive than the economy, because its own agencies compete to press their demands on the White House and the Congress. More important, the Bush and Reagan administrations, and to some extent the Carter administration before it, have sought to reduce the size and activities of some parts of the federal government, and to transfer some others to state and local governments. In these efforts the federal government appears to be trying to cut back the state—as well as to alter or end some of its functions. Conversely, attempts at decentralization may represent schemes to create a viable but smaller state in America, for the Reagan administration sought to eliminate, or to return to the states and localities, costly and controversial programs, those expensive to fund or likely to cause political difficulties, as well as those that the government and its supporters opposed on ideological grounds. In fact, the centralization of some other governmental activities and the vastly increased power over the federal budget of the Office of Management and Budget could support the hypothesis that an American state is just beginning to appear.

If a European-type state is in the offing, or if American scholars can Americanize the concept, it may turn out to be a worthwhile analytic tool, but meanwhile its use suggests a single-mindedness on the part of the federal government that does not often exist in reality, even in the White House. Indeed, federal urban policy, so-called, has often reflected the fact that individual federal agencies act at cross-purposes to one another, and that some of them are at times fairly obedient servants of influential state and local governments, political leaders, and/or private firms and industry lobbies.

My doubts about the nature of the state are not meant to deny that corporations and other capitalists usually have more influence in Washington than anyone else. Nor does the relative weakness of the federal government prevent it from assisting corporations in achieving their profits and other goals. Indeed, because of the power of corporate pressure groups and lobbies and the absence of a viable labor movement and labor party in the United States, the corporations may, in sum, have more power over the federal government than they do over European states, although they are also less united and less homogeneous in their immediate and concrete interests than they are in most European countries. Even so, the question of how much power the national government exerts in and over the economy, and for whose benefit, is much harder to answer here than in West Germany, France, or Sweden.

Another question has to do with the variations in corporate-government relations. For many years, the conservative wing of the Republican party represented small and medium-sized corporations, while the large firms normally supported incumbents in both parties, favored more liberal Republicans, or played a minor role in party politics and dealt directly with the federal agencies that were relevant to them. For reasons of efficiency alone, federal agencies themselves prefer to deal with large corporations—and with large organizations generally—than with small ones. At the same time, Northeast and Midwest firms of all sizes have found that the federal government often supports their competitors in the Sun Belt, partly because of the political strategies of some recent Presidents and of the political power of the South before then, but also because of a deliberate federal effort that began with the New Deal to spur economic growth in the poorer parts of the country whenever possible—even if the federal money does not always reach these parts, or the poor people in them.

A final question has to do with the purposes or motives, as compared with the consequences, of federal actions. Neo-Marxist analysis, like neo-ecology, is basically functionalist in outlook, and therefore pays greater attention to consequences than to purpose. This approach may be desirable in order to understand how social systems actually operate, but it can misinterpret situations in which consequence and purpose diverge, especially situations in which such divergence is unintended. Alternatively, the functionalist assumption can result in the conclusion that purpose is irrelevant or hypocritical, and while official purposes may often be irrelevant or hypocritical, this is not always the case.

Conversely, some neo-Marxists appear to be interested in determining motives, but they infer motives from consequences, and since their analysis aims to discover undesirable consequences of capitalist actions, they inevitably infer undesirable motives. To put it another way, they ascribe conspiratorial or other immoral motives to corporate (and governmental) behavior, much like some journalistic muckrakers, and thus fall into the same overly simple policy implication: that if motives were more altruistic, corporate and government actions would have more desirable consequences. They also ignore the possibility that actions based on undesirable motives can at times have desirable consequences.

IDENTIFYING THE VILLAINS

NEO-MARXISM AND neo-ecology may be distinctive among functional approaches insofar as both are interested in identifying systems or agents that are the villains in the crises or deficiencies of the central city, but of course they find different ones.

The Chicago ecologists did not deliberately look for villains, although they shared the class, ethnic, and racial biases common among academics of their era, and ascribed much of the crime, delinquency, and vice they discovered to "social disorganization," an implicitly moral shortcoming that they found predominantly in poor immigrant populations. They also identified another villain, at least by implication: the deliberate but unnatural acts of government that interfered with the natural economic and social processes of private enterprise and informal groups.

Neo-ecologists have made government an explicit villain, particularly when it regulates, taxes, or otherwise interferes with private enterprise. They also argue that, because unregulated economic growth was effective in reducing poverty earlier in the century, private enterprise can, and would, launch more effective antipoverty efforts now than government. In this respect, as in others, neo-ecology resembles the economic ideology of conservatives and neoconservatives, although some neo-ecologists appear to be more sympathetic toward the plight of the poor. For example, the previously mentioned scheme to retain the poor of the older central cities and encourage them to move to areas where jobs are more plentiful is not as harsh as conservative planned-shrinkage proposals or the drastic reductions in jobs, income grant, and welfare programs carried out by the Reaganites. To be sure, the neo-ecological mobility scheme is impractical, if only because there are already large numbers of untrained poor people— many of them black—in economically growing areas, especially in the Sun Belt, who have nevertheless not found jobs; in addition, the scheme ends with the same closing-out of urban welfare agencies as the standard conservative policy.

Like other conservatives, the neo-ecologists are wrong to concentrate their criticisms on government. Many government programs have failed because of opposition by business groups and taxpayers to funding levels that would make such programs successful, including antipoverty programs. Other federal programs, notably in housing, have been hurt because excessive financial incentives had to be paid to private enterprise to obtain its support or cooperation. Government is hardly blameless, but neo-ecology is reluctant to see that government shortcomings are frequently the result of pressure from powerful others, including private enterprise. It also forgets that many successes of private enterprise were achieved with government subsidies, or in markets that became noncompetitive as a result of government regulation.

In recent years, some neo-Marxists have also identified the federal government as the major villain, fairly when it volunteered to act as handmaiden to capital accumulation, unfairly when it was forced to do so. Nonetheless, the principal neo-Marxist villain remains capitalism itself; and, even as analyses become more sophisticated and reject some of the simplicities of classical Marxism, there remains the faith that capitalism is sufficiently villainous or still beset with enough contradictions that its future remains uncertain. Obviously, neo-Marxists cannot predict the future of American capitalism any better than anyone else, but despite what has happened in Eastern Europe, most are neither ready to give up on socialism sui generis or to foreclose the possibility of some role for it in the American future.

ECONOMY, STATE AND PEOPLE—THE CASE OF SUBURBANIZATION

SOME OF my other disagreements with both paradigms can be illustrated by what they say about American suburbanization and suburbs. These observations also help to introduce the final section of the paper, on the search for other paradigms.

Although the classical ecologists noticed what they called decentralization, they produced little research about either residential or industrial suburbanization, both of which were proceeding rapidly during the 1920s when the Chicago School began to flower. Today's neo-ecologists pay much greater attention to suburbanization. Seeing it as a successful instance of private enterprise at work, they approve of it, and of low-density development in general. They do not consider sprawl a serious problem and question whether high-density central cities can or should be restored to economic vitality.

The neo-Marxist paradigm is decidedly antisuburban. Its supporters believe that many Americans either do not or should not want to live in low-density conditions, but, for reasons already described in the earlier discussion of nonmetropolitan growth, should stay in the central cities, with the money saved used for the elimination of poverty and slums.

Perhaps because of their value differences, the two paradigms also support different explanations of suburbanization. The neo-ecologists emphasize population movements and technological innovation, but also see the phenomenon as a response to consumer demand and the new footlooseness of both people and firms. If neo-ecology emphasizes *pull* factors, then neo-Marxism stresses *push* factors, suggesting among other things that workers were pushed to the suburbs to defuse their militancy, and firms by growth and cost-reduction requirements that also caused technological innovation.

A comprehensive empirical test of the competing explanations remains to be done, but on this particular topic, neo-ecology is closer to the empirical truth than neo-Marxism. An early form of residential suburbanization began in America shortly after the founding of cities, when successful capitalists built themselves new houses beyond the existing residential areas. Moreover, they did so for reasons that still explain residential suburbanization today: they wanted more land, as well as peace and quiet; they sought to escape central city noise, dirt, and poverty; and they were eager to announce their good economic fortune in a highly visible manner. These patterns have not changed significantly, but during the nineteenth and twentieth centuries they occurred among an ever-larger proportion of the population, most extensively in the generations after World War II.

Lower-density industrial development, on either side of the city limits, began later in American history and more slowly. While ecologists overestimated the effect of technological innovation on suburbanization, Marxist analysts have underestimated the possibility that, at times, new inventions by themselves can change or speed up existing processes of growth. Industrial suburbanization was also spurred by the desire of employers and workers to escape the central city, but convincing evidence that workers' militancy was a significant factor has not yet appeared. By the end of World War II, the economic and technological incentives to suburbanize escalated further; and it is possible that, even if many of the people who participated in the postwar residential exodus had wanted to stay in the city, the suburbanization of industry might eventually have pushed many of them into the suburbs anyway.

Still, the first postwar suburbanization was largely residential, and I would argue that pull factors were more important than push factors, all things considered. Of course, central city residents could not have left for the suburbs without the help provided by FHA and VA loan guarantees, tax deductions, new highways, and other federal programs. Builders were also aided by these federal supports, not to mention the availability of the cheapest land and the highest profit margins on the other side of the city limits. Nonetheless, government and the building industry were responding to a widespread and strongly felt popular suburban appetite, which had already manifested itself during the 1920s, before government aid was available. Indeed, the suburban appetite was so massive and intense that the government could not easily have channeled the postwar housing demand into the central cities. Elected officials who wanted to express their gratitude to returning war veterans and who wanted to be reelected could not have housed the young families in central city walk-up or elevator apartments.

Given the dramatic postwar housing shortage, one could argue that the government, which was then launching a brand-new housing program and was operating in a seller's market, could have insisted on placing people in new central city apartments. Those lacking another choice would have had to go along, but those who could afford to choose would have gone to the suburbs, or would have had to be bribed with very low rents to take the urban apartments. Again, it is hard to imagine that elected politicians could either have given ultimata to returning veterans or have voted the funds for urban bribes when the obvious political benefits were to be gained from suburban bribes. Moreover, in the 1960s, after the federal government realized what the exodus was doing to the central cities, it invented a subsidized housing program, "608," that tried to encourage builders and middle-class tenants to stay inside the city limits, but it collapsed quickly from corruption and insufficient demand.

SUBURBANIZATION AS A SYMPTOM

ALTHOUGH THE conventional wisdom holds that post–World War II suburbanization played a major role in the subsequent crises of the older central cities, I think that most of the problems would have developed even if the federal government could somehow have located the needed new housing in these cities. Admittedly, the financial health of the central cities would not have declined so precipitously; for they would have retained profitable (and unprofitable) residential taxpayers as well as those retailers and employers who would not have moved out had the young white middle-class people they served or employed remained in the city.

The emergence of national and international economic organizations and processes that have driven firms out of the older cities and out of the country would, however, not have been held back. In fact, the older central cities might have lost jobs even more quickly, for the firms encountering higher production costs in middle-class–dominated cities might have headed to Southern rural areas or to Southeast Asia earlier. Conversely, a massive middle-class presence in the central cities would have maintained and even increased the political power of these cities in Washington; but, even so, it is hard to imagine the federal government being able or willing to exert the power to stop large firms from moving jobs out, or to subsidize small firms to prevent their demise.

The urban poor would not have benefited, either. If the white middle class had remained in the central cities, the northern migration of blacks and Hispanics after World War II might have been smaller because of the lack of affordable housing as well as likely white middle-class opposition to their coming in the first place. Because they needed jobs and urban industry needed cheap labor, they might have come anyway, but they might have wound up in suburban slums or shack towns. The racial and class segregation that developed between central cities and their suburbs would simply have been reversed, making American cities more like European ones in this respect.

Even the poor already in the central cities would not have been helped, for a white middle-class majority population would have maintained and perhaps even increased patterns of class and racial segregation to maximize its separation from poorer and darker-skinned residents. The so-called white suburban noose around the central cities would have remained, and grown further, inside the city limits. City governments responding to this majority constituency would have carried on similar patterns of segregation and differentiation in public services inside the central city. Some poorer urban residents would of course have obtained middle-class levels of garbage removal and some poor black children would have attended white middle-class schools, but most would have obtained the same inferior and segregated services they have always received.

The suggestion that drastic changes in the economy and economics of manufacturing could have been prevented by a government housing policy that discouraged suburbia is as unrealistic as the assumption that the white middle class would have put an end to class and racial inequality had it stayed in the central city. In fact, that population would have lobbied federal and state governments for subsidies and powers to protect, isolate, and segregate itself from the urban poor.

The foregoing analysis is hypothetical, but it also suggests an empirically testable proposition: the conditions in today's central cities and suburbs are symptoms and effects of national patterns of economic and racial inequality. The suburban exodus may not have ameliorated these patterns, but it did not cause them.

SOME IMPLICATIONS FOR NEO-ECOLOGY
AND NEO-MARXISM

WHILE MOST ecologists underplayed the massive role of government in postwar suburbanization, most Marxists were reluctant to see how much that role was effect rather than cause, guided by economically and politically significant public preferences. Politicians, bureaucrats, and capitalists re-sponded to these preferences because they meant votes, public funds, and profits, and because each payoff was obtained more easily and with less risk by following rather than altering or initiating public preferences. Be-sides, no one knew then or knows now how public preferences as wide-spread and intensely felt as those for low-density housing could be altered. Advertisers and dramatists in the commercial mass media, who are often suspected of knowing how to initiate, alter, or otherwise manipulate public preferences, actually do not often do so successfully. Sometimes they invent new products or cultural practices, and for reasons they themselves cannot explain, their inventions are big money-makers. More often they fail, and consequently, they try whenever possible to launch a number of innovations, be they cereals or pop songs, concurrently, hoping that one will catch on. Alternatively, they look for a new cultural practice and find a place on its coattails, but all other things being equal, they cannot risk "getting ahead" of their audiences or buyers. In any case, the idea that the good life was to be found in the suburbs rather than the central city was not incorporated into popular mass media fare until after the post–World War II suburban exodus was well on its way.

Admittedly, neither government nor private enterprise always responds to public preferences, and the preferences themselves are related to and influenced by economic and political conditions. First, the structural differ-entiation generated by and in modern economies has resulted in values of individualism, familism, and privacy, among others, which generate prefer-ences for the individually owned house. Second, that same differentiation has made many people able and willing to break or loosen other familial, as well as ethnic, religious, and related ties, and has allowed them to move next door to strangers of similar age, class, and race, knowing that they now had more in common. Third, the postwar affluence raised hopes and expectations of both social and residential mobility, not to mention higher comfort and greater convenience. Fourth, that affluence also supplied large numbers of people with permanent jobs, giving them the occupational security to live in communities far away from alternative sources of employ-ment.

All of these processes, and several others which would need to be added by a more detailed analysis, are in a general sense structural, reflecting patterns in the economy and polity that both neo-ecology and neo-Marxism consider. Even so, while these patterns made the proliferation of suburban home-ownership possible, the preferences connected to the patterns can be traced back to earlier times. The striving for upward mobility, the loosening of familial and communal ties in favor of greater autonomy for the nuclear family and the search for friends, as well as the more general rejection of ascription for achievement in many spheres of life—all these can be found already among the ancestors of suburbanites, either when they were emigrating to America or when they were heading for one or another American frontier. The desire for greater comfort and convenience, for a home, and for property and other goods over which people have some control actually precede the modern economy, and I would not be surprised if some go far back in human history.

I do not mean to explain American suburbia by invoking an old or modern set of cultural preferences, but the preferences cannot be left out of the analysis either. They are hardly sufficient explanations, for even if Europeans had expressed the same preferences, the necessary land and funds to implement them were not and are not now available on a wide scale in any European country. Although I suspect that many Europeans would have expressed—and acted on—the same preferences had they been asked, they were not asked. A long-standing housing shortage that the United States has never known (except in New York City) also created a long-standing government monopoly over housing in Europe, and monopolists have never needed to pay much attention to public preferences. Nor did those who controlled the state in European countries have other incentives to respond to these preferences. As one result, the postwar European suburbs were developed at high densities with apartments often assigned to people who lacked the money, status, and influence to obtain units in the central city.

FUTURE PARADIGMS IN URBAN SOCIOLOGY

THAT CONTEMPORARY American urban sociology is currently dominated by two paradigms is not ideal, but even so, it is a sign of progress. For most of its existence, the field was in effect monopolized by ecology, and while that monopoly may have been responsible for the flood of empirical work from about 1920 to about 1940, it must also be charged with the field's decline thereafter. Once urban growth and neighborhood change no longer made academic headlines and ecology was unable or unwilling to look at or explain other phenomena in the central cities or the suburbs, urban sociology suffered from a lack of interest that did not end until the beginning of the War on Poverty, the ghetto uprisings, and the fiscal crises.

Needless to say, a paradigmatic monopoly is never desirable in any field, and even the present duopoly is only a minor improvement, particularly because the two paradigms are so similar in their economic emphases even if they are highly divergent in ideology. Since both paradigms are essentially ways for understanding urban and societal growth and change, empirical researchers without explicit ideological and political agendas might find a way to draw useful elements from both. After all, most change is brought about by a mixture of large forces and agents that both benefit from and manipulate these forces, with the mixture of kinds of forces and agents varying in different situations and places and at different times. Some combination of the two paradigms that also adds relevant social and cultural variables would make it easier to understand urban growth and change, but as Marxists would be the first to point out, there is more to the study of cities than growth and change.

Actually, since both of the ruling paradigms are connected to larger political paradigms and were birthed to some extent by national political conditions, their future is not entirely certain. Neo-ecology is partly a child of the Reagan era, and may change with future White House administrations and congressional majorities, even if ecology itself has been around so long that its demise is hard to imagine.

The future of neo-Marxism is more uncertain, in part because of the revolutions that have taken place in Eastern Europe. To be sure, American neo-Marxism emerged from *American* intellectual life, and I am not sure if any neo-Marxist urbanists have defended either the state socialism or the urban policies of Eastern European countries in the last decade or two. Moreover, the more Eastern Europe—and Western European scholars— give up Marxist analyses, the more America may aim to hold on to what is best in neo-Marxist analyses, even as the policy and political implications of these analyses will probably look more and more like those of social-democratic scholars, here and elsewhere.

Whatever the future of the two current paradigms, additional ones—or at least the addition of social and cultural variables to the present ones— are urgently needed. Before describing the outlines of one I consider particularly important, I want to suggest some qualities and emphases needed by additional paradigms in order to assure a constructive future for urban sociology. To begin with, such paradigms must improve on ecological and Marxist analyses in connecting macro- and microphenomena, and in identifying the processes that connect these phenomena. Although the paradigms must eschew the temptation of reifying cities, or treating them as holistic systems, they must also retain the notion of settlement types and try to explain who does what with and to whom inside these settlements, and why. Ideally, the analysis should deal, even at the macrolevel, with identifiable actors or agents, be they individuals or organizations, in order to identify policy targets for policy researchers, although agents should not automatically be villains and heroes. A complete analysis must, however, include the structural contexts within which these agents operate, the incentives and constraints with which they are faced, and the choices they have.

The identity of the major agents is an empirical issue, although I have little doubt that corporations and government agencies will usually head the list. Even so, that list will also need to include organized and unorganized interest groups, voter blocs, voluntary associations, and the like. Aggregates of ordinary people belong on the list as well, stratified and divided by interests and backgrounds, and by the roles they play in that array of institutions and locations rightly or wrongly called urban. Nor can major social institutions such as the family and, in parts of the United States, influential churches be ignored. The economic emphases of the existing paradigms are obviously valid, but they must be complemented by sociological and ethnographic frames, if only because the "Economic Man" model underlying both paradigms is unduly narrow.

As I tried to suggest in the analysis of postwar suburbanization, people's preferences that are intensely felt and widely pursued cannot be left out either, particularly if the organized or unorganized populations holding them can generate the economic and political power to implement them. Still, the analysis would not be complete without the structural contexts within which these preferences come into being, are pursued, and are achieved or not achieved. Preferences themselves must be studied in relation to aspirations and expectations, alternative choices open to people and alternative choices that people ignore. In addition, the analysis has to identify the people who lack the ability to develop and realize preferences or to make choices, and who live under conditions in which necessity often dictates only one feasible solution.

These few sentences are too diffuse and general either to constitute the beginnings of paradigms or to apply to urban sociology alone. The latter is intentional, for as should be clear momentarily, my agenda here extends beyond urban sociology. I am not even sure whether there is justification for urban sociology as a distinctive field, at least on intellectual grounds. It has remained a field partly because it alone among sociological endeavors has emphasized spatial concepts, variables; and factors. This has not been accidental; for, insofar as central cities and suburbs have functioned as political and administrative units, they have been able to allocate and manipulate land uses and locations.

Urban sociology should not monopolize spatial analysis, however, for every human institution, from the family to the corporation, uses land and is concerned with location. Space is as prerequisite to social behavior as time and communication. Still, unless greater interest in spatial analysis develops across sociology, urban sociologists will be virtually the only ones paying it major attention. Space, being itself "empty," is of minor interest except when it is scarce, but who controls space and who can afford what kinds of space for what purposes and at what locations are significant questions even when land or location are not so scarce. How various kinds of spatial arrangements affect people, or fail to, is also important, but only after research is done on how those who own and control space decide what buildings and uses are put on it, what people do with and to each other inside those buildings and uses, and what meanings they attach to the buildings as well as what goes on inside them.

One might hope, however, that neither the traditional attempt to abstract spatial variables from society nor the spatial determinism that developed in classical ecology will be revived. As I first argued in the early 1960s, the terms *urban* and *suburban* do not by themselves explain anything. One should also hope that, someday, there will no longer be any poor people and cities can be turned to more constructive uses than storing them. In that case cities may be less distinguishable from suburbs and other settlement types than they are now. In this view of urban sociology, its main raison d'être is understanding, and contributing to, policy to eliminate poverty and segregation—with the intent that both will wither away as quickly as possible.

TOWARD A USER-ORIENTED PARADIGM

GIVEN THE current politics of the current paradigms, perhaps the most urgently needed new paradigm is a social-democratic one, which emphasizes social-democratic policies, seeking inspiration from those that have worked well in Western Europe even if they cannot be copied directly in this continent-sized country. Beyond that, a social-democratic urban sociology would be more empirical than neo-ecology and neo-Marxism, because it would not have the same prior ideological commitments to particular concepts for studying cities. The dedication to the welfare state and to democratic participation in the polity and the workplace stressed by American social-democratic thought would, however, inspire some of that empirical research and supply topics of studies and relevant concepts.

Although I consider it important to try to develop a social-democratic urban sociology, I want to go in a somewhat different direction; for one concept I consider highly relevant to urban sociology, including a social-democratic one, is *user orientation*. That concept centers on a distinction between the suppliers of public services—and of commercial products, ideas, policies, political decisions, etc.—and the people who use these. There are various kinds of suppliers, for example manufacturers, distributors, sellers, as well as professionals who supply services or policy advice, generals who supply military force, and politicians who supply decisions. Suppliers may be both individuals and organizations. Although my distinction is not mutually exclusive, since people and institutions in supplier roles may also be users at other times, I think of users here as people who are mainly users (or as European social scientists put it, consumers). They are likely to earn their living doing routine or dirty work for suppliers and are thus not, in my thinking, really suppliers. In short, my emphasis here is on poor, working-class and lower-middle-class people. (Upper- and upper-middle-class people pursue professional or managerial careers in which they function as suppliers, although in their off-hours, they too are users, and a more comprehensive analysis cannot ignore them in that role, if only because they are *affluent* users.)

The concepts of users and user orientation are applicable to all fields of sociology and are not relevant solely to urban sociology. Still, it may not be coincidental that even as I was first working on the ideas summarized in this part of the paper, the English urban sociologist Peter Saunders was thinking along somewhat the same lines, and quite independently. Urban sociology is distinctive, albeit not unique, in that it has historically concerned itself with suppliers, for example with those who own land, determine land uses, own and build buildings, and decide what activities will take place inside them, etc. Neo-ecology and neo-Marxism are basically supplier-oriented approaches, paying comparatively little attention to ordinary people who use the city and how they use it. Users *per se* are viewed as passive, peopling impersonal forces or serving as pawns in capital accumulation drives, while a user-oriented concept such as housing preference is of minor priority. A user-oriented paradigm is thus particularly necessary in urban sociology.

There is space here for only a handful of examples of a user-oriented approach, and for illustrative purposes I will focus mainly on the combination of working- and lower-middle-class users sometimes called middle Americans. In a user-oriented analysis, for instance, the current concern, both by neo-ecologists and neo-Marxists, with capitalism-state relations would have to be replaced. Middle Americans are interested primarily in private-public relationships, with the family (or household) and its immediate social and spatial networks and environs, including the workplace, constituting the private, and the large bureaucracies, corporate, governmental, and others, constituting the public. A user-oriented sociology would try particularly to understand how public, i.e., capitalist and governmental, organizations can serve and service private needs.

This in turn requires an analysis that describes and explains how public bodies serve and fail private ones (in the working- and lower-middle class), but the analysis would have to concentrate on the service and its defects, beginning from the perspective of the users (be these customers or clients or constituents) and tracing the relationships and problems with the public bodies. This sociology would pay less attention than current ones to how public bodies are structured and function, or how they produce or reproduce—or reach users. Instead, the analysis would begin with the interests of users, as perceived and felt by them, looking at producers and suppliers of services in terms of their ability and willingness to pay attention to, or ignore or manipulate, user demands and preferences. While the researchers might still be interested in "delivery systems," they would first want to know what is and is not being delivered to the users, as the latter view it, analyzing the organizations and individuals doing the delivering and operating the system in terms of the values, expectations, and views of various users. In effect, the researchers would be looking at what comes out of the delivery system instead of what is put into it.

One vital question for a user-oriented urban sociology is what public and private services different people actually want. While middle-American citizens have so far accepted "free" services, many have also protested tax levels. Consequently, a user-oriented urban sociologist would emphasize research on service preferences and priorities at different cost and tax levels. It is possible that many people would prefer fewer educational or recreational services than they now get or use, although whether such preferences should be honored by policymakers is a different issue. A user-oriented urban sociology would further seek to learn what people want or will accept in the way of supplier-user relations; whether and when they want to be clients of professionals, customers of entrepreneurs, constituents of bureaucrats, or participants in user-dominated cooperatives and self-help schemes.

These studies are, of course, in large part concerned with policy. In addition, when user-oriented researchers ask macrosociological questions, whether about delivery systems or capitalism-state relationships, they do so for microsociological purposes: to obtain a client's, customer's, taxpayer's (etc.) view of the world, instead of a professional's, entrepreneur's, or planner's view. Moreover, the sociological approach sketched here would need to jettison the currently conventional center-periphery portrait of the social system, in which the center is occupied by the state, the economy, the set of norms that signify society and the elite suppliers who look after each of these, while the periphery consists of the rank-and-file citizenry and its microlevel social systems. The alternative portrait would locate the prototypical middle-American household at the center, moving state, economy, and society to peripheral albeit highly powerful systems and symbols, which exist to serve and exploit, and to be served and exploited by, the occupants of this center.

That the powerful would now be at the periphery would not automatically reduce their power, or the extent to which they could influence and dominate people's lives. All I mean to suggest is that the citizenry does not share the perspective of most social scientists, or their fascination with state, economy, and society. Most citizens have a narrowly focused and self-interested concern with supplier delivery systems and elites; they want to exploit these and to be served by them, as well as to minimize their own exploitation. If citizens want anything from sociology, it is informational help in escaping exploitation and domination, and in maximizing their control over their own lives.

A user-oriented approach, or a fully worked out user-oriented paradigm, is not intended to replace all other paradigms, but to add balance. Further, even people who are mainly users are also occupants of other roles, in households, families, workplaces, and other institutions. Additionally, a user-oriented approach does not replace concepts such as class, age, gender, race, and the like, or the intellectual, policy, and political issues connected with these concepts. Finally, the user-supplier distinction is not meant to set aside that between labor and management, or, more generally, to avoid ideology. While the distinction does not fit neatly into the Right-Left spectrum, it does not ignore that spectrum. Instead, it may shed a somewhat different light on it, pointing to some of its shortcomings. For example, both neo-ecology and neo-Marxism are, like classic ecology and Marxism, ideologies of suppliers. Insofar as it represents any interests, ecology tends to favor those of corporate and other capitalists. Marxism spoke originally for various suppliers of revolution, but these days it speaks mainly for academic and other intellectual suppliers of Marxist analyses. Just as ecology has been basically unconcerned with the interests of the customers of private enterprise, so Marxism has worried little about the welfare of the public in whose name public ownership was demanded.

USER ORIENTATION AND LIBERALISM

I SUGGESTED previously that neo-ecology and neo-Marxism are, among other things, commentaries on and prescriptions for the national political economy, and as such they are conservative and radical, respectively, broadly speaking. A user-oriented approach lacks a single prescription for that economy since it would report the varying views for various users. If the users under study are middle Americans, the prescriptive outcome of the research would be economically liberal, in basic support of the welfare state, although their liberalism diverges from that of upper-middle-class people, particularly with respect to some cultural, social, and political values.

Middle America is a concept and middle Americans are an aggregate rather than a cohesive or homogeneous population. At a very general level, however, some middle-American values can be identified. One, which I have elsewhere called popular individualism, includes the desire for some personal self-development and privacy but in the context of a social life with family and friends. Concurrently, that individualism means as much distance from big business, government, and labor as possible, as well as from bureaucracy, and in fact all forms of organized society in which middle Americans are controlled by others, including liberal professionals. Thus, adherents to popular individualism are rarely eager for collective action or collective solutions. It is no accident that they often fail to provide massive political support for multifamily housing, public parks, and similar collective solutions which are hallmarks of upper-middle-class liberalism.

Most middle Americans are not entrepreneurs and cannot afford to take economic risks. They want economic security for themselves, and on the one hand favor a welfare state that emphasizes employment-related security. On the other hand, however, they would like fewer government services and, especially, lower taxes so that they can maximize their personal spending power. In effect, they would prefer a welfare state paid for by others, although they will support antipoverty efforts as long as these do not threaten their own jobs, incomes, neighborhoods, and social status. Ironically, most poor people want nothing more than to achieve the economic security levels they see in Middle America.

Insofar as middle Americans are probably the dominant plurality in the American population, and their individualism the numerically dominant set of values in the country, they, their individualism, and liberalism require far more attention from researchers than they have so far received. More important, that attention would provide research findings, and if policy oriented, policy leads, to help achieve a viable American economic liberalism that might be a first step to a social-democratic society.

THE HISTORICAL COMPARISON OF CITIES: SOME CONCEPTUAL, METHODOLOGICAL, AND VALUE PROBLEMS

WHAT IS A city? How does one compare today's cities with those of the Renaissance or the Periclean era? Are they even comparable given that economies, states, and so many other elements of society have changed? Can one select a viable sample of cities through history considering that those of the Greek era were small towns, and were also the capitals of their own states to boot? And how can one draw a sample of past and present cities when today's are no longer centers of military power as they were in the past?

This paper began with an invitation to a conference on the city in history, but when I started writing, I began to have a number of doubts, some of which are listed in the previous paragraph. These doubts were not about the historical comparison of cities as such, but about how best to compare the variety and diversity of settlements that share above all the fact that they are now called cities. My doubts raised some interesting questions, a number of which may be useful for comparative urban research in general, as well as for our conception of kinds of human settlements. This paper is

A previously unpublished paper prepared for Professor Gerald Else's conference on The City in History: Idea and Reality, in March 1973. I have written a new lead and made a number of other revisions as well.

concerned, however, with the cities of past and present, and with three sets of questions: (1) definitional questions about what is actually being compared in the study of cities over time; (2) sampling questions about how one selects cities for a comparative study; and (3) value questions about the values that should enter into such a study.

THE DEFINITIONAL QUESTIONS

MY FIRST set of questions asks whether, for comparative research purposes at least, an operational definition of the city is feasible, particularly over time, so as to make comparison possible. This question stems from the urban sociologist's considerable difficulty in defining what a modern city is, and how it may be distinguished from other, noncity settlement types. To begin with, there is the relatively minor problem of boundaries: is the city defined by its city limits, or is it the metropolitan area, and if so, how does one determine the boundaries of that area?

Second, there is the more difficult problem of distinguishing cities from noncities, for this inevitably requires establishing some criteria for "cityness" or "urbanity." The ecologist Louis Wirth used such criteria as size, density, and heterogeneity, but as I noted in chapter 4, each of these creates some problems. For example, size is an easily applied indicator, but American sociologists, at least, have never agreed on the minimum size of a city, and while none accept the old Census cutoff point of 2,500 people, there are many suburban satellite or bedroom communities that are considerably larger than settlements conventionally thought to be cities.

It is, of course, possible to resort to nonecological criteria, such as functional ones, but here too problems abound, for modern cities are too variegated in function to make it possible to suggest that some functions are urban while others are not. Most suburbs are bedroom communities, but then so are most residential areas within the city limits but outside the inner city. Historians have sometimes defined the essential function of the city as the creation of culture, but if this definition is used, most American cities do not qualify, since American culture is created almost entirely in New York, Los Angeles, and of course today on university campuses, many of which are not even located in cities.

Third, how does one grasp, conceptually and methodologically, the fantastic complexity of cities, so as to condense it for an operational definition that can be used for comparative purposes? Is a city defined by its land uses, its economic structure and activities, its political structures, or the myriads of formal and informal social organizations, networks, and subcultures within which its people live? Ecologists can solve the problem by looking at the city spatially, as a system or an aggregate of land uses; however, given our knowledge now of the limitations of this approach, other components of the structural complexity of the city must be considered. Moreover, how does one deal with the internal variation in cities: for example, the fact that a rich New Yorker lives quite differently—and thus essentially in a different city—than a poor one, and much more like a rich person in a homogeneous, low-density suburb? And even if one retains the spatial approach, which aspects of a city's land uses are to be included in an operational concept of the city and which are to be left out? Merchants tend to see the city as the central business district; travel agents—and tourists—as its famous landmarks and tourist traps; and art historians, as its museums, galleries, and historical monuments. However, the sociologist and the social historian have much more difficulty in deciding what areas of the city deserve study, particularly since the more prosaic residential, commercial, and industrial districts account for probably 90 percent of the land uses, the population, and the economic, political, and social activities that go on in the city.

The definitional difficulties increase when comparisons with past cities are attempted. One obvious problem is size, which forces comparison of the huge cities of today with many classic cities which, by modern standards, are only large-sized towns. Another is density, since many historic cities were far denser than most modern ones, excepting perhaps Manhattan and Calcutta. Heterogeneity is inapplicable, too, since historic cities were more homogeneous in economic activities than almost any of today's cities. While many historic cities housed diverse populations, modern cities are often ethnically and racially more diverse, but in other respects less so, now that the population cannot be separated into slaves and free persons, or divided into estates. A functional approach is no more helpful, for while historic cities could be identified as military centers or centers of formal culture, how does one compare them to modern American cities that have large police forces to maintain internal order but no army camps, and that, as already noted, create precious little formal culture, high or low? These problems are compounded when the "temporal directions" of a comparative study must be decided on; if the research begins with the oldest cities and moves forward to present times, the study requires a definition that may fit the oldest cities but not the modern ones; and if the work starts with the

modern city and works backward, many of the ecological, functional, and
structural characteristics of today's cities disappear quite rapidly as the
research moves away from the industrial era.

Presumably, a comparative researcher could decide to ignore all these
definitional problems and simply study those settlements that have been
described as cities throughout history. Methodologically, this is the easiest
solution, but such a study would not be comparing the same human settlements; it would be comparing similarly-labeled settlements, and would thus
be describing only semantic uniformities. Researchers would run the danger of comparing old apples with modern pears simply because both are
called fruits in our language.[1]

THE SAMPLING QUESTIONS

MY SECOND set of questions deals with a basic problem in comparative
study: how to sample from the large number of cities, past and present,
and by what criteria. In studying historic cities, the sampling problem is
both lessened and complicated by the availability of data; historians know a
great deal about a few cities but very little about the large majority of them,
and virtually nothing about those that have not yet been dug up by archaeologists. This nicely reduces the number of cities that can be studied fruit-
fully, but it also complicates the sampling problem, since the universe is so
badly skewed by the availability of data, not to mention the selection
process by which archaeologists decide where to dig, and the geological
processes that have pushed many ancient cities so far below the contemporary landscape that we do not even know of their existence.

Other problems come up in sampling modern cities, many of which
cannot be solved until an operational definition of the city is arrived at.
Assuming this definition can be achieved, the comparative researcher must
still decide whether to select those cities that can best be compared to
those of the past, or whether to limit the study to the biggest or most
famous cities of past and present, or whether to draw a sample stratified
by various criteria so that the more prosaic and uncelebrated cities, which
make up most of the universe of both modern and historic cities, are not
excluded.

Most urban historians seem to have solved the sampling problem by
ignoring it, for their work has largely been devoted to case studies of
individual cities. I do not want to scoff at the case study approach, for given
the limitations of time, money, personnel, and available data, case studies

may be the most feasible solution at the present time, and may in fact be the best way of getting further research under way quickly. This approach is not very satisfactory for comparative purposes, however; for the sample is then based on the decisions by which case study cities are selected, and any comparative statements can be made only with the most extreme qualification.

Case studies can too easily yield biased samples; among U.S. urban sociologists, for example, the tendency has been to study central business districts, inner-city neighborhoods, and particularly ghettos and ethnic and old working-class enclaves. Thus, almost nothing is known about what I have previously called the outer city. Historians, on the other hand, seem to have selected cities that were either centers of political and military power, or of high culture, or both. This not only creates some value problems to be considered shortly, but it also raises two other questions for a comparative study. One, if case studies of such cities are aggregated for comparative purposes, is the sample a sample of cities, or a sample of certain important—or famous—social functions that are often located in cities, but that are equally often located only in some very special cities? Then a comparative study is one of centers of power and/or culture, but not of cities. Two, such a sampling reflects a variant of the ecological fallacy, for it ascribes to a given city a function which can be found in that city but does not describe it entirely, and actually leaves out most of the activities of that city. For example, New York, or rather Manhattan, is today a center of financial power and of high culture, but describing even Manhattan alone in these terms surely leaves out at least 75 percent of the sum of activities taking place in that borough.

THE VALUE QUESTIONS

MY THIRD set of questions has to do with the overt and covert values that do and should underlie comparative historical research, and with the value implications of research conclusions. Covert values obviously enter into even intendedly value-free research by the topic selected for study, the concepts with which the topic is framed, and the methods by which it is studied. There is nothing wrong with this infusion of values as long as they do not remain covert, and researchers understand to what extent their conclusions are affected by these frames and values. Such values are part and parcel of the definitional and sampling problems discussed previously, for any definition of the city chosen must leave out some aspect of the urban complexity, and any but the most random sample must slight the universe, and both decisions can have value implications. For example, if the definition of the city emphasizes the city's role in the creation of culture, it not only leaves out the other urban functions and populations, but it also suggests that cities are important because they have given rise to or housed artists and intellectuals.

There is also a problem of overt values; in fact, there are two. One is that the values can be argued with, and if they affect the sampling, then the sampling will differ with different values. The other is that frequently scholars do not study cities as human settlements but as symbols expressing particular values. Since the scholars sometimes seem more interested in the values than in the settlements, they study cities that manifest these values, at least to them. In fact, they have limited their definition of cities to the settlements expressing these values, and then have sampled, studied, and praised the cities for achieving these values. Two values in particular have dominated what little I have read of the history of classical cities: the glorification of centralized power and the celebration of high culture and especially of architecture valued by today's high culture.

In doing some limited library browsing for this paper, I read R. E. Wycherly's *How the Greek Built Cities,* and although I am writing about him only because I read him before writing this essay, his book seems to me to illustrate these values—and to suggest the possibility for other values. With respect to the first value, the glorification of centralized power, Wycherly writes, for example:

> At the end of the second millennium and the beginning of the first, the level of civilization (in Greece) was comparatively low. Political organization, we may imagine, was rudimentary. There was no great ruler, no Minos or even Agamemnon exercising wide control but large numbers of local chiefs or kings. The inhabitants lived in groups of simple village-like communities.[2]

Wycherly here praises the great rulers of history and downgrades the local kings and chiefs and concludes that the level of civilization was low. However, one could argue just the opposite: that the level of civilization was quite high because Greece at that time was without power-seeking figures who resorted to war or exploitation, and instead of killing each other, people seem to have lived fairly peaceably in their "simple village-like communities." I may be unfair to Wycherly, but he appears to argue that cities are good because they are associated with great rulers and villages are bad because they are not, while from the perspective of other values, such as peace and the absence of killing by the state, cities may be bad and villages, good.

Generalizing far more—and perhaps too—broadly, too much historical writing has defined civilization as the exercise of central power, militarism, and war, among other things, and since civilization is generally a Good Thing, it has thus, intentionally or otherwise, praised central power, militarism, and war. Moreover, the settlements about which historians expressing such values have written have been the headquarters of kings, generals, and other politicians who have, whether of their own volition or because they were driven by economic and other forces, resorted to what radicals today would describe—if not always correctly—as imperialism. As a result, much of the history of ancient cities is the history of Athens, Rome, and their equivalents in Asia, Africa, and South America.

If I were undertaking a comparative study of cities, I would begin with a quite different definition of civilization, in which a high level is marked by a high median income among the population, a high degree of economic and social equality, a low number of wars and warlike acts, and the least unnecessary taking of human life—judging political organization as highly complex if it played any role in achieving these values, even if it was not centralized. And if I were to select a sample of civilized cities for study, classical Athens and Rome, or Cold War era Washington and Moscow, would not belong in the sample.

A similar point can be made about the broader cultural bias that is sometimes found among classical historians, which can also be illustrated from from Wycherly's work. His book contains eight chapters; the first two are general and then follow four on the fortifications, agoras, shrines, and official buildings, gymnasia, stadia, and theaters, 143 pages in all. Only 11 pages are devoted to houses, however, and just 11 more to fountain buildings and water supply structures. I report these page numbers because to me they reflect a bias, in part toward the monuments that the previously mentioned kings and generals built, and more generally toward the monumental architecture which expresses the norms of high-culture architecture, at least in our time—and conversely, a bias against the vernacular architecture in which ordinary people lived, and which expresses the norms of popular culture. I do not know whether Wycherly decided to allocate the pages he did to the different kinds of architecture because of the differential amount of information available about each, or because he felt that monumental and high-culture architecture were more important, but toward the end of his book, he writes:

The Greeks of the 5th century put their best architecturally into temples and public buildings and were content with modest private dwellings. . . . The modern planner pays particular attention to the residential parts of a town and makes it one of his principal aims to see that they are pleasant, healthy and convenient places to live in. In the scheme of the Greek city, the houses were subordinate.[3]

This paragraph suggests two comments. First, Wycherly ascribes motives to the Greeks of the fifth century without offering any data about them; for from his book, at least, one cannot tell whether these Greeks chose to put their best architecture into temples and other public buildings and decided to be content with modest private dwellings, or whether the elite made this choice and the rest of the population was forced to live with it, even though many people might have wanted to spruce up their houses and make do with fewer temples, etc.

Second, the paragraph reflects the author's preference for the monuments of the powerful but also for monumental high-culture architecture. As such, Wycherly is fairly typical of some classical historians I have read, who treat the city mainly as a rationale for—and subsequently a museum of—what they deem to be good architecture, in the process ignoring not only the popular architecture of people's houses, but also the city as a settlement in which people live. I would agree with Wycherly's modern planner and judge the architectural level of a city not by its monuments but by the space, comfort, and beauty of its residential architecture—particularly that housing the population earning around the median income or less. Furthermore, if I were to select cities for a comparative study over time, I would want to study those that expressed the best in popular architecture as defined above. Possibly Athens, Rome, Washington, and Moscow would again take a backseat, and even if I studied these cities, I would be interested in different neighborhoods than the historical admirers of monumental architecture.

These observations probably apply more to students of classic cities of previous generations, for today, the approach to history that also treats it as an evaluator of civilizations appears to be going out of fashion. Still, covert values are intrinsic to all research, and researchers conducting a comparative study of cities past and present must ask themselves what values are buried in the definition and sampling they choose. They must also ask what overt values they do and should defend in the research, and even if no overt values are included, what value implications derive from the findings. This is particularly important today, for given the problems of the contemporary American city, it is tempting to make a comparative study into a search for good old days, even if such good old days never existed. Despite the current state of the American city, the quality of life it offers most of its residents, even the poor and moderate-income ones, is still better than what was offered them by past cities.

To repeat, value choices are in the end personal and will vary with each researcher, but still, if the research claims to be scientific, it is wrong to limit the study of cities to those that housed a now-famous elite, or to emphasize the political activities and monuments of the elite in a more random sample of cities. A proper comparative study of the city must deal with its entire population and its entire culture or set of subcultures, whatever the researcher's own values.

CONCLUSION

THIS PAPER has raised a number of questions but offered pitifully few answers. If I were forced to give answers, however, I would suggest that it is probably impossible to arrive at a valid or reliable operational definition of city, and for two reasons. First, the term *city* is relational and can be defined only vis-à-vis the other settlement types that exist in a given society. Second, the city is, as I suggested earlier, a complex of different social structures and functions, without a single "essence," whereas a rural settlement is defined by a particular kind of economic function; it is, unlike the city, a one-industry settlement by definition.

Consequently, a systematic comparative study must either cover all settlement types or draw findings from a large sample of cities, thus evading the definitional problem by including many different types of cities; or it must limit itself to functionally defined cities and indicate that the findings apply not to all cities but only to one type. For example, it would be possible to compare cities that have been centers of power, as long as such a study were careful not to generalize its findings to all cities. Conversely, it may be desirable to eschew structural comparisons of the physical, social, and other structures of cities over time, and to emphasize a functional approach—to select a number of functions that are performed by all societies, and to see how they were performed and in what kinds of settlements. Thus, one might want to study the marketing function over time, or the order-keeping function, or the creation of culture, to determine how and where they have been performed in historic and modern times.

Finally, my reservations about the comparative study of cities do not apply to all current topics in this field. The origin-of-settlement types can be studied without having to solve the definitional problem; the idea of the city can be studied by accepting and investigating the various definitions of cities that have been offered over time; and the form of the city can be looked at both as a phenomenon in the history of ideas, particularly with respect to deliberately planned settlements, and as a response to the functions that have been performed by specific settlements. However, any comparative study of forms must deal somehow with the definitional and sampling problems I have described, for what one chooses to define as a city and how one samples cities will influence the forms being investigated. Studying the quality of life requires answers to the sampling and value questions, for what criteria one includes in the slippery term *the quality of life* imply an evaluation of the city; in addition, whose quality of life is to be studied is not only a value problem but a matter of including all the diverse populations of the city, so that the researcher does not come to conclusions about the quality of life in a given city by studying only the life of the rich or the poor.

Actually, all these questions could even be raised about today's American cities alone, even solely the big ones, because their functions and populations are in such flux that a number of adjectives have had to be added to the term *city* itself. Thus, we talk about the terms *inner* and *outer city* now, not to mention *central city*. The semantic complexity in the suburbs of America's cities may be even greater, for as they become denser and acquire sizable office, industrial, as well as commercial centers, a panoply of new names is being suggested. I have not tried to keep track of them, but one of the most dramatic is *technoburb,* suggested by the historian Robert Fishman.

Even these developments are not as new as they seem, for American cities have long been complicated and decentralized. Thus, the Chicago School ecologists of the 1920s were already looking at what they called secondary and tertiary shopping centers, albeit inside the city limits, for evidently the central business district could not handle all of Chicago's shoppers. In addition, the decentralization of urban functions had gone far enough that terms like *satellite cities* were being used to describe some of the smaller, nonsuburban cities not far from Chicago's city limits.

The questions I have raised deal more with changing and increasing urban structures and functions than with naming patterns, and perhaps the best time to ask them will be in the future, when the comparative study of cities is a mature discipline, with hundreds of researchers working in the field. Today, this field is only beginning, and like any infant industry, it must be encouraged to do whatever can be done with small amounts of money and personnel. As I indicated earlier, at this stage, much can be learned from case studies, and even from comparative research based on narrow definitions of the city and on skewed samples. Indeed, a lot of research will need to be done before it is necessary to grapple with the questions I have raised.

· S E V E N ·

ROBERT MOSES:
THE MASTER BROKER

W HEN JOHN LINDSAY first ran for the New York City mayoralty, he campaigned against the "powerbrokers," charging that these villains —whom he never named—were largely responsible for the city's problems. Robert Caro's monumental but sprawling biography of Robert Moses borrows Lindsay's term and the idea behind it to argue that Moses was solely responsible for New York City's building program between about 1930 and 1968, that he decided how and what to build mainly to obtain more power, and that he was therefore responsible for what Caro calls, in his subtitle, the fall of New York. This thesis compliments Moses by accepting his own assessment of his importance to the city, but fails to pay sufficient attention to the role of the economic and political system within which Moses worked, and which ultimately made his success possible.

The basis of that system is public works money, which flowed particularly generously during the Depression and the post–World War II era when Moses built his most important projects. Public works money not only produces public works, however, it also creates jobs and profits for many people, in construction, banking and insurance, among others. Above

A slightly expanded version of "The Master Builder," which first appeared in *Partisan Review*, vol. 41, no. 2, 1975. I have added a postscript.

all, public works money is necessary to the urban political organization, for it has no dependable source of funds to finance election campaigns and the day-to-day expenditures of political parties, politicians, and party workers.

To be sure, urban politics can be funded in other ways, but public works projects are especially suitable, because they involve huge and long-term expenditures, and because the complexity of the planning and building process allows funds for legitimate political activities, as well as for honest and dishonest graft, to be skimmed off the top without undue public notice. Equally significant, the finished projects are viewed as desirable indicators of municipal "progress" by many voters, who will therefore support the politicians that take credit for building them, and who will not object to some corruption as long as they are built.

Caro's bitter celebration of Moses' abilities is understandable, for the man was extraordinary, brilliant to the point of genius, with inexhaustible energy, a strong personality, and a stubborn vision: to create a comprehensive park and highway network for the city. A driven man, he was also vindictive, manipulative, and unscrupulous; a bully prepared to use immoral means to satisfy his vision wherever necessary. Although Caro describes him as a youthful idealist later corrupted by power, he was actually from the start bereft of altruism or empathy. His Ph.D. thesis, which argued for transferring power from politicians, bureaucrats, and citizens to selfless upper-class experts like himself, already indicated that he saw himself as a superman who alone knew what was good for people, and after a postgraduate fling in municipal reform, he devoted the rest of his life to practicing what he had originally preached.

Nevertheless, Moses' particular genius, and a major reason for his success, lay in his ability to pursue his ends by satisfying the demands of powerful economic and political blocs and citizens, without, however, becoming their servant. He attached himself to Al Smith shortly before he became governor of New York, and from him obtained the legal authority and the first funds to build parks and parkways. His initial success gave him enough surplus funds to make plans for future projects, and to be ready with such plans when the federal government began to funnel construction money to the city during the Depression. By then, he had also built an empire that was completely free from public accountability, except to the bondholders who financed his highway projects, so that he had total control over large amounts of construction money at a time when the city was bankrupt. As a result, it could only build the projects Moses wanted built; more important, all the businessmen, lawyers, union officials, and politicians whose livelihood came from public funds were dependent on his largesse, and gave him their allegiance in exchange for the contracts, campaign funds, etc., only he could provide. Caro suggests that whatever Moses' personal feelings about these people, he worked closely with them, and paid them off in order to be able to build.

At the same time, Moses created for himself the image of a selfless and nonpolitical public servant who derived no personal gains from his labors. (He did not need such gain, thanks to his family's affluence and the unlimited expense and entertainment accounts on which he drew in his various official capacities.) As Caro describes it, most New Yorkers, including Robert Moses himself, fell for this carefully constructed public image, notably the press, and especially the *New York Times,* whose executives and top editors supported him blindly until the last years of his reign.

Still, the primary reason for Moses' success was the coincidence of his vision with the interests of the city's increasingly affluent white middle class. First, Moses gave them the parks and beaches at which they could spend their new leisure time, and to which they could drive on his parkways in their new cars; just as important, Moses anticipated and shared their antipathy to mixing with poor and especially poor black people, effectively barring the poor from these facilities by not permitting buses on the parkways. Later, the white middle-class New Yorkers who had moved to the suburbs before and after World War II could use these parkways and the other highways Moses would build to commute to the city, and once again, Moses helped see to it that they would have no poor neighbors by preventing the construction of mass transit. And toward the end of his career, Moses built urban renewal projects—and cultural centers—for affluent people who wanted to stay in the city. In return, the middle-class population of the entire metropolitan area gave Moses whatever political support he needed to maintain and enlarge his power, so much so that none of the nominally more powerful politicians who wanted to fire him could do so, including Mayor LaGuardia, Governor Lehman, and even President Roosevelt, as well as several post–World War II politicians who fought with him.

Perhaps many New Yorkers would have been less enthusiastic about Moses had the press been able to report his immoral methods and had it wanted to publicize the often needless destruction of existing neighborhoods to accommodate his highway plans, but it is also possible that the beneficiaries of his projects would not have shed tears over the bulldozing of individual neighborhoods, even middle-class ones, as long as their own were preserved. Projects that offer citywide benefits are rarely held back by localized opposition even now, and in any case, the exploitation of the displaced, and the displaced themselves, are always quickly forgotten once new construction has risen on the cleared sites.

Caro's claim that New York's building program could not have materialized without Moses is belied by the fact that after World War II, most other American cities constructed exactly the same highways and urban renewal projects, and while many copied Moses' plans, they too were responding to the demands of middle-class voters, and wanted the jobs, profits, and political funds that flowed from the construction projects. Moses was unique in his ability to dominate the building process, but he was also aided by the extreme decentralization of New York City politics, its weak mayor system, and its lack of home rule, all of which helped to create power vacuums that he immediately filled. Moses built more and more quickly than anyone else, but many of his projects would eventually have been built anyway, even without him.

In the course of his career, Moses made innumerable enemies, not only among the displaced poor, but also among other New Yorkers who were left without the facilities and services—for example, hospitals, which could not be provided because so much of the city's budget was preempted by Moses' projects. Eventually, their protests caught up with him, and Moses' power began to decline in earnest after Lindsay was first elected mayor with the help of a sizable ghetto vote. Moses contributed to his own demise by allowing highly visible corruption in his urban renewal projects, and once the reporters had uncovered it, they revenged themselves, in Watergate style, for the many ways in which Moses had attacked and shackled them for over a generation. Nelson Rockefeller finally toppled Moses, although not because he was hungrier for power, as Caro suggests, but because he had the backing of David Rockefeller, who represented the bondholders, and because he was willing to continue to build, thus obtaining the allegiance of Moses' supporters, and making Moses himself superfluous.

If Caro is wrong to argue that Moses alone caused the fall of New York, he is also wrong to insist that New York has fallen. Caro's own vision for New York is a high-density city, with as few automobiles, expressways, and suburbs as possible, but the suburbanization of the city began before Moses was born, and the further suburbanization he facilitated has made life considerably more pleasant for the city's middle classes. Their New York has not fallen, but has only moved beyond the city limits, and from their perspective, Moses' one-man planning was exemplary, for it created a relatively integrated park and highway network that avoided some of the faults of piecemeal planning in other cities. Caro's stubborn vision of how New York should have been developed leads him to condemn almost all of

Moses' schemes, however, and prevents him from appreciating why Moses was so popular with the suburbanites of his time.

Of course, from the perspective of the New Yorkers then and now living in the city, many of Moses' projects were a tragic mistake; for they need, not the highways and Long Island parks Moses built, but the housing he tore down and the mass transit proposals he sabotaged. In addition, Moses hurt the city by permitting bondholders and others to make unreasonable profits which are still being paid out, and by his systematic assaults on the democratic process, even though the protests these generated ultimately helped to bring about the somewhat more democratic approach to public construction that now prevails. Ironically, in the last chapter of his book, Caro begins to reconsider his judgment of Moses, wondering whether Moses' ability to produce, even by undemocratic means, is not superior to the more democratic approach of the Lindsay administration, which resulted in much debate but little building. After seven years of work on this book, Caro may have been more affected by his subject's obsession with building than he himself realizes, but he is also right to imply that democracy and efficient public building are not entirely compatible. Still, the interlocking public authority system which Moses established is particularly unresponsive to the public will, and Caro properly recommends that it be eliminated.

Unfortunately, Caro's emphasis on Moses' villainy persuades him to judge Moses' actions and decisions as purely moral choices, implying that a well-intentioned builder would have made better plans. This is naive, for given the distribution of economic and political power in the city during the Moses era, even the most altruistic or democratic planners could not have acted completely differently—if they wanted to build, and while they might have caused less harm than Moses, none could have implemented Caro's vision, or held back the suburban exodus.

Moreover, Caro's understandable and praiseworthy need to document Moses' guilt makes him so eager to explain Moses' plans as expressions of a psychopathological drive for power, and later for spite and revenge, that he often neglects to report the man's own reasons for his plans. He fails to ask, for example, why Moses made decisions which, by Caro's account, seem totally irrational and even politically harmful to Moses, or to consider what political and other calculations went into Moses' planning. Fortunately, Caro has dug out so much hard-to-find and previously secreted information about Moses, as well as about the city in which he worked, and has reported it in such detail that his findings can be used without accepting his overly moralistic and psychological explanations. Caro's reportage, although at times distorted by his need to exaggerate Moses' power, is a superb achievement, but Caro should have given more credit to the power structure which enabled his powerbroker to build as he did, for it is the principal villain in the morality play he has written.

· P O S T S C R I P T ·

AS I NOTED in the introduction, I included this review as an antidote for the revisionism that may be taking Robert Moses out of the villainous category to which Robert Caro's book had assigned him. Moses's one-hundredth birthday remembrances a few years ago produced a number of positive reviews of Moses and his works, perhaps because of the undoubted greatness of some of that work and the obvious talents of Moses himself, but I think also because of a felt need by some people for a superman to help solve New York City's many problems.

At that time, I reread this review and decided that the revisionism was unjustified, and on all counts. Moses was responsible for some very harmful projects, especially inside the city, for many of his triumphs were built on Long Island. In addition, his talents were more than matched by his very sizable faults, such as his proclivity toward autocracy and dictatorship as well as his disdain for New Yorkers and the heartlessness he showed toward those victimized by his projects.

Given these personal shortcomings, he probably would be glad to serve as "Planning Superman" were he still alive today, but I doubt whether he could perform very well in that role now. What New York City needs most in the 1990s is more decent jobs for its poor people and money to construct the housing and infrastructure that have remained unbuilt in the last two decades. Moses could do the building, but he would not be able to find the money actually to do the building. His skill lay in attracting already-appropriated public funds into the city, not in raising new monies.

Judging from Caro's scholarship, Moses could not even put a halt to or steer in a more positive direction the overbuilding that has been taking place in New York as this is being written: in luxury housing for about a quarter of a century, in office buildings since the mid 1980s, and in hotels since the late 1980s. I think there is enough evidence in Caro's book to suggest that Moses would have gone along with the overbuilding, even though he might have been able to get some of the developers to put some money into restoring old Moses projects or building a few new ones. I doubt, however, that Moses would have used such money to build housing for the poor and moderate-income population, or to help the homeless. His vision of the city appears to have excluded the poor, and there is no reason to wish either for his return or for another Moses.

Even a nicer superman or superwoman should not be wanted, because except in the comic strips, absolute power still corrupts absolutely, and most American cities, New York included, still need more democracy than they now have. Besides, Caro showed conclusively that Moses' talent was not as a superman but as a skillful bureaucrat-politician who could extract the utmost from his fellow bureaucrats and politicians, and the public budget, to get what he wanted.

Today, the bureaucracy and the polity have become more complex, in part because of the decline of old political machines and the increase in the number of interest groups that take part directly or indirectly in the governing of New York. I am not sure that a conservative upper-class autocrat like Robert Moses could function in today's city, although I am sure that he should not have been allowed to function, at least in the role that made him famous and infamous.

PART THREE

CITY PLANNING, SOCIAL PLANNING, AND SOCIAL POLICY

· I N T R O D U C T I O N ·

IF THE PHYSICAL environment plays only a minor part in people's lives, then traditional "physical planning" at best plays only a limited role in helping people improve their lives. In 1990 one reaction might be that this is just as well, since government's ability to help is not as great as we once thought, and its willingness to do so is limited sharply both by its own agendas and by the pressures to which it must react—from those of the business community to those generated by ever-present community conflicts.

In the 1950s, most planners were much more confident about what they could do and optimistic that they could do it—and this author was no exception. Some of us thought we could do much better than physical planners, and one outcome of this optimism was the alternative approach I called goal-oriented planning.

The basic idea behind goal-oriented planning is simple: that planners must begin with the goals of the community—and of its people—and then develop those programs that constitute the best means for achieving the community's goals, taking care that the consequences of these programs result in as few undesirable behavioral or cost consequences as possible.

This conception of planning I owe to Martin Meyerson and to a study that he, John Dyckman, and I began in the mid-1950s with a grant from the Russell Sage Foundation, testing his conception by an analysis of planning for health, education, and recreation facilities. Our first step was to identify the goals and behavior patterns of various actors connected with these facilities. These actors we thought of as the *suppliers* (for example, recreation officials), the *users* (of parks and playgrounds), and the *community,* by which we meant the decision makers and residents qua citizens (and members of interest groups), but also the public interest.

Once goals had been determined, largely through sociological analyses, we hoped to use empirical behavioral data to determine what programs would best achieve the various goals of these actors and with what consequences, the eventual aim being a handbook to tell the planner what programs and consequences were related to a specific goal. Beyond that, we sought to evaluate the goals of the various actors, determine which ought to be pursued by the community in planning for the three kinds of facilities, and suggest the order of priority for this pursuit. For example, in recreation planning, we wanted to tell the planner not only what programs would achieve the recreation goals of the suppliers and the users of public recreation but also what kind of goals the community ought to be pursuing

to provide its residents with an opportunity for satisfying leisure behavior
—which might well ignore the traditional park and playground facilities
offered by the suppliers and might even preclude formal facilities. We hoped
eventually to carry out such analyses not just for the individual facilities we
were studying but for all community functions in relation to one another, so
that the planner had some criteria for deciding whether to invest the
community's incremental dollar or acre—or unit of political capital—in
housing, or education, or industry, or sewage disposal, or a tax cut. Indeed,
the study was so ambitious that we could never achieve closure, and so it
was never published.

Our research was generated by two basic ideas, both Meyerson's. First,
he argued that city planning was irrational: that the programs it was proposing often did not achieve the goals it was advocating and led to undesirable
consequences for the community as well. Second, he pointed out that the
so-called planning "standards" by which planners determined what facilities
ought to be provided by the community—for example, that one acre of
playground should be allotted for every thousand people, or that three
(1950s) dollars per capita should be spent annually for public library operations—were only implementing the goals of the suppliers of recreation and
library facilities. As a result, the suppliers obtained larger shares of the
municipal budget, political power, and community prestige, but often neglected the demands of users, planning facilities that were underutilized or
that appealed only to a narrow proportion of the total population. Moreover,
applying these standards for capital investments meant commitments to
operating expenditures and the provision of services without considering
the consequences of such commitments. For example, the conventional
standards for hospital construction also committed the community to existing hospitals—and thus existing medical practices. Planners, Meyerson
suggested, should not accept either past solutions or the implicit decisions
they contained. Instead, they should ask the basic planning question: for
what health goals for which members of the community should what kinds
of public resources be allocated and in what order of priority?

Few of our basic ideas were original, since Herbert Simon and other
social scientists had begun to work on them earlier. Planners were unfamil-
iar with them, however, although later, they became almost commonplace
in the profession, at least at the lip service level. Planners talk loosely
about the goals they are seeking to implement, much as politicians do when
they are campaigning, but neither grapple often with the fundamental questions we were trying to ask.

Asking such questions was not very difficult, and today it is easier still, but whether or not they can ever be fully answered—especially systematically or operationally—remains to be seen. The methodological problems of ascertaining and quantifying social goals are serious and while connecting goals with programs seems feasible, determining how to predict consequences, good and bad, may never produce more than good guesstimates.

The hardest puzzle, however, is how to deal with the fact that in a heterogeneous community—and few communities are not heterogeneous—citizen goals are always diverse and often in conflict with one another, and which goals of which citizens ought to be ranked in what order in the community's public allocations is hard to determine. Such questions are political, of course, but they ought to be answered systematically as well as democratically, and no one has yet invented a viable method to complement the politicians' apparently ad hoc solutions. True, "Management and Budget" offices, like the very powerful federal Office of Management and Budgets, now carry out a kind of goal-oriented planning, but the goals are usually narrow and often overly economistic, with benefit-cost analyses driving their methodologies.

The essays reprinted here grapple with only some of these issues. The first is a sociological analysis of the planning profession from 1890 to 1967, prepared as much for social scientists and the general public as for planners and policy designers. Written originally for the *Encyclopedia of the Social Sciences* published in 1968, it tries, among other things, to explain why planning was originally physical, and why it was beginning to change in the 1960s.

The remaining essays present and discuss the goal-oriented approach. Chapter 9 describes the approach, while a postscript looks at goal-oriented planning from the perspective of 1990, focusing on how and why it can still be useful, albeit as an apolitical standard with which to compare the results of political decision making. Both chapter 9 (and a related essay excerpted in its appendix) were drafted in Puerto Rico, where economic planning had blossomed after World War II and had even been given priority over physical planning. Then, in the late 1950s, Governor Muñoz Marín, concerned that the Central Planning Board's emphasis on economic and physical planning was wreaking havoc with the quality of life on the island, asked the board to plan for the preservation of Puerto Rican culture. Although his purpose seemed to have been to save a dying traditional, agrarian—and quite aristocratic—culture, the local planners, Puerto Rican and mainland in origin, and the many consultants invited to work with them interpreted his request more broadly. They tried to figure out what goals ought to be pursued by the Puerto Rican government for its society, and in the process, they reinvented the now-popular term *social planning,* although what they meant by it had little to do with today's "mainland" definition, which is a euphemism for planning activities that benefit the poor.

The last two chapters are both followups to chapter 9. Chapter 10 is a second paper about goal-oriented planning, initially written fifteen years later, but now rewritten considerably. It pays more attention to politics than its predecessor—but still not enough to work out the complex dialectics between expertise and power, as well as between elite ideas and more democratic ones. Admittedly, by the 1990s, solving city problems has become so difficult—in part because the days of urban growth are over—that politicians pay more attention to planning ideas, and at times even to planners, than when I first wrote this essay. However, as cities become poorer and poorer, developers obtain more and more influence because of the money they can add to the tax coffers (and campaign budgets). Concurrently, planners spend less of their time planning than supplying the expertise with which politicians control and hem in developers to the extent that they are able, and willing, to do so.

Chapter 11 grew out of a conference devoted to the relations between the academic social sciences and the growing policy-oriented research fields. Twenty years later, those fields, together with evaluation research, have expanded greatly, but much of their theoretical and conceptual repertoire still comes from the academy. While there is no dearth of immediately and narrowly practical policy research, a sophisticated action-oriented theory of how to develop and implement policy ideas and findings—and to chart the connections with political decision making—still seem to be missing. Planning theory has not developed sufficiently to fill the gap, either, and actually seems to live off new academic social science thought as well. My essay does not fill the gap, but at least it aims to identify the problem.

· E I G H T ·

CITY PLANNING
IN AMERICA:
1890–1967
A SOCIOLOGICAL
ANALYSIS

IN ITS GENERIC sense, planning is a method of decision making which proposes or identifies goals or ends, determines the means or programs which achieve or are thought to achieve these ends, and does so by the application of analytical techniques to discover the fit between ends and means and the consequences of implementing alternative ends and means. Planning can be used to shape an individual's decisions, but most often it is carried out by large social systems to determine long-range ends and means. City planning applies this method to determine public investment and other policies regarding future growth and change by municipalities and metropolitan areas.

Although the city planning profession and the city planning agency are inventions of the twentieth century, city planning has existed ever since people began to build towns and to make decisions about their future. In most societies, but particularly in America, there has been little consensus about these decisions. The diverse classes, ethnic groups, and interest groups who live in the city have different conceptions of how the city ought

Reprinted from *People and Plans*. I have added the dates now in the title and a postscript; in addition, I have made a few small changes in the manuscript, including putting it entirely in the past tense.

to grow and change, what aspects of city development ought to be encouraged or discouraged by public policies, and who should benefit from policy and allocation decisions. Consequently, these groups have attempted, directly or indirectly, to influence the ends, means, and techniques of planning and even the role of the planners. A sociological analysis of American city planning must therefore ask: who plans with what ends and means for which interest groups? Since the variables in this paradigm are affected by changes in the population and power structure of the American city, the analysis is best carried out historically.

American city planning can be said to have begun with the laying out of the infant country's first cities, usually by engineers who mapped grid schemes of rectangular blocks and lots, largely for the benefit of land sellers and builders.[1] Most American cities came into being without prior planning, however, and with only sporadic attempts to regulate their growth. By the middle of the nineteenth century, therefore, the major cities were marked by ugliness, inefficiency, and disorder. The provision of utilities and other municipal services could not keep up with the rapid increase in population, and the cities became overcrowded and congested, with vast slums in which epidemics, unchecked crime, and political corruption were commonplace. Shortly before the Civil War, these conditions stimulated the formation of a number of civic reform movements which were the forebears of contemporary city planning and of the ends and means it still emphasizes today.[2]

The reform groups were made up of predominantly Protestant and upper-middle-class civic and religious leaders, whose major end was the restoration of order. They sought physical order through slum clearance and the construction of model tenements to improve housing conditions[3] and through the park and playground movement which tried to preserve the supposedly health-giving features of the countryside by building parks and other recreational facilities in the crowded areas. They sought social order through the erection of educational and character-building facilities such as schools, libraries, and settlement houses, hoping that these would Americanize the immigrants and make them middle class in order to eradicate crime, vice, and even the harmless forms of lower-class hedonism. They promoted political order through the "good government" movement, which advocated nonpolitical methods of urban decision-making to eliminate the new political machines and the fledgling socialist movement. On a less manifest level, they were attempting to maintain the cultural and political power they had held before the arrival of the immigrants by imposing on the city the physical and social structure of the Protestant middle class, particularly as it then existed in rural areas and small, preindustrial market towns.

The means by which they proposed to achieve these ends included new legislation to regulate and control city growth; the use of public administration and later scientific management procedures to run the city; and the establishment of "facilities" such as parks and settlement houses, which would improve living conditions and alter the behavior of their users. After the reformers had built a few model facilities with private funds in the slums of several Eastern cities, they realized that they lacked the resources to alter the entire city by this approach and so began to use their considerable social status and what remained of their political influence to propose that the cities take over their programs as municipal functions. In this process, they developed principles and "standards" to make sure that the facilities would be provided in the proper quantity and quality. For example, as early as 1890, the "playground movement" had begun to formulate standards specifying the number, size, and equipping of playgrounds, and in 1910, it proposed that there be one playground of two to three acres within a half mile of every child and at least thirty square feet of playground space for every child in that service area.[4] Groups promoting other facilities developed similar standards, revised versions of which are still in use today.

The reformers' efforts were supported by other interest groups in the city who were threatened by the expanding slums and their immigrant population and who proposed two additional ends: beauty and efficiency. Architects who had set up a City Beautiful movement during the 1890's developed park and civic-center schemes to enhance the downtown districts of the city; for example, the Burnham plan for Chicago.[5] These plans were supported by downtown business and property interests, who wanted to promote land values in these areas and also advocated efficiency in government to keep taxes low. They were joined by property owners in high-income residential areas who were concerned about the invasion of commercial and industrial establishments and slums into these areas as the city continued to grow. They called on the cities to pass zoning legislation which would prohibit such influx and regulate what kinds of buildings and land uses were permissible by setting up zones for different land uses. Most of these proposals were also backed by the upper- and middle-class voters, who were similarly threatened by the growth of the city. They particularly favored zoning, for while pursuing order and efficiency, it also segregated land uses by class and effectively kept lower-class housing and industry out of their residential areas.

By the end of World War I, planning and zoning had become municipal responsibilities. Since their advocates usually opposed the political machines, these functions were incorporated in quasi-independent city-planning and zoning commissions, headed by lay boards of civic leaders and businessmen. Because of the emphasis on land use and the provision of facilities, the commissions were staffed principally by civil engineers and architects, who were called city planners. Soon thereafter, universities began to set up departments of city planning, almost always in architectural and engineering schools, to train people for the new municipal function and profession.

The new agencies and professionals codified and operationalized further the ends and means they had inherited from the reformers, principally through the comprehensive or "master plan," which programmed desired alterations in the land-use pattern and the facilities system and proposed legislation and administrative tools to achieve the alteration. The first of these plans appeared in 1914. Since the preparation of the master plan remained a principal function of city planning agencies through the 1960s, and since the elements of that plan changed relatively little between 1914 and 1968, it is worth spelling out what went into a master plan and, more important, what was left out.

The typical master plan was a portrait of the future condition of the city. It began with a demographic and economic analysis of the city, including a project of future growth and the size of population to be planned for. Then there were chapters and maps that described the present deficiencies: slums; "mixed" land uses; shortages of open space and of recreational and other facilities; traffic congestion; and the lack of adequate legislation and administrative machinery to control growth. The planning chapters outlined the future ideal: a city without slums, divided into zones for each major land use—commercial, industrial, and residential; efficient highway and mass transit systems; and properly distributed open space and public facilities provided on the basis of "facility standards." In the final section, the proposals for individual municipal functions and land uses were synthesized into a master-plan map, with recommendations for its implementation. These included a zoning ordinance to order land use as prescribed in the master plan; building codes to discourage slums; subdivision ordinances to regulate the building of new areas; a list of the needed facilities; proposals for governmental reorganization to coordinate development activities; and a rhetorical appeal to citizens and politicians to participate in and support the realization of the plan so as to achieve an orderly, efficient, and attractive community.[6]

In addition, the master plan proposed ends and means to improve the quality of urban life, which were embodied in its basic building block, the so-called neighborhood unit. This unit was a residential area whose size was determined by the enrollment of the public elementary school located at its center. It was planned to be purely residential, although some shopping facilities for everyday needs and a playground were provided; it was free from through traffic and was bounded by and thus separated from other neighborhoods by the major traffic arteries.[7] The typical master plan divided the city into neighborhood units; groupings of such units, called a community or district, served by district shopping centers, parks, libraries, and other facilities; and the downtown area, with its stores, offices, and central educational, cultural, and administrative facilities, sometimes combined into a civic center. The neighborhood was usually planned to be of low density, with single-family or row houses; apartment buildings were envisaged in or near the downtown area, and industrial districts were separated from residential and commercial areas as much as possible.

The master plan was essentially a technique for achieving the nineteenth-century ends of beauty, efficiency, and order and the small-town, middle-class neighborhood life favored by the reformers. It differed from their proposals by a greater emphasis on the ordering of land use and by the introduction of the concept of comprehensiveness, that is, the coordinated regulation of all phases of city development, public as well as private, so as to bring about an ideal city.

Many hundreds of master plans have been completed since 1920, some quite detailed and based on sophisticated analyses, and most of them developed on an assembly-line basis by public agencies and private consultants, especially for the smaller cities. Despite the diversity of urban life, most of the plans have been so similar that texts could be written about their preparation.[8] In terms of its impact, however, the master plan was a failure. Although individual recommendations have often been implemented, no master plan ever became a blueprint for the development of the city.

The failure of the master plan can be traced to the ends and means emphasized by the planners and to their view of the city, its growth processes, and the politics of planned change. Perhaps the crucial fault of the master plan was its environmental or physical determinism. Like the nineteenth-century reformers, the master planners assumed that people's lives are shaped by their physical surroundings and that the ideal city could be realized by the provision of an ideal physical environment. As architects and engineers, the planners believed that the city was a system of buildings and land uses which could be arranged and rearranged through planning, without taking account of the social, economic, and political structures and processes that determine people's behavior, including their use of land. This belief was supported by architectural ideology generally and also by plans for utopian and ideal cities which were constantly being proposed by architects and architecturally trained planners.[9] It was reinforced by an oversimplified interpretation of the findings of the urban ecologists, who seemed to correlate social pathology with the physical characteristics of residential areas, and by the thinking of real estate economists, who saw planning as the achievement of high land values and found these in the residential districts of the home-owning upper and middle classes.[10] The maximization of land values was also favored by the city officials who employed the planners, because it increased tax revenues, and by the property owners who supported the planners, because it meant higher profits for them.

The ends underlying the planners' physical approach reflected their Protestant upper- and middle-class view of city life. As a result, the master plan tried to eliminate as "blighting influences" many of the facilities, land uses, and institutions of working-class, low-income, and ethnic groups. Most of the plans either made no provision for tenements, rooming houses, secondhand stores, and marginal industry or located them in catchall zones of "nuisance uses" in which all land uses were permitted. Popular facilities considered culturally or morally undesirable were also excluded. The plans called for many parks and playgrounds, but left out the movie house, the neighborhood tavern, and the local club room; they proposed museums and churches, but no hot-dog stands and nightclubs; they planned for industrial parks, but not loft industry; for parking garages, but not automobile repair stations.

The units into which the plan divided the city were determined by transportation routes and other physical boundaries and did not reflect the natural areas of established social groups or the ecological processes of neighborhood change, invasion, and succession. Neighborhood boundaries ignored class divisions in the population, except as these were manifested by differences in house types. The planners made a conscious effort to break up ethnic enclaves in order to achieve nineteenth-century goals of Americanizing the immigrants.

The planners' certainty about how people ought to live and how the city ought to look resulted in a nearly static plan, a Platonic vision of the city as an orderly and finished work of art. Favoring low density and small-town living, the planners sought to achieve the cessation of residential mobility and the control and minimization of future growth. The only land uses programed for future growth were those favored by affluent residents, high-status industrial and commercial establishments, the real estate interests catering to these, and the tax collector.

The planners' inability to recognize diverse populations and values also prevented them from seeing the role of politics in implementing the plan. Believing that their solution was the best blueprint for the future, they thought that they needed only to publish their report, obtain support from the civic leaders and businessmen who sat on the boards of the planning commission, and then impress elected officials that the plan expressed the public interest. The planners' opposition to partisan political methods of decision making convinced them that the plan was "above politics" and that anyone who rejected it was acting from selfish and therefore evil motives.

Although the implementation of the plan would have required huge outlays of public funds and drastic political and economic as well as physical rearrangements, the master planners did not seriously consider that the ends they sought were opposed by many of the voters. The planners did not realize that most city residents place less value on public open space than they do; that they do not live their life around the elementary school; and that they are not interested in rearranging the land-use pattern at great expense to achieve an order that is most visible on a map or from an airplane and to produce an efficient city that tends to benefit the business community rather than the ordinary resident. Worse yet, the plan called for a middle-class life-style for all, but it did not recommend economic programs to enable low-income people to move out of tenements and buy single-family houses. As a result, master plans rarely generated any widespread enthusiasm among the voters, but always aroused considerable political opposition from the groups who would have to pay economically, socially, and politically for the proposed changes without reaping any benefit from them.

The master planners were also hampered by conditions not of their making. For one thing, their authority to plan stopped at the city limits, although the growth processes which they sought to control covered a much wider area, and the people and facilities for whom they planned were beginning to move to the suburbs before master planning was even invented. Also, the planners were poorly funded, so that their conclusions were often based on whatever data, however inadequate, were already available. Yet their methodology was ultimately also a function of their own ends, means, and techniques. Their belief in physical determinism limited their analysis to the determination of the land-use implications of their demographic and economic projections; and their faith in the ends and means they proposed discouraged their concern with alternative ends, with the fit between ends and means, and with the consequences of their recommendations. For example, in planning for recreation, they applied the facility standards of the recreation movement without computing the cost in land, and capital, and operating costs and without even realizing that the professional associations who formulated these standards had a vested interest in maximizing the facilities they advocated. Case studies of the planning process show that the planners often made their recommendations on arbitrary grounds, without understanding their consequences[11] and without using the research they had undertaken.[12]

Yet if master plans had little impact on city development, some of the planners' ideas were adopted. Zoning was supported so enthusiastically by realtors and home owners that many planning agencies spent all their time administering the zoning ordinance and could not work on master plans. The planners' neighborhood concept was adopted, in somewhat altered form, by the builders—and the purchasers—of the post–World War II suburbs, as was their idea that streets in which small children played ought to be free from through traffic. The planners' argument that excessive land coverage inevitably produced traffic congestion, that off-street parking was necessary, and that zoning too much land for commercial use in the hope of increasing tax income would also leave much land lying needlessly fallow were eventually accepted by city officials in principle, although often subverted by politically powerful private interests in practice. Also accepted was the basic master planning concept that there ought to be a comprehensive development plan for the city which coordinated the construction of housing with the construction of the needed public facilities, enabling the city fathers to evaluate private individual development proposals and choose the best sites for public improvements. Being politically weak, however, the planner could not stand up to the powerful economic interests which opposed the implementation of these principles, and being apolitical, they frequently could not develop compromise solutions which would have salvaged at least some of their proposals.

Master-planning activity reached a new high after World War II, when towns near the central cities began to be enveloped by the new suburbia and called on planners to control the growth, often to prevent the influx of newcomers who would lower the status level of the community and require higher tax rates to build new schools and other facilities for them.

At the same time, however, planners working in the cities began to lose confidence in the master plan. Isaacs had questioned the very basis of the neighborhood unit by pointing out that it favored racial segregation,[13] and

Bauer had argued that master planning, zoning, and subdivision regulations were contributing to the class and racial stratification of the new suburbs.[14] Yet the most persuasive skepticism about the master plan was produced by difficulties in its implementation and the static quality of the end product. As cities began to grow and to rebuild after the long hiatus of the Depression and World War II, many of the development proposals that came before their planning commissions either conflicted with the plans or could not be evaluated by the standards and other criteria built into it. Since the proposals were made by politically influential groups or promised new tax revenues, the conflict between them and the plan was usually resolved in their favor. Some planners argued that in order to be useful, the master plan had to be constantly revised and updated, but others began to suggest that planning should not be a method of describing the ideal city but a process of decision making and that master planning was only one tool among many to be employed in this process.

The new conception of planning only foreshadowed a radical transformation in planning theory and practice which overturned many of the traditional ends, means, and techniques that the planners took over from their reformer ancestors. This transformation came about because of changes in the condition and problems of the city, in the employers and clients of planning, and in the planners themselves.

By World War II, the growth of most older American cities had ended. After the war, as prosperity and the subsidies of the Federal Housing Administration enabled the white lower-middle-class and working-class population to become homeowners in suburbia, the city increasingly became the residence of a small number of rich people, a still large but declining middle-income population, and a rapidly rising number of poor nonwhite residents. The latter were forced to live in ghetto slums, and these as well as the pathologies associated with poverty reduced the livability of the city and created new problems for city officials. Low-income neighborhoods and residents could not pay the taxes needed to provide them with municipal services, and the exodus of middle-class residents, stores, and industries to the suburbs also deprived the city of its most profitable sources of tax income. Thus the city was forced to find new ways of maintaining itself even while it tried to cope with the exodus and the problems of the new low-income population. In Democratic administrations, some help came from the federal government, which participated in municipal activities through the financial support of new city programs.

City planning also benefited from federal subsidy, and the federal government became its major source of financing. Washington began to involve itself in planning activities during the Depression, when a National Resource Planning Board was established temporarily to undertake national and regional resources planning,[15] the National Resettlement Administration built four new so-called greenbelt towns, and the Public Housing Administration was established to tear down slums and build housing on the cleared sites. After World War II, the federal government began to fund local city planning activities themselves, most extensively for transportation planning and urban renewal.

Master planners had concerned themselves with transportation ever since car ownership had begun to increase urban congestion and suburbanization. Following the war, however, the new spurt in car buying and the growth of suburbia resulted in the building of expressways, subsidized by federal grants, in every American city. They were intended not only to reduce congestion on local city streets but also to bring the suburbanite back to the city to shop, especially when suburban shopping centers began to make inroads on downtown retail trade and on the municipal tax revenue from that area. The new expressways made it more convenient to use cars to travel to the city, but also further encouraged the exodus to suburbia. As a result, they not only failed to reduce congestion but took more customers away from the already declining mass transit systems and central business districts.

Consequently, by the late 1950s, a number of large cities began to formulate massive transportation planning studies which aimed to determine the location of future expressways and the revitalization of mass transit as part of a metropolitan area transportation system to serve the city and its suburbs. Since new transportation facilities stimulate other urban development and thus affect land-use patterns and the economic base of the cities,[16] the transportation planners were in effect formulating a new kind of master plan.[17]

In this process, they introduced several innovations into planning. Well financed and able to measure the amount and flow of traffic with relative ease, the planners obtained large masses of data and brought the newly available computer into planning to analyze them. Moreover, since the aim of their plan was limited to serving the transportation needs of the area and the achievement of the economically most productive and most efficient land-use patterns, they were working with a smaller number of ends than the master planners. This enabled them to formulate a number of alternative schemes, rather than a single one, using the computer and later the simulation model to choose among the alternatives for a final plan.[18] Because the studies were staffed by transportation experts, economists, and operations researchers, rather than by architects and master planners, the ends and means of traditional city planning were of lesser importance.

Finally, their plans were metropolitan. Because so much of the traffic flow was generated in the suburbs, transportation planning could not end at the city limits, and regional planning bodies were set up to do the studies. Metropolitan planning had been advocated by city planners and public administrators for a long time, for even the control of growth and the achievement of order and efficiency required a metropolitan government to coordinate municipal services and planning for the city and its suburbs in a single supergovernment, which would do away with the duplication and conflict among the many hundreds of local bodies.

Although private regional planning associations were set up in many cities and the Rockefeller Foundation financed a seven-volume New York Regional Plan in the 1920s, the appeals for both metropolitan government and planning fell on deaf ears. First, it was—and still is—difficult to define a metropolitan region, or any other region, for that matter, for the boundaries shift with the function whose ecological pattern is being studied. Thus, the region within which the urban economy affects its hinterland differs from that best suited to the creation of an effective police network or sanitation system. More important, however, the suburbs rejected any plan which would force them to share their power with or give up their local authority to the city. Since the cities had been predominantly Democratic and working class and the suburbs were then predominantly Republican and middle class, political and class conflicts were endemic and were magnified when cities became increasingly nonwhite. [19] Moreover, the suburbs had no great interest in metropolitan planning or coordination. Affluent homeowners can well afford the duplication of municipal services and are unwilling to accept any infringement on their local autonomy, not to mention the possible arrival of lower-status and nonwhite city residents in exchange for a slight saving in taxes. [20]

The second, and in some ways more significant, stimulus for change in city planning theory and practice came out of urban renewal. In 1949, the federal government set up the urban-renewal program which funneled considerable amounts of money to the cities to make possible the elimination of slums. Intense political opposition to public housing—especially from the real estate industry—prevented it from making any significant inroads on the slums, and the federal government therefore turned to private enterprise, hoping that it would rebuild on land that had been cleared and written down in price by federal grants. The program received strong local support from cities which expected that new building programs would increase their tax revenues and from downtown businessmen who saw urban renewal as a way of replacing the slum dwellers of the inner city with more affluent customers and later as a way of modernizing downtown districts with federal aid.

The theory behind urban renewal was the traditional nineteenth-century one that if slum dwellers were relocated in decent housing, they would give up their lower-class ways and the social pathologies thought to "breed" in the slums. Since inexpensive housing was in short supply, however, and the private redevelopers of cleared sites were building mainly luxury housing, the displaced were often forced to move into other slums, and they usually had to pay higher rents. In clearing entire neighborhoods, urban renewal also destroyed viable social communities, thus saddling the displaced with emotional costs as well. Nor did the first rebuilding projects contribute significantly to the housing stock and the economic and financial condition of the cities.[21] In the large cities, the unanticipated consequences of slum clearance created so much political opposition that by the start of the 1960s, when the market for luxury housing had been sated, the promiscuous use of the bulldozer was halted. Instead, renewal agencies began to experiment with rehabilitation, so as to minimize relocation, and in the late 1960s, the federal government began to provide new subsidies to builders and residents—albeit on a minuscule scale—for example, 221 (d) (3) below-market loans for the former and rent supplements for the latter—in order to increase the supply of low- and moderate-cost housing.

Initially, renewal had been carried out on a project-by-project basis, but once the choice sites desired by private builders had been used up, city planners were asked to develop a more comprehensive urban-renewal program. The selection of future renewal sites required the determination of the best reuse of the sites as judged by citywide considerations, and the federal government provided planning grants to the cities to create "workable programs" which had to demonstrate how individual projects fitted into a larger, more comprehensive renewal plan before federal renewal funds were made available. Subsequently, the federal government broadened its requirements—for example, by including social considerations in the choice of sites—and set up the Community Renewal Program. In 1966, the federal government made the integration of social and physical considerations in urban renewal complete by setting up the Demonstration Cities Program. Later retitled Model Cities, the new program was planned to provide yet further subsidies to enable sixty to seventy American cities to rebuild and rehabilitate the physical and social structures of their major slum ghetto neighborhoods. In addition, private enterprise was encouraged to participate more actively in the rebuilding of the slums, particularly through community-development corporations. In 1967, all these programs were still in the planning phase, although it was already evident that they would not be successful until the federal government was able to grant subsidies on a billion-dollar scale to provide housing, as well as jobs and income supports, for poor people.

In many cities, the community renewal programs resembled the traditional master plan; but in others, the failure of urban renewal to help the slum dwellers, the federal encouragement of more socially oriented planning, and the new ideas and grants developed in connection with the War on Poverty awakened planners to the need to solve the more basic problems of the low-income population.

The principal innovations were in the choice of ends and means and in the techniques of planning. Urban renewal was no longer conceived solely as a process for eliminating slums but as a means of dealing with the problems that force poor and nonwhite people into them. Many Model City schemes explored various programs of job creation, opening up housing, educational, and other opportunities to nonwhites and improving social services in the hope that these, together with housing programs, would eliminate the deprivation of the slum dwellers as well as the slums. New ends, such as equality of opportunity and greater distribution of public resources to the poor, were suggested to complement the ends of order and efficiency, particularly since the ghetto protests were leading to the realization that social order can be maintained only through greater economic and political equality. The planners' means were new as well, for programs intended to help people were added to those for changing the physical environment.

The extension of economic and other opportunities, even on a small scale, bore little resemblance to traditional planning solutions, and the outcome of the planning process was no longer envisaged as a master plan, but as a set of incremental or developmental programs that would improve present conditions, formulated so that they could be coordinated with the ongoing decision-making processes of city officials. [22]

Physical determinism was thus being replaced by a broader systems approach which sought to deal with the causes of the problem. In this conception of the planning process, land-use studies were no longer the primary form of planning research. For example, the renewal planners were turning to surveys of the present behavior and future wants of the populations for whom they were planning, analyses of the quality of opportunities and social services available to them, and economic as well as political studies to determine the feasibility and the consequences of the programs and policies they recommended.

This conception of planning also presaged a change in the role of the planner. The city planner was no longer a nonpolitical formulator of long-range ideals, but was becoming an adviser to elected and appointed officials, providing them with recommendations and technical information on current decisions. This new role was an outcome of conditions and forces that preceded innovations in the planning method. Shortly after the war, a number of cities assigned city planners the task of preparing five-year capital budgets, although the annual capital budget was still drawn up at city hall. This assignment not only shortened the time span in which planners were working but took them out of their nonpolitical ivory towers and made them aware of the political considerations in the allocation of public funds. It also brought the planner much closer to the elected official, for at the same time, many planning commissions were being reorganized into planning departments which took their place in the mayor's cabinet. This also decreased the planners' traditional distance from politics. Urban renewal activity quickened this change, for the funds that became available to cities as a result of the federal program encouraged mayors to give more power to urban-renewal agencies and sometimes to appoint redevelopment coordinators who supervised all housing, planning, and development activities.

The planner's rising influence in the 1960s must also be traced to other changes in the city and in city hall. The new problems of the city, and the gradual replacement of the remaining working-class machine politicians by middle-class, college-educated politician-administrators, supported by professionally trained bureaucrats, made city governments more responsive to expert advice, while the reduction of class differences between the planners and the new politicians improved communication between them. In addition, downtown business and property interests supported some of the new planning, partly because they, too, faced new problems they could not solve themselves and partly because they shared the planners' concern with the revitalization of the central business district. Moreover, planners were becoming more sympathetic to the city and were giving up their traditional antiurban ideology. As the suburbs threatened to engulf the city and to endanger the survival of the upper-middle-class cultural and civic institutions which have traditionally been located in the city, planners became advocates of urbanism. They supported schemes to bring the middle class back into the city, and in the suburbs proposed apartment and townhouse development to provide real or symbolic expressions of "urbanity."

Finally, with federal funds becoming a major source of support for local planning, and with state planning agencies and metropolitan ones also participating in local planning activities, planners were no longer as closely tied to the small group of local business and civic leaders who had traditionally supported them against their political opponents. This encouraged them to pay more attention to the needs of other and less vocal interest groups in the city and, during the War on Poverty, particularly the low-income population. This was part of a more general reevaluation of the relationship between the planner and the citizens, which began with the realization that the traditional appeal for citizen participation in planning was often only a demand for citizen ratification of the planner's decision. Now, some planners talked about proposals and experiments for direct citizens' participation in planning for their own neighborhood.[23]

The changes in the conditions under which planners work were complemented, and even preceded, by changes within the planning profession and in the recruitment of planners, including the entrance of social scientists into city planning.

The entry of social scientists into city planning began in the 1930s, when social scientists helped to conduct national and regional planning studies in various federal agencies. After World War II, the University of Chicago drew on some of them to establish a planning school which taught national as well as city planning and was the first to stress social science rather than architectural techniques. Subsequently parts of this curriculum spread, albeit slowly, to other planning schools and attracted students with social science backgrounds, so that in the 1960s architect and engineers were becoming a minority in the student body.

The Chicagoans approached planning as a method of *rational programming*. Briefly, they argued that the essence of planning was the deliberate choice of ends and the analytic determination of the most effective means to achieve these ends—means that make optimal use of scarce resources and, when implemented, were not accompanied by undesirable consequences. Ends, the Chicagoans argued, are imposed not by planning ideology or by *a priori* determinations of the public interest, but by political and market processes and by other forms of feedback from those affected by planning. Means and consequences were determined through predominantly empirical analyses and by other studies that tested the fit of means to ends and predicted the consequences of these means.[24]

Rational programming had much in common with concepts of planning and methods of rational decision making being developed in political science, public administration, and management, which reduced the differences between city planning and planning for other clients and ends. In turn, this enabled city planning to use the personnel and approaches of other disciplines, including operations research, decision theory, cost-benefit analysis, input-output studies, information theory, and simulation modelling as well as sociological and manpower analyses for understanding the behavior, attitudes, and ends of the clients of planning.

The new conception of planning also affected general land-use planning, creating a greater concern with the social and economic functions of land use and leading to incremental policy formulations for rearranging it. Even urban design, traditionally based primarily on aesthetic considerations, now paid some attention to the social processes that shape what city planners call the the urban form. [25]

Nevertheless, traditional master and land-use planning received new support through the revival of a nineteenth-century concept: the new town. Originally conceived as a way of moving urban slum dwellers into the countryside and halting the growth of cities, the new town of the 1960s was conceived as a relatively self-sufficient and independent community located beyond the city limits which would provide local employment opportunities for many of its residents, thus reducing their journey to work, the city's traffic congestion, and the alleged defects of the suburbs as so-called bedroom communities. [26] The development of such new towns as Columbia, Maryland, and Reston, Virginia by private builders in the 1960s gave master planners new hope that if the master plan and related traditional schemes could not work in established cities, they might be applied on the tabula rasa of a new-town site. Even so, it seemed likely that, ultimately, some of the same political and market forces that prevented the implementation of the urban master plan would also frustrate important features of the new-town master plans, especially if they did not meet the requirements of the funders and the wishes of the people who had to be attracted as home buyers. [27]

In the late 1960s, rational programming was being advocated and used by professors and academic researchers in the profession. It was, however, not yet accepted by most city-planning commissions and departments and was thus far from being incorporated at the level of day-to-day planning practice. Instead, the city planning practitioners typically reacted to the new theory—and the new urban problems—by adding programs of "social planning" to the traditional land-use or "physical planning approach." In its American usage the term *social planning* came from social welfare, where it referred to interagency coordination of social work programs. In city planning, the term was used to describe "planning for people," however, and especially for low-income ones, probably because physical planning catered so largely to building programs for more affluent city residents. The dichotomy between physical and social planning is theoretically unjustifiable, because physical plans affect people, rich and poor, as much as do social plans. Even so, some planning agencies added social planning divisions to their staffs, and a professional literature on social planning came into being. [28]

The first social planning activities were intended to meet the requirements of the urban renewal program and to correct the inequities of slum clearance for the slum dwellers, but subsequently they were used to coordinate city planning and renewal with the community action activities and other programs of the War on Poverty. Frequently, however, social planning was only a modernized version of previous attempts to impose middle-class ways on the low-income population. "Human renewal" educational and social work schemes to "rehabilitate" the slum dwellers while—or even in lieu of—improving their living conditions, thus subverted the antipoverty efforts into yet another device for maintaining the inequality of the low-income population. This led to proposals for bringing planners into closer contact with the low-income population. For example, Paul Davidoff suggested that because most planners were employed as technicians to pursue the interests of the so-called Establishment—that is, city hall, the political party, and the business community—other planners ought to become "advocate planners" [29]—that is, technical consultants and even spokespersons for the low-income population—paralleling a similar proposal in the legal profession. [30] In addition, a number of planners pointed out that because of the profession's ties to the Establishment, it had evaded its responsibility to take action on racial discrimination and economic inequality. [31] In several cities, planners worked with local civil rights groups and community organizations in poor neighborhoods and also formed a national professional association, Planners for Equal Opportunity, to complement the more conservative American Institute of Planners. They also rejected orthodox beliefs about how to plan for the slum ghetto, for example, by questioning the profession's advocacy of integrated housing as a means of improving the living conditions of the mass of poor blacks. [32]

These activities also initiated the explicit politicization of the city-planning profession. It appeared that the profession was being split into progressive and conservative wings, the former calling for social planning to reduce economic and racial inequality, the latter defending traditional physical planning and the legitimacy of middle-class values. The rational programmers constituted a third wing, favoring an approach to make it possible to plan for all interest groups, but they, too, were split over the issue of working with or against the Establishment.

In their day-to-day practice, city-planning agencies tended to favor the conservative wing and the traditional land-use approach to planning, although they were both threatened and influenced by the progressives and the rational programmers. Not only were the agencies in existence to conduct land-use planning, but most of the directors and senior staff members had been trained in this approach, and most of the leading practitioners in the profession still came from architectural and civil-engineering backgrounds. Rational programmers and progressives were more often found among the junior staff, and they had less influence on agency activities. Moreover, since planners were employees of municipal bureaucracies, they were expected to conform to agency policy on the job, and in some cities they were even restrained from off-hours participation in activities and groups that questioned or opposed agency policy. This naturally reduced the impact of progressive ideas on local planning activities.

In 1967, the future direction of city planning was uncertain. As architecturally trained planners become a minority in the profession, city planning may make more use of the concepts and methods of rational programming and will pay more attention to the social and economic problems of the city. It is also possible, however, that established city-planning agencies will continue to maintain the physical-planning tradition and that new agencies, staffed by professionals from other disciplines, will be assigned to deal with the social and economic aspects of urban growth and change.

I should note that the preceding analysis was influenced by my personal involvement in the progressive and rational programming wings of the planning profession. Many traditional city planners, pointing to their new influence and constantly rising agency budgets, argued not only that the ends of creating efficient and attractive cities through physical planning were still valid but also that *they* spoke to the needs and wants of the majority of the metropolitan area population, which was now affluent enough to want both these ends. Others argued that physical planning to attract the upper-middle class back to the city was crucial if the city was to continue to play a significant role in American civilization.

Although research on residential aspirations and the results of renewal activities suggested that it was probably impossible to reverse the middle-class exodus from the city,[33] there could be no question that physical planning was needed in every city, if only to modernize it, raise its efficiency in housing and moving workers and residents, and prevent further deterioration of its financial and physical condition. The ends of physical planning were most relevant to the suburbs and to the newer communities of western United States, although even they did not always favor the particular kinds of order, efficiency, and attractiveness that physical planners had traditionally sought. In the older American cities, however, poverty, unemployment, and racial and class discrimination were not only the most crucial problems but also major causes of the low quality of city living, the middle-class exodus, and the city's financial difficulties. The inequalities and resulting pathologies among the urban low-income population must therefore be eliminated before the attractive, efficient, and slumless city for which physical planners have been striving is to be realized. When the latter can be persuaded of the validity of this concept, it may be possible to achieve a synthesis of the so-called social and physical planning approaches to create a city planning profession that uses rational programming to bring about real improvements, not only in the lives of city residents but also in the condition of the cities themselves.

· P O S T S C R I P T ·

THIS ESSAY IS particularly time bound, and in two ways. First, it was written in 1967 at a time when planning was growing and changing, and the result is a quite Whiggish—and academic—essay which dealt largely with the changes that would be important in planning's fairly glorious future. As a result, I probably focused insufficiently on the often prosaic everyday work of planners that in effect supplied the bread-and-butter work for most professionals.

For example, while I devoted a number of pages to the decline and fall of master planning, I ignored the states and communities in which a master plan was required by legislation—and probably still is. I also did not say enough about the extent to which planners are concerned, through zoning and other methods, with trying to influence growth, either increasing it or slowing it down. The direction of the influence of growth was, however, less often determined by planners than by the community's business, political, and civic leadership, the voting citizens in cases in which they exerted their power—and the health of the economy in which the community was embedded. In any case, at this writing, planners still do mandated master planning and still try to influence growth in one or another direction.

The second way in which the essay is time bound is in misjudging planning's actual future, and the importance of both social planning and rational programming. I wrote the essay at a time in which the War on Poverty looked as though it might still move up from the skirmish stage, and I felt that it, Model Cities, and what was happening in the ghettoes would have a major impact on city planning.

Of course, the reality turned out to be quite different. The ghetto upheavals brought about a sudden and hurried influx of funds into the city, but in 1968, a Republican administration took over the White House and began to undertake the traditional Republican withdrawal from urban programs, particularly those that would benefit the low-income population. (In the meantime, the ghetto upheavals had ended, and the federal funds that now came into the city in this connection supplied urban police forces with more modern offensive and defensive weapons in case the upheavals began again.)

Although more subsidized housing was completed in 1972 than in any other year in American history, all of it had been scheduled in Lyndon B. Johnson's administration but it took a long time to go through what was then called the pipeline. Once President Nixon was reelected in 1972 and before he became embroiled in his Watergate troubles, he declared a moratorium on the construction of public and most other kinds of subsidized housing for the poor, a moratorium that has still not ended at this writing.

By then, some of the programs most relevant to city planners had also been stopped. Model Cities, which looked as if it would justify a radical departure for planning and related programs, first suffered the traditional watering down that takes place when Congress sees a good scheme and every representative wants one in his or her district. Thus, a program intended for a handful of experimental or demonstration cities was stretched to accommodate a much larger number, but before that stretching was even tried, the monies for Model Cities and the War on Poverty—not to mention the all-important White House leadership—began to be diverted to the destruction of Vietnam.

One of the other new ideas mentioned in this essay, new towns suffered a similar fate. Once the idea caught on, many new towns were proposed, but new towns require high initial capital outlays and cash flows, which private enterprise was unwilling and probably unable to provide for such an innovative—and risky—venture. Once the federal government began its move out of housing programs, the new-town plans had to be abandoned. Of the two new towns already under construction, Reston went broke and the new buyer finished it as an ordinary suburban community, so that only Columbia was completed more or less according to plan, thanks in large part to the genius and stubborn persistence of James Rouse. (However, even he could not persuade Columbia's residents to pay much attention to the neighborhood boundaries and facilities he had so lovingly nurtured.)

Ironically enough, postwar new towns had already been built in America earlier, by William Levitt and his associates in three Levittowns (one in Long Island and two near Philadelphia), and Philip Klutznick and his associates in Park Forest, near Chicago.

These were not considered new towns by the planners and others who had kept the English and the U.S. New Deal new-town tradition alive, probably because no well-known professional new town planners were involved in them. Thus, even though the towns were planned quite comprehensively, and William Levitt planned an industrial zone for his last Levittown, these four communities, as well as some other new towns in California—and probably elsewhere—never received the professionals' approval. Indeed, the Levittowns were the target of much abuse from planning and other professions during their first years and became symbols of all that was evil about postwar suburban communities.

Here my essay must end, for I moved out of academic planning and into sociology in 1971 and thus cannot properly update what has happened to urban planning, practice and academic, since then. Some of the fairly simple conceptions behind social planning and rational programming appear to be part of the conventional planning wisdom in 1990, and even the concern with democratization and egalitarian goals has not disappeared, although these goals are not among the dominant concerns in planning—or other professions—these days.

I should also add that since I wrote my essay, urban and social historians have done considerable work on the history of American city planning, the Progressives, and even on suburban planning. I have read only a little in these literatures, and have not drawn on them for this postscript, but of the books with which I am familiar, I might mention Christine M. Boyer, *Dreaming the Rational City: The Myth of American City Planning* (Cambridge, Mass.: MIT Press, 1986); Paul Boyer, *Urban Masses and Moral Order in America, 1820–1920* (Cambridge, Mass.: Harvard University Press, 1978); Robert Fogelsong, *Planning the Capitalist City: The Colonial Era to the 1980s* (Princeton: Princeton University Press, 1986); Robert Fishman, *Bourgeois Utopias: The Rise and Fall of Suburbia* (New York: Basic Books, 1987); Bernard J. Frieden and Marshall Kaplan, *The Politics of Neglect: Urban Aid from Model Cities to Revenue Sharing* (Cambridge, Mass.: MIT Press, 1975); Kenneth T Jackson, *Crabgrass Frontier: The Suburbanization of America* (New York: Oxford University Press, 1985); and Daniel Scheffer, ed., *Two Centuries of American Planning* (Baltimore: Johns Hopkins University Press, 1988).

THE GOAL-ORIENTED
APPROACH
TO PLANNING

C ITY PLANNING GREW up as a movement of upper-middle-class-Eastern reformers who were upset by the arrival of the European immigrants and the squalor of their existence in urban slums and the threat which these immigrants, and urban-industrial society generally, represented to the social, cultural, and political dominance the reformers had enjoyed in small-town agrarian America. These early planners did not concern themselves much with explicit goals; they were a movement with missionary fervor which had no need to question its goals. Instead, they devoted themselves to developing programs calling for a change in the physical environment, for they believed that physical change would bring about social change.

As reform groups and businessmen gave city planning increasing support, it became a profession. Its physical emphasis naturally attracted architects, landscape architects, and engineers; these developed planning tools that were based to a considerable extent on the beliefs which the movement had accepted. Thus, they made master plans which assumed

Reprinted from *People and Plans*. I have made a few small changes, and have added as an appendix parts of my "Memorandum on Social Planning," which had been the next chapter in *People and Plans*. I have also added a postscript.

that once land-use arrangements had been ordered "comprehensively," the social and economic structure of the community would also change.

They also made up standards which provided a formula by which the amount of land needed for a specific use could be determined in relation to the numbers of people involved. These standards were assumed to be means to the planners' goals. However, no one ever asked what these goals were and whether or not the standards would achieve them. For example, recreation planners advocated one acre of playground per thousand people because they were in favor of "wholesome recreation" and believed the playground provided it. But the planners did not consider whether they had a right to attempt to regulate leisure behavior, whether wholesome recreation was a desirable goal, whether the playground had anything to do with providing recreation, or whether enough children actually used the playground (for wholesome or other pursuits) to justify the costs of the playground in land and public funds. Actually, the public recreation standards, like most of the others, were made up by a single-purpose organization, itself descended from the reformist recreation movement, whose goal was to maximize the amount of land and public funds to be allocated to its services. Since city planners were ideologically and socially close to these movements, they accepted the standards without question. If they had applied all the community facility standards which they usually favored all at once, they would have discovered that there would not have been enough land left in the community for housing and industry nor enough money in the public till to run the rest of the community's operations.

During the first half of the twentieth century, few planners seem to have been bothered by these inconsistencies. Nor did they notice that the standards and their other techniques and solutions offered little help with the most important problem which the politician had to resolve: how to allocate limited public resources among a variety of pressing demands for land and funds, not all of which could be satisfied.

The kind of general planning that seeks to deal with these planning and political issues I label *goal*-oriented planning. I would define goal-oriented planning as developing programs or means to allocate limited resources in order to achieve the goals of the community (and its members) ranked in order or priority. The crucial elements in this definition are *goals,* the *programs* to achieve them, the *consequences* of achieving these, especially cost in relation to resources, and the criteria of ordering goals and programs in the *priority* of those to be achieved first, or later, and those to be given up. I cannot describe the whole approach here, but shall focus on two major aspects of this approach: the determination of goals and the determination of programs to achieve goals.

The most difficult problem is to determine whose goals and which goals are to be achieved. I noted before that in the past planners had their own goals for how people should behave, but that they were almost never explicitly concerned with goals. The goal-oriented approach calls for exactly the opposite; it stresses the need to make all goals explicit, and suggests that the goals to be achieved are those which the members of the community consider desirable.

However, the members of the community are not always agreed on goals. Renters want services; owners want tax reduction. Store owners in the central business district want high-income residential areas to surround this district; low-income residents without job security want to live near the district so that they can be close to the centers of transportation and a variety of jobs. People also have different goals depending on whether they are suppliers or users of public services. For example, public-recreation officials want people to seek their leisure in parks, playgrounds, and recreation centers; children seem to prefer the streets; teenagers, commercial recreation; and adults, the facilities in their own homes. The community as a whole also has goals for recreation; it wants to eliminate individually or socially destructive forms of leisure behavior. Thus, it is necessary to decide whose goals are to be implemented, whose are to be set aside, and, where possible, whether conflicting goals can be combined in some way so that as many as possible are achieved. More often, however, conflicting goals force the community and its decision makers to choices which will aid one interest at the expense of another.

The planner does not determine goals; this is the job of the community and its elected representatives. Even so, the planner should try to help these representatives in the process of goal determination by analyzing their present activities to show them what implicit goals they are pursuing —and with what consequences—and by making studies of the behavior patterns and attitudes of the citizenry that would provide data on the goals of the various sectors of the community's population.

In his or her goal-determining function, the planner is thus a technician-aide to the elected decision maker. This assumes, however, that the decision maker is a truly representative leader. Planners used to assume that politicians were inherently evil and perhaps many still think so. I imagine, however, that some and perhaps many planners now understand that they may represent sectors of the population with goals that differ from those of the planner, and that in any case, they are under different pressures than planners. Nonetheless, it may happen that politicians are elected without being representative and are thus able to pursue the goals of only the most powerful or most affluent portion of their entire constituency or their own personal goals without being responsive to any constituency. Once the planner is convinced that the goals of the community itself are not served by such a decision maker—and this is not an easy judgment to make—his or her other roles as citizen and professional give him or her the right, and even the duty, of fighting for what he or she thinks is right and of using all means at his or her command, including political ones, for this purpose. In this fight, the planner should continue to remain the servant of the community and especially of the politically neglected members of the community.

The most important role of the planner is, however, to tell the community and its leaders that if they want to achieve Goal X, they must institute Program Y, requiring certain costs and resulting in certain consequences, and if they want to achieve Goal A, they must implement Program B.

The second aspect of the goal-oriented approach is the determination of programs to achieve goals. For example, when the community's goal is to eliminate the economic, social, psychological, and residential problems of slum dwellers, the programs usually suggested by planners have involved slum clearance and the relocation of the residents into standard housing. We now know, however, that conventional programs do not necessarily achieve their goals. The economic and other problems of slum dwellers do not disappear when they are displaced from slum housing and relocated into standard housing, or when they are moved into brand-new public housing. If we really want to improve the condition of slum dwellers, the money used for slum clearance should be diverted to programs which would result in higher wages for slum dwellers, provide them with education for the social and economic skills needed in the city, and develop other programs that will alleviate social and psychological problems associated with poverty.

Similarly, if the community wants to maximize public health, planners must do more than plan for hospitals, health centers, and sanitation devices. First, the goal itself must be defined more clearly. Is the community concerned with prolonging the life of the old or chronically ill? Is it interested in maximizing the health of those who cause epidemics? Is it concerned with saving those who would otherwise die during infancy? Once goals have been spelled out, programs must be defined in relation to them. Municipally provided hospitals and health centers cure people, but often fail to reach those who are most in need of cures. If the latter are the greatest menace to public health and to themselves, however, it is necessary to develop the kind of facilities and programs that they will use.

The point I want to emphasize is that goals must be defined operationally, and programs must be created which will actually achieve these goals. In this connection, the planners' job is to bring together data from all kinds of disciplines which can be used to develop such programs. If we want to build a bridge that will not collapse, we have sufficient engineering data to develop a program almost guaranteed to achieve that goal. Now, planners must collect or stimulate the collection of data to develop programs for the achievement of more complex goals. For some goals, planners will have to call on sociologists, anthropologists, psychologists, students of consumer behavior, and others, as well as on the architects, engineers, municipal finance experts, and public administrators whom they have traditionally used as resource persons. Many of the data needed for such program planning are not yet available, and in such cases, planners must develop the best assumptions and estimates about phenomena for which they have no data. Then, when the planning has been implemented, they should follow up the results, to see whether or not their assumptions were right. Thus, data are created for similar goal-program relationships in the future. If planners can experiment, they should try two different programs to achieve the same goal and then do follow-up research to discover which one worked better.

This discussion of the goal-oriented approach to planning has been too brief to consider how to determine benefits and costs for each program. Nor has it touched on the most difficult problem of all: how to help the political decision makers in the final phase of the process, when they have to allocate resources among competing goals and in what proportion, and when they must determine which goals are most deserving of high priority and implementation and which must be postponed or given up.

In its brief history, planning has developed from a missionary movement to a profession based on the beliefs, of that movement, but with a strongly architectural and engineering emphasis. In terms of the approach I have outlined, planning would be a profession resembling in many ways the discipline of an applied social science. While it would depend on the social sciences for many of the data relating goals and programs, it would be an art in formulating its special synthesis of these data. Obviously it would continue to require traditional physical planning, with architectural and design techniques, in the implementation of spatial programs.

However, planning as I have defined it is, or should be, only one species of a larger genus of community decision-making, for the process proposed here is applicable to all phases of goal-seeking decisions. Ideally, all community decisions should aim toward achieving the goals that the community deems important and should be arrived at in the ways outlined above. I do not favor the planners' taking over the community's decision-making functions; rather, I suggest that the planning approach described here can be used for all kinds and levels of community decision-making and by all types of decision makers, political, citizen, as well as professional.

Two important qualifications must be appended. First, the presentation of an approach is relatively simple; its application is not; but an approach does not really exist until it can be used in actual decision-making, and many obstacles stand between my statement of the approach and its application. Second, I suspect that political decision-makers may already use an approach similar to the one I am suggesting. What one might call their "political benefit-cost accounting" is not altogether different from goal-oriented planning, even though politicians make their decisions without explicitly formulating goals, determining what programs will best achieve their goals, or measuring the benefits and costs of alternative programs. Still, before planners reject political decision-making processes, they should analyze them to determine how close the results are to the results that would stem from goal-oriented planning methods.

Nevertheless, whatever the problems of the goal-oriented approach, it is clear that planning and community—or societal—decision-making blend into each other and that every community decision is in some way related to the goals which planners are concerned with, just as planning must end up with a community or societal decision. In the long run, then, planning should become an applied social science and an art of community or societal decision-making.

APPENDIX

ANY METHODOLOGY for goal-oriented planning must fulfill three criteria: First, it must help to provide answers to planning decisions which are eventually embodied in budget and legislation decisions. The answers necessary can be summarized in the following list of questions:

1. How much—i.e., quantity of resources?
2. Of what—i.e., programs?

3. For whom—i.e., for what clients?
4. Why—i.e., to achieve what goals?
5. For how much—i.e., what social and economic costs?
6. Under what conditions—i.e., with what other consequences, especially demands made on the people for whom the planners are planning?

Second, the methodology must provide techniques for goal choice, for the selection of programs to achieve these goals, and for determining the consequences of these programs on costs and the functioning of the society.

Third, the methodology dealing with goal choices must be flexible to allow for the multiplicity of goals and interests in society and for the changes these are undergoing over time. Concurrently, however, the methodology must provide criteria or values that are absolute in the heuristic sense, so that goals and alternative programs can be evaluated against them.

There are essentially two approaches to goal-oriented planning. One approach begins with a goal choice and proceeds thence to programs and consequences. The other begins with various alternative programs, analyzes their implicit goals, and then revises the programs to achieve explicitly stated goals. The first approach may be outlined as follows:

1. Statement of goal in operational terms.
2. Development of program alternatives to achieve the goal.
3. Analysis of three types of consequences of implementing these program alternatives:
   (a) Goal achievement: do the programs achieve the goals?
   (b) Costs: What are the costs, in various kinds of resources, for effectuating the programs?
   (c) Other consequences: what kinds of benefits and what kinds of financial, social, political, and other human costs—or undesirable consequences—and for whom, do these programs have on other aspects of the society and on the achievement of other high-priority goals?
4. Comparison of programs: which of the alternative programs functions best and most efficiently with respect to:
   (a) Achievement of goals.
   (b) Maximization of benefits over costs.
   (c) Minimization of undesirable consequences.
5. Comparison of goal in relation to other goals:

   (a) Comparison at the level of costs: is the goal worth the costs and the shifting of resources from other goals?

   (b) Comparison at the level of goals: is the goal worth the detrimental consequences, if any, on the achievement of other goals?

   (c) Development of goal priority: how does the goal rank with others in a priority system?

6. Final planning decision:

   (a) Acceptance or rejection of goal and program, with given consequences.

   (b) Alteration of goal and program to minimize undesirable consequences.

This approach has some limitations; it assumes that the planners can rank the society's or community's goals in order of priority and then develop programs for these goals. Moreover, this approach tends to neglect existing programs. Conversely, starting with goals allow planners to think about goals without the restraint of existing programs and is therefore useful for the development of new ideas. For example, if the planner's goal is to accelerate the acculturation of poor rural migrants to urban life, new programs can be developed to attempt to achieve this goal, rather than to assume without proof that tearing down the rural houses of such people and rehousing them in the city will help achieve the desired objective.

The alternative and more feasible approach to goal-oriented planning begins with present program alternatives and evaluates the goals implicit in them. These alternatives may be existing or proposed programs contained in a legislative proposal, a budget draft, or a master plan. The methodology can be outlined as follows:

1. Statement of all proposal alternatives, if possible in operational terms.

2. Analysis of the consequences of each alternative if it were implemented:

   (a) Goals: what goals would be achieved for different sectors and client groups in the society?

   (b) Goals: what goals would not be achieved if the alternative were not implemented?

   (c) Costs: what are the costs, in social and economic resources? If possible, these should be stated as estimates of cost per unit of achievement, or per client, or per unit of scarce resources.

   (d) Other consequences: what effects would each program have on other aspects of the society or community? Which are desirable and undesirable and for whom?

3. Analysis of goals.
    (a) Are the goals implicit in the programs the proper goals, i.e.,
        those being sought?
    (b) If not: revise program alternatives until they are in line with the
        goals actually sought.
    (c) If yes:
        (1) Which of the alternatives achieves more important goals at
            the least cost in the scarcer resources and with fewest unde-
            sirable consequences?
        (2) Which alternative, if not provided, would result in more un-
            desirable consequences for the society or for a number of
            members thereof?
        (3) What alterations can be made in one or the other alternative
            to achieve the goals of both at least cost, financial and social?
        (4) What innovations can be suggested to achieve the important
            goals of both at least cost?
4. Presentation of alternatives to decision makers.
    (a) Analysis of each alternative, with reference to goals, costs, and
        other consequences.
    (b) Recommendation for choice to be made on a *technical* basis: if
        decision makers want to achieve goal A, then they should choose
        program A, etc.
    (c) Recommendation for choice on an *evaluative* basis, indicating
        which programs will contribute most to the achievement of over-
        all societal values.
    (d) Recommendations for choice on *other* bases. Here the planner is
        no longer technician, but governmental-political adviser, and
        might suggest his or her choice of alternatives, giving reasons for
        this choice, especially where it differs from the choice suggested
        by the analysis under 4(c) above.

Which of the two approaches is more useful will depend on the kinds of
problem that require solution. As already indicated, the first approach is
probably more useful for innovation, while the second is more useful for
evaluation of proposed alternative programs.

The heart of the planning process is to encourage the development of
programs that will achieve the goals desired. Too much of current planning
revolves around programs that are legitimated by tradition, rather than by
any knowledge of whether they achieve the desired goal. Thus, it is
important to develop a new tradition of asking, for any goal: what are the
programs that would really achieve this goal, irrespective of existing programs? Likewise, for any program: what goals does this program actually

achieve; what clients does it attract, and does it provide them with services they want or need? Or is it simply a program that satisfies the values of those who supply it, but does not appeal to any need or demand among intended users? Continued raising of such questions by planners who have no prior emotional or ideological commitment to any specific answer will produce visible benefits at the level of planning analysis.

It would be unrealistic to pretend that data for these analyses are now available or will be available in sufficient amounts in the future. Nevertheless, if the analyses themselves are valid, the lack of data should not be a deterrent to asking the right questions.

· P O S T S C R I P T ·

THIS ESSAY WAS first written in 1958, but in 1990, it is clearer to see that the approach has several faults as well as some sterling virtues.

To begin with the faults, one is its mechanical quality. To a large extent this was the result of trying to produce a general model or formula, for certainly I, and my colleagues, knew full well that society is not a mechanism and cannot be understood—or changed—with mechanical metaphors. However, at the time we were working, the profession was dealing with far more primitive models, or rather with simplistic formulas that were not even premechanical.

A second fault of the approach is its complexity, for determining all the community's goals, establishing their relative priorities, finding the right programs, predicting future consequences—and then reassessing the goals and priorities is an immense task, if indeed it can actually be done. Presumably, computers can now or will someday be able to do all the juggling, but determining people's and organizations' goals and separating the actual or operational ones they seek from the professed ones they preach will always have to be done by humans.

The goal-oriented model's third shortcoming is its failure to deal with the relationships between planning and politics, and to think about how goal-oriented planning relates to the less systematic planning for political goals carried on by elected and at least high-level appointed officials, as well as other politicians. We were not trying to edge politicians out or replace them, and it may have been the model's complexity that kept us from dealing with this all-important topic.

Nonetheless, and despite our intent to see the planner as the researcher-technician servant of the community, the approach came out overly elitist. While the method eschews the idea of the planner (or policy analyst and designer) as decision maker, it gives the planners a large and complicated role in the community, making them virtually indispensable. Even if they aim to be user oriented, for example, they are going to have to do a lot of research in order to figure out what users need and want. Conversely, there is very little of a decision-making role for the users—but then in the mid-1950s participatory democracy or advocacy planning had not yet been invented.

Goal-oriented planning's fourth major fault is just the reverse of the second; its simplicity. As already noted, ongoing communities or societies do not work in as mechanical a manner as the approach implies and never achieve the consensus the approach assumes in formulating community goals. Even getting people and bureaucracies to think in terms of actual goals is not that easy. Indeed, the rational bureaucrat will profess and propose whatever goals are necessary to raise his or her agency's budget, and an ethnographer may be necessary to determine operational ones.

Nevertheless, these and other faults notwithstanding, I still consider goal-oriented planning to be valuable, and for three reasons., First, the approach is radical, in the literal sense of the term, forcing planners, and if it is done well, the citizenry and the politicians, to ask fundamental questions about the community and its future: its actual goals, the extent to which existing programs are achieving these, what new programs could better achieve them, and what programs, old or new, would have the fewest undesirable consequences and the most desirable ones. Even discussing what makes consequences desirable or undesirable and for which components of the community and which sectors of the population still needs to be done. Many existing public programs hurt people, and those who are either inarticulate or very busy with more urgent concerns will never protest that they are being hurt.

Planners do not normally have time, or much incentive, to ask radical questions, and politicians even less so, but somebody ought to be asking them regularly, and on a more systematic basis than social critics.

Second, because goal-oriented planning seeks to establish an empirical relationship between a goal and the programs that can achieve it, the planners can help the community be more efficient and effective. They can also tell the community that if it really wants to achieve a particular goal, or eliminate a specific problem, it *has to* undertake a certain set of actions, or else the goal will simply not be achieved.

Moreover, establishing empirical goal-programs scenarios will enable planners to tell the community all the programs, short range and long range, that are going to be needed for major goals; what the probabilities are that the various programs can achieve the primary goal; and when goal-program relationships cannot be established. Then the planners can tell the community that specific goals cannot be achieved, either for lack of knowledge, or due to insuperable economic or political obstacles. If planners and politicians can know that there is no way of reaching a particular goal, they can either muddle through or counsel patience, avoiding both false promises and the undue expenditure of time, money, and effort on what cannot be done. This assumes, however, that the planners' can persuade political leaders, who rarely like to admit failure, to allow them to report to the community what cannot be done. The goal-oriented approach also gives planners a *standard* to tell them—in cases when programs to achieve a goal are known—what could be done, if the political, economic, and other resources were available. Of course, this standard applies only to an apolitical community that is devoted to achieving goals, and is both willing and able to overcome all obstacles in its path, including those who hold the economic, political, or social power to maintain various status quos.

That standard is very useful to planners, for example in telling a community that it is possible to reduce many kinds of street crime if the community really wants to pursue that goal as far as necessary to achieve success.

However, using the standard can also be risky and dangerous, for it is only a formula to make the point that if you want Goal X you must go with Programs Y to Z. Such a formula can rarely be applied literally to real communities, because these rarely achieve consensus on specific goals, so that in effect, the standard says that if you want Goal X for Groups A to G, Groups H to R may object to programs Y to Z being imposed on them for a goal they do not particularly care about. Not everybody in the community may want to pay the costs of reducing street crime.

Politicians may resent being measured with or against a standard, and while that standard is a good strategic device to criticize inept or corrupt community leaders, the standard does not lend itself very well to *political* planning for the majority of leaders who are neither inept nor corrupt. In effect, planners have to empathize, taking the politicians' role even while discussing with them the results of applying a planning standard that is essentially nonpolitical. Conversely, if they are politically able to do it, planners can use the standard for didactic purposes, telling the community that and how a particular goal can be achieved if people really want it. That may mobilize citizens who want to see that goal achieved to become active in behalf of the needed programs.

Perhaps the standard is most useful for planners' education, for if they know that programs Y to Z will achieve goal X but see that the community will not act, they can learn what the economic and political obstacles are to the goal's achievement—and they may be able to learn how to overcome them. At the least, they will know more about how politics and economics affect planning, which is always a useful lesson.

Even so, when planners have empirically based knowledge about goal-program relationships, they also have an important and potentially powerful planning tool. The more such knowledge they can collect, and the more they know what programs can achieve what goals, the more useful planning will become in the long run, for the profession will be able to develop the policy catalogs of established goal-program relations discussed briefly in chapter 10.

Third, the goal-oriented approach is systematically and explicitly concerned with consequences, and with determining them empirically in much the same way as goal-program relationships. Moreover, knowing the consequences of different programs is as essential as knowing the goals programs can achieve, for deleterious consequences can scuttle otherwise effective programs. Thus, much of what I have said above about goal-program relations also applies to program-consequences relationships, and need not be repeated here.

To be sure, many consequences cannot be studied empirically and can only be predicted. However, over the long run, predictions will either turn out to be right or wrong, and in any case can be checked against what actually happened so that empirical determinations can be made for the future. What can thus be learned about consequences also belongs in the policy catalog.

Fourth, even the most unrealistic feature of the approach, putting all community goals in order of priority, may become more possible as computers become more sophisticated. At that point, determining and prioritizing goals will also be a useful exercise, for if nothing else it enables people to think concretely about what goals they want for their community and for themselves. In addition, it is a potentially democratic exercise, for if the planners do their work comprehensively and conscientiously, and engage in empirical data gathering about goals, the goals of the large numbers of citizens who are unable to be heard at city hall will obtain some voice. Finally, it is a particularly important exercise because politicians typically have to figure out how to minimize conflicting goals and conflicting demands for the same resources. Consequently, they have a strong incentive to limit the number of goals to be included in their political planning so as not to make that planning more difficult than it already is. Planners cannot extricate the politicians from this dilemma, but they can remind elected officials what goals are being left out or being left at the bottom of the heap.

There is one danger in all this: that because the goal-oriented approach can supply planners with empirically based goal-program-consequences relationships, they may fall back into the profession's old trap of thinking that it knows everything better than everyone else and should therefore be in charge of the city's growth, change, and overall decision-making for the future. No one today thinks planners should have such power, and it would be tragic if the goal-oriented approach, which can be a marvelous heuristic exercise to improve the quality of planning and the usefulness of planners, moved the profession back in the direction of the old trap of false omniscience.

PLANNING, SOCIAL PLANNING, AND POLITICS

THIS ESSAY HAS two aims: to take a look at social planning, and to view it in its relation to politics and public decision making generally. Before dealing with social planning, however, it is necessary to discuss planning itself.

TWO DEFINITIONS OF PLANNING

PLANNING HAS usually been defined in two quite different ways, which can be labeled *substantive* and *process*. Substantive planning is concerned with the achievement of specific goals or the implementing of specific programs. The process definition sees planning as a method of decision making, which can be applied not just to cities but to any ongoing human activity.

Substantive planning aims to improve society in a specific way; process planning seeks to make improvement more rational, by the use of modern analytic concepts and techniques as well as logic and common sense. My own very simple model of process planning is described in chapter 9.

Previously unpublished, this is a greatly revised version of a paper first prepared for the Graduate School of Planning of the University of Puerto Rico in March 1973.

159

Substantive planning can be analyzed from the point of view of process planning, for even if its emphasis is on substantive goals, it also involves a planning process, for example to develop programs for substantive goals. In practice, however, substantive planning has not seriously attempted to be rational as a process. Instead it has resulted in plans that are sometimes goals and more often programs, but in the former case it has rarely operationalized the goals; and in the latter case it has often suggested programs without considering either what goals they would achieve or what consequences they would produce.

For example, encouraging gentrification has sometimes been a programmatic activity of substantive planning, and too often even planners have been caught up in the widespread (elite) enthusiasm about gentrification to think about the goals it achieves and the consequences that accompany it. Thus, planners ought to consider whether their community goals are to raise the socioeconomic class level of an area, to improve areas aesthetically, at least by upper-middle and upper-class standards, or to encourage a community's professional services industries—or its economic development—by increasing the housing supply likely to be chosen by young professionals. Yet other goals are buried in gentrification, and each one should be analyzed to determine if is something the community wishes to satisfy—and if gentrification is the best way to satisfy it. There is also the matter of consequences; for example, what happens to the current residents of an area to be gentrified, as well as to adjacent residential and other areas which may be helped or hurt in a variety of ways by the nearby gentrification.[1]

Likewise, replacing residential land with parkland may be a good idea in cities which are short of the latter, but sometimes parks are not used very often, either because people in the surrounding catchment area most likely to use a park have weekend homes, or are too fearful about their safety. Thus, planners must ask what goals they want the park to satisfy, and for whom, as well as what goals would be met if the residential area were maintained or improved.

TWO KINDS OF SOCIAL PLANNING

THE DISTINCTION between substance and process can be applied to social planning. For example, the original assignment which the Puerto Rico Central Planning Board gave to its consultants in 1958 (one of whom was this writer) was substantive: to add what were described as social goals to what was then a planning activity dominated by economic goals. The social goals themselves were never specified in detail; the board's assignment was an outgrowth of Governor Muñoz's *Operación Serenidad,* which suggested that planning ought to maintain and encourage Puerto Rican culture and to plan for people as other than economic beings—and workers in "Operation Bootstrap," the title given to the island's special economic development program. On the U.S. mainland, where the term *social planning* came into vogue at the beginning of the 1960s, it took on a somewhat different meaning: to consider the needs of poor people.[2]

Social planning as a process is somewhat more difficult to describe. The term itself is quite vague, since insofar as human beings are social beings, all goals are social, and all programs have social consequences. The only way social planning can be usefully applied is at the level of programs: one can distinguish among economic, physical, and social programs, although in practice, social programs have often been treated as a residual category, the term embracing all noneconomic and nonphysical programs. If job-creation programs are economic, and housing programs are physical, then educational, social-welfare, health, and recreational programs are social, and that is how the term has customarily been used. This is not a very helpful division of programmatic activities, however, except perhaps for administrative purposes.

Whatever advantages this may have for administrators, it has some disadvantages for planning. Thus, it took almost ten years for planners associated with the War on Poverty to realize that the best social planning for the poor required economic programs; that the first needs of the poor are not for special education, cultural uplifting, or counseling to eliminate "cultural deprivation," but for programs that provide them with decent and stable employment and income grants when employment is not available or when the poor are unemployable.

Admittedly, this shortcoming in the definition of social planning was not the only or even main reason for the delay; actually, many federal and local politicians were reluctant to give money directly to the poor, if only because of the historic fear that the poor would use it to buy liquor or some other consumer good not thought desirable by middle-class society. Giving money to professionals to help—and uplift—the poor was politically easier, for then the money would be spent wisely, as judged by the nonpoor majority, and by people trusted by that society.

The substantive conception of social planning has one important virtue, however; it identifies a particular client population that is to be benefited by planning, and for which programs can then be worked out, as well as consequences determined.

CLIENT-CENTERED PLANNING

IN FACT, one of the most important distinctions among kinds of planning ought to be on the basis of the clients of planning. Planning itself should be client centered, an idea that is implicit in what Janet Scheff has called client analysis.[3] To a certain degree, distinctions between kinds of planning are already made on this basis; corporate planning means planning for the corporation, and city planning is planning for the city. A corporation is a much more clearly defined client than the city, or even than "the poor," and city planning has suffered from the fact that since no one can plan for everything and everybody in the city, what aspects—and clients—of the city are actually being planned for by city planners has been left vague.

Defining planning in terms of clients, or users, has two major advantages. First, it identifies quite specifically who the beneficiaries of planning are to be. Second, it facilitates the kind of thinking that allows planning to proceed in terms of clients' goals. Social planning has too often been based on what middle-class planners thought best for the poor, whereas if one begins the planning process by talking about planning for the poor, there is, conceptually at least, room for some consideration for their own goals and priorities.[4]

Client-centered planning has at least one obvious disadvantage: it atomizes society (or the city) into different client groups and makes it difficult to plan for the society and the city as a whole. I do not see this solely as a disadvantage, however, for planning has suffered greatly from its attempt to be holistic, and in two ways. First, it has taken on an impossible task; except in a very small society or city, it is impossible to plan for the whole. Second, it has taken on an intellectually questionable task, for too often, planners who thought they were planning for an entire city or society were actually planning for only a portion of the population—traditionally the politically and economically more powerful or insistent. This kind of innocence is no longer so frequent in planning as it once was, but when and where it still exists, citizen protest groups often let the planners know their mistake. This is all to the good, but it can make planners look naive or inept and they should be neither.

In addition, traditionally, planners often assumed that they could automatically plan for the entire community or for the public interest, but this, we now know, is utopianism of a dangerous kind. In a large heterogeneous society like the United States, or in a large heterogeneous city, there are few goals or programs that are clearly in the public interest, and more often than not, goals or programs that are claimed to be in the public interest turn out to be primarily in the interest of those who make such a claim.[5]

A client-centered approach to planning would spell an end to the idea of conventional comprehensive planning; instead, planning would be concerned with the needs of different client groups in the society. Each such group might have its own planners, paid for by its own, and when necessary, publicly provided funds.

But if planning is done for an aggregate of client groups with their own planners, how then are all the diverse plans are put together? First, there is no reason why any of the planners who work for individual client groups cannot try to put all the plans together into a comprehensive scheme, although such a scheme would presumably favor their own clients. (This may appear to legitimize self-interest above holism, but while it does so, I am not at all sure whether most contemporary planning models are very different, even though their formulators may not realize it.)

Second, perhaps planners should not attempt to put all the diverse plans together, but leave the actual central planning power in the hands of elected officials—which, again, is already more or less the case. Nor is it necessarily undesirable, at least in a properly representative democracy where the elected officials represent all existing interest groups. In practice, the politicians will then probably hire their own set of planners and reinvent central planning on a new basis.

Not all planning can be client centered, however, and in the end, someone must still come up with a single highway plan or a mass transit scheme. Nonetheless, if planning were client centered, planners beholden to different clients would begin the planning process by having to debate whether more highways should be built, instead of being required by their employers to start drawing plans. True, the final outcome of the debate might not be much different than it is now, for even if planners with poor clients demanded mass transit, planners for other clients would have probably enough power to get the highways built, and perhaps even enough to run them through poor neighborhoods. Still, there would have been some open political debate, and the outcome would have been determined in the political process rather than by the judgments of planners working for highway agencies, or by politicians using planners to legitimate their decisions. Important planning decisions may in the end always be made by politicians, but client-centered planning might force these decisions into the political arena and require planners to deal with what are essentially political issues as political issues rather than technical ones.

PLANNING AND POLITICS

THAT THE important planning decisions are made by elected officials rather than planners is hardly a new idea. Although both substantive and process planners have sometimes viewed themselves as being nonpolitical, or as suprapolitical and "above politics," planning is by its very nature a political activity. Insofar as planning is concerned with goals, it deals with a fundamental political issue in any society: what goals that society ought to pursue; insofar as planning is concerned with consequences, it deals with an equally fundamental political issue—who is to benefit by public decisions and who is to pay the financial and other costs. In fact, because planning is ultimately a decision-making process affecting the allocation of resources, including scarce ones, it must be a political process.

The relationship between planning and politics differs for the two kinds of planning I have discussed. Substantive planning has generally functioned primarily as a reform movement, and this has not really changed since the early days when planning was allied with the business community and the civic leadership against the political machine. Today, planners are more likely to function as professionals or technicians, but it is hard not to find one who does not also have some ideas about reforming one or another aspect of the community. There is nothing wrong with this state of affairs, as long as planners are aware of what they are doing, what goals, reform and otherwise, they are inserting into the process, and what goals they are being asked to achieve in their technician roles.

The process definition of planning has a quite different relationship to politics, for it attempts to set up a separate decision-making process which is apart from or advisory to politics. For example, the goals-programs-consequences model of planning described in chapter 9 assumes implicitly that planners can make or can help to make the crucial decisions about goals and the programs by which to implement them without taking note of the political process—a naivete of which many systems analysis and other models are also guilty. Actually, it would be more correct to say that process models of planning assume that planners have or should have the political power of determining goals, programs, and consequences. To put it another way, such models work best if planners have a great deal of political power and can control society, for the rational consistency between goals, programs, and consequences that is inherent in a process model can only be achieved if planners have control over all three components of the planning process. As such, planning may even be an attempt (presumably mostly unconscious) by planners to try to control society, not just to seek power but to improve society in their own image.

With a few notable exceptions, planners have never had much political power, and it is not likely that they will ever have it. In America, as in most other modern societies, power is held largely by those who own or control the society's economic resources, and in a democracy, much of the power that is not held by the owners or controllers of economic resources is in the hands of elected officials, and their primary campaign funders and constituents. In cities, the primary campaign funders are apt to be large-scale developers, and they become especially influential when a city's economy is slow and the developers' potential contributions to tax revenues become politically and otherwise attractive.

Admittedly, planners have rarely sought to obtain the kind of power held by developers, or other economic and political elites but even when they have sought that kind of power, what they can actually get is limited by three factors that are inherent in planning.

First, planners are normally bureaucratic employees with advisory duties, either in public agencies or in private interest and pressure groups, and as such they are beholden to their employers.

Second, planning by its very nature deals with activities that are set in the future; however, since no one can know the future with absolute certainty, professionals who try to predict it on the basis of present knowledge have a difficult time persuading people that their plans are reasonable or that their predictions are valid, even if they are. For example, during the "baby boom" of the 1950s, planners often proposed the building of new elementary schools, having predicted on the basis of official birth rate figures that six years later, babies born in any given year would need classroom seats. In this instance, planners were not even predicting, for they knew with certainty that the classroom seats would be needed, but nevertheless, they had great difficulty persuading school boards to build the additional schools until these babies had actually reached school age—and then it was too late.

Third, insofar as planners are engaged in long-range planning, they are engaged in an activity that is often politically irrational. Some corporations that control their markets may have enough power to do long-range planning—whether or not they do it—but political institutions usually lack that degree of power and control. They need to remain flexible to react to short-run events, not to mention the next election, and long-range planning, or even the formulation of a fixed policy, reduces their flexibility.

As a result, planning can never be more than one small input into the political process, and this is true whether planners work for a central planning agency or are advisers to a president or mayor or advocates for a community group.

Indeed, what is most important is not what the planner does, but whom he or she works for.[6] The debates about the definition of planning and the nature of the planning process have much less impact on planning practice than who hires the planner and for what duties. As long as the planner is a bureaucratic employee or even a private consultant, the client who pays the planner's salary or fee has the major role in determining what is to be planned for whom—or, in terms of my process model, which goals are to be sought and to whom benefits and costs are allocated. In many instances, the planner may be far more than a technician, and may often be asked to suggest goals and criteria for benefit-cost allocations; in the end, however, his or her suggestions must be useful to the client, and to the role that that client plays in the larger political process.

In effect, then, planning has already taken on the client-centered role which I advocated earlier in the paper, except that the number of clients have been far too limited and the kinds of clients too skewed, economically and politically. What client-centered planning helps to encourage is that planning becomes pluralistic.[7]

PLANNERS AS GOAL-PROGRAM TECHNICIANS

WHEN ALL is said and done, planners can perhaps make their most significant contribution and even maximize their political influence as technicians, that is, by demonstrating what programs best achieve what goals. Rather than viewing their role as setting or advising on goals, planners should exploit what I think is their major source of political leverage: their professional expertise. And that expertise, I would argue, is in rational program formulation, pointing out what programs are most rational vis-à-vis a given goal.

The technician role should not be dismissed lightly because, for example, it appears to intrude on the imagined autonomy of the planner, or because it seems less professional or prestigious than goal-setting. In fact, developing the technical expertise to make planning into a true profession is an immensely complicated and intellectually exciting task, which involves developing programs and estimating consequences for a huge variety of goals, national as well as local. In another essay I wrote as follows:

> The task is the development, literally, of national policy catalogs, describing in detail the effective policies for a large number of specific goals—of various political shadings—in all the substantive areas, together with their costs and other consequences. As I envisage it, each policy catalog would deal with one substantive area, listing the activities and resources needed to achieve every conceivable goal, innovative and contentional, radical and conservative, and the like for that area. Once developed, these catalogs will constitute the basic technical contribution to the planning process, distinguishing planning from other decision-making methods, and the individual professional will plan by adapting the policies to the distinctive situation in which he or she is operating. Needless to say, the creation of the catalogs will require a tremendous amount of experimentation, action-research, and basic research, to be carried out largely by policy-oriented social scientists and planning researchers.
>
> These activities call for a level of specialized knowledge in many fields that is far beyond the capability of even the best-informed planning generalist. Instead, they will become the mandate for a number of policy-planning professions ranging from job creation, leisure, health, and transportation to income redistribution and political reorganization.[8]

Even so, the technician role still allows the planner to participate in goal-setting and to act political in affecting goals. The distinction I made previously between goals and programs is at best an analytic one; in the real world of practice, programs cannot be formulated without affecting and partly reformulating goals, or without shaping other goals. For example, if planners can demonstrate, with the help of social scientists, that a major cause of most street crimes is poverty and inequality, the programs they will propose extend far beyond the elimination of crime alone, for eliminating poverty and reducing inequality will also benefit the vast majority of the poor who never commit street crimes.

It may not be possible for planners and social scientists to demonstrate convincingly that poverty and inequality are major causes of street crime, although I think enough is now known to make such a demonstration. However, the nonpoor citizenry and its elected officials may not accept the argument. They may decide it is cheaper, for them, to live with street crime—particularly as long as it hurts the poor more than the rich and even the middle classes, since there is not much street crime in the suburbs—than it would be to eliminate poverty much less inequality. Eliminating poverty would, for example, require them to pay higher taxes, and to accept various changes in the economy to provide jobs for the now jobless. At this point, the planner is powerless, but he or she has performed his or her role and carried out his or her responsibility, and neither planners nor anyone else with little political power can persuade those with a great deal of power to do what they do not want to do.

Finally, this definition of the planner's role does not mean that planners need to refrain from suggesting what goals a society ought to pursue, or who is to benefit or pay costs. Planners are also always citizens, and in that role they have political rights and responsibilities they can and should pursue. The difficulty, as every planner knows, is to reconcile these rights and responsibilities with the political limitations under which bureaucrats have to work, or to put it frankly, whether to speak out or be quiet to prevent losing one's job. The planner-citizen can use data and other technical expertise to legitimate speaking out—and indeed to make that voice more effective—but still, there have always been and presumably always will be times and places where speaking out can result in getting fired.

In the end, the choice between speaking out and holding on to one's jobs has to be a personal one. Even so, as long as most planners are municipal officials, they must lobby and do whatever else is necessary to strengthen the civil liberties and rights of such officials, so that they are able to plan and speak without fear of job loss. Such lobbying will clearly be a political act, but then planning itself is often a political act, even though it is not, and should never be, synonymous with politics.

· E L E V E N ·

SOCIAL SCIENCE
FOR
SOCIAL POLICY

D URING THE 1960S, planners, systems analysts, policy specialists, and
others at work on the formulation or design of public policy began to
develop a niche for themselves in government, particularly in Washington
and in the larger American cities. At the same time, social scientists
became interested again in policy research, partly to train the policy designers but also to conduct studies that support, broaden, and criticize government policies. Much of this research has itself originated or taken place in
government agencies, but it also reemerged in the universities, so much so
that institutes of policy studies promptly began to replace institutes of urban
studies on the campus.

Nevertheless, intellectually speaking, policy research is still in its infancy, deriving its theory and concepts largely from the existing academic
social sciences. However, since policy researchers are concerned with
changing society rather than understanding it, they must have—and create
—a policy-oriented social science, independent of but related to and not
estranged from the academic or basic disciplines.

Reprinted by permission of Transaction Publishers from *The Use and Abuse of Social Science,*
Irving Louis Horowitz, ed. Copyright (c) 1971 by Transaction Publishers. I have made some
revisions and added a brief postscript.

I want here to describe some of the characteristics of a policy-oriented social science. My analysis begins by considering the nature of social policy and policy design, and then suggests some conceptual and theoretical requirements of a policy-oriented social science, mostly through a discussion of the shortcomings of academic social science—or what is often called basic research—for policy research. A final section lists these requirements in summary form. The analysis of both types of social science will draw largely on my own discipline of sociology.

THE NATURE OF SOCIAL POLICY AND POLICY DESIGN

BY SOCIAL policy I mean any proposal for deliberate activity to affect the workings of society or any of its parts. Properly speaking, the term *social* is superfluous, because all policies that affect more than one person are social. However, the term is often used to distinguish some types of policy from others—for example, economic or environmental policy—and because it has been appropriated by sociologists for their policy term, just as political scientists took over public policy as theirs. As I understand it, social policy differs from planning or social planning only in scale; a plan is nothing more than a set of interrelated social policies.[1]

The distinctive quality of social policy, as I view it, is its aim for what might be called programmatic rationality; it seeks to achieve substantive goals through instrumental action programs that can be proven logically or empirically to achieve these goals. Political activity, on the other hand, must by its very nature emphasize the politically rational, which is as likely to turn to expressive programs as instrumental ones.[2] For example, politicians may well resort to symbolic appeals for "law and order" when faced with a public demand for crime reduction, even if these appeals do not achieve the substantive goal. Designers of social policy, however, will be concerned first and foremost with programs that actually lead to a reduction in crime.

A MODEL FOR SOCIAL POLICY DESIGN

INHERENT IN these observations is a model of social-policy design that not only describes the components of the social-policy process but also spells out the kinds of social-science data needed by the policy designer. As I conceive it, social-policy design has three major components: goals, programs, and consequences, and the policy designer works toward the achievement of a (social) goal by the development of programs that can reasonably be predicted to achieve that goal, accompanied by an optimal set of consequences.[3]

The policy researcher's role in this process is to provide conceptual and theoretical inputs, the necessary empirical data, the best guesstimates when sufficient data are unavailable, and a critical analysis of the policy design when it is completed.

In the model I have summarized, the policy researcher participates in the same three stages of the process as the designer. At the stage of determining goals, the researcher may have to do some intensive interviewing in the sponsoring agency, for sponsors are often vague about the goals they seek, and when the sponsor is an agency, there is likely to be disagreement about goals as well. Without knowing how different parts of an agency feel, the policy designer may find that he or she has designed a program that will not engender the participation or allegiance of the total agency—for example, the lower bureaucracy of a public agency, or the less active members of a ghetto protest group. And if the goal requires participation or allegiance from clients outside the sponsoring agency, information will be required on how they feel about the goal. For example, if a sponsor seeks to improve the quality of housing among poor people, the agency ought to know what kind of housing these clients want and will accept: whether they will live in public housing or would prefer rent subsidies to help them compete in the private housing market. If more than one goal is being sought by the various participants in the policy design, as is usually the case, the researcher can also help the designer in determining which goals are most important, if all cannot be incorporated into a single policy design.

In addition, the policy researcher must make the designer aware of latent goals, particularly institutional maintenance or growth; for sponsoring agencies rarely pursue a policy that does not at least maintain their present level of resources or power.

The major need for policy research is, however, in the other two stages of the policy-design process. First, the policy designer needs information about which programs will achieve the goal, and wherever possible, empirical evidence to this effect. Ideally, the policy researcher should be able to provide what I have elsewhere called a policy catalog, that is, a list of programs relevant to all possible conceivable goals from crime reduction to economic equality that have been proven, by empirical research, to achieve these goals.[4] Since both goals and programs are nearly infinite, putting together such a catalog would require an immense amount of action research, social experimentation, and evaluation studies. The policy catalog would allow a policy researcher to supply a policy designer with generalized programmatic statements, based on as many cases and studies as possible, which the designer can then apply to the specific situation or community in which he or she is working.

When the goal in question is the elimination of a social problem, the policy researchers waits until the community agrees on what the problem is and how it should be perceived. The researcher may not agree with the community's conception, and particularly if it is expressive or has been constructed to eradicate a villain, the policy researcher must try to reconstruct the problem in a substantive direction. Concurrently, he or she must provide findings on the substantive problem's major causes, those explaining most of the variance, and on the immediate causes, for the most rational programs are those that eliminate the major causes, while the most easily implemented programs are usually those that get at immediate causes.

Moreover, policy research ought to provide the policy designer with a model, as empirically based as possible, of all the components and stages of the social-political process by which a social problem is eliminated or a goal achieved. This model should include all the *activities* involved in the process, the *agents* (institutional and other) whose normal social role is to bring these activities into being or who can be recruited to do so, and the *levers* (incentives and sanctions) needed to activate these agents. Needless to say, activities, agents, and levers must all be spelled out in highly specific terms, the ideal being a step-by-step model of the process by which a present state is transformed into an end-state.

Finally, the policy researcher must provide information, or at least estimates, of the consequences of a given program, from first order to nth order effects, preferably in terms of benefits and costs of all participants, direct and indirect, in both the program and its implementation. (By indirect participants, I mean especially the bystanders in a process, who may not be directly involved but who always play a role in the political climate that can spell success or failure to a program.) Ideally, the previously described policy catalog should also provide information on the various consequences of each program, and here the research task is even more massive, for effects research is difficult to do, at best, and many of the important consequences of any program cannot be isolated empirically. Thus policy designers may have to be satisfied with informed guesses on the part of policy researchers.

The major types of research needed are about financial and political consequences. Policy designers must have data to help them determine the money costs of a program, but they must also have some estimate of indirect costs paid by various participants, as well as financial benefits that might accrue to others. Data are also needed to estimate political consequences for direct and indirect participants, that is, for whom a given program will result in increases or decreases of political power. Political must be defined broadly, however, for data are also needed on the status consequences of a policy, for any program that results in a loss of status to some indirect participants in the process will inevitably result in political opposition to the policy.

In addition, the policy researcher needs to trace all other possible consequences of a program. Ideally, he or she should know how the beneficiaries and all other participants will be affected by it, that is, to what extent their own behavior and important attitudes may change as a result, if only to assure the political survival of his or her policy. Policy researchers must also have such data to make sure that programs do not cause unintended harm to intended clients or other participants in the social process being generated. For example, the policy researcher must know that a birth control program will not wreak havoc with other aspects of the conjugal relationship among the intended beneficiaries; that the cooling of interethnic or interracial conflicts among teenage gangs in a mixed neighborhood does not just transfer such conflicts to the adults; or that a racial integration program on the job or in the community does not result in a white exodus. Such data are needed, as noted before, to revise programs so that optimal consequences result, or to encourage the design of additional programs to deal with unintended but harmful consequences.

Needless to say, much of the policy research I have suggested here will never be done, and in most policy design situations, policy researchers can draw only on their understanding of society, the social process, and the effects of deliberate intervention in the process to offer help to the designer. But even this modest role cannot be carried out properly until we begin to develop policy-oriented social science.

THE UNSUITABILITIES OF ACADEMIC SOCIAL SCIENCE

ONE WAY of thinking about the characteristics and requirements of policy-oriented social science is to look at the unsuitabilities of academic social science for policy research. That such unsuitabilities exist is obvious; academic social science seeks to understand society, not to intervene in it, resulting in many organizational, theoretical, and methodological features that cannot be applied to policy research.[5] This is not a criticism of academic social science, for understanding society is a prerequisite to intervening as well as a useful task per se, and besides, policy-oriented social science needs its big academic sibling for help and legitimation.

It is of course impossible to generalize about as large and variegated a phenomenon as academic social science, but it is possible to identify some prevailing theoretical and conceptual features that make it unsuitable for policy purposes. These are: its detachment, "impersonal universalism," high levels of generality and abstractness, and last but not least, its political perspectives. Moreover, as noted earlier, I will limit my analysis to sociology.

DETACHMENT

ACADEMIC SOCIOLOGY, like most academic social science, views itself as detached from society. For example, academic sociologists rarely make studies to affect the workings of society; instead, they are more likely to study the people who do so. By detachment, I do not refer here to the illusory attempt at objective or value-free research, but rather to a general perspective: that of the outside observer who is examining a society in which he or she is not expected to take action, except as an individual citizen.

The detached perspective is not helpful in policy-oriented research, for it generates theories and concepts more suitable for the bystander to the social process than the participant. Although it is essential for participants to take the bystander role from time to time, in order to understand the contexts within which they are working, to evaluate the worthwhileness and effects of their participation—and just to see what they are doing from a different perspective—still, the policy researcher must help the policy designer with dynamic conceptions of the social process so that the latter can find a foothold from which those responsible for implementing a policy can intervene. Parsonian theory may be useful in understanding how society as such is put together, but it does not, despite its concern with "action," supply concepts that help the policy designer initiate action. Even C. Wright Mills' classic study of the power elite, though hardly detached in terms of values, does not enable a policy designer to come up with policies or political strategies to reduce the power of that elite. To be sure, Mills' works were very influential in politicizing young people in the 1960s, and in that sense, Mills was policy oriented, but it is given to few to be able to influence the social process as he did, and I am concerned here with more prosaic policy researchers aiding more prosaic policy designers.

IMPERSONAL UNIVERSALISM

ONE OF the correlates of detachment is what I call impersonal universalism, by which I mean the concern with identifying the broad impersonal causal forces that underlie events. Academic sociology developed in reaction to older personalistic theories of human behavior, for example the Great Man theory, and sought to show that individuals cannot be understood apart from society. This mode of explanation was and still is highly useful in discouraging the overly facile application of moral opprobrium to socially caused actions, and it is useful for policy design in that it tends to focus on major causes, but policy designers also need a less universal and less impersonal approach. They need to know about social structures, but they also need to know about the social agencies that can bring about change. For example, although there can be no doubt that urbanization and industrialization are responsible for many structural changes in the family, policy designers in the area of family policy cannot do anything significant about these broad forces and require analyses that deal with more manageable causes.

Policy designers also need less impersonal theories, for they must, after all, design policies to be implemented among persons. The policy designer works in a sociopolitical context in which moral judgments are made, praise and blame are dealt out, and hypotheses about the motivations of actors are all-important. Consequently, he or she must be able to understand how impersonal causes are translated into—and affect—moral judgments and motives. Similarly, while it is useful for policy designers to know that all human beings play a multiplicity of roles and that conflicts among roles can lead to social and individual strain, they must design policies for people as combinations of roles and must know how to judge the consequences of a policy for a person who is at once a worker, home owner, landlord, mother, and a deacon of her church.

HIGH LEVELS OF GENERALITY

THE UNIVERSALISM of academic sociology also produces levels of generality that are often too high for the needs of policy. Although many of the social problems with which policy designers deal may well be the results of urbanization, they must have research which tells them what specific aspects of urbanization are at play and how they affect people. Urbanization can mean many things: for example, the actual move from country to city, living at higher density than in the country, having more heterogeneous neighbors, holding an industrial rather than a rural job, participating in more complex divisions of labor of many kinds, or encountering the life-styles and forms of social participation that are typically found in the city. A social problem resulting from rural in-migration will have to be treated quite differently from one resulting from living at high density, and what is the policy designer to do when confronted with a group that, though it holds industrial jobs and lives in tenements in a heterogeneous neighborhood, still practices the peasant life-style it brought from Europe or Asia?

Similarly, the policy designer is absolutely lost when confronted with a concept like social change, for it lumps into one term all the various activities in which he or she is involved. Like the Eskimo who requires more than twenty different words for snow, the policy designer must have very specific concepts of social change, which spell out for individuals, groups, and institutions who or what is changing from what original position to what subsequent one, in which aspects of a person's life or group's activities, and with what consequences for the rest of his life or their activities.

CONCEPTUAL ABSTRACTNESS

THE HIGH levels of generality at which much of academic social science operates also breeds conceptual abstractness, which results in concepts that cannot be applied to the real-life situations in which the policy designer works. Such concepts as social structure, culture, and institution are helpful in the academic's task of generalizing about human behavior, but policy designers can only work with specific human organizations that play roles in the policy they are designing. They cannot deal with political institutions but must deal with city hall, political parties, and citizen groups. They will often be helped by information about what such groups have in common as political institutions, and what roles they play in the structure of power, but policy must eventually involve individual organizations, and they must know where the power lies in a specific situation if they are to be able to act.

One of the most important concepts in modern sociology is class, but this concept is also of little use to the policy designer. Since classes do not exist in America as concrete entities, policy cannot be designed to act on them directly; policy designers must have data that is analyzed in terms of the specific and concrete variables that they can affect. They must break down the concept into some of its many possible variables and components: income, occupation, education, power, and prestige, for they can only design policies that affect people's earnings, jobs, schooling, political position, and status. Likewise, policy designers find little of relevance in the descriptions of the class structure and the class cultures that sociologists develop; they can do something about poverty and poor schools but not about lower-class norms, and the sociologist's careful qualification that class cultures and life-styles overlap cannot help a policy designer who must know how a specific group of people will react to a policy. He or she wants to know what this reaction is, not whether it is lower class or working class. He or she needs to know how different types of poor people will feel about the choice between a poorly paying or dirty, dead-end job and being on welfare; whether these feelings are part of a larger lower- or working-class set of norms is only of parenthetical interest. Moreover, his or her interest in whether people can be classified as lower or working class is limited to the consequences of the hierarchical fact that working-class people are higher in the sociopolitical pecking order than poor people, and may express discontent if the distinctions between the strata are altered by an antipoverty program.

Abstract academic concepts are not irrelevant to policy; often they are crucial but not sufficiently developed for the policy designer's purposes. A good example is the sociologist's emphasis on the distinction between manifest and latent phenomena and formal and informal groups. A great deal of highly useful research has shown the impact of latent functions and informal group life. By and large, however, policy makers can deal only— or best—with formal groups and their manifest activities, and they must know therefore how to develop policies that affect their informal and latent components.

The final and perhaps most important drawback of conceptual abstractness is the inaccessibility of the relevant data. Until there is a plethora of policy-oriented and academic research, the policy designer will have to work with the data that are available, and these are usually limited to basic and not very subtle kinds, for example, census statistics. Thus, the highly developed conceptual virtuosity of the academic sociologist who has studied a low-income class community or a delinquent group is of little relevance to the policy designer who may know no more about a poor neighborhood than is available in census tract statistics or a health and welfare council analysis, or about delinquents than he or she can dredge up from police records or case worker reports. This is not the fault of academic sociology, of course, but policy designers need to know what they can make of the data they have.

THE POLITICAL PERSPECTIVE OF ACADEMIC SOCIOLOGY

LAST BUT hardly least, the political perspective of much academic sociology also makes it unsuitable for policy research and design. I am not concerned here with partisan politics, intended or unintended ideological bias, or the more concrete political and ideological value and implications that usually enter into all research, whether manifestly value free or not, in the selection of topics, concepts, and hypotheses. These issues always receive discussion, and besides, policy design is not wedded to a particular political outlook. Although most social scientists currently interested in what they call policy research tend to be liberals, other social scientists doing a form of policy research they call systems analysis are more frequently conservative, if not in intention at least in their work.[6] Moreover, policy design can also be reactionary, radical, or anarchist. It is even possible for policy designers or researchers to be politically neutral, acting as technicians who develop programs and consequences for goals determined by others. In this case, they are neutral only in intent, for they are actually adopting the political values of those who determine the goals.

Whether the goals are conservative, liberal, or radical, all policy designers and researchers must accept one political value—the desirability of intervention—and in so doing, they depart from the paths of academic research. Policy design and research must be concerned with *what can be* or should be, whereas academic researchers see their task as studying *what is,* or if they are predictive, what will be. This is only another way of saying that policy research must be normative, but this in turn demands a different perspective. For one thing, policy researchers must have a thorough understanding of what is, but only for allowing them to see how the present can be changed and at what points they can help the policy designer intervene. They must develop conceptual bridges to enable the designer to make the transition from what is to what can be, from the present to some desired future.

Academic sociology's emphasis on what is also results in what might be called a perspective of adaptation; it is mainly interested in studying how people adapt to the situations they face, and whether they are satisfied or dissatisfied with these situations, but it is not much interested in considering how people would adapt to different circumstances, or what circumstances they want. To put it another way, academic sociology has largely studied behavior, and attitudes about that behavior (how people feel about what is).[7] It has not often studied aspirations, or what people feel they and society should be, however. Ironically, despite the great influence of Talcott Parsons on American sociology, most of his colleagues have ignored one of his central themes: that individuals and groups are goal seeking, striving to achieve their aspirations. The policy researcher must of course place great emphasis on aspirations, for here is one major bridging concept between what is and can be.

Academic sociology is also especially sensitive to obstacles to change, not because researchers are conservative, but because of its emphasis on what is. Policy designers must be aware of such obstacles, too, but they must also have research on the readiness for change, a subject about which academic sociology has been relatively silent. Similarly, studies of cultural factors in behavior have often defined culture as a conservative influence, partly because it has been assumed that culture is naturally persistent and hard to change. As a result, there has been too little research on the intensity with which cultural norms are held and, except in ethnic acculturation studies, on how culture changes when opportunities improve. For example, there have been many studies of the culture of the poor, but few that investigated changes in culture when poor people obtained higher incomes, or what happened to behavior when people escaped from poverty.[8] These are the kinds of studies policy designers must have; they need to know what forms of situational change bring about cultural change and vice versa, and they require measures of the intensity or nonintensity and persistence or nonpersistence of all of the components of culture, social structure, and personality. Instead of academic sociology's passive stance, policy research must take an active one toward the subject of study.[9]

Another unsuitable perspective of academic sociology is its systemic bias, that is, concern with the social system rather than with its parts. For example, most functionalists emphasize the functions and dysfunctions of social phenomena for the society as a whole, paying less attention to the functions and dysfunctions these phenomena have for individuals and groups within the society.

Likewise, when sociologists say that society defines certain activities as criminal or that it encourages deviant behavior to reinforce conformity to its norms, they reify society as a social unit that acts for its members. This reification is based on the ideas of Emile Durkheim, who developed the concept of society from his studies of small independent tribes living in a clearly bounded territory with a distinctive social structure and often without a formal government, but such an approach is not applicable to large interdependent nations.

This is clear when one looks at American society and asks not what it is but what it actually does as a society; for an identifiable unit that acts as a society does not exist. Of course, the State, that is, government, sometimes acts as a body, occasionally on the basis of considerable consensus, but more often by shoehorning a set of political minorities into a temporary majority so that a decision can be reached by majority vote. However, that decision is made by the State, not by society, and when sociologists use the term society, they really mean the State—although even *it* is rarely a homogeneous monolith, but rather an array of agencies that do not always act in concert. Thus it is not American society that deprives the drug addict of easy access to his or her fix, and not even the State, but certain governmental agencies, who may argue and feel that they are supported by the majority of the population, but actually only speak in the name of the State and those citizens who favor taking a hard line toward the addict. This becomes evident when one looks at governmental decisions for which consensus is lacking—for example, tax reform or the prohibition of marijuana. In these instances, agencies of the state are pursuing actions favored by only part of the nation, and no one would suggest that these actions are approved by society.

The systemic bias encourages findings that identify the activities and interests of dominant social groups with society as a whole, and tends to underestimate the amount of disagreement and conflict. Aside from its implicit or explicit political position, however, this bias produces data that are of little help to the policy designer. Unless he or she is working for the federal government or for city hall and is asked to design policies that enhance control over the areas for which they are responsible, he or she needs research based on a more pluralistic perspective. Most of the time, the policies that designers are concerned with are intended for selected clients, and the consequences of almost any program will result in benefits for some groups and costs for others. They must therefore know more about specific populations, interest groups, and institutions than about society.

A final drawback of the academic perspective for the policy designer is its relative inattention to theories and concepts of power. Because of the emphasis on what is and the systemic bias, sociologists in the past have not dealt sufficiently with the role that power plays—in maintaining what is, in holding the social system together, and in the life of nonpolitical institutions generally.

Policy designers who usually work in a political institution are constantly aware of the role of power in any social group, and because they are concerned with implementing as well as designing policy, they need research on the nature and use of power, for example, by groups who would oppose a specific program. They must also know how power can be used to implement policies—and when the power of sanctions or of incentives is called for. They particularly need data on the extent to which the use of governmental power is effective in overcoming cultural obstacles to change. Often, cultural norms—for example, in support of racial or sexual discrimination—are weaker than they seem and can be overcome by the exercise of governmental power.

SOME POSITIVE FUNCTIONS OF ACADEMIC SOCIAL SCIENCE

I HAVE dwelt at length on the ways in which academic social science is unsuitable for policy design and research, but its positive role in policy must also be acknowledged, if more briefly. Indeed, policy research could not exist without basic research.

From what little is known so far of the sociology of policy design, it is clear that both policy designer and researcher frequently become so involved in the bureaucratic and political contexts in which they operate that their own perspective extends only as far as their side of the political game. Also, both are forced to pay so much attention to minor details that they lose sight of the larger picture. And when the political battles are over and their policy is implemented, both can become so enchanted with their victory that they fail to see the faults of their policy. The War on Poverty is a good example, for many thoughtful researchers and policy designers became wedded to the policies they were able to get passed by Congress and soon forgot how little relevance these policies had for eliminating poverty. Moreover, because of the bureaucratic and political contexts in which they work, policy designers and researchers often find it difficult to be innovative, to scrap bad policies, or to come up with ideas for new ones.

Ideally, these faults would be best dealt with if policy researchers could look at their problems with the detachment, universalism, generality, and abstractness of the academic, for they would then be able to see their policies from both sides of the political fence, evaluate them coolly for their ability to achieve the intended goal, and look for innovation when it is needed. Since it is unlikely that most policy researchers can be both policy oriented and academic in their perspective at the same time, they need to rely on academic researchers to function as outside critics, although these academics should obviously have a general interest in policy as well as theory.

But policy research needs its academic counterpart in at least three other ways. First, one cannot design policy for intervening in society without first understanding society, and generally speaking, the better the academic research, the better the resulting policy research and design. This is particularly true at present, when policy research remains an infant industry that must build on what academics have produced before. But I suspect it will always be true, for most policy research will, by definition, be specific and concrete, and must therefore look elsewhere for more general and abstract theories and generalizations.

Second, one of the major contributions of academic research, at least potentially, is its serendipity: its ability to spawn fresh ideas, unexpected findings, and productive new tangents. To put it more simply, academic research will probably always be more innovative than policy research, and as such may also be a major source of innovation in policy research. This is especially true because almost all academic studies have some implications for policy, even if they are unintended, and unrecognized by the academic researcher. A good policy researcher should be able to spot these implications—or the leads to implications—in even the most abstract academic study.

Third, academic research is and probably always will be the methodological model for policy research, since policy researchers are typically forced to come up with quick answers and can therefore do only quick or "dirty" research. It is quite possible that they will make some significant methodological innovations for policy research, but it is also true that when it comes to rigor, academic researchers will provide the technical models and will themselves be the role models for their colleagues in policy research. Moreover, once the policy researchers have made the value commitments inherent in policy research, they must follow the same norms of rigor in data collection and analysis that obtain in the academic sphere as much as they can, although normally they have far less time for research than academics. Policymakers and politicians would usually like the findings the day before the start of research.

SOME CONCEPTUAL AND THEORETICAL REQUIREMENTS FOR A POLICY-ORIENTED SOCIAL SCIENCE

ACADEMIC RESEARCH may often be unsuitable for policy purposes, but clearly, policy research cannot develop without it. [10] If policy research ever becomes a viable institutional activity in action agencies, and if policy-oriented social science disciplines are able to become independent from and roughly equal in size and especially competence to academic disciplines, they will not need to rely and model themselves as much on the latter. Until this state of affairs is reached, however, they will have to rely on the academy, and particularly academic policy research. (It is neither the same nor does it have the same mandate as policy research in an action agency, but it can provide an important bridge between the academic or basic disciplines and the researchers inside an action agency.)

My analysis of the unsuitability of academic social science for policy has already indicated or implied most of the major requirements of a policy-oriented social science, so that it is possible to list these here in summary form.

First, the purpose of policy-oriented social science is to provide the policy designer (as well as the policy implementer) with "general" and "specific" research. The former would deal with such general issues as the nature of social policy, the role of the policy designer in its various institutional contexts, the relationship between policy and the ongoing social-political process, and the nature and problems of intervention in that process. General research would presumably be the distinctive task of academic policy-oriented social scientists. Specific research, done both in the academy and in action agencies, would provide detailed data on specific substantive policy fields, such as health, housing, family life, and so forth, cataloguing for each issue the programs that would achieve specific goals and the resulting consequences.

Second, specific research must be based on highly specified theories and concepts which can, wherever possible, analyze the concrete groups, organizations, and institutions with which the policy designer must deal.

Moreover, such theories and concepts must lend themselves to maximal operationalization, so that the findings that result from them can be easily applied to the policy process.

Third, a fundamental necessity of policy-oriented social science is a model of the social-political process that is tailored to the needs of the policy designer. Such a model must have the following features:

> It must view the social-political process as composed of goal-seeking groups and individuals, and must therefore provide concepts about the nature of goal formation: the relationship between goals and behavior on the one hand, and goals and underlying values on the other.

> It must analyze the sociopolitical process in terms of the specific activities (rather than abstract behavior patterns) by which goal-seeking groups and individuals proceed, and the incentives and restraints that impinge on them and their activities.

> It must attempt to explain the process in terms of specific causes, particularly major and immediate ones; for the policy designer seeks to encourage or overcome these causes in the programs he or she proposes.

> It must be a normative and future-oriented theory of action, which analyzes both what is and what can be, developing concepts that allow the policy designer to develop programs that bridge the present and the desired future. In each case, the theory must spell out the obstacles to change, the agencies and norms behind these obstacles, the strength or intensity of these obstacles, and the kinds of rewards or sanctions by which they could be overcome. (The theory must also specify what cannot be, identifying those elements of the sociopolitical process that cannot be changed by policy design and the available political capital.)

> One of the central concepts in the theory of the social process must be power, for the policy designer must understand how power functions in both political and nonpolitical institutions, and what kinds of power can be exerted, by whom on whom, to implement programs.

Fourth, policy-oriented social science cannot delude itself that it is value free, for it must provide the policy designer with the means to achieve values stated as goals. However, the data-gathering process must follow the dictates of intellectual rigor prevailing in academic social science; otherwise, it is possible that the policy researcher will supply the policy designer with findings that underestimate the difficulties and the obstacles to implementing programs.

Fifth, policy-oriented research must be particularly concerned with the values of all those participating in or affected by a specific policy, not only to discourage policy designers from imposing their own or the sponsor's values on the beneficiaries of the policy, but also to make sure that the designed policy bears some relevance to the aspirations of those affected by it. This is not to say that policy design must honor all existing values, for policies that provide benefits to some will also create costs to others. The policy researcher must therefore collect data not only on what values are held by people affected by a specific policy, but also how intensely these are held, and what incentives or sanctions would change them if necessary.

Finally, one of the prime values underlying policy-oriented social science and its research methods must be democracy. Policy researchers, like policy designers, must be responsive to the values and aspirations of the people for whom they are designing policy, but their relationships with people involved in both research and policy design phases must also eschew the elitism sometimes found in academic social science which treats the researched as "subjects." People who want to participate in the research itself must be allowed to do so whenever possible, and policy research and design must be predicated on the notion of planning with, not planning for, people.

· P O S T S C R I P T ·

TOO MUCH OF what I wrote in 1971 is unfortunately still true. Academic policy research grew immensely during the 1970s and 1980s, and increasingly, even some academic or "basic" research papers end up with a few policy recommendations. Evaluation research conducted both by academics and by a variety of public and private practitioners and consultants has grown yet more. Nonetheless, too many of these projects still operate within either the theoretical or conceptual basis of academic social science, while evaluation research tends to supply simple measures of whether the policy or action project has achieved its official goals.

One of the problems in evaluating today's policy and evaluation research is that most of what is published is written by academics. The people who carry out policy and evaluation research for private firms and public agencies either do not write about what they do because they are too busy or because they are hemmed in by proprietary requirements—or political ones in the case of public agencies. When they do write for publication, often they either write only articles that report—and perhaps even boast of—their successes, or they write academic pieces to get themselves and their employing agency into an academic journal.

For policy research, the academic bias has some advantages, at least as long as the research model remains academic, for then researchers both in private and public agencies obtain legitimation by showing that their work remains close to what is considered proper research in the academy—even if it is quick-and-dirty as it must often be.

Still, I think it is time for the policy researchers and the practitioners, as they are increasingly called, to develop their own theoretical frameworks. They have to learn to look at the objects and subjects of their study less from the abstract and detached academic perspectives I have described. Instead, they need to approach their research with theories and with concepts that will enable them to come up with effective and feasible recommendations—and fewer of the kind that their "line" colleagues or other users of their research can dismiss as irrelevant or impractical and unrealistic. True, the inherent conflicts between agencies and users will also affect in-house researchers, for sometimes they may not be able to satisfy both their superiors and the users—a problem that becomes both political and ethical.

I have myself been an academic policy researcher too long—and thus too far removed from the organizations in which policy is turned into action —to be able to develop the alternative sociology and social science that I think is necessary. I may even be on a quest that cannot be achieved, if at all, until policy researchers are completely cut off from academic research, and also from enough academic graduate studies, so that they can learn how to analyze organizations in terms of policy research priorities rather than from the perspective of, for example, "organizational theory."

My quest could, however, be dystopian, for the kind of policy research theory and conceptual repertoire I believe is necessary might also make the large private firms and public agencies—who would be the first to apply these—more effective in achieving their goals. When and if these goals make illegitimate demands on the rest of society—for more resources, more power, less privacy for individuals, etc.—any progress in policy to achieve them would hardly be desirable. Perhaps here is an instance in which we may at times even be best off with an inept status quo.

ANTIPOVERTY POLICIES I: HOMES, SCHOOLS, AND JOBS

· I N T R O D U C T I O N ·

IN THE LAST three decades, much of my work both as a planning and a sociology professor has revolved around various aspects of and effects of antipoverty policy. My family was poor during my early adolescence, and I saw much harsher poverty in the ghettos of Chicago at that time. Even so, poverty became visible for me as a research and planning problem only in the late 1950s, during my research in the West End of Boston, where I first realized how poor people had to live in what was by then an affluent society, and how close to poverty even the working class West Enders always were. The difference between working class and poverty status was the job, how well it paid, and how secure it was.

Since than, I have always thought that the central problem of our cities was decent and secure jobs for everyone, and income grants for those unable to work or unable to find it—and that many other urban problems would almost solve themselves if such jobs and grants could be supplied. I have also thought that when private enterprise could not supply such jobs, the government had to step in, and I still think so now—even if that liberal point of view is said by some to be outdated. The alleged obsolescence of liberalism is usually forgotten the moment enough voters are in economic trouble, but as a planner, I think poverty needs to be attacked all the time. While it would be nice to believe that private enterprise and the tax reduction policies it advocates can reduce poverty, private enterprise has never been willing and the tax policies it favors have never been able to do so. Thus, the burden has to fall on government, for only it has the resources. One contribution planners, policy analysts and social scientists can make is to help government—and private enterprise—supply the funds and the political support lacking in the last War on Poverty.

If there is a single theme in the final two parts of the book, that is it, because most of the essays are critical of some aspect of the conventional wisdom with respect to poverty or antipoverty planning. The first, chapter 12, which I wrote in 1958, was one of the earliest critiques of the federal slum clearance program, and it was written at a time when just about every white planner honestly thought that urban renewal was good for the people who lived in "slums." I am reprinting the essay because even if old-style federal urban renewal is probably permanently dead, the governmental and private treatment of the poor—and the poorly housed—has not changed very much. Indeed, more pervasive and potent forms of residential displacement of the poor have developed since the 1960s, culminating in the rising homelessness that began in the 1980s. These are described in chapter 13, which is in effect a postscript to chapter 12.

Chapter 14 questions the conventional wisdom regarding education and poverty. During the War on Poverty itself, the historic American belief that more education is a magic cure for everything was trotted out again, and it continued to be thought of as a major antipoverty policy after that war had been killed off. I wrote then (in the mid 1970s) as I do now in a revised version, that education cannot be a magic cure, and that it works most effectively for children in families where decent jobs have already supplied a minimum of economic security. Only when that minimum is available can most children, poor or middle class, develop the motivation and rationale for working hard in school. Conversely, poor children with jobless parents learn quickly that education is not likely to have a payoff for them, whatever the parents themselves may say to them. While a minority of very ambitious and academically bright poor children can use the school to escape poverty, too many of the rest tune out until they get pushed out or can drop out, meanwhile educating themselves on the streets for the knowledge they need to survive in their world.

In effect, then, jobs are the crucial prerequisite to education, as they are to so much else in America. At the same time, I have long feared that there are no longer enough jobs to go around, and that the scarcity of jobs will only get worse. My fears were first aroused by the automation scare of the mid-1960s, but they have been revived by the ability of computers to eliminate jobs—even though they may initially also spawn new ones—and by the departure of manufacturing and service jobs for low-wage countries in the Third World. These trends will only become more serious as the number of low-wage countries increases, all of them competing with one another to attract First World jobs, and as new labor-saving technology is invented. Sometimes it appears as if one purpose of capitalism and what is destined to replace state socialism is to eliminate as many human workers as possible from their industrial—and postindustrial—economies.

A principal dilemma of job creation policy is whether to create decent jobs that can be performed by the unskilled or semiskilled—with minimal training—who are generally most often jobless, or whether to train the jobless for the skilled jobs more likely to be available. The right answer is of course both, but creating new unskilled jobs goes counter to the conventional economic wisdom. Even so, as I suggest in chapter 15, a lot of public-works projects that can be carried out by the unskilled are needed. At the same time, however, unskilled people should also be trained for skilled jobs, which means finding a way around the shortcomings of education described in chapter 14—as well as the racial discrimination that keeps too many skilled jobs, and the right training for them, away from nonwhite applicants. Nonetheless, the best medicine for joblessness remains making sure that the supply of jobs far exceeds the supply of people ready to fill them. This is not only difficult in our kind of economy but also runs up against another historic—and false—American belief: that there are always more decent and secure jobs than there are workers willing to take them.

Chapters 15 and 16 try to find policies for solving present and especially future job scarcity, the former by discussing the deliberate creation of jobs, the latter by work sharing, the reduction of work time for all in order to save or create jobs for others. Chapter 15 goes back a long long way; for in 1964, I wrote a short article listing some jobs that could be created to deal with what I called the "automating society." (I wrote it for *The Correspondent*, a small journal David Riesman had started to argue against nuclear war and for a peaceful economy.) I tried again in the mid-1970s with an unsolicited paper for the Carter-Mondale election campaign. I don't think anyone from the campaign ever even acknowledged receipt of the paper, but then the two candidates and their staffs had other, more urgent problems.

Chapter 15 is a nearly total rewrite of this essay, but its basic argument, that in the long run America has to move toward more labor-intensity in the economy, remains the same. Chapter 16 is also oriented toward the longer run, although when I first began to think about worksharing in the early 1980s, the U.S. jobless rate had reached 10 percent and was still rising. In some Western European countries, where unemployment had increased above 15 percent and was heading for 20, governments had begun to experiment with schemes for the thirty-six- and thirty-two-hour week. The experiments lasted long enough to provide some experience with work sharing, some of which is reported in my essay. That experience, and the extensive amount of policy research carried out in Europe, will stand in good stead if and when worksharing is going to be needed. Despite its drawbacks, worksharing is far superior to condemning a quarter or more of the population to permanent or near-permanent joblessness.

Both essays discuss policy ideas that are not immediately practical, but that need to be discussed anyway. As I suggested in the preface, raising impractical ideas is one obligation of academics, and if the ideas become useful in the future, practical people will be around to make them feasible.

The final chapter in this section questions the conventional assumption that poverty is purely an economic phenomenon. The essay speculates about the possibility that poverty exists and persists because it has other purposes, most of them unrecognized, and that we, the middle and upper classes, have a variety of uses for poverty and the poor. If my speculations are right, these uses are additional obstacles to ending poverty that have to be confronted by antipoverty policies of a kind not yet considered. The original paper was written in the late 1960s, when I was trying to explain to myself and others the short life of the War on Poverty, and was looking beyond the obvious political and economic reasons. The uses of poverty I described have not gone away, which is why I have reprinted this essay virtually unchanged.

· T W E L V E ·

THE HUMAN
IMPLICATIONS OF
SLUM CLEARANCE
AND RELOCATION

T HE WEST END of Boston is a now-famous neighborhood in planning
history which was declared a slum and selected for "clearance" by
Boston's planners and city officials in the mid-1950s. I came to the West
End, not to study the area's destruction, but to conduct a sociological
community study of the community before relocation, as part of a larger
and longer NIMH-sponsored research project entitled "Relocation and Mental
Health: Adaptation and Stress." However, since I was in the West End
from October 1957 to May 1958, shortly before the beginning of relocation,
I also collected data about the area's forthcoming clearance.

I gathered my data by living in the neighborhood as a participant-ob-
server, conducting formal and informal interviews with many West Enders
as well as with redevelopment officials. After the West End was torn down,
I gathered some additional data through visits to old friends and neighbors,
now scattered throughout the Boston area.

My conclusions were based on observational and interview evidence.

Reprinted from *People and Plans*. I have made a few revisions in the introduction and even
fewer in the rest of the essay. I have retained the original article's present tense, reflecting
the late 1950s, when urban renewal, or redevelopment as it was then still called, was a popular
planning policy.

The long-term research project later measured the effects of clearance *and* relocation principally through a set of before-and-after relocation interviews with a sample of five hundred West End residents. Many of the findings of this study were published subsequently and they substantiated the observations and predictions I made about the economic, social, and psychological effects of slum clearance and relocation on the West Enders.[1]

When this article first appeared, its conclusions were greeted with considerable skepticism and even hostility from city planners and renewal officials. After the larger West End study and research in other cities produced similar findings, however, they developed a new argument: that the West End project was one of the most poorly handled clearance and relocation projects of the 1950s and that its effects could therefore not be considered as applicable to other, supposedly more adequately handled, renewal projects. Hartman's careful comparative analysis of a number of relocation studies[2] and my own observations in several cities indicate, however, that the relocation of the West Enders was handled relatively well and was certainly no worse than relocation projects in other large cities. Thus, the findings of the West End studies cannot be explained away. Moreover, because the West Enders were white and of a somewhat higher socioeconomic level than most of the people displaced by renewal elsewhere, the West End findings may actually understate the negative impact of clearance and relocation activities in other cities. Indeed, blacks probably suffered considerably more from slum clearance without proper relocation than the West Enders. Their incomes were lower, their housing choices after displacement were even more limited because of segregation, and many lacked the extensive familial contacts of the West Enders, so that they were more dependent on the people they had come to know and trust in the neighborhood.

BOSTON'S WEST END

A NUMBER of large American cities are currently initiating or carrying out renewal projects which involve the clearance of a neighborhood and the relocation of a large number of families. This paper attempts to analyze and evaluate some of the social and planning problems in this process, as they were observed in the redevelopment of Boston's West End. It is submitted as a case study, because many of the conditions described exist also in other American cities.

The forty-eight-acre West End project area[3] is part of a seventy-two-acre working-class residential district in downtown Boston.[4] The project area is covered almost solidly with five-story apartment buildings, which replaced older three-story single- and multifamily structures around the turn of the century. The land coverage is very high, as is the ground density.[5] However, the apartments were built at a time when families were much larger, so that for many households the floor density is low. In the last twenty-five years, the West End has been mainly an area of first and second settlement for Italian and Polish families. In 1950, the area was estimated to have 12,000 residents. At the time of the city's "taking" the land under eminent domain in May 1958, about 2,800 households and 7,500 residents remained.[6]

The redevelopment plan proposes total clearance, except for a half dozen community-wide institutions and buildings of architectural interest. The area is to be redeveloped with up to 2,400 apartments, most of them in elevator buildings, at rents currently estimated to be $45 per room, and with parks, shops, and parking areas for the new tenants.* Massachusetts General Hospital is also expanding its plant and parking areas on an adjacent site.

THE REDEVELOPMENT PLAN

A PLANNING analysis of this redevelopment project must begin with the question of whether or not the area is a slum. The term *slum* is an evaluative, not an empirical, one; and any definition must be related, implicitly or explicitly, to the renewal policy in which it is used. Popular definitions of the slum include two criteria: the social image of the area and its physical condition. Federal standards for determining eligibility for renewal funds focus almost exclusively on the latter. However, it is the local agency which selects the area to be proposed for clearance; and, in most communities, the area's physical condition is a necessary but not sufficient criterion. What seems to happen is that neighborhoods come to be described as slums if they are inhabited by residents who, for a variety of economic, cultural, and psychological reasons are considered undesirable by the majority of the community.[7] The community image of the area gives rise to feelings that

---

*Note: According to consumer price indexes published in the February 1990 Economic Report of the President, rents at the end of 1989 were 360 percent those of rents in 1958. Thus, the per room figure of $45 would have been $162. Actual winter 1990 rents in Charles River Park for the average two-bedroom apartments were $1140–1375, and in the more luxurious Longfellow Place building, $1390–2398.

something should be done, and subsequently the area is proposed for redevelopment.[8] Usually, the physical condition of the area is such that it is eligible for redevelopment; however, there are areas, such as Boston's North End, which meet physical criteria but are socially and politically strong enough to discourage any official or politician from suggesting them for clearance.[9]

The federal and local housing standards which are applied to slum areas reflect the value pattern of middle-class professionals. These professionals, like the rest of the middle class, place greater emphasis on the status functions of housing than does the working class. Their evaluation of the behavior of slum residents is also based on class-defined standards, and these often confuse behavior which is only culturally different with pathological or antisocial acts.[10]

Generally speaking, these standards are desirable bases for public policy, despite their class bias; and many of them should be applied to the poorer areas of the city, *if* they were followed by a program which provided the residents of these areas with better housing. Presently, however, these standards are used to tear down poor neighborhoods; but the better housing for the residents is not provided. This assertion will be supported by the analysis that follows.

Slum and Low-Rent Districts: A Redefinition

Consequently, unless urban-renewal policy is drastically altered, other definitions of the slum should be developed. Existing physical standards fail to make a distinction between *low-rent* and *slum* districts, or low-rent and slum housing, community facilities, street patterns, and so on. This distinction is an important one. *Slum dwellings and the like may be defined as those which are proved to be physically, socially, or emotionally harmful to their residents or to the community at large. On the other hand, low-rent dwellings, and so forth, provide housing and the necessary facilities which are not harmful, to people who want, or for economic reasons must maintain, low rental payments and are willing to accept lack of modernity, high density, lack of privacy, stair climbing, and other inconveniences as alternative costs.*[11]

A set of equitable social standards is more difficult to define, because of the problem of causality. In most cases, people move into what are known as slum areas because they have problems or unacceptable behavior patterns; economic, social, and psychological conditions, rather than the slum, cause these. The social environment may "infect" a few people previously without problems, but this is much rarer than commonly thought. However, for purposes of definition in connection with renewal policy, it is possible to distinguish between undesirable patterns which are related causally to the neighborhood and those which are not. *Thus, for renewal purposes, a slum may also be defined as an area which, because of the nature of its social environment, can be proved to create problems and pathologies, either for the residents or for the community at large.*

For example, if children are drawn into illegal activities and it can be *proved* that the neighborhood, rather than conditioins of lower-class life, was responsible, that neighborhood might be called a slum.[12] The same would apply if residential overcrowding inhibited privacy and led to intra- or interfamilial conflict. However, overcrowding is normally caused by socio-economic deprivations that force people to live under such conditioins, rather than by the neighborhood itself; and clearance does not solve this problem.

The West End as a Low-Rent District

In my opinion, and given existing renewal policies, most of the West End cannot be described as a slum. I would estimate that at the time of the land taking, probably from 25 to 35 percent of the buildings in the project area were structually unsound, uninhabitable because they had been vacant for some time, or located on alleys too narrow for proper sanitation and fire prevention.[13] Some of the deterioration was due to the fact that in 1950, when the plans for eventual redevelopment were first announced, landlords were advised not to make extensive repairs on their properties. Many residents claimed—with some justification—that parts of the area deterio-rated rapidly as a result, especially where apartments or entire buildings became and remained vacant in the years that followed.[14] However, reduc-tion of maintenance during the period of rent control and the housing shortage, especially by absentee landlords with big holdings, also con-tributed to the decay.[15]

Nevertheless, the majority of the structures provide low-rent rather than slum dwellings. Rents are extremely low—often below those charged in public housing; and during the postwar prosperity, most West Enders were able to modernize the interiors of their apartments.[16] The low rents enable the many people in the area who have never escaped the threat of work layoffs to keep their fixed housing costs low enough to survive such a layoff, and the location of the area is within walking distance of the central business district where most of the residents are employed. Also, the minimal rents and the familiar neighbors enable the many old people in the area who retired on social security and some income from a building to maintain independent households.

The exteriors of the buildings have not been well maintained. This is in part because West Enders pay little attention to the status symbols connected with housing. The proximity of family and ethnic group and the availability of local institutions catering to their needs are valued by residents more highly than the status image of the neighborhood.[17] Nor do they regard the high density as a problem, except for parking. Privacy is not evaluated here as highly as it is in middle-class culture, and West Enders consider it more important to have large numbers of relatives, friends, and neighbors at hand. Cultural differences between middle- and working-class families thus affect the applicability and validity of some of the planner's housing standards.

Nor does the West End satisfy the social criteria which would make it a slum. There are people defined as "problem residents" in the area, because of the spillover from the adjacent skid row and because the low rents have attracted transients, single-parent families, and new immigrants. For some years now the West End has been the main first area of settlement for newcomers to Boston, and it has thus served an important, though unrecognized, function in the city.[18] Problems and pathologies associated with poverty are also present.[19] But these problems are not created by the neighborhood. In fact, for the newcomers the West End has provided an opportunity to avoid the problems that they would have faced in the other major location for first settlement, the South End. Moreover, the highly developed system of informal social control in the West End makes it possible for people with different standards of living and ethnic backgrounds to live together peaceably, tolerant of those with problems.

Some Other Reasons for the Redevelopment Decision

The certification of the West End for redevelopment was not due solely to its physical and social characteristics. Because of its central location adjacent to Beacon Hill and near the downtown retail area, real estate men had long felt the West End was "ripe for higher uses." The Charles River frontage was considered desirable for high-rent apartments. Moreover, the desire of the hospital and other powerful Boston institutions that the low-income population be moved out of the area, the city's desperate need for a higher tax base, its equally urgent search for some signs of economic revival,[20] and the belief that the shrinkage of the central retail area could and should be halted by settling "quality shoppers" nearby—all contributed to justify clearance of the area. The fact that a developer was available made the plan a potential reality. Meanwhile, other Boston neighborhoods in which the housing is more deteriorated and even dangerous received a much lower priority for renewal, because they are not suitable for high-income housing or because there is less interest among the community's major decision-makers.

Costs and Benefits of Redevelopment

The proposed redevelopment will be profitable for the builders and will add to Boston's tax base; and it should provide a psychological lift to the city. Several questions can be raised, however, about its overall benefit to the community, especially when some generally unrecognized and perhaps unintended consequences are taken into consideration. An examination of some of these probable consequences follows:

1. The project has been planned on the assumption that high- and middle-income residents are of benefit to the city, whereas low-income residents are only a burden and a source of public expense. This assumption ignores the vital economic and social functions played in the city economy by low-income people and by the availability of low-rent housing. The reduction of the city's low-rent housing supply by close to 3,000 units makes it more difficult for the present and future industrial force of a low-wage city to find centrally located, economic housing. The need to relocate 2,800 households in the reduced supply will thus overcrowd the remainder, or increase further the outmigration from the city.
2. The economic benefits from the redevelopment may be counteracted by the loss of property values and tax yields in the areas from which tenants will be drawn. Moreover, the central business district which is intended to benefit by the redevelopment may actually lose because *(a)* the redevelopment plan calls for a sizable shopping center; *(b)* the people likely to rent the new apartments probably already do much of their shopping downtown; and *(c)* the West Enders who will leave the city will probably shop in outlying centers, whereas previously they did all but their food buying in the downtown stores.
3. West Enders with social, economic, and other problems are faced by yet further problems brought on by the need to move from a familiar,

permissive, and inexpensive neighborhood. Although some will undoubtedly find better housing, others will be forced to the real slums of the city or will overcrowd other low-rent districts to the point where they become slums. The need to move and to pay higher rents will increase the burdens of these West Enders and of the community agencies helping them now.

More detailed analyses of the project would have to be made to determine whether or not the benefits outweigh the costs for the community as a whole and for the sectors of the population affected by the project.

The Hidden Costs

However, such analyses would not take into consideration the hidden social, economic, and other costs paid by the West Enders in being forced out of their neighborhood with nothing more than the $100 moving allowance.

1. West Enders must bear the financial burdens that result from having to pay higher rentals for new apartments that are unlikely to be better in quality than the old ones. For many West Enders, this will require drastic budgetary changes with consequent deprivations in other spheres of life.[21] Because of the shortage of rental housing, some people will be encouraged to buy houses in the suburbs at prices beyond their ability to pay. Moreover, because of the negative publicity leveled at the West End by the press, apartment-hunting tenants from there are likely to be faced with rent gouging by landlords who know that West Enders are at the mercy of the market as well as with discrimination or refusals because they are "slum dwellers."[22]

2. Landlords who were able to live modestly from the rentals of one or more West End buildings will lose their incomes; the amount of money they will receive for these buildings is not likely to be large enough to allow them to purchase others.

3. Many small businessmen in the area will lose their incomes and livelihood. Although federal relocation regulations allot them $2,500 for moving expenses if they reestablish their business, many will be unable to find a new location, since Boston is already oversupplied with small stores.[23] Many of these businessmen are too old to be hired by employers, so both economically and psychologically their future is grim.

4. There are social and psychological losses that result from the breakup of the neighborhood. Clearance destroys not only housing but also a functioning social system, the existence of which is not even recognized by current relocation procedures. The scattering of family units and friends is likely to be especially harmful to the many older people. The younger West Enders feel that they can adjust to a new neighborhood, but they expect that many of the older ones will not be able to do so and will die during the process.[24]

The variety of costs which West Enders will pay as a result of clearance and relocation (to be discussed below) represent hidden subsidies to the redevelopment program. In effect, the present low-income population will subsidize the clearance of their neighborhood and the apartments of their high-income successors, both by their own losses and by the share they must pay of the federal and local tax money used to clear the site. To balance these costs, the only benefit to be received by most residents is the moving allowance.

Some West Enders will undoubtedly benefit from the development by being able to find better apartments. Others will gain by being given a push toward a move to the suburbs they had wanted to make anyway, but that they had delayed because of inertia; however, many of the families in this position had already left the West End between 1950 and 1958.[25]

THE RELOCATION PLAN

WHILE CONSIDERABLE attention has been devoted to the planning of the physical redevelopment phase of the project, less planning has been done for the relocation of the present West End residents. The local relocation plan, approved by federal officials, is based on the assumption that the 60 percent of the population eligible for public housing will accept such units and that private housing is available for the remainder. Neither of these assumptions has yet been tested, and both were open to serious question in May 1958.

Many eligible West Enders are unwilling to go into public housing. This is so in part because they have been affected by the negative image given public housing by the Boston newspapers, because they will be unable to live with relatives, friends, and neighbors from their own ethnic group, because they consider public-housing tenants to be below them in status, and because they do not wish to be subjected to administrative regulation of their activities.[26] Nor is it entirely clear whether there are sufficient vacant public-housing units for even those West Enders who will accept them.[27]

As a result, considerably more than the 40 percent estimated by the relocation planners will be competing for low-rent and low-cost *private* housing. Moreover, no adequate study has been made of the private-housing market,[28] so at the time of the land acquisition, no one knew how much of such housing was available.[29] In addition, since most West End people are used to living amidst their own ethnic group, those of Italian descent (approximately 45 percent of the present population) would like to move to a handful of Italian communities in the Boston area. However, these probably cannot house more than a small percentage of the reloca-tees.

As a result, many people inside and outside the West End believe that there is not sufficient relocation housing to meet either the needs of the 2,800 West End households or the federal regulations calling for their rehousing in decent, safe, and sanitary dwellings.[30]

Consequences of Relocation

The relocation procedures that have been developed from the nationwide experience of the past few years also present some problems in relation to the culture and the needs of the West End residents. These problems are discussed below and are in addition to the four types of problems described earlier.

1. Relocation procedures were developed by middle-class professionals and thus assume the self-sufficiency of the nuclear family household. In the West End, however, many of these physically individual house-holds are tied to those of other families by strong bonds, either of kinship or peer-group membership. If households are relocated indi-vidually, so they are not accessible to these other households with whom they live, negative social and emotional consequences may result. For many of the old people, accessibility means pedestrian accessibility, and thus they will suffer most from being separated from West End relatives and neighbors. Younger people can come together again by car or public transportation, but only if they are relocated in relatively accessible neighborhoods.[31]

2. Differences exist between relocation officials and West End residents in the evaluation of physical and social "standardness" of housing.

Thus, what the former define as physically standard may be located in areas which the latter will consider socially undesirable. Since social criteria are more important to many West Enders than physical criteria, they may reject on this basis the units offered to them by relocation officials. Conversely, they may relocate themselves in dwelling units that are substandard by federal provisions, but not by the West Enders' priority of social over physical values.

3. As presently indicated, the scheduling of relocation is based on the requirements of the clearance program. If relocation takes longer than expected, this may force officials to interpret the federal relocation provisions as written and limit the apartment choices of the relocatees to the number required by law.[32] Given the differences in housing standards between officials and residents, some people may be forced to move into dwelling units and neighborhoods they do not want. Others may be hurried into panicky "voluntary" relocation with much the same results.

4. Since relocation procedures do not allow for the transfer of the social system, the shock of the relocation process itself is likely to affect negatively a number of people who have never lived anywhere except in the West End and whose social and emotional ties are entirely within the neighborhood.

Cultural and Political Obstacles to Communication

A fifth problem involves communication difficulties between the redevelopment agency and the West End residents that threaten to make the prospective relocation even more painful. This problem deserves more elaborate discussion than accorded others because these difficulties are an expression of more fundamental problems.

During the eight years in which the Housing Authority and its successor, the Redevelopment Authority, endeavored to implement the redevelopment plan, considerable hostility developed among the residents toward the city agencies. This hostility was based primarily on opposition to the destruction of the West End. However, there were other causes. Working-class people are frequently hostile toward governmental authority in general and feel that the politicians as well as the city officials seek to deprive them of things they value or are trying to cheat them out of their belongings.[33] This attitude was strengthened in the West End by the fact that in a city inhabited by people of Italian and Irish descent in about equal numbers, the latter retain control over its government and political life. Moreover, as a result of the transformation of the Boston City Council from a ward to an at-large system in 1950, the West End was for all practical purposes disfranchised.[34]

The Housing and Redevelopment Authorities acted as strict administrators of the law and failed to take residents' attitudes into consideration. For example, their communication with the West End followed local and federal regulations, and they were extremely careful not to give out any information about which they were not absolutely certain or which was not required by the rule books. The informational vacuum thus created in the West End was filled with rumors. Moreover, the officials assumed that West End residents were as expert as they in understanding the complex administrative processes of redevelopment and could thus interpret properly the cryptic news releases which the agency issued periodically.[35]

However, since West Enders have little contact with bureaucratic procedure, they tend to interpret such procedure in personal terms. Because of their generally suspicious view of city governmental activities, they reinterpreted the agency's communications accordingly. For example, the long years of delay between the announcement of redevelopment and the final taking were generally assumed to be due to the city's desire to confuse the residents, scare them out of the West End, and thus reduce the acquisition costs of property and the relocation problem.

The redevelopment officials did not seem to consider the effects of their announcements, especially since vocal opposition to the redevelopment was minimal. This was interpreted by the agency as a general acquiescence on the part of West Enders toward the fate of their neighborhood.

Actually, since 1950, the residents had read so many news stories announcing an early start of the redevelopment that many were convinced it would never take place. Although a small group of determined West Enders had begun to fight the city's plan in 1954, they received little support from residents for this reason.[36]

The pattern of poor communication on the part of the redevelopment officials and the negative interpretation of any communication by the residents continued after the Authority had set up a project area relocation office and had announced the taking of the properties by eminent domain. The agency continued to be vague on those topics of most importance to the residents: for example, on the relocation and clearance schedules. This was particularly frustrating to those people who, finally relieved of eight years of uncertainty, now wanted to plan ahead.[37] Other West Enders took admonitions to move as soon as possible to mean that the relocation office was set up to scare people out of the area. Suggestions about the availability of vacant housing in areas of lower socioeconomic status than the West

End were reinterpreted to mean that the city wanted to push West Enders into the worst slums of Boston. The redevelopment agency's official notification to landlords that their structures had been purchased for one dollar under eminent-domain procedures, plus its failure to include this token payment or to explain why it was not included, convinced many people that the city was not keeping its promises to treat them fairly and was going to cheat them out of their payments. Likewise, the way in which the redevelopment agency took the land caused considerable hurt among the older immigrants. They could not understand how the buildings they had worked so hard to own could suddenly be taken away from them, with no assurance as to when they would be paid or how much. Moreover, at the same time they were told to pay rents for their own apartments in these buildings or face eviction. Thus, many of the landlords who earned their livelihood from the rents they collected were at the same time deprived of both a source of income and the funds with which to pay the rent demanded from them.[38]

Although the residents and redevelopment officials attributed the communication failure to each other's negative motivations, the difficulties were based on cultural factors. The redevelopment agency was concerned mainly with following local and federal regulations governing relocation. These regulations said nothing about understanding the consequences to the residents of its official acts. Thus, the agency had no real opportunity for learning how the West End received its letters and announcements or interpreted its actions. However, it is questionable whether such an opportunity would have been exploited. The officials concerned were not policymakers; they were hired to carry out their prescribed duties. They felt sorry for some of the West Enders, especially those with serious problems; and they tried to help them in various ways not required by their job. But, since they believed that relocation would improve the living conditions for most of the residents and that the redevelopment was for the good of the city, they could not really understand why the West Enders were hostile and often unwilling to cooperate.

These beliefs about the virtues of relocation and the unilateral desirability of redevelopment are written into existing local and federal renewal policy. *As a result, when redevelopment officials take action affecting project area residents, they are not required to take into account the attitudes and the situation of the residents.* There is no opportunity for the correction of such actions by feedback from the residents. As a result, the relocation procedures developed so far in most American cities include no techniques that would ease the burden of the people who are to be moved.

Relocation, the Residents' Subsidy of Redevelopment

American redevelopment planning so far has proceeded on the assumption that relocation is secondary to redevelopment. Thus, great pains are taken with planning for clearance and the reuse of the site, but plans for the present occupants of the site are treated as by-products of the redevelopment proposal. For example, the local and federal redevelopment agencies had detailed maps of the West End's street and utility system, but they did not seem to know the simple fact that a number of owners living in the area depended on the rents they collected for their income.

Perhaps the clearest indication of the relatively low priority of relocation in the redevelopment process is the fact that the funds allocated to relocation are less than 5 percent of the total cost of taking and clearing the land, and this represents only about 1 percent of the cost of clearance and redevelopment. The real cost of relocation is very much higher, but is paid in various ways by the people being moved out. Under present conditions, the redevelopment of American cities is economically possible only because of the hidden subsidies provided by the residents of the areas to be cleared.

SOME RECOMMENDATIONS

THIS CRITIQUE is not directed either at renewal or at relocation per se, but at the present policies which use public funds to subsidize—if only indirectly—the erection of high-rent housing and penalize the low-income population, without clear proof that these policies are in the public interest.

Moreover, the specific criticisms made of Boston procedures are not intended to blame any individuals within the local or federal agencies. It is important to emphasize that what has happened cannot be attributed to evil motives. No laws have been broken, and many officials have acted with what they thought were the best intentions toward the West Enders! [39] However, good intentions can lead to harmful consequences if the basic procedures are at fault. Thus, the responsibility for what has happened rests to a considerable extent on the system of procedures that has emerged from years of legislative and administrative decision-making since the passage of the 1949 Housing Act and on the unintended or unrecognized consequences of these procedures when they are actually implemented. However, this system is tied to the economic and political structure, which must therefore also be implicated. For example, since redevelopment agencies must provide sufficient incentives to attract a redeveloper, some of their policies, such as site selection, must be shaped by the demands, or the anticipated demands, of these redevelopers.

Proposals for Redevelopment

Urban renewal and the rehousing of slum dwellers are necessary and desirable objectives. However, the means of achieving them ought to be chosen in relation to these objectives, rather than to extraneous ones.[40] Thus, redevelopment should be pursued primarily for the benefit of the community as a whole and of the people who live in the slum area, and not for that of the redevelopers or their eventual tenants.[41] The recommendations that follow are based largely on this principle. Although they stem from the Boston observations, many of them are undoubtedly applicable to renewal and relocation procedures in other large cities.

1. Renewal projects should be located first in those areas which are slums as defined above, that is, in which it can be proved that the housing and facilities present social and physical dangers to the residents and to the larger community. The availability of a redeveloper ought to be a consideration, but one of lesser priority.

2. Before areas for renewal are finally determined, independent studies should be made which provide proof of the area's character, but take into account the values and living patterns of the residents.[42] These studies should be made by persons who have no connection with either the project area or the redevelopment agency.

3. Renewal proposals which call for the clearance of an entire neighborhood should be studied closely to determine whether the existing social system satisfies more positive than negative functions for the residents. If this is the case, planners must decide whether the destruction of this social system is justified by the benefits to be derived from clearance.

4. Projects which require large-scale relocation[43] should be studied in a similar manner. Such projects should not be initiated until the community has built sufficient relocation units to assure the proper[44] rehousing of the residents. If private enterprise is unable to provide them, city, state, and federal funds will have to be used. Moreover, if relocation housing is built prior to the renewal project, and in sufficient quantity, and if it is financially and otherwise attractive, it is likely to draw enough people out of slum areas to reduce the market value of slum structures. Consequently, some of the costs of provid-

ing such relocation housing will be returned by reduced acquisition costs at the time of renewal.

5. If a community is unwilling or unable to provide the required relocation housing, it should not be permitted to engage in renewal operations.

6. City planners ought to recognize the functions performed in the city by the low-income population. They should make sure that sufficient housing is available for them and in the proper locations (including some near the central business district) for their needs and those of the city. The federal government should encourage the renewal of such housing by increasing its subsidies when the renewal plan calls for the rehabilitation or construction of low-income dwellings.

7. Greater emphasis should be placed on the rehabilitation of low-rent housing, and less on its clearance. Such rehabilitation should be based on standards that provide decent, safe, and sanitary—but economically priced—dwelling units. In order to make this possible, existing standards should be restudied, to distinguish requirements which bring housing up to a standard but low-rent level from those which are "fringe benefits" that price rehabilitated units out of the low-rent market. [45]

8. In the future, if renewal becomes an accepted urban governmental activity, experiments should be made with:

   (a) Flexible subsidies, so that federal contributions are increased if the reuse is low- or middle-income housing; and reduced if it is luxury housing.

   (b) Requirements that redevelopers construct or finance some relocation housing, especially if they propose to redevelop the site with housing out of the price range of the present site residents.

Proposals for Relocation

If the purpose of urban renewal is to improve the living conditions of the present slum dwellers, relocation becomes one of the most important phases, if not the most important, of the renewal process. This principle suggests a number of proposals for procedural change:

1. The relocation plan should take priority over the renewal phases of the total plan, and no renewal plan should be approved by federal or local agencies until a proper relocation plan has been developed.

2. This relocation plan should be based on a thorough knowledge of the project area residents, so that the plan fits their demands and needs and so that officials have some understanding of the consequences of

their actions before they put the plan into effect. The federal agency ought to reevaluate its relation to the local agencies, raising its requirements for approval of the local relocation plan and relaxing its requirements for such phases as rent collection. The latter would make it possible for the local agency to be more sensitive to special needs of the project area residents.

3. Any renewal plan which requires the clearance of an area and large-scale relocation should contain provisions for the rehabilitation of site structures if changes in market conditions suddenly reduce the amount of land required by the redeveloper.[46]

4. Local and federal agencies should provide interest-free or low-interest loans to relocatees who wish to buy new homes.

5. These agencies should provide similar loans to project area landlords whose present buildings provide decent, safe, and sanitary housing, to allow them to purchase new buildings in other areas or to rehabilitate such buildings and to make them available to project area residents.

6. Landlords with units eligible for relocation housing anywhere in the community should be encouraged to rent to relocatees through such incentives as rehabilitation loans, subsidies for redecorating, and the like.

7. When project area rents have been low, so that residents' housing costs are raised sharply as a result of relocation, the federal and local agencies should set up a rent moratorium to allow relocatees to save some money for future rentals. The length of this moratorium should be based on the gap between project area and relocation area rentals.

8. Liquidation funds in lieu of moving allowances should be provided to small-store owners and other businessmen who will not be able to reopen their firms elsewhere. Other federal and local programs should be made available to provide occupational retraining and other vocational aids to those who want them.

9. Communication between the redevelopment agency and the residents should be set up so that:

   (a) The amount of information given to site residents is maximized, and the development of rumors due to information vacuums is prevented.

   (b) Officials are trained to understand the inevitably deprivatory nature of relocation for the residents, so that they have more insight into what relocation means to the residents and can develop a more tolerant attitude toward their reactions of shock and protest.

10. The relocation staff should be strengthened by the addition of:

(a) Social workers who can provide aid to residents faced with additional problems resulting from relocation and can make referrals to other city agencies that deal with such problems.[47]

(b) Real estate technicians who can develop a thorough inventory of the city's housing supply and can also weed out unscrupulous landlords who are likely to exploit the relocatees.

11. In relocation projects that involve the destruction of a positive social system, experiments should be conducted to:

(a) Find ways of relocating together extended families living together in separate but adjacent households, provided they want to be moved en masse.

(b) Make it possible for important project area institutions and organizations to reestablish themselves in those neighborhoods which have received the majority of relocatees or in central locations where they are accessible to scattered relocatees.

(c) Develop group relocation methods to allow members of an ethnic group who want to stay together to move into an area as a group. This is especially important if there are neighborhoods with available relocation housing in which there are presently no members of that ethnic group.

12. Previous relocation projects suggest that most people relocate themselves, and only a small proportion are relocated by the agency. In the future, procedures should be revised on this basis. Then, the major functions of the relocation agency should be:

(a) To make sure that the supply of relocation housing is sufficient to give relocatees a maximal choice of decent, safe, and sanitary dwelling units at rents they are willing to pay and in neighborhoods in which they want to live.

(b) To provide information and other aids that will enable relocatees to evaluate these dwelling units and to make the best housing choice in relation to their needs and wants.

(c) To offer relocation services to those who want to be moved by the agency.

Implications for the Future of Urban Renewal

Many of these proposals will increase the cost of relocation, which will in turn raise the cost of renewal. This is equitable, since project area residents should not be required to subsidize the process, as they do presently. In time, the higher cost of renewal will become the accepted rate. Moreover, since redevelopers often stand to make considerable profit from their renewal operation, they should be asked to bear part of this increased cost.[48]

Current renewal and relocation procedures have been discussed mainly in terms of the inequities being borne by the project area residents. However, these procedures can be shown to have undesirable consequences for renewal itself. For example, projects based on inadequate relocation plans simply push site residents into the next adjacent low-income area and create overcrowding that leads to the formation of new slums. Thus, the city is saddled with additional problems and new costs, which eventually overwhelm the apparent short-run benefits of the renewal project. Moreover, poorly handled relocation frequently results in political repercussions which can endanger the community's long-range renewal plans. Consequently, the critique and proposals suggested here have implications not only for the site residents but for the future of urban renewal itself.[49]

· T H I R T E E N ·

FROM THE
BULLDOZER TO
HOMELESSNESS

T HE ERA OF the public bulldozer is for the most part dead and gone, but even if the government no longer tears down the housing of the poor directly, it takes their housing away from them in a variety of ways. Private enterprise does both, usually because of government's inability to interfere in the housing industry, and sometimes with government's assent.

The ways in which private enterprise cuts into the supply of low-cost housing and thus displaces the poor vary with the times and the state of the economy. This essay, written originally in 1981 to estimate the total displacement brought about by urban renewal, also sketches the various other ways in which displacement has taken place since the days of the bulldozer, ending with the massive homelessness that began in the 1980s.

THE EFFECTS OF URBAN RENEWAL

NOT LONG after the first edition of *The Urban Villagers* was published in 1962, public opinion began to turn against slum-clearance projects of the

Reprinted with permission of the Free Press, a Division of Macmillan, Inc., from pages 384 to 395 of *The Urban Villagers: Group and Class in the Life of Italian-Americans,* Updated and Expanded Edition, by Herbert J. Gans. Copyright © 1962 by the Free Press. Copyright © 1982 by Herbert J. Gans. The present version has been considerably revised and updated.

kind that had destroyed the West End, persuading some that my book was an example of successful policy-oriented research. Authors are probably the least able to assess the impact of their work, but books and articles normally influence professional and elite, rather than public, opinion.[1]

Most likely, the bulldozer approach to urban renewal was actually terminated by the immense difficulty of relocating, even improperly, large numbers of poor people; by the opposition from white neighborhoods experiencing the arrival of black displacees;[2] and last (but hardly least) by ghetto protests against further "Negro removal." Moreover, the Newark disorders of 1967 were caused in part by a plan to clear several blocks in the Central Ward ghetto for a new medical school; and the Detroit riots that same year took place in a neighborhood overcrowded with displacees from cleared parts of the city.

Since the late 1960s, the bulldozer approach has been used almost entirely in small cities and towns, and the occasional big-city clearance projects that take place usually involve small areas and few displacees. Even so, displacement remains a brutal process. People are still losing familiar neighborhoods and old neighbors; the developers, eager to start demolition and reconstruction, often force the displaced to move out quickly; and inexpensive relocation housing is harder to find than ever.[3]

No one has yet computed the total number of households displaced by urban renewal. However, my review of official displacement and relocation data suggests the following: from 1956, when HHFA (HUD's predecessor) announced that 33,000 families had so far been relocated by the six-year-old program, until about 1963, on the average about 30,000 families and 10,000 individuals (or 40,000 households) were displaced annually. From 1964 to 1971, the number declined to 20,000 families and 10,000 individuals a year; between 1977 and 1980 it was gradually reduced to about 15,000 families and individuals combined.[4] I estimate that from 1950 to 1980 the officially displaced totaled about 735,000 households. However, since many people moved prematurely because of misinformation, fear, and other reasons between the time an area was scheduled for renewal and official displacement got under way, it is necessary to increase the official figure by 25 to 33 percent. The total number of households displaced and low-cost dwelling units eliminated through 1980 must therefore be at least a million.[5] And this does not include the households forced out by the urban expressway building program that took place before and during the peak years of urban renewal.

OTHER FORMS OF DISPLACEMENT

SINCE THE virtual end of urban renewal, other forms of displacement have either become more numerous or just more visible. Some are the results of other governmental action, far more follow private ones, but all also— and always—take place because poverty and powerlessness make it impossible for low-income people to compete successfully for housing when it, or land, is scarce. Which activities are to be considered displacement is itself in dispute. The narrow definition limits displacement to direct changes in the housing units that force poor and other tenants to leave: *gentrification,* the purchase and rehabilitation of low-cost housing by affluent people for their own use; *conversion,* developer-initiated gentrification for multifamily occupancy; and *abandonment,* the vacating and likely destruction of inexpensive housing.

The broader definition adds involuntary departures caused by indirect changes in the housing market: evictions; massive rent increases and tenant harassment which amount to de facto eviction; public subsidy programs for the middle class that bid up the price of housing; and inflationary pressures on private and public housing that drive rents up beyond what people can pay. A yet broader definition would include economic cutbacks that lead to joblessness or reduced welfare payments and thus force people to look for cheaper housing—or finally to become homeless. Of course, not all displacement involves poor people, and some of the displaced poor are being moved out of harmful housing. A few even find other inexpensive apartments. *Nonetheless, when households are displaced from inexpensive dwelling units, these units are usually lost forever to low-income tenants; and, as a result, the total supply of housing they can afford is reduced further.*

How many people are displaced annually and have been displaced in the past is unknown. Because of differences in definition, difficulties in counting the displaced, and the lack of economic or legislative interest in accurate figures, national estimates have varied considerably.[6] A 1979 HUD study concluded that between 1974 and 1976, 500,000 households were displaced annually.[7] However, a 1981 California Legal Services analysis using a broader definition and counting people forced out by rent increases suggested that over 800,000 households are displaced every year.[8]

Whatever the definition, the number remains large, but because by the 1980s displacement was almost entirely private, data are no longer available. Chester Hartman, a principal student of displacement has been using an estimate of 500,000 households a year, but indicates that this is strictly a guesstimate.[9]

There is disagreement as well about the scope of different forms of displacement, but in the 1970s, rent increases by private landlords probably account for a plurality, if not a majority, of displacements. The 1979 HUD report estimated that from 1974 to 1976, private-sector action was responsible for 87 percent of the displacements and public-sector action for the rest.[10]

Among the forms of displacement that occur because of direct changes in dwelling units, abandonment has been a primary cause ever since urban renewal slowed down, while gentrification and conversion have probably remained of minor significance. However, accurate numbers are unavailable, and in some economically vital cities, abandoned units may have been reclaimed, for the poor and others. Robert Burchell's 1978 survey of officials in the 150 declining American cities thought to have experienced noticeable abandonment turned up about 263,000 units.[11] A much larger figure, 625,000 to 875,000 dwelling units, results if Peter Marcuse's 1981 estimate of New York City abandonment is extrapolated to the country as a whole.[12] His later estimate, published in 1986, this time in numbers of people, totaled 380,000 to 500,000 when New York City figures were again extrapolated.[13] Moreover, these estimates dealt only with then-current abandonment; no one has ventured to guess how many additional units were emptied earlier but torn down, or converted to uses other than housing low-income people.

The most widely quoted estimate of gentrification offered by HUD, in 1979, was 0.5 percent of all urban housing units, or 100,000 at the end of the 1970s.[14] This figure was probably low, and besides, the rate of gentrification and conversion surely rose in the 1980s. In 1986, Marcuse estimated New York City's displacement from gentrification to be between 10,000 and 40,000 households a year, and if each household is equal to a dwelling unit and the national figure is five times New York's, 50,000 to 200,000 units were then being gentrified every year.[15] By the late 1980s, however, the number must have gone down, at least in cities where jobs for young professionals were also declining.

While abandonment almost always uproots poor people, gentrification frequently displaces near-poor and moderate-income households and whites. Conversion often takes place in previously nonresidential structures, but when it occurs in old industrial buildings, small firms are forced out of business and low-wage workers lose their jobs.

THE DYNAMICS OF ABANDONMENT
AND GENTRIFICATION

ABANDONMENT IS of two kinds: tenant initiated and landlord initiated. In cities with sufficient vacant inexpensive housing, poor people who can afford to move try to improve their housing condition. In the process, the worst slums of all are sometimes abandoned because no one else is willing to move in.[16] Although purely tenant-initiated abandonment is rare, it is a method of housing improvement for the poor.

Landlord-initiated abandonment is, however, a form of displacement. As buildings age and require more maintenance and as maintenance costs and local taxes increase, low-cost housing can become an unprofitable invest-ment, particularly if tenants are unable or unwilling to pay more. The stereotypical conception of the greedy slumlord who owns and "milks" large numbers of buildings is still sometimes accurate, but many tenements are owned by individual landlords who barely manage to keep their heads above water.[17]

In any case, when profit margins become too low or nonexistent, big and small landlords, notably absentees, often divest themselves of, or "walk away" from, their buildings, depriving tenants of heat, hot water, and other services.[18] Before long, some tenants begin to leave, in effect becoming involuntary displacees. Now, the abandonment process spirals. Vacant apartments attract vandals (who tear out copper pipes and other salable items), partying teenagers, and arsonists. Then the other tenants must leave as well. The abandonment of one structure scares the remaining occupants of the block, so that even when other buildings remain physically viable, fear can drive tenants out and keep replacements from coming in. Although neighborhood cohesion or social control, and quick municipal action to seal up vacant buildings, can prevent panic and further abandon-ment, often the rest of the block empties quickly. Ultimately, entire neigh-borhoods may undergo abandonment. (This is what happened in parts of New York's South Bronx, which became a national symbol of abandon-ment.)[19]

Abandoned buildings, blocks, and neighborhoods exist in every aging industrial city and even in small, middle-aged towns.[20] In some areas, including the South Bronx, local residents have obtained and rehabilitated abandoned buildings, investing their own labor, or "sweat equity," but these projects require so much dedication, organization, labor, and money that the total number of buildings saved in this way remains minuscule.

However, by the end of the 1980s, some of the buildings began to be rebuilt by private enterprise, and by New York City, which finally launched a serious effort to build affordable housing. Many of the city-built units have been allocated to homeless people, especially those who had to be moved out of Manhattan welfare hotels for economy and other reasons. (Some of these hotels were then gentrified.)

Gentrification is basically a private version of urban renewal. The term comes from England, but it is apt because affluent people are taking over the homes and neighborhoods of less affluent ones. (The initial American term was "revitalization," which presumably referred to healthier property values and tax receipts, not to the replacement of the lifeless poor by the lively rich.) Gentrifiers usually buy old town houses or single-family houses built originally for upper-middle-class and upper-income families which have become tenements or rooming houses. They have also sought row houses originally built for middle- and working-class families, because these are smaller and therefore cheaper to build. Converters look for once-luxurious apartment houses and hotels, but also for solidly built rooming houses, office buildings, factories, lofts—and, in Manhattan, they rebuild nearly anything, even the dark and airless nineteenth-century tenements originally constructed to house the working poor.

The people who move into gentrified and converted dwellings are mostly young, well-to-do, and free spending. Their arrival not only increases property values, prices, rents, and tax receipts, but also spurs the establishment of new stores and other businesses in the areas they take over. Gentrification spirals as readily as abandonment, for once "pioneers" have gentrified the first two or three houses on a block, others come quickly before house prices rise out of reach, and one gentrified block can lead to a gentrified neighborhood. Consequently, the process has received enthusiastic support from local officials and business people. Favorable publicity from the news media has enhanced the visibility and exaggerated the amount of gentrification, which in turn has encouraged illusions of an urban renaissance—and, at the start of the energy crisis, fantasies that masses of suburbanites would come back to the gentrified city. Scattered case studies of gentrified areas in the 1970s suggested that fewer than 10 percent of the new occupants were returned suburbanites; and now, as then, far more urban neighborhoods are undergoing abandonment than gentrification. Indeed, gentrification is very much affected by the larger economy, especially, as already noted, the growth or decline of the professional parts of the service economy.

DISPLACEMENT AND REPLACEMENT

THE PRECEDING sections mean to suggest that a major component of American housing practice for the poor is displacement. Practice is not policy, but even government housing policy has traditionally been more devoted to housing improvement, whether by clearance or rehabilitation, which normally forces out poor people, than to supplying more housing for the poor.

A reckoning of how much low-cost housing has been constructed in comparison to the number of units lost through displacement can only be approximate. One can safely assume that private builders have not constructed a significant number of totally unsubsidized dwelling units for the poor, or the near-poor, in the past decades. The government has built about a million units of public housing since 1949, and most of the apartments are normally rented to people with incomes at or below the poverty line.[21] During the 1960s and 1970s, the government also made possible the construction of about 175,000 units under "Section 221 BMIR," about 400,000 units each under "Section 235" and "Section 236," and 170,000 under "Section 8." These and smaller low-cost housing programs have altogether added about 1,200,000 units. Initially, many were allocated to moderate-income tenants, although in the 1980s, more were being occupied by low-income people.[22]

Since the number of units built by public-housing agencies and the number of households displaced by urban renewal during the past thirty years cancel each other out, the net addition to the low-cost housing supply is the total number of "221 BMIR," "235," "236," and "Section 8" units now occupied by the poor and the near-poor, to which one must add the dwelling units constructed by state and local governments and by nonprofit agencies. The total figure is unknown, but even if all the 1.2 million units mentioned in the previous paragraph were assigned to this population, they could not possibly take care of the low-income people among the 500,000 to 800,000 or more households who are displaced and made homeless every year. The net effect of housing practice and policy is a continuing shrinkage in the supply of housing that the low-income population can afford.

DISPLACEMENT AND HOMELESSNESS

IF ONE looks at the numbers of poor people who are displaced every year and the concurrent failure of the government to build low-income and affordable housing, the emergence of homelessness in the mid-1980s should have been predictable. In fact, with hindsight it is surprising that there was so little of it in the 1970s. However, the people who were spared from losing their homes then were hit en masse shortly after the arrival of the Reagan administration, when the decline of the low-wage economy, the rise of joblessness, and especially in that economy, coincided with the drastic cuts in welfare and other government aids to the poor, as well as the continuing rise in rents and the additional disappearance of low-income housing.

All of a sudden, then, a problem became visible that had in fact been developing for at least a decade. In retrospect, it should have been predictable before, since as early as fall 1981, the President's Commission on Housing was reporting incredible rent-income ratios among the poor: nearly a quarter of all poor households were paying 50 percent or more of their income for rent, and another third were paying between 30 and 50 percent. (By 1990, two-thirds of all the poor paid more than half their incomes for rent.)[23]

Although conservatives were quick to blame the new homelessness on a familiar scapegoat, rent control, this contradicted their earlier charge against rent control, that it mainly benefits the middle class. The Right also blamed homelessness on the emptying of mental hospitals and the increase of drug addiction, but the mental hospitals were first emptied in the 1960s, and the rise in homelessness began before the arrival of crack cocaine—and long after the rise and fall of heroin in the 1970s.

What really happened is that the continuing expansion of the downtown business district took away further skid row housing while gentrification took other kinds of rooming houses in which poor single men and former mental hospital patients had been living in recent years. However, the most important cause of homelessness was probably the persisting rise in rents even as poor people saw jobs disappear and welfare rolls and benefits shrinking. At that point, entire families joined the single men who traditionally made up the homeless population.

A large social science literature on homelessness has emerged, one part of which has attempted to estimate the total number of homeless. As always, counting exercises are complicated by definitional problems.[24] For example, a narrow definition would limit itself to those who have lost their homes permanently, while a broader one would include those who have lost them temporarily but can get them back with a rise in their fortunes—unless they have been homeless sufficiently long that no landlord will take them back.

Those normally defined as homeless are both without homes and without shelter, but in addition, there are people who have lost their homes but still have shelter with relatives or friends. While they are officially and euphemistically known as the doubled up, they should be counted among the homeless as well, particularly because they may be evicted if their money runs out or if overcrowding begins to cause problems. However, they are not now counted, so that no one even knows how many people are doubled up, how many of those obtain their own homes again, and how many of them become literally homeless instead—and then appear in the official statistics.

In any case, homelessness is very much a process, and most of the counting has by necessity been cross-sectional. Furthermore, almost all the studies have been of individual cities, and national studies, or even national estimates are far fewer. The best national study comes from the Urban Institute, and its authors estimate that as of spring 1987, there were at most half a million homeless—far fewer than the 2 to 3 million proposed by some advocates of the homeless.[25] The Urban Institute did not attempt to study the hard-to-reach homeless or the doubled up, but Michael Stegman's 1988 study of the New York rental housing market estimated that about 110,000 households were then doubled up.[26] Assuming New York figures need to be increased fivefold to yield a national estimate, more than 500,000 household would have to be added to the homeless rolls, and many more individuals, since most of the doubled up are single-parent families of three to five people.

Moreover, all the local and national numbers can increase quickly with new downturns in the low wage economy, further cuts in welfare, and an additional rise in rents at the low end of the rental market. Conversely, the numbers could shrink with good economic news or the federal government's building of additional low-cost units.

One difficulty in adding to the supply of low-cost housing, especially outside the ghettos, is the "NIMBY" problem, reflecting the fears of higher crime, the loss of status, and the decline of property values thought to be caused by the homeless. Whether these fears are justified or not makes little difference, because the nonhomeless are reacting to their own and media images of the corroding effects of homelessness. Indeed, homelessness is a very accurate term, for the homeless have not just lost the roofs over their heads, but *their* roofs. They have been deprived of their customary shelter, i.e., the physical dwelling unit and their physically necessary belongings, including a mailing address and mailbox. They have also been deprived of their social belongings, for example, those that define and express their social identity and position, their neighborhood identity and other material and social goods—including social and emotional supports—essential to being an accepted member of society. In addition, the family has been burdened with additional stigma, and loss of self-respect, and in many cases its members have been scattered, knocking out the most vital part of their social and emotional support system. Thus, all the normal, and well-known, effects of poverty are multiplied many times by homelessness.

Furthermore, the level of stigmatization is such that in many cities, the homeless are thought to need training to live in permanent housing again, as if a complex skill had been permanently lost or had never been achieved. While long-lasting homelessness may have negative emotional and social effects, no one knows how long that period has to be and how it varies for different kinds of homelessness—and how much retraining to live in a permanent home, if any, the diverse kinds of homeless require. Meanwhile, the idea that the homeless need to be "hometrained" before they deserve permanent housing supplies a political underpinning for programs to build shelters and transitional housing where the homeless live under supervision, and to keep them out of permanent housing in regular neighborhoods. While some homeless may need supervision and counseling, I would argue that unless they are mentally ill, homeless people should be assumed able to live on their own in permanent housing unless there is clear evidence to the contrary.

The current ideas about housing the homeless not only hurt the homeless themselves, but they also justify the creation of whole new levels of officially supplied housing below that, in name and quality, of public housing. Permanent housing is now the equivalent of public housing, but below that is transitional housing, which may be permanent in quality, but is given the poor only temporarily. Further "down" are various levels of temporary shelters, welfare hotels, armories, and other strictly impermanent and often dangerous arrangements, some of which may turn out to be housing of long duration for the homeless. In effect, new housing classes are being created, all of them under the previously lowest such class.

IMPLICATIONS FOR HOUSING POLICY[27]

I AM not opposed to all urban renewal—or gentrification and conversion—schemes, as long as these create jobs and tax benefits that go to the poor, involuntary displacement is kept to an absolute minimum, and the displaced are generously reimbursed and first supplied with decent housing costing less than a quarter of their income.

I doubt, however, that such a policy will be implemented, that the displacement of the poor and the further destruction of inexpensive housing will soon end, or that the federal moratorium on building or subsidizing units for the poor, the near-poor, and the moderate-income population, which Richard Nixon began in 1973 and which his successors have continued, will be lifted.

From the perspective of 1990, the housing policy that came to an end with the Nixon moratorium had some shortcomings that need to be kept in mind for the future. First, what applied to urban renewal applies to publicly funded low-income housing of all kinds: policies that raise the rents so that poor people must cut back on other necessities are harmful, however excellent the new housing.

Second, the distinction I made in chapter 12 between harmful and low-rent housing remains significant, and I believe that rehousing occupants of physically and otherwise harmful slums is as important as ever. However, moving occupants of low-rent dwellings into "better" housing, including that praised as examples of "good design," may do more to beautify the city for the affluent than to help poor people. Some improvements in health and morale often follow after people obtain better units, but there are limits to the social and emotional effects of housing.[28] For example, there is no evidence to suggest that people, poor or affluent, normally become abler parents, more compatible neighbors, harder workers, or emotionally healthier simply because they obtain better housing. To be sure, poor mothers can supervise the outdoor play of small children more effectively from row houses or garden apartments than from highrises, but once children reach their teens, mothers may lose them to the street culture whether they live in tall or low buildings. A larger dwelling unit, which supplies enough personal space and individual privacy, may prevent or ameliorate some familial tensions, help children to study, and permit adults a private sex life, but space is an economic, not an architectural, resource which requires money that the poor lack and will not be given.

Third and perhaps most important, better housing does not, by itself, do much to reduce people's poverty. Although American "housers" and other reformers have long believed in this and other magical effects of good housing, the occupants of even the best-designed public-housing project remain just as poor, as subject to the pathologies associated with poverty, and as stigmatized as slum dwellers. [29] If one applies the unfortunately forgotten distinction by S. M. Miller and Pamela Roby between antipoverty policies which function as *investments* and help people escape poverty, and *amenities,* which only make their lives more pleasant, better housing is not an investment. [30] Nor is it a high-priority amenity, especially when "better" also means more expensive. Housing per se is a major amenity, however. Not only do poor people consider housing important for making life as comfortable as their poverty allows, but they view the home as a haven for the family from a very threatening outside world. [31] Even so, they want to define decent housing by their own criteria, and housing their budget cannot stand is not decent.

Since housing is not an investment for escaping poverty, a housing policy should not be mistaken for an anti-poverty policy. In fact, an effective antipoverty policy would also be the ideal housing policy, since the formerly poor could then participate in the same private-but-subsidized market in which other Americans obtain good housing—or did so in the past. Ironically enough, even the homeless need nothing so much as an antipoverty policy, because without a steady job or income in lieu of a job, they cannot afford anything except shelters—which in effect means that they are still being kept homeless.

Until everyone can actually afford to obtain their housing in the private-but-subsidized housing market, the federal government should build, or encourage the building (as well as rehabilitation) of low cost housing for the homeless, all those still living in harmful housing, but also for those poor, near-poor, and even moderate-income income people paying more than 25 percent of their income as rent.

Not all of these will need new housing, but adding low cost housing to the housing supply will increase the vacancy rate and reduce overly high rents for those who can least afford them. Moreover, housing programs would also create jobs by restoring the national infrastructure—and I think housing is as much a part of that infrastructure as bridges. (See chapter 15.) How much new or rehabilitated housing will be needed depends on a variety of factors, but some units should be made available to moderate-income people, and some should even be built for the middle class, to reduce its housing costs, and to obtain its political support.

New building and rehabilitation are expensive; therefore the total amount of affordable housing can also be increased by subsidizing some existing units, either in the form of tax supports or vouchers. These should be given to poor people to allow them somewhat the same kind of choice of housing and location all other Americans now exercise, with the amount of rental support pegged to whatever levels necessary in various local housing markets. I see voucher programs as rent supplements, not as incentives for poor people to move out of substandard into standard housing, although housing improvement vouchers could also be provided, with extra incentives for people ready to bear the costs of moving into and staying in better but also higher-priced dwellings.

In many cities, vouchers will not work because the vacancy rate for inexpensive housing is close to zero, and the extra funds made available to people in vouchers would simply be drawn away in higher rents. In such places, the government must also build directly for the poor, in mixed-income projects wherever possible, with upper-income and middle-income tenants helping to subsidize the poor, but also in public-housing projects, especially for people who now live in harmful housing. Ideally these projects should be lowrise, unlike the giant high-rise projects of the post–World War II era as much as possible. This is not always feasible, however, and tenant-control and tenant-management programs to keep housing decent and safe exist even in big high-rise projects. In those cities where it is impossible to build such projects on scattered sites, and where housing for the poor is particularly scarce, some may have to be built in poor neighborhoods, nonwhite, mixed and white.

Since the cost of building new or rehabilitating abandoned housing will be expensive, governments must also learn how they can discourage the destruction of further low-income housing, and the displacement that follows. As noted earlier, clearly harmful housing that cannot be fixed up may still have to be torn down, but such housing is becoming scarcer all the time. As for harmful neighborhoods, these appear to be increasing, but unless the harm comes from the natural environment, it makes more sense to deal with the sources of harm, for example, a local drug industry, than to clear a neighborhood as a way to remove the drug dealers.

Whatever the housing programs chosen, however, it must be understood that they cannot replace an antipoverty policy. Ending people's poverty is always better than supplying them with "better" housing while keeping them poor. Whatever the harm, alleged and real, associated with substandard housing, it is much less than the harm caused by being poor.

· F O U R T E E N ·

THE ROLE
OF EDUCATION
IN THE ESCAPE
FROM POVERTY

I N THE CONVENTIONAL American wisdom, education has long been
viewed as a major—and almost guaranteed—device for upward occupational mobility, the idea being that what young people learn at school will
enable them to obtain a viable foothold in the world of work. As a result,
education has also been conceived as a critical agent in the escape from
poverty, and many of the programs in the War on Poverty of the 1960s
emphasized improvements in the education of the poor.

Like some other social scientists, I am dubious that education can play
as significant a role in the economic and occupational mobility of this population as is usually hoped. Consequently, I doubt that schooling, at least of
the kind offered today, can be a significant force in the escape from poverty.[1] Although too little is known even about exactly what education does
in the upward mobility of the middle class, even less is known about what it
does among and for the poor. While some poor children (and adolescents)
have always been and are now able to escape from poverty because of their
superior performance in school, most poor children follow one of these
patterns: they do not have access to good quality schools in which a

Reprinted, with a number of revisions and a postscript, from Norman Ashline, et al., eds.,
Education, Inequality, and National Policy (Lexington, Mass.: D.C. Heath, 1976).

225

superior performance is a stepping stone to occupational success; they are kept out of good jobs by the many noneducational forms of status—and the credentials to which they also lack access; or, they graduate into a labor market in which jobs, especially blue-collar ones, are increasingly scarce for everyone. Further, too many poor children do not do particularly well in school to begin with, partly because the schools have not yet learned how to teach them, but also because they sometimes do not want to teach them, intentionally or otherwise.

Much of the discussion about education among the poor has sought to put the blame on the schools, on poor children, or on their parents; but ultimately, little is to be gained by blaming anyone, for the fault rests mainly with much larger and more powerful forces. In American society, as elsewhere, public education has functioned, if not always intentionally, to support the existing stratification system, channeling many children into the strata of their parents and into those occupations most in demand in the current economy, and only a handful of children have been able to transcend the general channeling process, except when their skills were particularly scarce.[2]

As a result, poor children go to schools that are, on the whole, inferior in many ways to middle-class schools, where they are often taught by teachers who do not consider them capable of learning. Some teachers are simply hostile toward the poor; a much larger number, however, adhere to widely accepted stereotypes of the poor as being stupid and apathetic, and then it becomes a self-fulfilling prophecy. Nevertheless, despite the considerable evidence that poor young children are as intelligent, curious, and hungry for learning as their middle-class peers—many of whom are not half as interested in learning as educators like to believe—some poor children *do* behave in schools as if they were stupid or apathetic. Aside from the fact that they sense, and react to, their teachers' stereotypes of them, they also enter the schools with several handicaps. Poor parents are so busy with survival, or so beset with crises, that they frequently do not have the time or energy to teach their children the kinds of play that are a crucial part of early learning of the kind that is supposed to continue in school. Other parents, having themselves been deprived of that kind of play, do not know how to teach it to their children. Many more lack the prior "book learning" that curriculum makers and teachers take for granted and thus do not teach.

Upon entering the schools, the children encounter an academic culture and a set of bureaucratic rules that not only diverge sharply from the culture and rules they have learned as necessary for survival and mobility in their neighborhood, but that also often seem to have little direct relevance to learning per se. Equally significant, as poor children get older, they become aware of the fact that the culture and rules of the school are also irrelevant to their future. As they discover that even with a diploma they may not find a decent job and the chance to escape poverty, they become alienated from the school and from learning, "enrolling" instead in what used to be called the school of hard knocks, in which they learn more of what they need to know for their survival as poor people.

To put it another way, poor youngsters realize that the school functions in part as a preparatory institution and anticipatory recruiting station for what economists call the *primary labor market* of well-paid, permanent, secure, and relatively interesting jobs; that neither their teachers nor the rest of middle-class society considers them eligible for this labor market; and that unless they are superior in skill or ambition, they may be relegated to the *secondary labor market,* of unskilled, underpaid, temporary, unstable, and dead-end jobs, the preparation for which is so minimal that it can be learned in the street culture of the urban slum.[3] John Ogbu, writing about blacks, has put this more graphically as a "job ceiling" beyond which the average poor black child is not likely to rise, and for which he or she should therefore not aspire if he or she is to be spared disappointment and frustration.[4]

One visible illustration of poor children's awareness of their future is the consistent finding that school performance, particularly among boys, declines as they become old enough to realize what is in store for them, so that by the time poor children enter their teens, many drop out of school, in spirit if not in body. Some resort to protesting what they consider to be imprisonment in a hostile institution, either by seemingly senseless verbal or physical violence or by more explicit hostility toward teachers and others. Some researchers have described these reactions as part of a culture of resistance or protest, but if it is a culture, it is one embedded in depression and despair—as well as anger. The childrens' anger comes from the realization that they are being treated unfairly; the despair, that their behavior is likely to hurt *them* more than anyone else.

Some teachers are able to overcome these patterns, either by personal charisma or by their ability and freedom to transform the curriculum into meaningful teaching. More important, they or the children they teach can see a direct path from the school to college and the world of work beyond. Sometimes, poor children appear to be born with such a vision, and the ambition it implies; more often, they are socialized by parents who are also able to isolate them from the street culture and from their peers who try, like all peers, to demand conformity to the majoritarian pattern. Sometimes, the children are lucky enough to become part of special programs which chart that direct path, for example, with scholarships of the kind invented by Eugene Lang—and with the constant monitoring of their progress on that path.

Still, unusual teachers, children, and programs are rare, and among all populations, affluent or poor. Such programs could be mass-produced, of course, but they rarely work as well as they do when they are demonstration programs, or experiments, or otherwise administered on a small scale. Moreover, it would be unfair to demand of poor children what we do not (yet) demand of the rest: that they will obtain good jobs only if they have the academic skills to go to college. It would also be unfair to demand from poor children the exceptional school performance that we do not demand from the rest of the population. In any case, unusual teachers, children, and programs are unlikely to be produced in large enough quantities to overcome the drawbacks of existing institutional arrangements, including those that seek to keep some people poor.

ESCAPING POVERTY—THE HISTORICAL EXPERIENCE

INSTEAD OF expecting the school to function as a major causal factor in the escape from poverty, I believe it is more useful to ask which institutions and agencies, education and other, have been and are most helpful in enabling the poor to enter the more affluent sectors of society. This question can be addressed in several ways, but I shall here use a historical approach: to discover how previous generations of poor people escaped from poverty, and to use this experience in constructing an alternative escape model. American history is, of course, a treasure trove for this purpose, for most of the people who came to America arrived as poor people and were able, somehow, to achieve a measure of affluence.

If one looks, for example, at the European immigrants who arrived in America in the last half of the nineteenth century and the first quarter of the twentieth century, it is clear (1) that most came as very poor people; (2) that insofar as their children went to school at all, they went to schools that were worse in all respects than today's schools for the poor; and (3) that they nevertheless were able eventually to escape poverty. I am referring here especially to what I call the "peasant immigrants," the people who came from the rural areas of southern, eastern, and southeastern Europe —for example, the southern Italians, Sicilians, Poles, other Slavs, Hungarians, and Greeks, among others—most of them unskilled and most of them with little or no education. Their experience is relevant, particularly because they were similar in many ways to the contemporary (nonimmigrant) poor, who were only a generation or so ago rural migrants from the South, Appalachia, and Puerto Rico. At the same time, they must be distinguished from *urban* immigrants, with some artisan industrial, commercial, or other urban occupational experience, perhaps with a little more education, and, in some cases, with a little capital in their pockets. During the nineteenth century, America became home for urban immigrants from many countries, including those who sent mainly peasant immigrants, but the most frequently mentioned, and thus most visible, urban immigrants have been the Jews, particularly those emigrating from eastern Europe.

The case of the Jews deserves somewhat more detailed discussion because many educators believe that they relied mainly on education to escape poverty, ostensibly because Jewish culture places especially high value on education. Recent historical research suggests, however, that immigrant Jewish children and the children of the first Jewish immigrants did not stay in school very long, so that fewer than imagined could have used education to achieve upward mobility.[5] In addition, the Talmudic education valued by the Jewish immigrants—actually only by the religious minority among them—was antisecular and discouraged learning for the sake of occupational mobility, so that it may not have been useful for moving out of poverty.

No one yet knows how many Jewish immigrants valued secular education, or whether they valued it more than other urban immigrants, but most of the Jewish newcomers were so poor that they had to send their children to work as quickly as the other immigrants—although there is some evidence to suggest that the second, or first native-born, generation of Jews attended school in large numbers and performed more successfully than other second-generation groups, at least among the peasant immigrants. Unfortunately, the many educators and other policymakers, then and now, who pointed to the Jews to support their claims for relying on education as a means of escaping poverty vastly overestimated the educational performance of the Jewish immigrants. They also failed to consider that other urban immigrants may also have escaped more quickly from poverty than the peasant immigrants, whether or not they went to school; and they ignored the difference between urban and peasant immigrants.

What exactly the urban experience of the urban immigrants contributed to their ability to escape poverty more quickly is not yet known, and that they were urban may not have been relevant at all. Most likely, their previous commercial or industrial labor market experience was relevant, as well as the previously mentioned education and capital, but none of these are inherently urban and could have been obtained in the small towns of Europe as well, or even in villages that had some marketing function. *Urban* is thus used quite loosely here.[6]

One historical fact is well established, however: the European peasant immigrants did not escape poverty via the schools. They came from countries in which education had been either inaccessible or irrelevant to them, and many of them made strenuous efforts to keep their children out of school in America, partly because these schools treated them with hostility and believed that they were unteachable, but also because parents needed or wanted the children to work and contribute to the family income. Furthermore, the jobs that were available to them did not require education.[7]

Instead of the schools, the peasant immigrants relied on the labor market; wherever feasible, as many family members as possible went to work at whatever jobs were available. Though many were never able to progress beyond positions in the secondary labor markets of their time, and many died prematurely from exhaustion, illness, and other consequences of being poor, some were able, by mere persistence, to achieve a modest family income—if not in the first, then in the second generation. They were able to escape from poverty not only by their own efforts, and because generations of previous poverty had prepared them for surviving at abysmally low standards of living, but also because their sole resource—unskilled labor—was in demand at that time. The European immigrants came, after all, at a time when America was undergoing particularly rapid industrialization and urbanization, so that except during the frequent periods of depression, there were jobs in building factories, transportation systems, and cities. In addition, the immigrants arrived at a time of incipient unionization, and the unions played a large role in the achievement of job security, and thus in the escape from the secondary labor market. Indeed, in those days unions were in many ways organizations of the poor, which they are not today.

Finally, I suspect that those immigrants who were able to stay—or move quickly—out of low-paying factory jobs and engaged instead in petty entrepreneurial activities, including peddling, were able to make their way out of poverty more rapidly than those who had to rely on factory work. The rapid expansion of consumer goods, industries, and retailing during the late nineteenth century often allowed peddlers to become shopkeepers fairly quickly; and although many of those who opened shops soon went bankrupt, others were able to move themselves or their children into the middle class. Needless to say, the urban immigrants were usually in a better position than the peasant immigrants to exchange the factory for the entrepreneurial enterprise, if only because they may have had some petty business experience in Europe.

Over the long run, of course, both urban and peasant immigrants from Europe were able to leave poverty behind, but even so, the peasant immigrants escaped from poverty more slowly than is generally believed; many were still poor or in the secondary labor market in the second generation, and only in the third and fourth generations have the majority established themselves in well-paying and secure blue-collar and white-collar jobs.[8]

Significantly, the slow escape from poverty initially took place without major changes in the attitude toward education. Since enough semiskilled blue-collar and service jobs were available, and since employers were not yet concerned with credentials unrelated to performance, the descendants of the immigrants did not give up the peasants' belief in the limited relevance of education. Equally important, they could not yet afford to do so; they still needed the children's contribution to the family income, and thus encouraged them to leave school as quickly as possible. By then child labor laws were sufficiently enforced so that the children often stayed in school until the legal leaving age. Whether they learned anything relevant to their later occupational activities, however, is still a moot question.

Only in the 1950s did these attitudes change. As blue-collar wages began to go up, parents no longer needed their children's paychecks. Later, as parents realized that automation and the decline in manufacturing would eventually lead to a reduction in decent blue-collar jobs, and that white-collar jobs could not be obtained without the proper credentials, they began to insist that their children graduate from high school, and then, that they go to college as well.[9] Such changes in attitude have escalated since the 1970s, and the third- and fourth-generation descendants from the European peasant immigration have since filled the publicly funded colleges and community colleges, along with blacks, Hispanics—and the first waves from the new immigrations. Parents who can afford private-school tuitions have sent their children to schools at which members of ethnic groups, save perhaps the Jews, were previously unknown.

These observations suggest a hypothesis about the role of education in upward mobility that is just the reverse of the conventional wisdom. Education, at least for the poor, is not a causal agent in the achievement of mobility, but one of its effects, and education may not be an aid to mobility until after parents have achieved a threshold of economic security in the primary labor market.[10] Only then are parents able and willing to encourage their children to go to school, and to be able to live in neighborhoods with schools worth attending; and perhaps most important, only then do children and adolescents conclude that education may indeed be useful to them. Whether the interest in and the willingness to use education require prior middle-income status, and whether the change of attitude applies to education in general or only to higher education, which is more directly relevant to occupational mobility, remains to be seen. Adolescent interest and willingness is only part of the equation, however. The other, just as necessary, is the availability of decent jobs and the willingness of employers to hire young people whose language still bears traces of growing up in a poor neighborhood, or who are dark skinned, i.e., black or Hispanic. Even so, the history of the European immigrants suggests that all other things being equal, economic success leads to educational success, not the other way around.

SOME POLICY IMPLICATIONS

THIS ANALYSIS is based on limited historical and mobility data, but if it is accurate, it suggests that education should play a different role in antipoverty policy than it did, for example, in the War on Poverty. Although there are dangers in trying to repeat history, the most effective way to eliminate poverty is through employment, with income grants in lieu of employment for those who cannot work or cannot find work, until poor people have enough economic security to be able to use education to achieve further mobility, either for themselves or for their children.

Since jobs, particularly for the unskilled, are now scarcer than they were during the time that the European immigrants escaped poverty, it will be necessary to resort to deliberate job creation. The jobs to be created should mesh with the needs of the private and especially the public economy, but they must also mesh with the long-range need of the poor: to become part of the primary labor market. In other words, such jobs must provide enough income, security, and opportunity for advancement to enable their holders to feel that they are participants in the economy and the society, so that their children will be able to advance further through education.

The historical record suggests that parental establishment in the primary labor market was a prerequisite and a takeoff point for using education to achieve further mobility, but whether history must repeat itself, or whether a different takeoff point can be found is as yet an unanswered question. No one now knows where the takeoff point is at which people feel that they are participants in the economy and society, so that their children will feel it is useful to go to school. Thus, research would have to be undertaken to determine whether that takeoff point requires parental establishment in the primary labor market, or whether it could be reached even if parents are still in the secondary labor market. Or for that matter, does it only require a specific level of family income, either through work or income grants, or a degree of income security, or some combination of work and income prerequisites?

The exact requirements for the takeoff point are particularly important in view of the fact that without major transformation of the contemporary economy, it is unlikely that many of today's poor can be employed. Perhaps the takeoff point may not even require jobs, but simply a degree of economic security, in which case it may be achieveable through a system of income grants providing a decent living to poor people unable to work or find work.

The history of the European immigrants also suggests that it may take two to three generations before some poor people are ready to reach the point at which they are able to make effective use of education for further mobility. However, whether this is a justifiable hypothesis remains to be seen; it is possible that under other labor market conditions, the European immigrants could have moved out of poverty more quickly. Also, today's poor people do not, for the most part, suffer from the language barriers the immigrants faced, and in addition, their aspirations and expectations are higher, so that they would bitterly resent any policy planning that asks them to wait for yet another two to three generations. In addition, it is always possible that educational breakthroughs will be made that will enable poor children to use the schools to escape poverty, although such breakthroughs would be irrelevant if the economy would not be able to employ them up to the level of their education. Conversely, many of today's poor carry one stigma not carried by the European immigrants; they suffer from racial discrimination, which hurts them both in the schools and in the labor market. Actually, many European immigrants were initially also discriminated against—for having a dark skin and "swarthy" features—but they were redefined as whites the moment they had escaped from poverty, a possibility out of the reach of today's poor blacks.

Finally, and most important, that the social process moved at a given pace in the past does not mean that it has to move at the same pace today. It may be that the children of today's black and Hispanic peasant immigrants can move more quickly than those of the European immigrants of the past, for black and Hispanic youngsters are now attending college all over the country. Presumably most are the children of the growing black and Hispanic working class—which remains invisible to white America and even to researchers because it does not cause problems—but the school-going cohort may also include children of the working poor and the welfare recipients.

Perhaps other things have changed. Public and private colleges have sought out nonwhite children in ways that the children of the European immigrants were never sought out. Also, today's high school graduates and college attenders have obtained some preschool learning at home, from parents, TV, and neighborhood centers—and maybe it now takes a lower level of parental economic security for children to stay in school. In addition, more is known about educational policy-making than even a generation ago, and perhaps in the long run, more successful programs to teach the poor—and persuade them to learn—can be created, and then mass-produced.

Meanwhile, there is another approach: to reverse the current pattern of having schooling precede entry into the labor market. Rather than keeping poor children in school even though they perform poorly there, it may be more desirable to enable them to go to work instead, in adolescence, and in some cases even earlier, with the idea that they can return later to school. Certainly many poor youngsters today, as in the past, would like nothing better than to leave school for a job, and there is no reason to believe that they cannot perform at least in most semiskilled jobs, particularly if they are supplied with job training once they are hired.

Revoking some school attendance and even child labor laws may appear to be a regressive proposal, but while history offers considerable evidence of exploitation of children before these laws came into existence, it is also true that young people were able to perform creditably in the labor market and offer income support to their families, particularly at times when adults could not find jobs. Even so, I am not advocating a return to a nineteenth-century practice, and any policy to put adolescents to work would have to be accompanied by stringent safeguards to prevent exploitation, both of them and of other workers, i.e., adults whom they might replace. Consequently, the youngsters should be given jobs that (1) fit their youthful needs, (2) call for job training, (3) provide opportunities for developing a career, and (4) do not allow employers to fire older, better-paid workers instead. Indeed, I am arguing not that poor young people should be put to work, but that they should be enabled to begin careers at an earlier age.

In addition, their jobs should have built-in educational components. First, the young workers should be encouraged to continue their education while working, and even to be aided financially to do so, assuming that there are schools available where they could learn. Second and more important, the young workers should be able to return to school on a full-time basis when they are older, and when they may be more interested in schooling than they are at present. Young people today who have gone to work at an early age are often sorry later that they did not stay in school, and although their judgment is based on hindsight, it does reflect a greater appreciation of the utility of education (or credentials) with increasing age. The return to school could take the form of a leave of absence from work, which many corporations already give their executive trainees, or of the equivalent of the GI Bill, which war veterans once received to prepare themselves for better jobs.

Although the school postponement program is envisaged to be mainly for men and women workers, it could also be used to help young women who become mothers and heads of single-parent families during high school, and who want to stay at home with their children or work or both while the children are young. These mothers might also be more interested in going to school when they are older.

If scholarships were available for such young people so that they could return to school in their twenties and thirties, with enough funds in the scholarship to enable them to support their families while they are in school, the educational investment would produce a higher payoff for them and for society than the present investment required for keeping—and often merely storing—poor adolescents in school in late childhood. Consequently a work —or motherhood—program for young people should be combined with a later educational program, with the federal government setting aside enough funds at the time adolescents go to work to allow them to return to finish their education—through college, or technical school. If they do not want to go to school, they should be offered other kinds of assistance, for example, help in starting a business, small or large, that would be useful in escaping poverty or in securing an escape that has already taken place. If nothing else, a cash grant in lieu of going to school should be considered, as long as the grantee spends it on his or her occupational future.

Allowing poor adolescents who are truant from school—or who have dropped out emotionally—to go to work might also have a salutary effect on the schools themselves. Teachers would no longer have to cope with unhappy and unruly youngsters and could devote themselves more fully to students who are ready to learn. In addition, the threat of losing students to the world of work, which would lead to a reduction in teaching jobs and school budgets, might encourage the schools to make education more relevant to poor young people in an attempt to keep them from going to work. Perhaps the schools might even begin to draw some educational lessons from the mass media and the peer group, both of which have long been able to educate children more effectively than teachers and textbooks. Conversely, the schools might become more involved in preliminary forms of job training, in order to give some anticipatory job socialization to youngsters who want to drop out to go to work. Finally, if the schools are likely to lose at least some of their students when the job market beckons, they could recoup the declining enrollments by matriculating young children at an earlier age, before kindergarten. Head Start, private-school nursery programs, and some day-care programs have shown that prekindergarten children are particularly eager to learn.

SOME CAVEATS

MY PROPOSALS have several difficulties and defects, of which at least three are worth mentioning. First, they imply differential educational treatment for the poor and the rest of society, for while poor youngsters would leave school to go to work, affluent ones would stay in school and prepare for college, thus widening the gap between the poor and the nonpoor. Such inequality of treatment is not desirable, although in this case it only formalizes what already exists informally, and enabling poor children to work at decent jobs seems preferable to having them sit in school without learning. Nevertheless, formally unequal treatment of poor adolescents can only be justified if it is automatically complemented by a later chance for education, if the adolescents who drop out go to work are able to return to school later. Even so, I would suggest that if the goal is the escape from poverty, equality of *results* or outcomes is more important than the time-honored educational belief—if not practice—in equality of *treatment*. If unequal treatment can bring about more equality of results, it is preferable to equal treatment that helps to perpetuate poverty.

Second, the argument I have made here can be used, when taken out of context, to justify pushing additional poor children out of school, whether jobs are available or not. Pushing children out of school is an unjustifiable policy even when jobs are available for them, however, and when jobs are not available, keeping poor youngsters in school is far preferable to forcing them out on the streets without work.

Third, the entire scheme presented in this essay rests, on the one hand, on a highly pessimistic assessment of the school, and on the other hand, on a highly optimistic assessment of the labor market and of the possibilities of job creation in particular. Given the disappointing record of job creation and income-grant programs for the poor, my implication that it is easier to intervene in the economy to incorporate the young poor in the labor market than it is to change the educational system may be totally inaccurate.

There is no doubt that the proposals made here suffer from misplaced optimism; and in actual fact, I am as pessimistic about the possibility that the poor can obtain decent jobs or income grants as that they can obtain a decent education. The powerlessness of the poor and their economic super-fluousness, at least in the current economy, strongly suggest that nothing significant will be done for them, either in the schools or in the economy.

As a result, my proposals are, for the moment, utopian. Nevertheless, even if they cannot be implemented, these proposals seem justified on another ground: that they will at least dispel the illusion, which has been created both for the poor and for the rest of society, that if and when the right combination of philosophy and technique is found, education can offer an escape from poverty. If that illusion, which Colin Greer has called the "Great School Legend," can be dispelled, it may be possible to achieve some progress by considering entirely new approaches, in which education takes a more effective role within a larger and broader antipoverty policy. Such approaches are beyond the scope of this essay, but they require not only the movement toward a full-employment, labor-intensive economy, but also some redistribution of wealth and income, as well as the greater equalization of work and in workplaces.[11] Poverty cannot be eliminated without a more egalitarian economy and polity, and only when such equalization has been achieved will it be feasible to bring about the educational equality that some educators have sought for so long.

· P O S T S C R I P T ·

TWO FURTHER caveats should be noted here, which have to do with the time at which I wrote the original paper—and both call for some updating. To begin with, the paper dealt only with the old European immigration that ended in 1925 and resumed on a small scale after World War II. Also, it focused almost entirely on the availability of unskilled and semiskilled manufacturing jobs of the kinds with which the European immigrants—especially men—eventually escaped poverty.

Before I discuss the two caveats in detail, however, another updating is required which may aid in solving some of the seemingly intractable problems of educating the poor. During the last fifteen years, it has become clearer that the right educational programs *can* work, and that, in addition, the slowness with which some of the European immigrants moved out of poverty can also be avoided. Another fifteen years of experience with Head Start has shown that if the right educational program can sufficiently change part of the immediate social environment of poor children, it can give them the head start they need for moving out of poverty. Likewise, the now rapidly growing program of sponsorship of older students initiated by Eugene Lang suggests likewise that a smaller, but in some way more insistent, change in that environment can propel poor children to college.

In short, children can adapt quickly to new opportunities, if the right ones are available. The dark side of the two programs only make this point more insistently, for as in the 1960s, the effects of Head Start wear off after a while, once its graduates are thrown back into the old environments. The band-aid solution is to lengthen, enlarge, and then mass-produce Head Start. However, the proper lesson of Head Start is to make sure that the old environments themselves are changed, and for all. Some right-wing writers have argued that the way to do this is to take poor children from their parents, an idea that is unfortunately also held by many of the professionals who lead and run foster care. Even so, the idea is appalling and has fascist undertones. Fortunately, however, it is unconstitutional: the Supreme Court has ruled that parents have the right to bring up their own children. The proper way to change the old environments is the reduction of poverty, even if that policy is not very feasible at this writing.

The sponsorship program leads to much the same conclusion. It is a well-financed and very intensive, one-on-one program, and although it has not yet been tried on a random sample of poor children, it appears to work with and for the ones who have been chosen so far. Like Head Start, its success proves that a drastic change of the social environment of poor youngsters is educationally effective, but unlike Head Start, it cannot easily be lengthened and mass-produced. Dedicated millionaires are in short supply. Teachers who could function as sponsors can probably be found, however, and they might be more effective if they were aided by mentors from the youngsters' neighborhoods. Still, to make the program work on a widespread basis, the monies for college must come from elsewhere and in larger amounts. Equally important, parents who need their children's income from jobs must also be supported—and once again, the right program must include the reduction of poverty on a wide scale.

Now to the two caveats. Since 1965, America has been the host for a second wave of immigration that is as large in size as the European one, and perhaps larger if one includes the many illegal arrivals. Only a few of the newcomers are from Europe, however, most having come from various countries in Southeast Asia but also the Near East, as well as from Central and Latin America and to some extent from Africa.

Some of these immigrants came as peasants, others came from cities and small towns or had had other contacts with modern industrial and commercial economies. Thus, it should be possible to see whether my observations about the economic fate of the European immigrants hold up for these newcomers, and what role education plays in their children's escape from poverty.

Several observations can already be made. First, those who came from middle-class backgrounds or with middle-class incomes have not had to worry about poverty. Although they may not have been able to obtain jobs using the skills—and professions—they practiced in their home countries, they seem to have fared well economically, particularly in retailing. Middle-class Cubans and South Koreans stand out as visible examples, for many of the former have prospered in Miami (even before and without drug money) while the latter have taken over or started many businesses in New York City and elsewhere.

Second, even immigrants who did not come with middle-class incomes and skills have escaped poverty via retailing, just as many did in the European immigration. Whether or not they had retailing experience at home, some found a niche in the ethnic and foreign-language enclaves that always supply many business opportunities until the newcomers speak English, and are ready to eat more American food and use other American goods as well. In addition, they have developed, or brought over, family and mutual-aid organization networks which provide small amounts of capital and/or large amounts of cheap labor—notably other family members—to help them. None of this is new, either, however.[12]

What may be new is their attitude and practice with respect to children's education, for I have the impression that far larger proportions are encouraging their children to obtain educations than was true among their peers in the original European immigration. If this is the case, it is probably a result both of the economy into which they are coming, and its great difference from the economy into which the Europeans came seventy to one hundred years ago. Moreover, fewer may be encouraging their children to stay in retailing, but we do not know either whether this is true, or what their children will actually do as adults. Probably more of the children of the European immigrants than we now think wanted to escape the long hours of petty retailing for less onerous and more interesting jobs, but they may not have had alternative opportunities.[13]

Third, today's immigrants have come into an America in which education is available everywhere, while at the turn of the century, it was still a scarce resource. After all, fewer than 5 percent of all Americans then graduated from high school. Consequently, more of today's immigrants may be sending their children to school even if they came from peasant backgrounds, either because of changed American conditions, or because they already wanted education for them in their home countries. In that sense, the peasant-urban distinction I made for the old immigration may no longer be as relevant, or not relevant at all.

Fourth, the same myth about the educational superiority of some new arrivals that developed in connection with the European immigration is developing now; for currently, Southeast Asians are today's Jews. Indeed, as Chinese, Japanese, Taiwanese, and Korean children win the national science prizes that once went in abnormally high proportions to Jewish children, new theories are being spun about why the Southeast Asians do so well in school—and by the same token, do so well in the economy. Eventually, most of these theories will be proven inaccurate, but in the meantime, the many children from these ethnic groups who are not doing well in school, and who are laggards in math and science, are forgotten— just as the poor school performers among the Jews were forgotten the last time.

Fifth, almost all the newcomers have nonblack skins, and except for the Haitians and some other Central and Latin American newcomers, suffer none of the stigma and other pains that America inflicts on blacks. Consequently, their economic mobility will not be held back for racial reasons. Concurrently, and like all the other immigrants who ever came to America, they benefit from their willingness to work longer hours for less pay than Americans. What will happen to their children, who will be American, and therefore eager to work for shorter hours and higher pay, is another matter, and some or many will join tomorrow's poor. Meanwhile, however, most of the black newcomers, save some of the West Indians, suffer from discrimination and segregation, and presumably, so will their Americanized children, many of whom can also expect to be poor.

The other shortcoming of the original essay, its concentration on manufacturing jobs, is more difficult to deal with. While the new service jobs which are to some extent replacing the disappearing factory work do not necessarily require higher skills, many do require more basic language and math literacy. In addition, employers demand at least a high school diploma, if in part only to screen out young people from low-income and especially black low-income homes. Thus, the need for poor children to go to school if they are to be employed later is greater than ever, and their reasons for not going, or for not performing adequately enough, become all the more tragic.

For me, the new economic context offers several lessons. One is that the basic thesis of the original paper remains accurate; for fifteen years after it was written, dropout rates have gone down slightly but learning rates are not keeping up well enough with the higher demands of the labor market and of employers.

Another lesson stems from the long-term complaint of urban office employers that too many of the young people who apply for entry-level clerical and technical jobs are too poorly educated to be hired, and these complaints will increase if the projected labor shortage of the 1990s becomes a real one. Job shortages, and all other kinds of demands for labor from poor people are all to the good, for they should communicate to younger children that the economy wants them, and that therefore education has direct instrumental value. Whether this idea is being communicated is not clear, because at this writing in spring 1990, other messages are coming through as well: that many employers and most unions that discriminated in the past still do so, that some old job ceilings still apply to blacks, and that immigrants who work longer hours for less money are taking black jobs. As a result, many children in ghetto schools are still going through the same self-destructive but otherwise rational rejection of schooling.

A further lesson, the third in this list, is that the roles people learn to cope with poverty and all its emotional side effects do not disappear just because of projected labor shortages. Evidently, children, and the street culture in which school dropouts and pushouts learn, need more and longer proof that conditions have improved, although we do not know what kinds of proof of what duration are needed. Poor people have good reason not to change their ways instantly, for they do not want to suffer additional disappointments and frustrations. Nor will they change their ways just because the rest of society demands it, and while the nonpoor do not change their ways any faster, they are not constantly being asked to do so before being deemed eligible for jobs.

The good side of a tight labor market is that there may be more pressure on the schools to try harder, and to pay more for better teachers working in smaller classes. Equally important, there is also pressure on the business community to get into the educational act and try to make up for the shortcomings of the educational system. While business has no special skills at education, it does know how to do job training, and perhaps necessity will enable it to find ways of job training that work well with poor dropouts —and that may even feed back into the future practices of educational system. To be sure, optimism must be restrained here, and the business community complaints about a functionally illiterate labor force are not new. Moreover, in the past many urban employers have eventually moved out of the city, either into lily-white suburbs, or into other parts of the country where labor is cheaper and white skinned as well. Whether this—or anything else—has changed is not yet clear. Also, as time passes, the children of the new immigrants, now Americanized, may be available for the clerical and technical jobs that would otherwise go to blacks, and blacks, now joined by Puerto Ricans, will be shunted aside once more.

Consequently, the need for government to do something about enhancing the economic security of today's nonimmigrant poor remains as urgent as it was when I wrote the original essay. Moreover, the needed programs have not changed much since the 1930s, when the Roosevelt administration created jobs for the unskilled by rebuilding and adding to the country's infrastructure, building schools, libraries, roads, and bridges, as well as draining rivers and repairing harbors. Much of what was built during that period and subsequently has been poorly maintained in recent decades and needs rebuilding or modernization—and will provide many jew jobs.

In the old days, these jobs would have been for men only but now that so much construction work is mechanized, many can employ women too. In addition, there are other "building" jobs that have traditionally gone to women but can be done by men as well. The most necessary is the rebuilding of non-physical infrastructures, and my favorite example is the revamping of the schools—to be accomplished by the hiring of additional teachers and other staff to make possible the establishment of truly small classrooms in the public schools, especially those serving the poor.

There are many other ways to create jobs; these are discussed at greater length in the next essay. From the point of view of this essay, the most important jobs are those intended for unskilled and semiskilled people who are trying to establish an economic base in the economy and obtain enough security for themselves and their children that the children will find reason to go to school, strengthen that base, and use education to find better jobs.

Creating work for poor people, many of whom have not held proper jobs for a long period or for their whole lives, is a difficult venture, and the initial failure rate will be high. Still, there is a famous precedent, which also employed the seemingly unemployable, and which worked because it had to: the war effort of World War II. Then the urgency was immediate and cost was no object, two advantages that do not exist today. Still, if today's poor are not integrated into the labor force now, they may never be, because the new immigrants and their children can fill all the vacant slots— and there are many more people all over the world who are ready to join this wave of immigration, or start the next one.

· F I F T E E N ·

PLANNING FOR A
LABOR-INTENSIVE
ECONOMY

L ONG-RANGE PLANNING or social policymaking ought to concern itself
with three kinds of topics: (1) seemingly permanent goals and long-
lasting problems; (2) goals and problems for which programs can only be
developed in the future; and (3) goals and problems that will have to be
dealt with in the future but that should be put on the public agenda now.

Unemployment seems to me to fit into each of the three topics; in
addition, it is also a current problem for too many Americans. Even though
the official unemployment rate has been so low in the late 1980s that
joblessness is not a salient political issue, it can become one very quickly
again. Furthermore, as I have pointed out before, I assume that it will
eventually become a major societal problem. When computers and robots
reach their full potential, and when the spread of industrialization in the
Third World creates many more countries with low-wage labor, America—
and Western Europe—will most likely develop a permanent shortage of
jobs. Indeed, today's persistently jobless are the first victims of the future
work shortage.

A completely rewritten version of "Jobs and Services: Toward a Labor-Intensive Economy,"
reprinted with permission of M. E. Sharpe, Inc. 80 Business Park Drive, Armonk, New York
10504 USA, from the July/August 1977 issue of *Challenge*.

Although economists like to treat labor (other than their own) as one of many commodities, long-term and permanent unemployment is an economic disaster—not only for the jobless and their families but also for their communities, and often their regions.

In addition, joblessness is a personal, social, and political disaster. It makes people feel useless and causes them to lose their self-respect, which quickly has social effects for it can lead to family breakup, as well as depression, mental illness, and alcoholism. Then too, joblessness means more crime and delinquency, although too few public officials make that connection. Last but not least, unemployment helps to support the drug industry, for the clinical depression induced by joblessness is probably responsible for much of the demand for the escapist effects produced by drugs.

The political effects of unemployment are less visible but equally dangerous, because they often disenfranchise the people so affected. For understandable reasons, the unemployed have little faith in politics and are especially difficult to organize or to persuade to vote. Also, joblessness is usually highest among the poor and the minorities who already vote and participate otherwise less than the more affluent even when they have jobs. Moreover, they remain numerical minorities in the electorate and, in the absence of third parties, are virtually captive voters for the Democrats, who can therefore pay less attention to their demands. Consequently, probably the most important political force with respect to unemployment are the working- and middle-class people who are employed, especially in good jobs, but who are fearful of losing those jobs.

The possibility of future unemployment comes at a time when the number of Americans who want to work is still rising, in part because of inflation, in part because women are attracted to the labor force by the good jobs now open to some of them. In any case, the so-called Protestant work ethic is not disappearing, for it is a nearly universal social and psychological imperative that has nothing to do with religion. Working is one ticket by which adults are admitted to membership in society so that they can obtain the crucial feeling of being socially useful. That feeling is in turn essential for self-respect and emotional well-being—at least until substitutes for these social functions of work are created.

At the same time, increasing numbers of Americans want satisfying jobs, and as educational levels rise, so do the numbers who want a career rather than just a series of jobs. In the past, work was, for many more people than today, only a means to an end, a way of financing family life and other "outside" activities; but since about the 1970s, many people have looked for the kind of job satisfaction that only a small minority of the labor force, notably professionals, could hitherto achieve.

THE LABOR-INTENSIVE ECONOMY

IF I am correct that we are at the start of a permanent job shrinkage, two possible types of solutions seem most relevant. One is *worksharing*, the reduction of work time by everyone to save and create jobs for the jobless, which will be discussed in the next chapter. The other, and more important one, is to figure out how to change the economy so that it produces many more jobs. Familiar solutions like higher productivity may also be useful, but only if that productivity does not result in more machines and fewer jobs. To put it into a nutshell, there must be an end to the long-term American romance with productivity at all costs, and industrialism's affair with labor-saving devices, whether in manufacturing or in service industries. The long-term solution, and the challenge for long-range planning, is to move the economy from its present capital-intensive direction toward a more labor-intensive one, and to do so in a world economy that needs to be but cannot easily be persuaded to move in the same direction.

I am not for Luddite policies to smash any machines, or for dismantling the tractor to bring back pick-and-shovel jobs. Nor do I believe that small is necessarily beautiful. Instead, I think planners of all kinds must figure out how to change the structure of the economy and the behavior of those who run it so as to replace the singlemindedly capital-intensive thrust and the reasons for its existence. Then productivity and economic health can be redefined in terms of the number of jobs saved or created, rather than simply GNP or per-capita wealth. Elected officials actually apply this definition all the time, at least when they are defending their constituencies against reductions in local military spending—but they have time to think only in terms of ad hoc Band-Aid solutions. The Full Employment acts of the 1940s and 1970s were steps in the right direction, but they also stopped or were stopped at the level of jobs, while legislation to plan how more people could be employed productively and in decent jobs was not approved by the federal government.

At this writing, when the official unemployment rate is at around 5 percent, joblessness receives little public attention, but even when the unemployment rate was higher, the idea of moving from a capital-intensive toward labor-intensive economy received very little discussion. Perhaps the idea is too impractical, because by itself such an economy cannot survive in a capital-intensive world economy, but perhaps too many people still remember when the American economy was much more labor-intensive than it is today, or they see the countries of the Third World where such economies still persist and spell much poverty, very low standards of living, and a lot of backbreaking work.

What I have in mind is obviously something very different: a "postindustrial" form of labor intensiveness, in which the dirty, backbreaking, and most boring jobs that can be done by machines are made capital-intensive, and more decent labor-intensive jobs are invented at the same time. It may be that the times are not yet ripe for such an approach, partly because joblessness is not yet viewed as a serious problem, but also because we must first end the worship of the machine and the celebration of all new technology.

Furthermore, too few people—intellectuals and others—have thought very much about how their work, or work in general, should be changed. For one thing, too many people are still trying to move from a series of jobs to careers; for another, too many others are dissatisfied less with their work than with their bosses or workplaces. As a result, work-related aspirations have not dealt with the nature of work but with fantasies about a leisure-filled life free from work. For these and other reasons, the political culture that would support movement toward a labor-intensive economy does not yet exist.

However, this need not discourage economic and social planners from starting to think about such an economy: how it would function; what new problems it would generate; what changes in manufacturing and service industries, and in their organization, it would require; and what kinds of workplace relations it would bring about. First and foremost, someone would have to think about whether and under what conditions a labor-intensive economy—or how much of one—is feasible, especially at a time when the United States no longer plays a dominating role in the world economy, and can no longer call its own economic shots.

Perhaps the basic idea is not even viable without a drastically reorganized political economy, because at times it seems as if the machines, or rather the financial and industrial organizations that oversee the use of machines have created a dynamic that cannot easily be ended. For example, if it is certain that machines almost always produce more and make less trouble than workers for those who own and manage the economic institutions, then everything that can be computerized or robotized will be, save some of the functions of the owners and managers themselves, and the more so in a world economy where individual national economies survive best by maximal cost cutting. In that case, an economic counter-dynamic and the political forces to empower it are much harder to imagine.

Still, there is such a counter-dynamic: people's need for work to feed and house themselves and their families, and the needs of economic organizations to have customers who can afford to buy their wares. In the very long run, these factors suggest that eventually the world economy is going to have to cope with the shortage of jobs, and *that* argument justifies both the goal of, and the planning for, a labor-intensive economy.

FIRST STEPS

THE BASIC planning issues can be divided into two. One is how to find and use the relevant economic and political mechanisms to slow down the capital-intensive thrust of the economy; the other is to figure out how to create new jobs, and the economic demands and arrangements for them. The latter is more difficult, in part because it is impossible to predict what kinds of goods and services that lead to labor-intensive work people will demand in the future when many new jobs will be needed. Indeed, all I can do is to suggest what might be done if the job shrinkage were at hand today. However, such an analysis is also useful as a way of thinking of new jobs for today's jobless and allegedly unemployable people.

Obstacles to the spread of the machines are easy to propose, but hard to implement. The most obvious policy is to remove all remaining tax incentives and other programs that encourage the building of more labor-saving machines, especially when labor-intensive solutions can be proposed instead. These can be encouraged further with tax benefits for employers, and if wages are not competitive, with wage supports for the affected workers as well. Outright tax and other sanctions against needless further automation might also be considered, although such a policy can easily become Luddite if it prevents the building, say, of computers that create more jobs than than they replace, or of machines that provide other benefits, such as the prevention and cure of dangerous disease.[1] A somewhat different approach would be to discourage the export of jobs other than those that native or immigrant Americans will not take, although this will probably require import duties and other protectionist devices that will have other costs. Putting obstacles in the way of low-wage countries is not to our advantage since they and their workers may also constitute markets for our goods and services.

In an era in which the government will be required to cut back the military, it may also be asked to end the traditional American practice of using defense as an employment opportunity. As long as there was sufficient political support for the cold war, the defense effort was the easiest and fastest political method for job creation, but if this era has ended, conversion analysts should be able to show that building new weapons is not the most efficient or cheapest job-creation mechanism. The defense industry is now highly capital-intensive, and far more jobs can be created in civilian enterprises for the same number of dollars—although it may take time to persuade the voters of this fact, and to reduce the power of the many interests that have developed around defense spending.

NEW SERVICES AND JOBS

STILL, THE primary challenge, and purpose, of this exercise is to try to create new services and goods that in turn create new jobs, and enrich the quality of life as well. Indeed, the enrichment goal is essential, or else the monies for the goods and services to be supplied by private enterprise, or the taxes for those to be supplied by government, will not come forth.

Whether the goods and services, and of course the jobs, are created by private enterprise or government—or whether they are created jointly to spread the risk—makes no difference from an employment perspective. In fact, the two can learn from each other. While government can supply start-up funds and set standards, private enterprise, which is good at smelling out marketable new goods and services, can help government in this respect; for if new public services are to be approved by taxpayers, they must be even more marketable than those established to make a profit.[2] Actually, the more useful the voters find the services with which they are supplied, the less antagonistic some will be to paying the needed taxes— even if it is very important never to overestimate the willingness of Americans to pay new taxes, what they say to pollsters to the contrary notwithstanding.

Job creation of the kind under discussion here involves the talents not only of planners but also of inventors, marketers, utopian thinkers, as well as socially oriented poets and artists.[3] In fact, people with such talents might someday come up with a way of eliminating jobs, especially the unsatisfying ones no one wants to do, as long as they can also invent substitutes for the social and psychological, as well as the economic functions of work so that people can support themselves and keep themselves busy.

The most easily imagined kind of labor-intensive work is infrastructural. Every new generation needs to repair and add to the *built* infrastructure, although such work is often postponed until enough serious accidents generate enough political outcries to force a start. Nevertheless, many jobs could be created to rebuild and add to the number of roads, bridges, highways, mass-transit systems (in some places), as well as to clean up and where relevant desilt rivers, lakes, and other bodies of water. Such jobs are very important because they will provide work—and training—for unskilled and semiskilled workers who now suffer most from joblessness. However, the jobs must be supplied in large enough numbers so that they cannot be performed by existing workers—and so that the latter can function as trainers and supervisors for the unskilled.

Many of these jobs will go to men, although they can also be done by women. Conversely, a different kind of infrastructural work would probably attract mainly women: to "rebuild" and modernize the data bases and records of local government, other public agencies, and even nonprofit ones, which cannot afford to computerize or otherwise modernize their records.

The majority of these jobs may be temporary, which means that they have to be so organized as to provide entry-level experience for large numbers of workers, and also to supply job training and later retraining so that as many of these workers as possible can later find jobs elsewhere in the economy.[4]

A related enterprise is work on the *environmental* infrastructure, and some of the above-mentioned building jobs will also help to clean up the environment. Others, such as replacing present oil-, gasoline-, and nuclear-energy systems will require new machines which do not create new jobs, but in many cities, electrically or otherwise energized micro–mass-transit systems, i.e., vans and jitneys, might mean more jobs even as they reduce automobile congestion.

Still, the most important environmentally relevant job-creating device may be to encourage people to shift to a new kind of small farming, which would fit neither the old family farm nor the totally commercial or giant industrial farm models—and which would strictly eschew any temptation toward pastoral romanticism. Above all, such farming would have to minimize the physical hardness and economic uncertainty that helped drive many people off the farms in the last hundred years, not always willingly. Also, it would need to be sufficiently mechanized to encourage people to want to try farming, making sure that there are enough cooperative work arrangements to eliminate the traditional isolation of the small farm, and to enable the farmers and their families to maintain whatever contact they wanted with urban/suburban America.

Many other kinds of new jobs can be "imagined." In the Great Depression, the Roosevelt administration's WPA established a precedent especially for additions to the *educational* and *cultural* infrastructure: that agency built schools, libraries, and community centers, among other things. Today the need is not for educational buildings but for new kinds of educational arrangements and services. All else being equal, students learn better in small classes than in big ones, something that the private schools serving the rich learned long ago. Perhaps some of the obstacles to educating the poor would be overcome by very small classrooms, where teachers could supply individual attention—and might put an end to the destructive expectation that the poor cannot learn. Children from working- and middle-class homes are also entitled to small classrooms; think of all the jobs that could be created in this way—for master teachers, assistant teachers, and trainees. In addition, one can imagine neighborhood libraries that stay open afternoons and nights for children who want to do their homework there, or who want to call on librarians for the help they cannot get at home.

In the 1930s, the WPA also hired writers and artists to add to the country's culture, and some similar efforts would be desirable today, on cultural and employment grounds. For example, most public art is now created by so-called serious, i.e., high-culture, artists, and sometimes their work is not popular with the community for which it has been created. Be that as it may, a case can be made for more pluralism in public art. For example, some very talented poor youngsters who are not selected for formal artistic training have developed their own art world, creating often unfairly maligned graffiti. Most graffiti may not deserve to be called public art, but some of it is very good, and its artists ought to be given paid work to create community and neighborhood public art like other artists. Yet further public art needs to respect the still very popular romantic style I think of as capitalist realism, which is associated with Norman Rockwell, for example.

Today, a case can also be made for additions to the *recreational* infrastructure, for example, the construction of swimming pools, and lakes where there is room, the adapting of rivers for swimming and boating, and the opening up of more forests and wilderness areas to reduce the ever-increasing overload on the national parks.

As the population ages, it travels and vacations more; but big and small cities, as well as their business communities, have already noticed the tourist dollars to be made from older Americans. Some economically declining or even dying cities can become museum towns that draw tourists, and can thereby save and create jobs for people who have a specially difficult time in the job market. I would also like to see government provide start-up funds for traveling circuses, carnivals, and community theaters and music halls that provide alternative entertainment to movies and television, but at the same time create jobs and train some of the next generation's movie and television entertainers.

Furthermore, there is good reason to add to what could be called the *helping* infrastructure. Even now, it is clear that in order to bring poor and other mothers into the labor force, a nearly completely new day-care industry will need to be invented. Equally urgent is the upgrading of the already existing informal day-care industry. The grandmothers, other relatives, and neighbors who now take cake of children can in most cases use both advice and extra money so that they can turn what they do into informal kinds of jobs.

Another industry badly in need of some revamping is the medical one. I suspect many people, and insurance companies, would be pleased if the government helped to establish an entirely new stratum of medical technicians—who would of course need a more prestigious name—but who would supply the routine medical service that most people need most of the time, and who would make house calls as well. If such technicians were trained to treat patients as people and not merely as sick bodies, and worked out of medical centers and clinics with the same approach, conventional doctors and hospitals might lose their present monopoly.

Along the same lines, Americans in need of routine temporary therapy —and of help in resolving routine conflicts with family members or neighbors—could use low-cost mental health clinics, again with a different name, which would combine some of the skills of the mental health profession with those of trained counselors or ministers as well as arbitrators. New jobs would be created alongside the better care, although some cults and pseudo-therapeutic movements would lose some adherents.

With an aging population and longer life expectancy, another kind of day-care industry will have to be established, providing home care for those who can no longer take care of themselves or do not want to move into nursing homes. Today's nursing homes are highly labor-intensive places, but for cost and other reasons, the care that can be given is often not tender or loving, and the worst nursing homes merely store the aged until they die. Many improvements are obvious, all of them involving new jobs —but of course new costs as well.

Finally, there is work to be done in the *bureaucratic* infrastructure, both of the government and the workplace. There must be a way to create more user-friendly bureaucracies—even if no new jobs result—for example, if there were more incentives to provide services, and fewer to find cheaters or develop unnecessarily adversarial relations. That might increase productivity in workplaces, which might indirectly create more jobs. For example, the IRS would clearly collect more taxes if it could learn to act in a more user-friendly fashion.

I have long felt that small local communities needed a few extra paid jobs, such as running the largest or most service-giving voluntary associations. Parents might relate better to their children's schools if they were helped and represented by a parental union which had one or more paid staff, for example, especially in communities where the PTA only represents the school's interests. On the national level, I favor what I think of as people's lobbies, which do for ordinary people in a variety of roles what corporate and professional lobbies do for their clients.[5]

The preceding analysis has been limited mainly to services, but a parallel one could be undertaken for the invention of goods that would create new jobs. Here private enterprise would have a much larger role, and government aid, including funds, would not be needed except for start-up loans that families cannot and banks will not fund.

In the last fifty years, commercial enterprises have been most adept at discovering new goods that people want to buy and turning their innovations into mass-produced goods. Then, about twenty five years ago, people with enough disposable income began to demand goods that are not mass-produced, which creates a fertile area for new jobs of all kinds, from finding and renovating old mass-produced goods that have suddenly become collectibles to baking and distributing kinds of breads once found only in isolated European villages. The jobs potential of American popular culture and its constantly changing fads and fashions seems nearly bottomless.

Inventing new jobs is easier than figuring out who will pay for them, and it is possible that maximizing the number of jobs has less to do with new goods and services than with finding the right economic structures. Perhaps smaller workplaces or more worker participation will generate more productivity to offset the economy of scale of the ever-larger private firms and public agencies that now dominate the economy and will presumably be even bigger in the future if nothing is done. Some people may even want to turn hobbies into small-scale commercial production, especially if they can combine it with working few hours a week in a bureaucratic workplace.

Many other questions about the possibilities—and problems—of greater labor-intensivity can and should be raised. This is beyond my expertise; my argument is limited to suggesting that it is time to start thinking about the possibility of a more labor-intensive economy, both on a national and international scale. That such an economy is now impractical is obvious; that it must always be so cannot now be proven or denied. Perhaps it cannot work, ever, but would it be proper to say that today's capital-intensive economy is working? An economy that has long depended on military expenditures for creating new jobs and at the same time condemns an increasing number of people to living on the dole and to hustling in the underground economy cannot be described as even muddling through.

· S I X T E E N ·

TOWARD THE THIRTY-TWO-HOUR WORKWEEK: AN ANALYSIS OF WORKSHARING

I F AND WHEN the computer, the robot, and the increasing number of low-wage Third World countries cause a serious reduction in the number of jobs in the U.S., new ways of dealing with the job shortage will be demanded—and will have to be supplied—at once. One of the new solutions for reducing high unemployment is *worksharing,* the reduction of work hours to spread the existing work so that old jobs are saved and new jobs are created because everyone is working less.[1]

Worksharing can take the form of shorter workdays, workweeks, work-years—i.e., longer vacations—but it can also be achieved through maternal and other leaves and by sabbaticals.[2] If necessary, the later entrance of young people into the labor force as well as earlier retirement can also be used as work-time reduction devices, but of course only at the expense of specific age-groups. Whatever the policy, however, all that is necessary is that enough people give up enough work time to justify the saving of old and the creation of new jobs.[3]

The idea is not a new one; in the U.S., union leader Samuel Gompers

Reprinted, with many revisions, from *Social Policy* (Winter 1985), pp. 58–61. The original article was a response to a call for the thirty-two-hour week by Roy Bennett in the Summer 1985 issue of *Social Policy.*

campaigned for the eight-hour day in the late nineteenth century as a way of creating more jobs, while early in the Great Depression, then Senator Hugo Black joined with Representative Connery on legislation to institute the thirty-hour week. FDR vetoed the idea at that time, but revived it as a forty-hour week late in the 1930s, after which interest in worksharing lay dormant until the automation scare of the 1960s.[4]

In the U.S., interest in the idea died out as soon as that scare ended, but in Europe it did not, at least among union leaders and scholars. During the 1970s, a vast research and political literature began to appear around work-time reduction, and in the mid 1980s, during a period of double-digit joblessness, the discussions of the previous decade produced action. Specifically, several Western European countries began to move toward a shorter workweek, the immediate target being thirty-six hours. But for a variety of reasons noted later, they got no further than thirty-eight or thirty-nine hours. Only Sweden has been able to cut work time significantly, less through workweek reductions than through a variety of leaves, so that annual work hours there are now about a quarter lower than they are in the U.S. It may be no coincidence that Swedish unemployment rates have been the lowest in the world, generally hovering around 2 to 3 percent.

No one can now predict when worksharing will be needed in the U.S. and other modern countries, but when the time comes, that policy will be needed quickly, and it will work more effectively the more countries adopt it together. In any case, systematic policy as well as political discussion of the idea ought to begin now, especially in the U.S., where worksharing has never even yet become a topic of academic discussion.

The discussion of, and research into, worksharing, ought to be positive, but above all it has to be practical and hardheaded, for like every social policy, it has both faults and virtues.

THE PROBLEMS OF WORKSHARING

First, worksharing creates fewer jobs than imagined. Although the thirty-two week is a 20 percent reduction in work hours from the forty-hour week, it cannot supply an equivalent proportion of new jobs. It would preserve some jobs now subject to elimination and create others by spreading the work, but altogether a 20-percent decrease in work time would probably save or add only 8 to 10 percent more jobs at best—although this is still a far better record than any other unemployment policy has yet achieved.

Because work-time reduction involves hiring more workers for the same amount of work, every firm would pay additional fringe benefits while also incurring higher costs in the hiring, screening, and turnover of employees. As a result, firms that have cut work hours have normally encouraged or required higher productivity, resorted to overtime, and found other ways of minimizing the number of new hires.[5] Proper legislation to regulate overtime and some government subsidy can counteract this tendency somewhat, and an 8-percent job-maintenance or -creation figure would bring about a noticeable drop in the unemployment rates. Nonetheless, even a more drastic cut in the workweek might someday be needed, or a combination of workweek and other reductions—although work-time reduction cannot by itself bring about full employment. In fact, it can only be effective as part of a more comprehensive set of job-saving and job-creating approaches.

Second, a proper worksharing policy is a costly proposition. To be sure, low-cost versions are available, for example those that require workers to take cuts in wages and fringe benefits proportional to the amount of work-time reduction. Indeed, such a policy was used by the Hoover administration.[6] Worksharing *without* wage and fringe-benefit cuts, which seems to me the only desirable and politically viable idea, will, however, increase the total wage bill of every firm. Some firms may not be able to pay it; others will refuse, finding it cheaper to automate or send the jobs abroad. This is probably the major problem of work sharing, and one that cannot be solved easily.

The problem will be less serious if a thirty-two-hour week—to use it as an example—is phased in on a one-hour-a-year basis, and might virtually solve itself over time. More likely, some employers will have to receive compensatory benefits for their higher wage costs. One possibility is shifting some fringe-benefit costs to other funding sources, for example, by instituting a national health service. Another possibility is to levy special taxes on the firms that cause the need for worksharing in the first place: those that replace workers with machines or send jobs out of the country. Taxing the profits they derive from firing American workers would either discourage them from doing so or help pay for worksharing. Of course, they might then be encouraged to leave the United States entirely, which is another reason why worksharing must eventually be an international solution. Firms that produce consumer goods and must have customers who can afford to buy them will have a special incentive in helping to pay the costs of worksharing. Most likely, a variety of methods must be used to deal with this worksharing problem.

Third, workers may not be as enthusiastic about worksharing as policy designers, at least until they see what it means to their incomes. For workers, a reduced workweek without a reduction in pay is an hourly wage-rate increase in which the pay increase has been exchanged for free time. As such, it is a time-for-money trade-off. In good economic times, a sizable number of American and European workers have indicated their interest in such a trade-off both in actual choices made and in polls.[7] In bad times, however, workers want to maximize the money in their pockets. Other workers, particularly young ones with growing families, can use more free time to be with their children, but they also need a maximal paycheck even more urgently and might thus be unenthusiastic about work-time reduction. A concurrent family-allowance program would solve some of *their* problems.

Conversely, older workers may oppose worksharing because it abrogates the privileges of seniority. In fact, American unions have been strong defenders of the seniority principle, and have, therefore, been traditionally less interested in protecting the rights of junior workers. As a result, too many unions have been unenthusiastic about worksharing. Moreover, new ways of preserving seniority have to be found that do not endanger the jobs of young workers, partly because some of them can now demand protection under affirmative action laws. Even so, a good deal of political and ideological work needs to be done, and corollary policies to counteract the problems of worksharing developed, in order to obtain support for worksharing from unions and their members as well as from nonunion workers—blue, pink, and white collar.

Fourth, the political paths and processes for implementing a thirty-two-hour week have to be charted. While an hour-a-year reduction in the workweek may not create too much political or economic stir, it might also fail to generate enough political enthusiasm. On the other hand, instituting a thirty-two-hour week at once would be a highly visible political issue that could someday obtain ready support—if and when unemployment itself becomes a viable political issue. The Black-Connery Thirty-Hour-Week bill passed the U.S. Senate in the spring of 1933, but FDR evidently thought it too radical a measure, for he had it tabled in the House of Representatives, even though its members were ready to approve it.[8] At that time, many employers were already practicing unilateral worksharing, by putting everyone on short hours and short pay to boot. A government worksharing bill would probably have helped both employers and workers. Even so, a sharp workweek reduction is a traumatic step for everyone, and staged reductions are a much better approach.

Other scenarios can and should be developed and discussed. One approach would be to initiate a set of diverse worksharing schemes alongside, or instead of, the annual one-hour reduction. In the United States, worksharing can also proceed by extending the annual vacation, still often only two weeks, to the four or six weeks most European workers have long enjoyed. Another possibility is to begin worksharing in parts of the economy. In the mid-1980s, the Belgian and Dutch governments took the lead and, hoping to act as role models, limited new government jobs to thirty-two hours a week initially. In effect, both countries were establishing a temporary two-tier work-time and pay system.

A different alternative would be to begin in industries with high unemployment rates, which would also target jobs more directly to the jobless. However, because such industries are economically weak already, a thirty-two-hour workweek would have to be accompanied by some government subsidies, probably to both workers and employers.

Furthermore, legal and legislative questions about the power of government to reduce the workweek must be answered. The Black-Connery bill simply forbade interstate or foreign commerce involving goods not produced under a thirty-hour-a-week schedule; the 1938 Fair Labor Standards Act required overtime wage premiums in interstate commerce after forty hours, thus encouraging the forty-hour workweek that became a reality after World War II. Whether the U.S. government can and should go beyond interstate commerce regulation must be answered by lawyers — but also by economists, particularly because of some possible dysfunctional economic effects of worksharing that will also impinge on enforcement. For example, small firms and highly labor-intensive ones beset by foreign competition will have special difficulties with work-time reduction, and seasonal industries must be exempted altogether. The policy can probably not even be enforced in small firms, and there is no way by which self-employed individuals and family firms — including the mom-and-pop food store — can be made to cut back their work time, although social and social-life pressures to conform to mainstream work hours would eventually make the thirty-two-hour workweek nigh universal.

Fifth, and last, is the development of the necessary political consensus. In many European countries, where labor, management, and the government sit down together to shape economic policy, that consensus is comparatively easily achieved, although what was true in the past may not apply to the future. In 1984, the West German steel and printing industry unions had to strike for a thirty-five-hour workweek, which ended in a virtual defeat for them and a settlement at thirty-nine hours.

In the United States, many major political obstacles need to be overcome. One is the powerlessness of the unemployed. Their numbers are small; they are dispersed over the country in urban and regional pockets; and many are black or Hispanic. Most likely, a consensus to do something about unemployment will not develop until the threat of joblessness scares a far larger number of people, particularly white breadwinners all over the country. However, even if and when that were to happen, these breadwinners may not want to share the work with racial minorities or with the many people involuntarily stuck in part-time jobs.

Worksharing faces two further political obstacles. The first is its current, almost total, invisibility. Another, perhaps more tenacious, obstacle is that worksharing is a pessimistic policy that, in effect, admits that economic growth will not return, and that new jobs cannot be created in sufficient number by other means. In the early 1980s, when U.S. joblessness had reached 10 percent, Ronald Reagan was able to persuade many Americans that economic growth could return—and it did return, even though at the price of an enormous growth in the federal debt and a huge deficit. In effect, the Reagan administration maintained the myth of magical economic growth, and it will take some time to persuade Americans that economic growth cannot always be turned on when needed.

Conversely, worksharing also contains some optimistic qualities, at least on paper, for it is the first step toward the age-old vision of liberating men and women from long hours on the job, drudgery, and dirty work. That vision has appealed to utopians over many centuries and, as it becomes more necessary, it should appeal to many others as well. No one knows now, however, whether a society in which work is not dominant is even workable. Although additional leisure-time activities will readily appear, work is today a major means for being socially useful, obtaining a place in the social structure, and maintaining social and emotional health. Substitutes for these functions of work still have to be invented. Also, the utopian vision must be amended to find ways of providing people with sufficient economic security and income, which will surely require fundamental changes in the economy that have not yet been considered in capitalist or socialist thought.[9]

SHORT-TERM WORKSHARING AND PUBLIC WORKS

THE THIRTY-TWO-HOUR week, or any other work-time reduction policy must be complemented by two other policies. One is short-term worksharing, usually called Short Time Compensation (STC), in which work-time reduction replaces layoffs. Typically, the workweek is reduced to four days under STC, with unemployment insurance funds paying the fifth day's wage or salary.[10]

STC is best suited to temporary economic downturns and appeals especially to firms eager to hold on to trained workers during these downturns. STC was first tried in Western Europe in the 1920s and is a standard policy now in most European countries. Its use is normally capped, typically for twenty or twenty-six weeks, but that cap can be lengthened during especially difficult times, and it can be eliminated altogether, at which point temporary worksharing turns into the permanent kind.

STC has not caught on in the U.S., though it is employed in a handful of states, and at one point in the mid-1980s, it looked as if it might become a popular policy to deal with temporary joblessness. At that time, Rep. Patricia Schroeder of Colorado took an active interest in it, but no one else ever joined her in Washington. Still, the policy is available, and has been well enough tested and researched in Europe that all its advantages and disadvantages are known and can be taken into account here if and when its time comes.

The other policy, which is absolutely essential as a backup to worksharing, is direct job creation, particularly through public works. Given the sociological realities of unemployment in America and the very real possibility that many of the employed might oppose legislation to share the work with many of the unemployed, other job opportunities for the latter must be available. Public works schemes have many additional advantages that need not be recited here, but they must also be designed to create work for those who lack the political power to benefit from the other job policies.

WORKSHARING AND THE FUTURE

Since worksharing is currently totally invisible in the U.S., it has also not become the political football that it became in Europe in the mid-1980s. Thus, it may be possible in the years to come to undertake research on how worksharing, or any other kind of work-time reduction, could be implemented here, what problems would be created by its implementation, and how these could be solved. As a result, tentative solutions might be found so that as feasible a policy as possible could be reduced for public discussion when and if worksharing becomes necessary.

Although it is impossible and not even desirable to isolate the idea and keep it from becoming controversial, no one would benefit if it were ground up in ideological battles, or tarred as either a management or a union idea, and a liberal or a conservative one, since it is inherently neither. Planners, policy analysts, and social scientists can do the necessary research and policy analysis, although general political support and even some funding from a variety of sources would help—and among other things to make the idea less invisible, too. For example, one of the major constituencies for worksharing—and for all full-employment policies—should be the huge consumer-goods–producing corporations, for they need to have a vital interest in any policy that provides income to their customers.

When the right economic and political time for worksharing arrives, it will surely arrive first in Europe before it becomes feasible here—and there will then be a further chance to learn from the European experience and adapt it to American conditions. Meanwhile, however, work-time reduction in all its varieties is a fertile concept for scholarly policy-oriented analysis!

· S E V E N T E E N ·

THE USES
OF POVERTY

I N THE LATE 1940s, Robert K. Merton applied the notion of functional analysis to explain the continuing existence of the much maligned urban political machine, for if it continued to exist, perhaps it fulfilled latent— unintended or unrecognized—positive functions.[1] Merton thought that it did. He pointed out how the machine provided central authority to get things done when a decentralized local government could not act, humanized the services of the impersonal bureaucracy for fearful citizens, offered concrete help (rather than abstract law or justice) to the poor, and otherwise performed services needed or demanded by many people but considered unconventional or even illegal by formal public agencies.

Today, poverty is more maligned than the political machine ever was: yet it, too, is a persistent social phenomenon. Consequently, there may be some merit in asking whether it also has positive functions that explain its persistence.[2]

Merton defined functions as "those observed consequences [of a phenomenon] which make for the adaptation or adjustment of a given [social] system." I shall use a slightly different definition; instead of identifying

Reprinted from *Social Policy,* March/April 1971. I have made some revisions to add clarity and to eliminate some jargon from the original version.

functions for an entire social system, I shall identify them for the interest groups, socioeconomic classes, and other population aggregates with shared values that "inhabit" a social system. I suspect that in a modern heterogeneous society, few phenomena are functional or dysfunctional for the society as a whole, and that most result in benefits to some groups and costs to others. Nor are any phenomena indispensable: in most instances, one can suggest what Merton calls "functional alternatives" or equivalents for them, i.e., other social patterns or policies that achieve the same positive functions but avoid the dysfunctions.[3]

Associating poverty with positive functions seems at first glance to be unimaginable. Of course, the slumlord and the loan shark are commonly known to profit from the existence of poverty, but they are viewed as evil men, so their activities are classified among the dysfunctions of poverty. However, what is less often recognized, at least by the conventional wisdom, is that poverty also makes possible the existence or expansion of respectable professions and occupations, for example, penology, criminology, social work, and public health. In the 1960s, the poor have provided jobs for professional and paraprofessional "poverty warriors," and for journalists and social scientists, this author included, who have supplied the information demanded by the revival of public interest in poverty that began in the 1960s, and again at the end of the 1980s.

Clearly, then, poverty and the poor may well satisfy a number of positive functions for many nonpoor groups in American society. I shall describe thirteen such functions—economic, social, and political—that seem to me most significant.

THE FUNCTIONS OF POVERTY

FIRST, THE EXISTENCE of poverty ensures that society's "dirty work" will be done. Every society has such work: physically dirty or dangerous, temporary, dead-end and underpaid, undignified and menial jobs. Society can fill these jobs by paying higher wages than for "clean" work, or it can force people who have no other choice to do the dirty work—and at low wages. In America, poverty functions to provide a low-wage labor pool that is willing—or rather, unable to be *un*willing—to perform dirty work at low cost. Indeed, this function of the poor is so important that in some southern states, welfare payments used to be cut off during the summer months when the poor were needed to work in the fields. Moreover, much of the political debate about the Negative Income Tax and the Family Assistance Plan of the 1960s concerned their impact on the work incentive, by which some government officials actually meant the incentive of the poor to do the needed dirty work if the wages therefrom were no larger than the income grant. Many economic activities that involve dirty work depend on the poor for their existence: restaurants, hospitals, nursing homes, parts of the garment industry, and fruit and vegetable farming, among others, could not persist in their present form without the poor.

Second, because the poor are required to work at low wages, they subsidize a variety of economic activities that benefit the affluent. For example, domestics subsidize the upper-middle and upper classes, making life easier for their employers and freeing the affluent for a variety of professional, cultural, civic, and partying activities. Similarly, because the poor pay a higher proportion of their income in property and sales taxes, among others, they subsidize many state and local-governmental services that benefit more affluent groups. In addition, the poor support innovation in medical practice as patients in teaching and research hospitals and as guinea pigs in medical experiments.

Third, poverty creates jobs for a number of occupations and professions that serve or "service" the poor, or protect the rest of society from them. As already noted, penology would be minuscule without the poor, as would the police. Other activities and groups that flourish because of the existence of poverty are the numbers game, the sale of drugs and cheap wines and liquors, pentecostal ministers, faith healers, prostitutes, pawnshops, and the peacetime army, which recruits many of its enlisted men from among the poor.

Fourth, the poor buy goods others do not want and thus prolong the economic usefulness of such goods—day-old bread, fruit and vegetables that would otherwise have to be thrown out, secondhand clothes, and deteriorating automobiles and buildings. They also provide incomes for doctors, lawyers, teachers, and others who are too old, poorly trained, or incompetent to attract more affluent clients.

In addition to economic functions, the poor perform a number of social functions.

Fifth, the poor can be identified and punished as alleged or real deviants in order to uphold the legitimacy of conventional norms. To justify the desirability of hard work, thrift, honesty, and monogamy, for example, the defenders of these norms must be able to find people who can be accused of being lazy, spendthrift, dishonest, and promiscuous. Although there is some evidence that most of the poor are as moral and law-abiding as everyone else, they may for economic and other reasons find it rational to live in common-law rather than formal marriage, and poor women may prefer to be single-parent family heads rather than marry men who cannot find work. In any case, the poor are more likely than middle-class transgressors to be caught and punished when they participate in deviant acts. Moreover, they lack the political and cultural power to correct the stereotypes that other people hold of them and thus continue to be thought of as lazy, spendthrift, etc., by those who need living proof that moral deviance does not pay.

Sixth, and conversely, the poor offer vicarious participation to the rest of the population in the uninhibited sexual, alcoholic, and narcotic behavior in which they are alleged to participate and which, being freed from the constraints of affluence, they are often thought to enjoy more that the middle classes. Thus many people, some social scientists included, believe that the poor not only are more given to uninhibited behavior (which may be true, although it is often motivated by despair more than by lack of inhibition) but derive more pleasure from it than affluent people (which research by Lee Rainwater, Walter Miller, and others shows to be patently untrue). However, whether the poor actually have more sex and enjoy it more is irrelevant. So long as middle-class people believe this to be true, they can participate in it vicariously when instances are reported in factual or fictional form.

Seventh, the poor also serve a direct cultural function when culture created by or for them is adopted by the more affluent. The rich collect artifacts from extinct folk cultures of poor people; and almost all Americans listen to the blues, spirituals, and country music, which originated among the southern poor. In the last twenty-five years they have enjoyed the rock styles that were born, like the music of the Beatles, in the slums. The poor also serve as culture heroes, particularly, of course, to the left; but the hobo, the cowboy, and the mythical prostitute with a heart of gold have performed this function for a variety of groups.

Eighth, poverty helps to guarantee the status of those who are not poor. In every hierarchical society someone has to be at the bottom; but in American society, in which social mobility is an important goal for many and people need to know where they stand, the poor function as a reliable and relatively permanent measuring rod for status comparisons. This is particularly true for the working class, which is concerned with the need to maintain status distinctions between themselves and the poor, much as the aristocracy must find ways of distinguishing itself from the nouveaux riches.

Ninth, the poor also aid the upward mobility of groups just above them in the class hierarchy. Thus a goodly number of Americans have entered the middle class through the profits earned from the provision of goods and services in the slums, including illegal or nonrespectable ones that upper-class and upper-middle-class businessmen shun because of their low prestige. As a result, members of almost every immigrant group have financed their upward mobility by providing slum housing, entertainment, gambling, narcotics, etc., to later arrivals—most recently to blacks, Puerto Ricans, Latin-Americans—and Asians.

Tenth, the poor help to keep philanthropy busy, thus justifying its continued existence. "Society" sometimes uses the poor as beneficiaries of charity affairs; indeed, some sectors of the upper class depend on the poor to demonstrate their superiority over other elites who devote themselves solely to making money.

Eleventh, the poor, being powerless, can be made to absorb the costs of change and growth in American society. During the nineteenth century, they did the backbreaking work that built the cities; today, they are pushed out of their neighborhoods to make room for various forms of "progress." Urban-renewal projects to hold middle-class taxpayers in the city and expressways to enable suburbanites to commute downtown have typically been located in poor neighborhoods, since no other group will allow itself to be displaced. For the same reason, universities, hospitals, and civic centers also expand into land occupied by the poor. The major costs of the industrialization of agriculture have been borne by the poor, who are pushed off the land without recompense; and they have paid a large share of the human cost of the growth of American power overseas, for they have provided many of the foot soldiers for Vietnam and other wars.

Twelfth, the poor "stabilize" the American political process by keeping U.S. politics more centrist than would otherwise be the case. As already noted, they vote and participate in politics less than other groups so that the political system is often free to ignore them. Moreover, since they can rarely support Republicans, the Democrats can count on their votes, and be responsive to more conservative voters—for example, the white working class—who might otherwise switch to the Republicans. In the process, job and income issues that concern the poor, but that might cost a lot of money and upset the other voters, are ignored or condemned as socialistic.

Thirteenth, the role of the poor in upholding conventional norms (see the *fifth* point, above) also has a significant political function. An economy based on the ideology of laissez-faire requires a deprived population that is allegedly unwilling to work or that can be considered inferior because it must accept charity or welfare in order to survive. Not only does the alleged moral deviance of the poor reduce the moral pressure on the present political economy to eliminate poverty, but radical alternatives can also be made to look quite unattractive if those who will benefit most from them can be described as lazy, spendthrift, dishonest, and promiscuous.

THE ALTERNATIVES

I HAVE DESCRIBED thirteen of the more important functions poverty and the poor satisfy in American society—enough to support the functionalist thesis that poverty, like any other social phenomenon, survives in part because it is useful to society or some of its parts. This analysis is not intended to suggest that because it is often functional, poverty *should* exist, or that it *must* exist. For one thing, poverty has many more dysfunctions than functions; for another, it is possible to suggest functional alternatives.

For example, society's dirty work could be done without poverty, either by automation or by paying "dirty workers" decent wages. Nor is it necessary for the poor to subsidize the many activities that they support through their low-wage jobs. Any change would, however, drive up the costs of these activities, which would result in higher prices to their customers and clients. Similarly, many of the professionals who flourish because of the poor could be given other roles. Social workers could provide counseling to the affluent, as they prefer to do anyway; and the police could devote themselves to traffic and organized crime. Other roles would have to be found for badly trained or incompetent professionals now relegated to serving the poor, and someone else would have to pay their salaries. Fewer penologists would be employable, however. Pentecostal religion could probably not survive without the poor—nor would parts of the second- and third-hard–goods market. And in many cities, "used" housing that no one else wants would then have to be torn down at public expense.

Alternatives for the cultural functions of the poor could be found more easily and cheaply. Indeed, movie entertainers and adolescents (as imagined by adults) are already serving as the deviants needed to uphold traditional morality and as devotees of orgies to "staff" the fantasies of vicarious participation.

The status functions of the poor are another matter. In a hierarchical society, some people must be defined as inferior to everyone else with respect to a variety of attributes, but they need not be poor in the absolute sense. One could conceive of a society in which the "lower class," though last in the pecking order, received 75 percent of the median income, rather than 15 to 40 percent, as is now the case. Needless to say, this would require considerable income redistribution. The contribution the poor make to the upward mobility of the groups that provide them with goods and services could also be maintained without the poverty-stricken having such low incomes. However, it is true that if the poor were more affluent, they might have access to enough capital to take over this role, thus competing with, and perhaps rejecting, the outsiders. Similarly, if the poor were more affluent, they would make less willing clients for philanthropy. But "society" can devote more attention to medical research and other health-related good deeds.

The political functions of the poor would be more difficult to replace. With increased affluence the poor would probably obtain more political power and be more active politically. With higher incomes and more political power, the poor would be likely to resist paying the costs of growth and change. Of course, it is possible to imagine gentrification and highway projects that properly reimbursed the displaced people, but such projects would then become considerably more expensive, and many might never be built. This, in turn, would reduce the comfort and convenience of those who now benefit from the housing and expressways.

In sum, then, many of the functions served by the poor could be replaced if poverty were eliminated, but almost always at higher costs to others, particularly more affluent others. Consequently, a functional analysis must conclude that poverty persists not only because it fulfills a number of positive functions but also because many of the functional alternatives to poverty would be quite dysfunctional for the affluent members of society. A functional analysis thus ultimately arrives at much the same conclusion as radical sociology: that social phenomena that are functional for affluent or powerful groups and dysfunctional for poor or powerless ones persist even if large numbers of people indicate they are against them and would like to see them eliminated.

ANTIPOVERTY PLANNING

WHILE MANY of the functions of poverty could in theory be replaced by functional alternatives, these are easier to propose than to implement. Moreover if the alternatives generate other costs for the affluent, the powerful, or a significant majority of the voters, they will not be accepted. In short, while poverty is not very expensive to eliminate, it serves enough other functions for a variety of people that become obstacles to its elimination.

Thus, poverty is always more than a failure of the economy or, for that matter, of capitalism. It served many of the functions I have just described in the once–state socialist societies of Eastern Europe—and it will persist because these functions have not been abolished with the end of state socialism. Many people blame poverty on the poor themselves and their various deficiencies; and, as a matter of fact, blaming itself serves an important function or two: it makes the blamers feel better, and it supplies a reason for not dealing with the economic aspects of poverty.

I do not mean to suggest that poverty cannot be abolished, but the planning task is more complex than has been imagined. Most likely, poverty and the social problems associated with it can probably be eliminated only when they become dysfunctional for the affluent, the powerful, and a significant majority of the voting public. For example, when the poor become a serious enough danger to public health or the quality of life and the people who count can neither escape it nor want anymore to live with it, society will look for financially and politically easy ways of eliminating the danger—and if these do not work, and no other ways of dealing with that danger can be found, then poverty may be eliminated.

In theory, poverty could also be eliminated when the powerless can obtain enough power to change society. This seems to be even harder to imagine, or to bring about, however, since as far as history can tell us, the poor have never been able to mount successful revolutions on their own. Slave revolts have sometimes ended with temporary victories for the slaves, and modern societies have conducted revolutions in the name of the poor, with some improvements as a result in the economic and social conditions of their poor residents. Perhaps because these revolutions have so far taken place largely in very poor countries, they have not yet been able to eliminate poverty, however. [4]

ANTIPOVERTY POLICIES II: RACE, ETHNICITY, AND CLASS

· I N T R O D U C T I O N ·

THE FINAL PART of the book is mainly about what Gunnar Myrdal and his associates called *The American Dilemma* in their classic 1944 volume, but which might today better be called *The American Impasse,* for racial segregation and discrimination have proven more stubborn than Myrdal believed.

One of the reasons race creates an impasse is that it is so tightly interconnected with poverty. Myrdal and his coauthors pictured it as a vicious circle, and as they put it in the language of the mid-1940s:

> White prejudice and discrimination keep the Negro low in standards of living, health, education, manners and morals. This in turn gives support to white prejudice. (1944 ed., p. 75)

Today we speak about the intersection of race and class, but circles are a more apt metaphor precisely because the two problems are so intertwined. Researchers have long been debating whether the main or sufficient cause of black poverty is the low class position—and associated lack of economic skills—of blacks, or whether it is their color that keeps them in their low class position. The debate is hardly resolved, but as far as I am concerned, the basic income statistics of the last decades alone suggest that race is the sufficient cause. There are far fewer poor whites than a generation ago, for except in a few regional pockets like the Appalachians, most have moved above the poverty line, whereas blacks have not. Such data plus the frightening figures about the decline of blacks in the labor force mentioned in the postscript to chapter 19 (p. 295) show that discrimination and racial exclusion are the primary explanation, although class, economic condition, and the economy that produce both are not far behind.

Analytic conclusions and policy strategies need not necessarily be the same, but policy researchers have been involved in a similar debate: whether economic or "racial" policies (which William J. Wilson calls race-specific), such as the reduction of prejudice, discrimination, and segregation have priority. This is not an either-or matter, however, for there are a number of economic and racial policies; and which of each, or what mixture of both, are best can also be discussed.

Myrdal himself suggested, wisely, to proceed on as many fronts as possible, for at different times, different policies may be more effective—and which ones are going to be effective at any given time cannot easily be predicted. In affluent times, *both* economic and racial policies seem to work, for whites seem to be more generous with public funds, and while they may not be less prejudiced, they appear to be less fearful of blacks, for example as low-status competitors for their homes and jobs. Thus, during the post–World War II era of affluence, economic growth helped whites and blacks alike, and President Johnson was able to obtain the passage of basic civil rights legislation just before that era ended.

At the start of the 1990s, when the economy is in an uncertain shape and when the consensus that existed during the affluent years of the 1960s is absent, the impasse is harder to deal with, and the circle is harder to break into.

If my analysis is right and race is the primary or sufficient cause of black poverty, in *theory,* racial or race-specific policies should be called for, but as I noted before, analysis and policy need not travel the same path. In *practice,* racial policies are in fact not the best solution to attack black poverty. One major reason is that such policies require institutional and individual behavior and attitude changes from a white majority that has little reason—not to mention incentives—for change. Conversely, economic policies do not require whites to live or associate with, or give up something for, people they have not themselves chosen; and in addition, economic policies add to all pies, white and black alike. Thus, they are more easily implemented, and they are the fastest way to improve the condition of the black poor.

This is no argument against the *concurrent* use of race-specific policies, however, because, for symbolic and political reasons, whites, blacks—and government itself—need to be reminded that government must uphold the laws of the land with respect to racial equality.

Nonetheless, economic policies may also be the most effective way to increase racial equality, at least in the long run. To be specific, if poverty could be reduced, "Negro standards"—to use Myrdal's words—would rise, and white prejudice would decline. For example, if a significant number of the black poor could move out of poverty, visible reductions in crime and drug abuse would take place and whites would become less fearful—and less likely to stereotype all poor blacks as criminals. Thus, at least some major class-components of racial prejudice would begin to disappear.

Prejudice has always declined when the parties involved have been of equal status, and the closer whites and blacks move toward equal socioeconomic status, the more likely that whites will pay less attention to skin color—particularly in a country with a growing population of Asians and Latins. At that point, admittedly still far away, racism will make less and less sense, and race-specific public policies may not even be needed.

Ethnicity is a minor player in all this, because for the very Americanized and much intermarried descendants of the white European immigrants who came between 1880 and 1925, ethnic identity can now be ignored, rejected, or freely chosen. If all goes well economically, the immigrants who have come since the 1960s, from Asia and Latin America as well as Europe, will slowly but surely follow the same trajectory; and only those immigrants whose skin is black—from Haiti and Africa, for example—will find that the trajectory is unavailable to them until racial discrimination declines.

Meanwhile, however, American blacks have finally been able to recognize, celebrate, and practice the latter-day versions of the cultures that their ancestors brought over from Africa. This is why I said in the preface that the new name blacks are now using, African-American, is basically an ethnic conception and should be welcomed as such. Not all blacks may want to be African-Americans, but then many of the descendants of the Italian, Polish, and other white immigrants do not always want to remember their European culture either.

The four chapters of this part of the book all touch on some parts of the broad picture sketched above. The first essay is the draft of a chapter of the government's "Kerner Report," prepared after the ghetto uprisings of the late 1960s. It responds to a debate of that period over the influence of race and ethnicity in the escape from poverty, and criticizes the conservative argument that today's blacks are like yesterday's immigrants. According to this argument, the only difference between the two populations is that blacks have not been in the urban labor market as long as the European ethnics. The implication is that if blacks would be patient, they would eventually make it up the American socioeconomic ladder just as the white ethnics had done—and with no more government help than the immigrants and their descendants had received. I thought this argument to be patently wrong.

The differences between the fates of blacks and of white immigrants have not changed dramatically in the two decades since I wrote that essay, which is why I reprint it here.* The second essay of part 5 is included for the same reason: because less has changed since the mid-1960s than is commonly thought. The essay is a critical analysis first published in *Commonweal,* of Daniel Patrick Moynihan's 1965 "Moynihan Report," in which he proposed that the black female-headed family was both an effect of male

---

*I reprint it with a mixture of pride and amusement, because while I wrote it at the request of the Kerner Commission staff, the commission was not allowed to acknowledge my authorship, or the other work I did for the commission. Having refused to pay my federal income tax as an antiwar protest the year before, I could not receive security clearance. To their everlasting credit, David Ginsberg and Vic Palmieri asked me to do the chapter anyway, but I assume I was not the only officially certified security risk whose work appeared in a government report.

black joblessness and a cause of the pathology in which the black family and community had become entangled. Young planners and policy researchers who think that the troubles of black America began around 1980 with "deindustrialization," "the feminization of poverty," and the arrival of Ronald Reagan need to realize that for blacks, deindustrialization or its equivalent—and their effects—began much earlier. What *has* changed in the 1980s is that the numbers Moynihan reported have risen, and that heroin and crack cocaine are literally destroying a number of poor black families.

While Moynihan was worrying about the female-headed family as a growing social problem, other government officials and citizens were concerned about the numerical rise in criminal and "deviant" activities that are often associated with poverty. In the 1960s, the elite white public discourse explained these activities as stemming from a special culture that distinguished the deviant and criminal poor from the rest.

The most famous of these is Oscar Lewis' culture of poverty, and I spent part of my time in the 1960s writing and talking to make the point that the problems of the poor—and the problems they made for others—were mainly the effects of poverty and that culture played only a limited role. The essay reprinted here came out of a special seminar on poverty chaired by Daniel Patrick Moynihan, and was one of a number of essays which attacked cultural explanations of poverty.

At the end of the 1960s, I thought that we had won the battle over the public discourse and that the idea that culture is the cause of poverty, which essentially blames the victims of poverty for being poor—had been vanquished. If this battle was actually won, however, the victory was brief; because by the start of the 1980s, a new term, the *underclass,* with many of the same connotations, became popular with academics, journalists, and others. Moreover, the definition of the underclass that came to dominate the public discourse, at least since the mid-1980s, was little more than an updated version of the culture of poverty.

The final essay in this book is thus in many respects a sequel to the preceding one. It is also a bit more urgent in tone, partly because the economic problems of the poorest blacks have become so much worse, and partly because *underclass* seems to me a more dangerous term than *the culture of poverty* and others used in the 1960s.

Popular terms are important mainly as possible indicators of how the elite and perhaps the larger public feel and think. If enough people see the underclass as the newest set of undeserving poor, their use of that term also identifies the people who are not deserving enough to be helped in their attempts to escape from poverty. Labeling needy people as undeserving as a way of depriving them of help is an old American solution, and it is also a cheap one, because then antipoverty programs do not need to be considered.

In reality, of course, this solution is not so cheap, because whatever the poor are called and however much antipoverty programs are cut back, some of the poor will protest or fight back in various ways. The protests rarely take the form of ghetto uprisings or marches that now symbolize the 1960s, but have become more economic, individualistic, and despairing. Some of the increasing non–white-collar crime is, among other things, a form of income redistribution—at least when it takes place outside poor areas. Drugs are a growth industry that compensates a little for the joblessness induced by the legal economy. Drug addiction itself, as well as the older addiction of the poor to alcohol, are in part a despairing protest against, and escape from, poverty, segregation, and hopelessness.

That justifies none of them. Furthermore, how they affect the quality of life, among the poor and the rest of us, is costly in many ways—especially once the price of extra police, courts, prisons, mental hospitals, and the like is factored in. Indeed, I would imagine that the total price is not much less than a set of effective antipoverty programs which would begin to reintegrate the poor into the economy and, incidentally, turn them back into full taxpayers.

· E I G H T E E N ·

ESCAPING FROM POVERTY: A COMPARISON OF THE IMMIGRANT AND BLACK EXPERIENCE

M ANY WHITE AMERICANS have asked why blacks cannot escape from poverty in the same way that the European immigrants made their escape in past generations. This question, which is often asked by the descendants of these immigrants, implies that if blacks had the moral virtues and emotional strengths of the immigrants, there would be no need for ghetto rebellions on the one hand, or for governmental antipoverty programs and integration policies on the other hand. Since the question is, in part at least, an argument against such governmental policies, the answer to it may not convert many of the questioners, for they would only find another reason to justify their antiblack feelings. Even so, the question deserves to be answered.

The major reason why blacks have not been able to escape from poverty under their own steam is the changed American economy. When the European immigrants came, America was just becoming an urban-industrial

---

This essay, which I wrote for the National Advisory Commission on Civil Disorders in January 1968, was turned by the commission staff into chapter 9 of the commission's report, known informally as the "Kerner Report." My draft, like the commission's entire report, still used the word *Negro,* which I have changed here to *black;* I have also made a few other changes to increase clarity. I have not added a postscript, for it would only duplicate parts of the postscript to chapter 14.

society. Indeed, the immigrants were admitted to America because the country was then beginning to build its major cities and industries, and it needed a great deal of unskilled labor. The immigrants performed this labor, and thus gained an economic foothold in the society, so that their children and grandchildren could move up to skilled, white-collar, and professional employment.

Since World War II, however, America has been a mature urban-industrial society, in which unskilled labor is much less necessary, and blue-collar jobs of all kinds are decreasing in number and importance. As a result, urban blacks have been unable to find the unskilled jobs that would permit them to gain the same economic foothold as the immigrants. They have also had difficulty in obtaining skilled jobs, partly because they lack the skills, and partly because they cannot gain entrance into the unions that control such jobs. Moreover, given the low quality of slum schools, blacks —like other poor people—have not been able to obtain the education that is now needed to qualify for a decent job. Although today's slum schools are probably no worse than the schools that the immigrants attended, the schools today have a task that they did not have when the demand for unskilled labor was high: to teach children from low-income homes more than the rudiments of literacy. In any case, since private enterprise is unable to create enough unskilled jobs by its own efforts, government must step in to find ways of incorporating the black poor into the economy.

The second major reason for the inability of so many blacks to escape from poverty is segregation. Blacks have always suffered from discrimination, and even before the arrival of the immigrants, they were restricted to the poorly paid, low-status service occupations. In fact, had it not been for discrimination, the North might well have recruited southern blacks after the Civil War to provide the labor for building the urban-industrial economy. Instead, northern employers recruited workers in Europe, and once the immigrants came, they were allowed to push the blacks out of the few urban occupations they had dominated, e.g., catering and barbering. It was not until immigration had been ended and until World War II that blacks were hired for industrial jobs, and by then the decline in such jobs had already begun.

Political factors also played a role in the immigrant escape from poverty. The immigrants came to America in large masses, and settled primarily in rapidly growing cities with powerful and expanding political machines. These machines saw that they could grow further by representing the immigrants, and by trading their votes for economic favors. Since the machines controlled public building in the growing cities, they could also generate employment, and the construction jobs went almost entirely to the immigrants. Later, each ethnic group often took over one or more of the municipal services as well. In New York for example, the Irish long dominated police and fire protection; the Italians, sanitation; and the Jews, public education.

In addition, the machines were decentralized, and developed ward-level grievance machinery and personal representation, so that the immigrants felt that they could make their voices heard and had some semblance of power. By the time blacks started to move to the cities in large numbers, the city building process had virtually come to an end, and the progressive reform groups had more or less won their war on the machines, so that the machines were no longer so powerful or so well equipped to provide jobs and other favors. Although the machines often retained their hold over the areas settled by blacks, the increasing scarcity of patronage jobs made them unwilling to give up the political positions they had created in these neighborhoods. As a result, New York's Harlem was ruled by white politicians for many years after it had become a black ghetto, and even in the 1960s, New York's Lower East Side, which has become predominantly Puerto Rican, has been run by Jewish and Italian members of Tammany Hall. The pattern is the same in most other American cities, so that blacks are still underrepresented in city councils, and at the higher levels of most city agencies. Segregation played a role here, too; the immigrants and their descendants felt threatened by the arrival of the blacks, so that they would not have been amenable to a black-immigrant coalition which might have saved the old political machines. The reform groups, although nominally more liberal on the race issue, were dominated by businessmen and middle-class city residents, and were opposed to coalition with any low-income group, white or black.

Cultural factors also made it easier for the immigrants to escape from poverty. They came to America from much poorer societies, with a very low standard of living. When most jobs in the American economy were unskilled, they did not feel so deprived in being forced to take the dirty and poorly paid jobs. Moreover, their families were large, and sometimes several breadwinners, some of whom never married, contributed to the total family income. As a result, family units could live off even the lowest-paid jobs and still put some money away for savings or investment, e.g., to purchase a house or tenement, or to open a store or factory. Since the immigrants had their own ethnic culture, and could not speak English, they needed stores that supplied them with ethnic foods and other services.

Also, most families were sufficiently intact most of the time to enable most parents to find satisfactions in family life that compensated for the bad jobs they had to take, and the hard work they had to endure.

Blacks came to the city under quite different circumstances. They were relegated to the jobs which no one else would take, and which paid so little that they could not put money away for savings, housing, or stores. They spoke English and did not need their own stores, and besides, the areas they occupied were already filled with stores. In addition, blacks lacked a large enough family that could act as an economic unit and they had fewer children, so that each household usually had only one or two breadwinners. Moreover, the poorer black men had fewer cultural incentives to work in a dirty job for the sake of the family. As a result of slavery and of long periods of male unemployment afterwards, poor black men often played secondary and marginal roles in their families. For these black men, then, there were fewer of the cultural and psychological rewards of family life. Being a marginal figure in the family, a black man was more often rejected by his wife when he was unemployed, or he deserted because he felt himself to be useless to his families.

Even so, most black men worked as hard as the immigrants to support their families, but the payoff just was not the same. The jobs did not pay enough to enable them to support their families, for prices and standards of living had risen since the immigrants came. Also, the city had been built up, so that the entrepreneurial opportunities that allowed some of the immigrants to become rich had vanished. And above all, they were at the mercy of segregation, which deprived them of the good jobs, of the chance to get into the right unions, of the opportunity to buy real estate or to obtain the loans to go into business, or of the possibility of moving out of the ghetto and to bring up their children in better neighborhoods. Indeed, it must not be forgotten that the immigrants were able to leave their ghettos as soon as they had the money, whereas many blacks who could afford to leave the ghetto had to remain there because segregation would not let them live elsewhere.

Finally, one must not exaggerate the differences between blacks and the European white immigrants, for they are not as great as white nostalgia makes them now seem. When the immigrants were immersed in poverty, they too lived in slums, and these neighborhoods exhibited fearfully high rates of alcoholism, desertion, illegitimacy, and all the other pathologies associated with poverty. Just as some black men desert their families when they are unemployed and their wives can get jobs, so did some Irish,

Italian, Polish, Greek, Jewish, and other men—even though affluence has clouded white memories of these phenomena.

Moreover, even today, whites tend to exaggerate how well and how quickly they escaped from poverty, and how badly and how poorly blacks have made their escape. The fact is that by the 1960s, among the Italians, Poles, other Slavic groups, and Jews who came to America in the last big wave of immigration, only the Jews, who came already urbanized, had totally escaped from poverty. The other groups, which like blacks came to America from rural backgrounds, usually took three generations to reach the final stages of the escape from poverty. Until the 1960s, the majority of Italians, Poles, other Slavs, and Greeks were employed in blue-collar jobs, and only a small proportion of their children attended college. In other words, only the third, and in many cases, only the fourth generation has been able to achieve the kind of middle-class income and status that allows it to send its children to college. Thanks to favorable economic and political conditions, these ethnic groups were able to escape from lower-class status to working-class and lower-middle-class status, but it has taken them three generations.

In the 1960s, blacks have been in the city for only two generations, and they have come under much less favorable conditions. Moreover, their escape from poverty has been blocked in part by the very slowness of the European ethnic groups; for their inability to get into the building trades and other unions, and their inability to move into better neighborhoods beyond the ghetto has been blocked by the descendants of the European immigrants who control these unions and neighborhoods, and have not yet given them up for middle-class occupations and areas. In short, one other reason why blacks have not escaped poverty more quickly is that their ascent is held up by the slowness of the European ethnic groups in moving into the college-educated middle class.

Even so, some blacks have escaped poverty, and they have done so in only two generations, although they are not so visible because in many cases, residential segregation forces them to remain in the ghetto. Still, the proportion of black men employed in white-collar jobs has risen from 10.2 percent in 1950 to 20.8 percent in 1966, and the proportion who now attend college has grown equally quickly. In fact, some blacks have probably escaped from poverty more rapidly than did the immigrants when they first arrived in America; and as Daniel P. Moynihan pointed out in the "Moynihan Report," this is creating a large and ever-increasing gap between black haves and have-nots.

This gap, and the awareness of being left behind on the part of the have-nots undoubtedly adds to the feelings of desperation and anger that breed rebellions and riots. The have-nots realize that declining economic opportunities and segregation make it possible for only a small proportion of blacks to escape poverty under their own steam, and that other means must be found to help the rest.

NINETEEN

THE BLACK FAMILY: REFLECTIONS ON THE "MOYNIHAN REPORT"

IN MARCH 1965, the United States Department of Labor published "for official use only" a report entitled *The Negro Family: The Case for National Action*. Written by Daniel Patrick Moynihan and Paul Barton just before the former resigned as Assistant Secretary of Labor to run unsuccessfully for president of New York's City Council, it was soon labeled the Moynihan Report by the Washington officials who were able to obtain copies.

Although not apparent from its title, the report called for a bold and important change in federal civil-rights policy, asking the federal government to identify itself with the black revolution and to shift its programs from an emphasis on liberty to one on equality. "The Negro Revolution," says Moynihan, "like the industrial upheaval of the 1930's, is a movement for equality as well as liberty," but the Supreme Court decision for school desegregation, the Civil Rights Acts of 1964 and 1965, and other legislation have only provided political liberty. The War on Poverty, which Moynihan describes as the first phase of the black revolution, makes opportunities available, but job-training programs that promise no jobs at their conclusion

---

Reprinted from *People and Plans*. Although I have changed *Negroes* to *blacks* in my observations in this essay, I have not done so with the official title of the Moynihan Report or the quotes from it. I have appended a postscript.

cannot produce equality. Held back by poverty, discrimination, and inadequate schooling, blacks cannot compete with whites, so that "equality of opportunity almost insures inequality of results."

Federal policies must therefore be devised to provide equality, "distribution of achievements among Negroes roughly comparable to that of whites," for otherwise, "there will be no social peace in the Untied States for generations."

But according to Moynihan, a serious obstacle stands in the way of achieving equality: the inability of blacks "to move from where they are now to where they want and ought to be." This inability he ascribes to the breakdown of black social structure and, more particularly, the deterioration of the black family. The remainder of the report is devoted to an analysis of that deterioration.

Soon after the report was published, President Johnson drew extensively on it for a commencement address at Howard University. He placed himself firmly behind Moynihan's proposal for a policy of equality of results, describing it as "the next and more profound stage of the battle for civil rights," and pointed to the breakdown of the black family as a limiting factor. He called for programs to strengthen the family and announced that a White House conference would be assembled in the fall for this purpose.

During the summer of 1965, public interest in both the report and the speech declined as new speeches and reports made the headlines, but after the Los Angeles riots, the Moynihan report suddenly achieved new notoriety, for its analysis of black society seemed to provide the best and the most easily available explanation of what had happened in Watts. Demand for copies increased, and the government released it to the press. Consequently, it is worth looking more closely at its findings and their implications.

From a variety of government and social-science studies, Moynihan concludes that the principal weaknesses of the black family are its instability, its proclivity for producing illegitimate children, and its matriarchal structure. Nearly a quarter of married Negro women are divorced or separated, and 35 percent of all black children live in broken homes. Almost a quarter of black births are illegitimate, and nearly a quarter of all black families are headed by a woman. As a result, 14 percent of all black children are being supported by the Aid for Families of Dependent Children (AFDC) program.

Although these figures would suggest that a smaller proportion of the black community is in trouble than is often claimed, they also underestimate the extent of the breakdown, for more families are touched by it at some time in their lives than at the given moment caught by the statistics. Thus, Moynihan estimates that fewer than half of all black children have continuously lived with both their parents by the time they reach the age of eighteen, and many legitimate children grow up without their real fathers. As Lee Rainwater points out, lower-class black women often marry the man who fathers their first or second child in order to obtain the valued status of being married, but thereafter they live in unmarried unions with other men.[1] Also, many households in which a man is present are nevertheless headed by women, for Moynihan indicates that in a fourth of black families in which a husband is present, he is not the principal earner. Perhaps the best illustration of the way in which available figures understate the problem comes from unemployment statistics which show that while the average monthly unemployment rate for Negro males in 1964 was 9 percent, fully 29 percent were unemployed at one time or another during that year. Moreover, the rates of family instability among whites are considerably lower and still decreasing, while they are on the rise among the black population.

The population that bears the brunt of these instabilities is, of course, the low-income one. Although the proportion of stable two-parent black families is probably increasing, "the Negro community is . . . dividing between a stable middle class group that is steadily growing stronger . . . and an increasingly disorganized and disadvantaged lower class group."

In that group, a significant minority of the families are broken, headed by women, and composed of illegitimate children. The black woman can obtain either employment or welfare payments to support her children, while the black man, saddled with unstable jobs, frequent unemployment, and short-term unemployment insurance, cannot provide the economic support that is a principal male function in American society. As a result, the woman becomes the head of the family, and the man a marginal appendage, who deserts or is rejected by his wife when he can no longer contribute to the family upkeep. With divorce made impossible by economic or legal barriers, the women may then live with a number of men in what Walter Miller calls "serial monogamy," finding a new mate when the inevitable quarrels start over who should support and head the family. And because the women value children, they continue to have them, illegitimately or not.

This family structure seems to have detrimental effects on the children, and especially on the boys, for they grow up in an environment that constantly demonstrates to them that men are troublesome good-for-nothings. Moynihan's data show that black girls do better in school and on the labor market than the boys and that the latter more often turn to delinquency, crime, alcohol, drugs, and mental illness in order to escape the bitter reality of a hopeless future. The girls are not entirely immune from ill effects, however, for many become pregnant in their teens; but since the girls' mothers are often willing to raise their grandchildren, the girls do not become a public and visible social problem.

The fundamental causes of family instability Moynihan traces to slavery and unemployment. Drawing on the researches of Frank Tannenbaum and Stanley Elkins, he points out that American slaveowners treated their slaves as mere commodities and, unlike their Latin American counterparts, often denied them all basic human rights, including that of marriage. More important, the structure of southern slave economy also placed the black man in an inferior position. He was needed only when the plantation economy was booming, and his price on the slave market was generally lower than that of the woman. Her services were always in demand around the household—or in the master's bed—and until her children were sold away from her, she was allowed to raise them. This established her in a position of economic and familial dominance which she has maintained, willingly or not, until the present day. All the available evidence indicates that since the Civil War, black male unemployment has almost always been higher than female. The gap has been widened further in recent years, especially in the cities, as job opportunities have increased for women, while decreasing for men, due to the ever-shrinking supply of unskilled and semiskilled work and the continuing racial discrimination in many trades. Since blacks are still moving to the cities in large numbers, the trends that Moynihan reports are likely to continue in the years to come.

Slavery made it impossible for blacks to establish a two-parent family, and its heritage has undoubtedly left its mark on their descendants. Even so, slavery is only a necessary but not a sufficient cause of the problem. Histories of the nineteenth-century European immigration, anthropological studies of the Caribbean matriarchal family, and observations among Puerto Ricans in American cities indicate that whenever there is work for women and serious unemployment among men, families break up as the latter desert or are expelled. The most impressive illustration of this pattern is a chart in the Moynihan report which shows that between 1951 and 1963, increases in the black male unemployment rate were followed, a year later, by a rise in the proportion of separated women.

Underemployment, being stuck in a dead-end job, and low wages may have similar consequences, and Moynihan points out that the minimum wage of $1.25 an hour, which is all that too many blacks earn, can support an individual, but not a family.[2]

In short, Moynihan's findings suggest that the problems of the black family which he sees as holding back the achievement of equality are themselves the results of previous inequalities, particularly economic ones that began with slavery and have been maintained by racial discrimination ever since. The report's concluding proposal, that "the policy of the United States is to bring the Negro American to full and equal sharing in the responsibilities and rewards of citizenship" and that "to this end, the programs of the federal government . . . shall be designed to have the effect, directly or indirectly, of enhancing the stability and resources of the Negro American family," therefore requires a drastic change of direction in federal civil-rights activities.

The Moynihan report does not offer any recommendations to implement its policy proposal, arguing that the problem must be defined properly first in order to prevent the hasty development of programs that do not address themselves to the basic problem. While this argument was perhaps justified as long as the report remained confidential, it may have some negative consequences now that the contents have been released to the press. The vacuum that is created when no recommendations are attached to a policy proposal can easily be filled by undesirable solutions, and the report's conclusions can be conveniently misinterpreted.

This possibility is enhanced by the potential conflict between the two major themes of the report: that blacks must be given real equality and that because of the deterioration of the family they are presently incapable of achieving it. The amount of space devoted to the latter theme and the inherent sensationalism of the data make it possible that the handicaps of the black population will receive more attention than Moynihan's forthright appeal for an equality of outcomes.

Thus, the findings on family instability and illegitimacy can be used by right-wing and racist groups to support their claim that blacks are inherently immoral and therefore unworthy of equality. Politicians responding to more respectable white backlash can argue that blacks must improve themselves before they are entitled to further government aid, and so can educators, psychologists, social workers, and other professionals who believe that the basic problem of blacks is "cultural deprivation" or "ego inadequacy," rather than lack of opportunities for equality. This in turn could lead to a clamor for pseudopsychiatric programs which attempt to change the black family through counseling and other therapeutic methods. Worse still, the report could be used to justify a reduction of efforts in the elimination of racial discrimination and the War on Poverty, watering down programs that were only just instituted and have not yet had a chance to improve the condition of the black population, but are already under concerted attack from conservative white groups and local politicians.

Of course, the deterioration of black society is due both to lack of opportunity and to cultural deprivation, but the latter is clearly an effect of the former and is much more difficult to change through government policies. For example, poor black school performance results both from inadequate, segregated schools and from the failure of the black home to prepare children for school, as well as from low motivation on the part of black children who see no reason to learn if they cannot find jobs after graduation. Even so, however difficult it may be to improve and desegregate the schools and to provide jobs, it is easier, more desirable, and more likely to help black family life than attempts to alter the structure of the family or the personality of its members through programs of "cultural enrichment" or therapy, not to mention irresponsible demands for black self-improvement.

In addition, it must be stressed that at present we do not even know whether the lower-class black family structure is actually as pathological as the Moynihan report suggests. However much the picture of family life painted in that report may grate on middle-class moral sensibilities, it may well be that instability, illegitimacy, and matriarchy are the most positive adaptations possible to the conditions that blacks must endure.

Moynihan presents some data which show that children from broken homes do more poorly in school and are more likely to turn to delinquency and drugs. Preliminary findings of a study by Bernard Mackler, of the New York Center for Urban Education, show no relation between school performance and broken families, and a massive study of mental health in Manhattan demonstrated that among whites, at least, growing up in a broken family did not increase the likelihood of mental illness as much as did poverty and being of low status.[3]

Families can break up for many reasons, including cultural and personality differences among the parents, economic difficulties, or mental illness on the part of one or both spouses. Each of these reasons produces different effects on the children, and not all are likely to be pathological. Indeed, if one family member is mentally ill, removing him from the family and thus breaking it up may be the healthiest solution, at least for the family.

Likewise, the matriarchal family structure with an absent father has not yet been proved pathological, even for the boys who grow up in it. Sociological studies of the black family have demonstrated the existence of an extended kinship system of mothers, grandmothers, aunts, and other female relatives which is surprisingly stable, at least on the female side. Moreover, many matriarchal families raise boys who do adapt successfully and themselves make stable marriages. The immediate cause of pathology may be the absence of a set of emotional strengths and cultural skills in the mothers, rather than the instability or departure of the fathers. A family headed by a capable if unmarried mother may thus be healthier than a two-parent family in which the father is a marginal appendage. If this is true, one could argue that at present the broken and matriarchal family is a viable solution for the black lower-class population, for given the economic and other handicaps of the men, the family can best survive by rejecting its men, albeit at great emotional cost to them.

Similar skepticism can be applied to premature judgments of black illegitimacy. Since illegitimacy is not punished in the lower class as it is in the middle class, and illegitimate children and grandchildren are as welcome as legitimate ones, they may not suffer the harmful consequences that can accompany illegitimacy in the middle class. Moreover, even the moral evaluation of illegitimacy in the middle class has less relevance in the black lower class, particularly when men cannot be counted on as stable family members.

Finally, illegitimacy and the bearing of children generally has a different meaning in this population than in the middle-class one. Rainwater's previously cited paper suggests that adolescent black girls often invite pregnancy because having children is their way of becoming adults and of making sure that they will have a family in which they can play the dominant role for which they have been trained by their culture. Although many older black women have children because they lack access to birth-control methods they can use or trust, I suspect that others continue to have them because in a society in which older children are often a disappointment, babies provide a source of pleasure and a feeling of usefulness to their mothers. If having children offers them a reason for living in the same way that sexual prowess does for black men, then alternate rewards and sources of hope must be available before illegitimacy can be judged by middle-class standards or programs developed to do away with it. Until more is known about the functioning and effects of lower-class black family structure, the assumption that it is entirely or predominantly pathological is premature.

It would thus be tragic if the findings of the Moynihan Report were used to justify demands for black self-improvement or the development of a middle-class family structure before further programs to bring about real equality are set up. Consequently, it is important to see what conclusions and recommendations emerge from the forthcoming White House conference and how the assembled experts deal with the two themes of Moynihan's report. It is also relevant to describe some recommendations that seem to me to be called for by the findings of that report.

The fundamentally economic causes of the present structure of the black family indicate that programs to change it must deal with these causes, principally in the areas of employment, income, and the provision of housing and other basic services. The history of the black family since the time of slavery indicates that the most important program is the elimination of unemployment and underemployment. If black men can obtain decent and stable jobs, then many—and far more than we think—can at once assume a viable role in the family and raise children who will put an end to the long tradition of male marginality and inferiority.

A second set of needed programs must provide equality of income for people who cannot work or cannot earn a living wage. The program for Aid to Families of Dependent Children, which at present fosters the instability of the black family, should at once be replaced by a policy of payments to all families in which the men cannot provide support. By giving larger payments to households in which husbands are present, family stability and the two-parent family could be encouraged. But all present forms of welfare payments ought to be replaced by a single system of income grants, based on the concept of the negative income tax, to be paid to all households below a minimum income, whatever the reason for their poverty.

A third set of programs should aim at equality of results in housing and other basic services. The enforcement of effective desegregation laws would enable many black parents who can afford to live outside the ghetto to raise their children amid other stable families. A massive federal rehousing program, combined with an expansion of the rent-supplement scheme, would make this opportunity available to yet others, including many female-headed households, struggling desperately to keep their children "off the streets" in order to isolate them from early pregnancy, delinquency, and despair. Until this happens, however, independent steps must be taken to desegregate the schools, so that black youngsters can escape the culture of inferiority which is endemic to segregated schools.

Some immediate steps can also be taken to change the female-dominated environment in which black boys grow up. If or when little can be done in the home, it is possible to increase the number of men in schools, recreation centers, settlement houses, and social-work agencies in order to give the boys contact with men who have a viable function and reduce the impression—and the fact—that women are the source of all instruction, authority, and reward in their lives. Adolescent boys and adult men can be hired as subprofessionals for this purpose. Similarly, voter-registration and political-organization programs ought to be supported, for politics is, even in the black community, a male activity, and the extension of real democracy to the ghetto would do much to make its residents feel that they have some power to change their lives and their living conditions.

Finally, a massive research program on the structure of the black family ought to be undertaken, to determine how and where it breeds pathology and to permit the development of therapeutic methods to aid those who cannot adapt to programs for equality of results. There will be men who are so ravaged by deprivation and despair that they cannot hold a job even when jobs are plentiful, but I am confident that if men can be given a viable occupational role, if family income is sufficient to guarantee a decent living, if blacks are freed from the material and emotional punishment of racial discrimination and allowed to participate as first-class citizens in the political community, a healthy black family structure—which may or may not coincide with the middle-class ideal—will develop as a result.

The insistence on equality of results in the Moynihan Report is therefore the most effective approach to removing the instabilities of the black family. Whether or not Moynihan's pleas, and that made by President Lyndon B. Johnson at Howard University, will be heeded remains to be seen. The economic, social, and political changes required to provide equality are drastic, and both the white and the black middle classes, not to mention the white lower class, have a considerable investment in the status quo which condemns the poor black to membership in a powerless, dependent, and deprived underclass. Some change can be initiated through federal action, but the implementation of civil-rights legislation and antipoverty programs also indicates that much of the federal innovation is subverted at the local level and that a significant portion of the new funds are drained off to support the very political and economic forces that help to keep lower-class blacks in their present position.

Federal and local officials must do all they can to prevent this from happening in the future, but they must be supported—and pressured—by professional, religious, and civic groups dedicated to racial equality. Also, the civil-rights movement must begin to represent and speak for the low-income black population more than it has done in the past, for if the black revolution and the social peace of which Moynihan speaks are to be won, they must be won by and for that population.

Yet, inescapably, the black problem is primarily a white problem, of the ultimate source of change must be the white population. Of the twin ideals of American democracy that Moynihan describes, it has traditionally opted for Liberty rather than Equality, including the liberty to keep the less equal in their place. It would be hard to imagine a sudden ground swell for equality from the white population; but if it really wants to prevent the spreading of violent protest through race riots and the proliferation of the less visible but equally destructive protest expressed through delinquency and drug addiction, it must allow its political leaders to make the changes in the American social, economic, and political structure that are needed to move toward equality. Unfortunately, so far most whites are less touched than titillated by riots and family breakdown and more driven to revenge than to reform when black deprivation does reach into their lives. In this desert of compassion, the Moynihan report is a tiny oasis of hope and, if properly interpreted and implemented, a first guide to the achievement of equality in the years to come.

· P O S T S C R I P T ·

ALTHOUGH A GREAT deal of research has been done on the topics of this essay since I first wrote it in 1965, there is still no agreement about how to explain the family structure of poor blacks. Of course, the numbers have grown considerably since a young Labor Department official became the senior senator from New York. An updating of the figures cited on p. 286 shows that the proportion of divorced or separated married black women has risen to 45 percent in 1987, while 59 percent of all black children lived in broken homes that same year. In 1986, 61 percent of black births were illegitimate, and as of 1987, 42 percent of all black families were headed by a woman.[4] The proportion of children born to black teenagers has also risen since 1965, and has in fact become defined as a major social problem only after Moynihan wrote his report.

Why have these numbers risen so dramatically since the 1960s? In part, they represent statistical rhetoric, because some of the percentages have also increased dramatically for whites, especially poor whites. However, most of the numbers for poor blacks are larger than those for poor whites, and while there is no agreement in the research community on the reasons, I believe that the increase is largely an illustration—and an effect—of the extent to which blacks—male and female—have been driven further to the margins and out of the economy. This is well demonstrated by what I consider the most depressing statistic of all: the decline in the labor force participation rate of young black males. In 1965, the participation rate, for black men aged twenty to twenty-four, was 81.6 percent, but by 1984 it had shrunk to only 58 percent. For whites, the decline was minuscule, from 80.2 percent to 78 percent.[5]

The labor force participation rate for young blacks has gone down so sharply mainly because of the lack of jobs, but also for other, equally depressing reasons. A large number of men in this age group are in prison, and others are out of the labor force because they are participants in those parts of the underground economies that may someday land them in prison. Yet others are dead, partly because violence is an ever-present part of extreme poverty, partly because they have been killed in drug industry turf wars.[6]

This labor force statistic also helps to explain the rise in teenage mothers. To be sure, the *necessary* cause of that increase is the general rise in sexual activity among teenagers, black and white, poor and rich, since the 1960s. Poor people have always been sexually more active, whatever their color or ethnicity, than the rest of the population, and usually they have begun that activity earlier as well—perhaps because their life expectancy is shorter than that of more affluent people. In addition, most—but not all —studies suggest that poor blacks are sexually more active than poor whites, although all researchers agree that they make less use of birth control devices and abortions, and also have less access to these.

The declining labor force participation rate is, however, the *sufficient* cause why pregnant young women see no reason to marry or even live with the young men who fathered their child; for poor women want bread-winner mates, and to many of these young men are clearly destined not to be very reliable breadwinners.[7] In the 1960s, that economic destiny was far less likely, which is probably why, as I reported on page 287, that the black women Rainwater studied tended to marry the fathers of their first children, only moving on to other men (whom they did not marry) when these fathers could not stay employed.

In addition, the women's own economic future plays a role in these statistics, for they see little reason to hold off motherhood for economic reasons. There is some indication that teenagers who have difficulty in school become mothers at an early age because they can sense that their job and other opportunities do not look as attractive as motherhood. Since there are still few taboos against early motherhood among many parts of the poor black community, some of the youngsters seem to feel that they might as well begin their entry into motherhood earlier than other Americans.

This may be a deliberate decision, as some economists are suggesting, but it is probably not grounded on economic considerations. Poor teenagers without much of an economic future may not have many reasons for staying in school, whereas becoming mothers will make them feel socially useful and respected. Likewise, those who have not received much love from their own parents may want a baby who they know will love them. Poor people have often welcomed children even if they could not afford them.

However, some of the teenagers' babies are unwanted, and poor black teenagers have more unwanted children than poor whites, either because they have less access to birth control and abortion, or because their job opportunities look worse. Most likely, both factors are involved, suggesting again that the single-parent family—today's phrase for the broken family—and teenage motherhood, are reactions to the distinctive poverty, lack of opportunity, and discrimination with which blacks are confronted.[8] Black rates of illegitimacy have been higher for a long time than those of whites, but the economic inequality of poor blacks is much more pervasive than that of poor whites, a fact that is hidden when only current incomes are compared.[9]

The best way to summarize this discussion may be to suggest that the single-parent family is what might be described as an outcome term, which covers a number of causes, processes, and formal or informal decisions that come together in a similar behavioral outcome. Consequently, it may be impossible to find a single explanation for the poor single-parent family, teenage or adult.

Conservative researchers believe, as one might expect, that this family format is a cause of black poverty, although there is no sound evidence that if poor young women postpone childbearing, and forego all sexual activity, until they get married that their job prospects will improve significantly. After all, their sexual abstinence will not create the needed jobs. There are too few jobs for unskilled black women, and too many black women remain unskilled because the economy has not, until the late 1980s, given them any hint that they might have a chance at decent and secure jobs that justify their trying to learn something in the schools which they must attend. If the serious labor force shortage some expect in the 1990s actually takes place, and racial discrimination declines concurrently, perhaps blacks can expect some increase in decent jobs, and then there may be some reduction in black teenage pregnancy, in school dropouts—and in the return to school of older single parents. Still, immediate reactions of this kind to a sudden change in the labor market—and one that may not be permanent—should not be expected from very many poor youngsters.

The conservative notion that marriage solves all problems does not even apply to nonpoor white women anymore. As far as poor young blacks are concerned, however, marrying the jobless young men with whom they associate makes no economic or other sense; and marrying them in order to have children is economically irrational, since they would then be ineligible for welfare, and especially for the much-needed Medicaid—without which they cannot obtain medical care. As a result, some conservative policy analysts have recommended ending welfare, but there is no reason to believe that sexual activity has ever been much changed by punitive public policy. Instead, more poor women would probably turn to prostitution or drug sales to earn a living, even as they produced children with lower birth weights and more illnesses.

Since social problems are created by those who decide what is to be problematic rather than by those who are declared to behave in a problematic fashion, the relevant questions to ask are why illegitimacy, the single-parent family, and adolescent motherhood have become such urgent social problems—and more important, to what extent these phenomena are actually harmful and for whom. One intellectual and social puzzle is why the framers of social problems still worry so about marriages and children being legitimated by the state, especially among people who have no property to inherit or pass on; for the lack of such legitimation seems to create few significant problems for the adults and children involved. Another puzzle is the concern with whether the children have one or two in-house parents, since there is still not enough convincing evidence that two parents, especially two who are constantly fighting, are beneficial for the children's emotional health. Two parents are better than one to help share the child-raising burdens; but whether a functioning father has to live with the mother, or whether a father, or some male who takes the father role, is actually needed for the children's proper development also remains to be determined. Until such questions are answered, there is no reason to believe that growing up in a single-parent family is problematic above and beyond the obviously problematic poverty in which the growing up takes place.[10]

Also, whether adolescent motherhood creates any significant costs for either mother or child above and beyond their poverty is not yet clear. For example, we do not know whether a twenty-six-year-old poor unmarried mother without parental training will be a better mother because she is ten years older than a sixteen-year-old with the same attributes. In an era in which professional people—who are the primary definers of social problems—have their babies in their thirties, the fact that increasing numbers of poor women will have them in their teens is understandably disconcerting, but that still does not prove that the practice is harmful.

I do not mean to justify illegitimacy, single-parent families, or babies having babies, but if these are either not harmful per se or are effects of poverty, then for planning and social policy at least the implication should be clear.

Until enough of the needed research and thinking are done, all that can be said with certainty is that illegitimate children, single-parent families, and teenager mothers violate dominant American norms, and thus hurt the feelings of those who hold these norms. As a result, the norm violators are thought to be undeserving, and as a result of *that* they are apt to be treated punitively, which may in turn result in behavior that is actually harmful. As already noted, jobless unmarried mothers who are deprived of all, or sufficient, welfare benefits may produce low–birthweight children or turn to criminal pursuits to earn money. Later on, the teachers of their children will most likely have lower expectations of how illegitimate children perform in school, which may help to explain frequent findings that such children do more poorly in school and drop out more often.

Future research could also determine that the traditional two-parent family is the most universally desired, or least harmful, for everyone, at least in America, rich or poor, in which case the salient government family policy can be developed. Meanwhile, only a cursory examination of middle-class families, white or black, is needed to indicate that most are married or were once married, that most of the children were born legitimately, and that almost all arrived after their mothers' adolescence had ended. This alone should suggest the continued validity of Moynihan's basic finding: that the single-parent family is an effect of joblessness and other kinds of poverty.

· T W E N T Y ·

CULTURE AND CLASS IN THE STUDY OF POVERTY: AN APPROACH TO ANTIPOVERTY RESEARCH

THE MORAL ASSUMPTIONS OF POVERTY RESEARCH

POVERTY RESEARCH, LIKE all social research, is suffused with the cultural and political assumptions of the researcher. Consequently, one of the most significant facts about poverty research is that it is being carried out entirely by middle-class researchers, who differ in class, culture, and political power from the people they are studying. Such researchers—and I am one of them—are members of an affluent society, who, however marginal they may feel themselves to be, are investigating an aggregate that is excluded from that society. Whatever the researchers' political beliefs—and students of poverty span the political spectrum—this difference in class position affects their perspective. Some of that perspective is inevitably built on random observations and untested assumptions and may include inaccurate folklore about the poor which he or she has unconsciously picked up as a middle-class person. As a result, "social science views [of poverty] are more elaborated, logically organized and sophisticated versions of . . . commonsense understandings"[1]

Moreover, poverty researchers, like other affluent Americans, have had

Reprinted from *People and Plans* with some clarifying changes and a postscript.

to grapple with the question of how to explain the existence of an underclass in their society. In a fascinating paper, Rainwater once described five explanatory perspectives which, as he puts it, "neutralize the disinherited" by considering them as immoral, pathological, biologically inferior, culturally different, and heroic. As his terms indicate, these "explanations" are by no means all negative, but they enable the explainers to resolve their anxiety about the poor by viewing them as different or unreal.[2]

Rainwater's list is a sophisticated and updated version of an older, more familiar explanatory perspective, which judges the poor as deserving or undeserving.[3] This dichotomy still persists today, albeit with different terminologies, for it addresses the basic political question of what to do about poverty. If the poor are deserving, they are obviously entitled to admittance into the affluent society as equals, with all the economic, social, and political redistribution this entails; if they are undeserving, they need not be admitted, or at least not until they have been made or have made themselves deserving.

The history of American poverty research can be described in terms of this moral dichotomy. Most of the lay researchers of the nineteenth century felt the poor were personally and politically immoral and therefore undeserving. Although some researchers understood that the moral lapses of the poor stemmed from economic deprivation and related causes, most offered a cultural explanation, indicting the non-Puritan subcultures of the Irish and eastern and southern European immigrants.[4] These frequently high-born observers, who were struggling to maintain the cultural and political dominance of the Protestant middle and upper classes against the flood of newcomers, proposed that poverty could be dealt with by ending the European immigration and by Americanizing and bourgeoisifying the immigrants who had already come.[5]

Social scientists took up the study of poverty in the twentieth century without an explicit political agenda and also changed the terminology. They saw the poor as suffering from individual pathology or from social disorganization; they treated them as deficient, rather than undeserving, but there was often the implication that the deficiencies had to be corrected before the poor were deserving of help.

This conception of the poor spawned a generation of countervailing research which identified positive elements in their social structure and culture.[6] Although many of the actual studies were done among the working-class populations, the findings suggested or implied that because the poor were not disorganized, socially or individually, they were therefore deserving.

The debate over the moral quality of the poor was particularly intense during the War on Poverty, with advocates of undeservingness seeing the poor as deficient in basic skills and attitudes. Educators who shared this view described them as *culturally* deprived; social workers and clinical psychologists found them weak in ego strength; and community organizers viewed them as apathetic. Professionals who believe the poor to be deserving argue that the poor are not deficient, but economically deprived; they need jobs, higher incomes, better schools, and "maximum feasible participation"—"resource strategy equalization" in Lee Rainwater's terms, rather than just services, such as training and counseling in skills and ways of living that lead to cultural change.[7]

Social scientists have debated an only slightly different version of the same argument. Some feel that the poor share the values and aspirations of the affluent society and if they can be provided with decent jobs and other resources, they will cease to suffer from the pathological and related deprivational consequences of poverty. According to Beck's 1967 review of the poverty literature, carried out at the height of the War on Poverty, many more social scientists then shared the feeling that the poor are deficient.[8] Yet others, particularly anthropologists, suggested that poverty and the low position of the poor resulted in the creation of a separate lower-class culture, or a culture of poverty, which makes it impossible for poor people to develop the behavior patterns and values that would presently enable them to participate in the affluent society.

Although few social scientists would think of explicitly characterizing the poor as deserving or undeserving, those who argue that the poor share the values of the affluent obviously consider them as ready and able to share in the blessings of the affluent society, whereas those who consider them deficient or culturally different imply that the poor are not able to enter until they change themselves or are changed. The anthropologist Walter Miller argued that the poor do not even want to enter the affluent society, at least culturally, and his analysis implies that the poor are deserving precisely because they have their own culture. Even so, those who see the poor as deficient or culturally different often favor resource-oriented anti-poverty programs, just as those who feel that the poor share the values of the affluent society recognize the existence of cultural factors that block the escape from poverty.

The ghetto rebellions of the late 1960s encouraged a popular revival of the old terminology, however. The black poor, at least, were now seen by many whites as undeserving, for they rioted despite the passage of civil rights legislation and the War on Poverty, and should not be rewarded for their ungratefulness. [9] Observers who felt that the black poor are deserving, on the other hand, claimed that the rebellions stemmed from the failure of white society to grant the economic, political, and social equality it has long promised and that rioting and looting were only desperate attempts by the poor to obtain the satisfactions that the affluent society has denied them.

The Poor: Neither Deserving nor Undeserving

Because of its fundamental political implications and its moral tone, the debate about whether the poor are deserving or undeserving will undoubtedly continue as long as there are poor people in America. Nevertheless, I feel that the debate, however it is conceptualized, is irrelevant and undesirable. The researcher ought to look at poverty and the poor from a perspective that avoids a moral judgment, for it is ultimately impossible to prove that the poor are more or less deserving than the affluent. Enough is now known about the economic and social determinants of pathology to reject explanations of pathology as a moral lapse. Moreover, since there is some evidence that people's legal or illegal practices are a function of their opportunity to earn a livelihood in legal ways, one cannot know whether the poor are as law-abiding or moral as the middle class until they have achieved the same opportunities, and then the issue will be irrelevant. [10]

It is also undesirable to view the poor as deserving or undeserving, for any judgment must be based on the judge's definition of deservingness, and who has the ability to formulate a definition that is not class bound? Such judgments are almost always made by people who are trying to prevent the mobility of a population group that is threatening their own position, so that the aristocracy finds the nouveau riche undeserving of being admitted to the upper class; the cultural elite believes the middle classes to be undeserving partakers of "culture"; and many working-class people feel that people who do not labor with their hands do not deserve to be considered workers. Still, almost everyone gangs up on the poor; they are judged as undeserving by all income groups, becoming victims of a no-win moral game in which they are expected to live by moral and legal standards that few middle-class people are capable of upholding. Deservingness is thus not an absolute moral concept, but in part a means of preventing one group's access to the rights and resources of another.

The only proper research perspective, I believe, is to look at the poor as an economically and politically deprived population whose behavior, values—and pathologies—are adaptations to their existential situation, just as the behavior, values, and pathologies of the affluent are adaptations to *their* existential situation. In both instances, adaptation results in a mixture of moral and immoral, legal and illegal, practices, but the nature of the mix is a function of the existential situation. Since the standards of law, and even of morality, of an affluent society are determined by the affluent members of that society, the poor are, by definition, less law-abiding and less moral, but only because they are less affluent and must therefore adapt to different existential circumstances.

If the poor are expected to live up to the moral and legal standards of the affluent society, however, the only justifiable antipoverty strategy is to give them the same access to resources now held by the affluent and to let them use and spend these resources with the same freedom of choice that is now reserved to the affluent.

The reminder of the paper will elaborate this perspective, particularly around the debate over class and culture among the poor, spelling out some of the implications for both social-science theory and antipoverty policy. I should note that by "the poor" I shall refer principally to people who have presumably been poor long enough to develop cultural patterns associated with poverty and are permanently rather than temporarily poor.

POVERTY AND CULTURE

THE ARGUMENT between those who think that poverty can best be eliminated by providing jobs and other resources and those who feel that cultural obstacles and psychological deficiencies must be overcome as well is ultimately an argument about social change, and about the role of culture in change. The advocates of resources are not concerned explicitly with culture, but they do make a cultural assumption: whatever the culture of the poor, it will not interfere in people's adaptation to better opportunities for obtaining economic resources. They take a *situational* view of social change and of personality: that people respond to the situations—and opportunities—available to them and change their behavior accordingly. Those who call attention to cultural (and psychological) obstacles, however, are taking a *cultural* view of social change, which suggests that people react to change in terms of prior values and behavior patterns and adopt only those changes that are congruent with their culture.[11]

Since academicians have been caught up in the debate over deservingness and undeservingness as much as the rest of American society, the situational and cultural views of change have frequently been described as polar opposites, and theorists have battled over the data to find support for one pole or the other. Clearly, the truth lies somewhere between, but at present, neither the data nor the conceptual framework to find that truth is as yet available.

The situational view is obviously too simple; people are not automatons who respond either in the same way or with the same speed to a common stimulus. Despite a middle-class inclination on the part of researchers to view the poor as homogeneous, all available studies indicate that there is as much variety among them as among the affluent. Some have been poor for generations; others are poor only periodically. Some are downwardly mobile; others are upwardly mobile. Many share middle-class values, others embrace working-class values; some have become so used to the defense mechanisms they have learned for coping with deprivation that they have difficulty in adapting to new opportunities, and some are beset by physical or emotional illness, poverty having created pathologies that now block the ability to adapt to nonpathological situations. [12]

The Shortcomings of the Cultural View of Change

The cultural view of social and personal change is also deficient. First, it uses an overly behavioral definition of culture which ignores the existence of values that conflict with behavior; and second, it sees culture as a holistic system whose parts are intricately related, so that any individual element of a culture cannot be changed without system-wide reverberations.

The behavioral definition identifies culture in terms of how people act; it views values as *behavioral norms* that are metaphysical and moral guidelines to behavior and are deduced from behavior. For example, Walter Miller sees values as "focal concerns" which stem from, express, and ultimately maintain behavior. As he puts it, "The concept 'focal concern' . . . reflects actual behavior, whereas 'value' tends to wash out intracultural differences since it is colored by notions of the 'official' ideal." [13] This definition, useful as it is, pays little or no attention to *aspirations,* values that express the desire for alternative forms of behavior.

The behavioral conception of culture can be traced to anthropological traditions and to the latent political agenda of anthropological researchers. The field-worker who studied a strange culture began by gathering artifacts, and as anthropology matured, he or she also collected behavior patterns. The cultural relativists, who wanted to defend these cultures against involuntary change, sought to show that the behavior patterns were functional to the survival of the group. How people felt about their behavior did not interest them unduly. They noted that infanticide was functional for the survival of a hunting tribe, but did not devote much attention to how people felt about the desirability of infanticide—or about less deadly patterns of culture.

This approach may have been valid at its time; it was in part a reaction against nineteenth-century idealism which identified culture solely with aspirations and was not interested in how people really behaved. The behavioral view of culture was also a useful tool to fight the advocates of colonialism, who viewed all cultures in terms of the aspirations of their own Western society and were ready to alter—or kill the holders of—any diverging culture they encountered to achieve their own goals. Moreover, the approach was perhaps empirically valid; it may have fitted the preliterate group whose culture had developed around a limited and homogeneous economy and ecology. Tribes who devoted themselves exclusively to agriculture or hunting developed cultures that fitted such single-minded economies. Such cultures gave their people little if any choice; they bred fatalists who did not know that alternative ways of behaving were possible, usually because they were not possible, and this left no room for diverging aspirations.

But such a definition of culture is not applicable to contemporary Western society. Many poor people in our society are also fatalists, not because they are unable to conceive of alternative conditions, but because they have been frustrated in the realization of alternatives. Unlike preliterate people —or at least the classic version of the ideal type preliterate—they are unhappy with their state; they have aspirations that diverge from the focal concerns underlying their behavior. Of course, they can justify, to themselves and to others, the behavioral choices they make and must make, and Walter Miller's insightful analysis of focal concerns indicates clearly how they "support and maintain the basic features of the lower class way of life."[14] Even so, people who are forced to create values and justifications for what they must do may also be well aware of alternatives that they would prefer under different conditions.

For generations, researchers made no distinction between norms and aspirations, and most research emphasis was placed on the former. Lay observers and practitioners were only willing to judge; they saw the behavioral norms along the poor which diverged from their own and bade the poor behave like middle-class people. In reaction, social scientists who had done empirical work among the poor defended their behavioral norms as adaptations to their existential situation or as an independent culture, but paid little attention to aspirations diverging from these norms. Walter Miller has taken perhaps the most extreme position; he implies that lower-class aspirations as well as norms are different from those of the rest of society, and if poor people express middle-class values, they do so only because they are expected to endorse the "official ideals."[15] Their real aspirations, he seems to suggest, are those of their own lower-class culture.

Subsequent research began, however, to distinguish between aspirations and behavioral norms. Starting with a debate among anthropologists over whether Caribbean lower-class couples in "living" or consensual relationships preferred formal marriage, several studies have shown that poor people share many of the aspirations of the affluent society, but also develop norms that justify their actual behavior. Rodman conceptualizes the divergence between aspirations and norms as "lower-class value stretch;" Rainwater argues that poor people share the aspirations of the larger society, which he calls conventional norms, but knowing that they cannot live up to them, develop other norms that fit the existential conditions to which they must adapt.[16]

In a heterogeneous or pluralistic society, the divergence between aspirations and behavioral norms is almost built in; where a variety of cultures or subcultures coexist, aspirations diffuse freely. Among middle-income people, the gap between aspirations and behavioral norms is probably narrower than among poor people; the former can more often achieve what they want. Even if they cannot always satisfy career aspirations, they are able to satisfy other aspirations: for instance, for family life. The poor have far fewer options. Lacking the income and the economic security to achieve their aspirations, they must develop diverging behavioral norms in almost all areas of life. Nevertheless, they still retain aspirations, and many are those of the affluent society's "American Dream."

Consequently, research on the culture of the poor must include both behavioral norms and aspirations. The norms must be studied because they indicate how people react to their present existence, but limiting the analysis to them can lead to the assumption that behavior would remain the same under different conditions, when there is no reliable evidence, pro or con, to justify such an assumption today. As Hylan Lewis puts it, in a book to which the present essay owes a great deal, "It is important not to confuse basic life chances and actual behavior with basic cultural values and preferences."[17] Cultural analysis must also look at aspirations, determining their content, the intensity with which they are held, and, above all, whether they would be translated into behavioral norms if economic conditions made it possible.

The second deficiency of the cultural view of change is the conception of culture as holistic and systemic. When a behavior pattern is identified as part of a larger and interrelated cultural system, and when the causes of that pattern are ascribed to "the culture," there is a tendency to see the behavior pattern and its supporting norms as resistant to change and as persisting simply because they are cultural, although there is no real evidence that culture is as unchanging as assumed. This conception of culture is also ahistorical, for it ignores the origin of behavior patterns and norms. As a result, too little attention is paid to the conditions that bring a behavior pattern into being or to the conditions that may alter it. Culture becomes its own cause, and change is possible only if the culture as a whole is somehow changed.

This conceptualization is, once more, a survival of a now-inappropriate intellectual tradition. Anthropologists started out by studying small and simple societies, which may have been characterized by a cultural system whose elements were interrelated. Whether or not this was the case, the desire to preserve preliterate cultures encouraged field workers toward holistic functionalism, for if they could argue that any given behavior pattern was an integral part of the system and that the entire system might well collapse if one pattern was changed, they could oppose the colonialists who wanted to change a tribe's work habits or its religion.

Sociology used much the same conceptual apparatus; it became enamored of such terms as *Gemeinschaft* and community, viewing these as organic wholes which could be changed only with dire results, that is, the creation of a *Gesellschaft* and the city, which were described as atomized, impersonal, and dehumanized groupings. Like the anthropological concept of folk culture, *Gemeinschaft* and the organic community bore little relation to real societies, and although these terms were formulated as ideal types rather than as descriptive concepts, still, they were largely romantic fictions generated by nostalgia for the past and by the opposition of earlier sociologists and anthropologists to urbanization and industrialization.[18] It is very doubtful whether any past society ever came close to being a folk culture or a *Gemeinschaft* or whether any modern society is principally a *Gesellschaft*.

The systemic concept of culture is also inappropriate. Modern societies are pluralist; whether developed or developing, they consist of a diverse set of cultures living side by side, and researchers studying them have had to develop such terms as *subculture, class culture,* and *contraculture* to describe the diversity.[19] Holistic functionalism is irrelevant, too; no culture is sufficiently integrated so that its parts can be described as elements in a system. In modern sociology and anthropology, functionalism can survive only by identifying dysfunctions as well as functions and by showing that cultural patterns that are functional for one group may well be dysfunctional for another.

An ahistorical conception of culture is equally inapplicable to modern societies. In such societies, some behavior patterns are persistent, but others are not; they change when economic and other conditions change, although we do not yet know which patterns are persistent, and for how long, and which are not. More important, culture is a response to economic and other conditions; it is itself situational in origin and changes as situations change. Behavior patterns, norms, and aspirations develop as responses to situations to which people must adapt, and culture originates out of such responses. Changes in economic and social opportunities give rise to new behavioral solutions, which then become recurring patterns, are later complemented by norms that justify them, and are eventually overthrown by new existential conditions. Some behavioral norms are more persistent than others, but over the long run, all the norms and aspirations by which people live are nonpersistent; they rise and fall with changes in situations.[20]

These observations are not intended to question the validity of the concept of culture, for not all behavior is a response to a present situation, and not all—and perhaps not even most—behavior patterns change immediately with a change in situation. A new situation will initially be met with available norms; only when these norms turn out to be inapplicable or damaging will people change: first their behavior, and then the norms upholding that behavior. Nevertheless, the lag between a change in existential conditions and the change of norms does not make the norms immutable.

An Alternative Conception of Culture

People's behavior is thus a mixture of situational responses and cultural patterns, that is, behavioral norms and aspirations. Some situational responses are strictly ad hoc reactions to a current situation; they exist because of that situation and will disappear if it changes or disappears. Other situational responses are internalized and become behavior norms which are an intrinsic part of the persons and groups in which they move and are thus less subject to change with changes in situation. The intensity of internalization varies: at one extreme, there are norms that are not much deeper than lip service; at the other, there are norms that are built in to the basic personality structure, and a generation or more of living in a new situation may not dislodge them. They become culture, and people may adhere to them even if they are no longer appropriate, paying all kinds of economic and emotional costs to maintain them.

The southern white reaction to racial integration offers many examples of such intensely internalized norms, although it also offers examples of norms that were thought to be persistent, but crumbled as soon as the civil-rights movement or the federal government applied pressure to eliminate them. Indeed, there are probably many norms that can be toppled by a threat to exert power or to withdraw rewards; the many cultural compromises which first- and second-generation ethnics make to retain the affection of their children is a good example. Conversely, some norms are maintained simply because they have become political symbols, and people are unwilling to give them up because this would be interpreted as a loss of power. Thus, acculturated ethnic groups often preserve ethnic cultural traits for public display to maintain their ethnically based political influence. The role of power in culture, culture change, and acculturation deserves much more attention than it has received.

Not all behavioral norms are necessarily conservative; some may make people especially adaptable to change and may even encourage change. Despite what has been written about the ravages of slavery and post-Emancipation segregation as well as the high levels of joblessness blacks encountered in the southern and northern cities, they went to work readily and at other times when jobs became plentiful. Likewise, the white business community, North as well as South, operates with behavioral norms that make it readier to accept racial change than others. They cannot adhere with intensity to any beliefs that will cut into profits.

To sum up: I have argued that behavior results initially from an adaptation to the existential situation. Much of that behavior is no more than a situational response that exists only because of the situation, and it changes with a change in situation. Other behavioral patterns become behavioral norms which are internalized and are then held in varying degrees of intensity and persistence. If they persist with a change in situation, they may then be considered patterns of *behavioral culture,* and such norms may become causes of behavior. Other norms can encourage change. In addition, adaptation to a situation is affected by aspirations, which also exist in various degrees of intensity and persistence and form an *aspirational cul-*

ture. Culture, then, is that mix of behavioral norms and aspirations that results in new behavior or maintains existing behavior within the context and limits of situationally set restraints and incentives.

Culture and Poverty

This view of culture has important implications for studying the poor. It rejects a concept that emphasizes tradition and obstacles to change and sees norms and aspirations within a milieu of situations against which the norms and aspirations are constantly tested. Moreover, it enables the researcher to analyze, or at least to estimate, what happens to norms under alternative situations and thus to guess at how poor people would adapt to new opportunities.

With such a perspective, one can—and must—ask constantly to what situation, to what set of opportunities and restraints, do the present behavioral norms and aspirations respond and how intensely are they held; how much are they internalized, if at all, and to what extent would they persist or change if the significant opportunities and restraints underwent change? To put it another way, if culture is learned, one must ask how quickly and easily various behavioral norms could be unlearned, once the existential situation from which they sprang had changed.

Moreover, supposing this change took place, and opportunities—for decent jobs and incomes, for example—were made available to poor people, what behavioral norms, if any, are so deeply internalized that they interfere, say, with taking a good job? Answers to this question lead directly to policy considerations. One alternative is to seek a change in norms; another, to design the job in such a fashion that it can be accepted without requiring an immediate change in strongly persisting norms. Since such norms are not easily changed, it may be more desirable to tailor the opportunity to fit the norm, rather than the other way around. For example, if the inability to plan, often ascribed to the poor, is actually a persisting behavioral norm that will interfere in their being employable, rather than just an ad hoc response to an uncertain future, it would be wrong to expect people to learn to plan at once, just because jobs are now available. The better solution would be to fit the jobs to this inability and to make sure that the adults, once having some degree of economic security, will then plan and will be able to teach their children how to do so.

The prime issue in the area of culture and poverty, then, is to discover how soon diverse poor people will change their behavior, given new opportunities, and what restraints or obstacles, good or bad, come from that reaction to past situations we call culture. Consequently, the primary problem is to determine what opportunities have to be created to eliminate poverty, how poor people can be encouraged to adapt to those opportunities that ·conflict with persistent cultural patterns, and how they can retain the persisting patterns that do not conflict with other aspirations.

Because of the considerable divergence between behavioral norms and aspirations, it is clearly impossible to think of a holistic lower-class culture. It is perhaps possible to describe a *behavioral lower-class culture,* consisting of the behavioral norms with which people adapt to being poor and lower class. There is, however, no *aspirational lower-class culture,* for much evidence suggests that poor people's aspirations are similar to those of more affluent Americans. My hypothesis is that many and perhaps most poor people share the aspirations of the working class; others, those of the white-collar lower-middle class; and yet others, those of the professional and managerial upper-middle class, although most poor people probably aspire to the behavioral norms of these groups—to the ways they are living now—rather than to *their* aspirations.

Under present conditions the aspirations that poor people hold may not be fulfilled, but this does not invalidate them, for their existence, and the intensity with which they are held, can be tested only when economic and other conditions are favorable to their realization. If and when poor people obtain the resources that they are seeking, much of the behavioral lower-class culture will disappear. Only those poor people who cannot accept alternative opportunities because they cannot give up their present behavioral norms can be considered adherents to a lower-class culture.

In short, such conceptions of lower-class culture as Walter Miller's describe only part of the total reality. If Miller's lower-class culture were really an independent culture with its own set of aspirations, its practitioners would presumably be satisfied with their way of life. If they are not satisfied, however, if they only adapt to necessity but want something different, then ascribing their adaptation to a lower-class culture is inaccurate. It is also politically undesirable, for the judgment that behavior is cultural lends itself to an argument against change. But if data are not available for that judgment, the researcher indulges in conceptual conservatism.[21]

Miller does not indicate specifically whether the adolescents he studied adhered to both a behavioral and an aspirational lower-class culture. He suggests that "the motivation of 'delinquent' behavior engaged in by members of lower-class corner groups involves a *positive* effort to achieve states, conditions or qualities valued within the actor's most significant cultural milieu,"[22] that is, that the adolescents valued the behavior norms for which they were rewarded by their reference groups.

Perhaps the adolescents from Boston's Roxbury area did not share the aspirations of the larger society; they were, after all, delinquents, youngsters who had been caught in an illegal act and might be cynical about such aspirations. Moreover, the hippies and other "youth cultures" should remind us that adolescents do not always endorse the aspirations of an adult society. The crucial question, then, is how did lower-class adults in Roxbury feel? I would suspect that they were less positive about their youngsters' delinquent activities, partly because they are more sensitive to what Miller calls "official ideals," but partly because they do adhere to a non–lower-class aspirational culture.

My definition of culture also suggests a somewhat different interpretation of a culture of poverty than Oscar Lewis' concept. If culture is viewed as a causal factor, and particularly as those norms and aspirations that resist change, then a culture of poverty would consist of those specifically cultural or nonsituational factors that help to keep people poor, especially when alternative opportunities beckon.

Lewis' concept of the culture of poverty puts more emphasis on the behavior patterns and feelings that result from lack of opportunity and the inability to achieve aspirations. According to Lewis, "The culture of poverty is both an adaptation and a reaction of the poor to their marginal position in a class-stratified, highly individuated society. It represents an effort to cope with feelings of hopelessness and despair that develop from the realization of the improbability of achieving success in terms of the values and goals of the larger society."[23] His conception thus stresses the defense mechanisms by which people cope with deprivation, frustration, and alienation, rather than with poverty alone; it is closer to a culture of alienation than to a culture of poverty. In fact, Lewis distinguishes between poor people with and without a culture of poverty, and in indicating that people can be poor without feeling hopeless, he seems to suggest that the culture of poverty is partly responsible for feelings of hopelessness. Moreover, he claims that if poor people can overcome their malaise and resort to political action—or if they live in a socialist society like Cuba, in which they are presumably considered part of the society—they give up the culture of poverty. "When the poor become class-conscious or active members of trade-union organizations, or when they adopt an internationalist outlook on the world, they are no longer part of the culture of poverty although they may still be desperately poor."[24]

Lewis' distinction between poverty and the culture of poverty is important, for it aims to separate different kinds of poverty and adaptations to poverty. Lewis' emphasis on alienation suggests, however, that his culture of poverty concept pertains more to belonging to an underclass than to being poor, while his identification of the culture of poverty with class-stratified, highly individuated societies suggests that for him the culture is an effect rather than a cause of membership in an underclass. The various traits of the culture of poverty that he describes are partly social psychological consequences, partly situational responses, and partly behavioral norms associated with underclass membership, but the major causal factor is the class-stratified, highly individuated society. From a causal perspective, Lewis' concept is thus less concerned with culture than with the situational factors that bring about culture; it is less a culture of poverty than a sociology of the underclass.

Whether or not the families who tell their life histories in Lewis' books adhere to a culture that is a direct or indirect cause of their remaining in poverty is hard to say, for one would have to know how they would react under better economic conditions. Such data are almost impossible to gather, so that it is difficult to tell how the Sanchez and Rios families might respond, for example, if Mexico and Puerto Rico offered the men a steady supply of decent and secure jobs. Since almost all the members of the families aspire to something better, my hunch is that their behavioral and aspirational cultures would change under improved circumstances; their culture is probably not a cause of their poverty.

As I use the term *culture of poverty,* then, it would apply to people who have internalized behavioral norms that cause or perpetuate poverty and who lack—or have despairingly given up—aspirations for a better way of life; particularly people whose societies have not let them know change is possible: the peasants and urbanites who have so far been left out of the revolution of rising expectations. The only virtue of this definition is its emphasis on culture as a causal factor, thus enabling the policy-oriented researcher to separate the situational and cultural processes responsible for poverty.

If the culture of poverty is defined as those cultural patterns that keep people poor, it would be necessary to include in the term also the persisting cultural patterns among the affluent which, deliberately or not, keep their fellow citizens poor. When the concept of a culture of poverty is applied only to the poor, the onus for change falls too much on them, when, in reality, the prime obstacles to the elimination of poverty lie in an economic, political, and social structure that operates to protect and increase the wealth of the already affluent.

Culture and Class

My definition of culture also has implications for the cultural aspects of social stratification. Class may be defined sociologically to describe how people stand in the socioeconomic hierarchy with respect to occupation, income, education, and other variables having to do with the resources they have obtained, but it is often also defined culturally, in terms of their class-bound ways of life, that is, as class culture. Generally speaking, descriptions of class cultures pay little attention to the distinction between behavioral and aspirational culture, on the one hand, and situational responses, on the other hand. Descriptions that determine people's class position on the basis of situational responses, but ascribe them to culture, make ad hoc behavior seem permanent and may assign people to class positions on a long-term basis by data that describe their short-run response to a situation. [25] For example, if poor people's inability to plan is a situational response, rather than a behavioral norm, it could not be used as a criterion of lower-class culture, although it might be considered a pattern associated with lower-class position. Class, like culture, should be determined on the basis of norms that restrain or encourage people in adapting to new conditions.

Class-cultural descriptions must therefore focus on behavioral norms, on the intensity with which they are held, and on people's ability to adapt to new situations. Moreover, if culture is defined to include aspirations, assignments of class position would have to take people's aspirations into account. Since these aspirations may be for working-class, lower-middle-class, or upper-middle-class ways of life, it becomes difficult to assign poor people to a single lower-class culture. In addition, if the previous criterion of ability to adapt is also included, those who can adapt to change would have to be classified further on the basis of whether their aspirations are for one or another of the "higher" classes. The resulting classification would be quite complex and would indicate more accurately the diversity within the poverty-stricken population than current concepts of lower-class culture. More important, the number who are, culturally speaking, permanently and inevitably lower class is much smaller than sometimes imagined, for that number would include only those whose aspirations are lower class and whose behavioral culture prevents easy adaptation to change.

This approach would, of course, limit the use of current typologies of class. Dichotomies such as working class and lower class, or upper-lower and lower-lower class, can be used to describe the existential condition in which people find themselves and the situational responses they make, that is, as *sociological* typologies of class, but they cannot be used as *cultural* typologies, for people who share the same existential situation may respond with different behavioral norms and aspirations.[26] Combining sociological and cultural criteria into a single holistic category not only underestimates the diversity of people but also implies that they are satisfied with or resigned to being lower class, so that class culture is used to explain why poor people remain lower class when in reality their being poor is responsible. No doubt cultural patterns do play a causal role in class culture, but they must be determined empirically. Any other approach would reify the concept of class culture and give it a conservative political bias that suggests the poor are happy with or resigned to their lot.

Moreover, dichotomies such as working and lower class are in many ways only a sociological version of the distinction between the deserving and undeserving poor, even if their formulators had no such invidious distinction in mind. These labels are also too formalistic; they only chart the social and economic distances between people on a hierarchical scale. The terms *lower* and *middle class* are positional; they do not describe people's behavioral or aspirational culture. In fact, they really refer only to the economic, behavioral, and status deviation of poor people from the middle classes, for most current models of the class system, especially cultural models, are based on the amount of deviation from middle-class norms and aspirations.

Ideally, definitions and labels of class should include substantive elements that refer to the major themes of each class culture and indicate the real differences of culture, if any, among the classes. If the data for a thematic cultural analysis were available, we might discover that there is no distinctive lower-class culture; there are only tendencies toward distinctiveness, many of which are but functions of the situations with which people must cope and might disappear altogether once situations were changed.

Sociologists cannot ignore present situations, however, even if they are undesirable, and despite my reservations about the concepts of class and culture, ultimately I would agree with Lee Rainwater when he writes: "If, then, we take subculture to refer to a distinctive pattern of existential and evaluative elements, a pattern distinctive to a particular group in a larger collectivity and consequential for the way their behavior differs from that of others in the collectivity, it seems to me that there is no doubt that the concept of lower class subculture is useful." [27] I would add only that I am skeptical of the existence of lower-class evaluative elements, or what I have called aspirational culture.

AN OUTLINE OF BASIC RESEARCH AND POLICY QUESTIONS

THE REMAINDER of this paper attempts to apply the frame of reference I have outlined by suggesting some of the questions that ought to be asked by researchers and by indicating the methodological implications of the approach.

Studies of the poor should give up the notion of culture as largely behavioral, with little concern about divergent aspirations; as holistic; and as a persistent causal factor in behavior. Instead, insofar as poverty research should focus on the poor at all—a point I shall consider below—it should deal with behavior patterns, norms, and aspirations on an individual basis, relate them to their situational origin, and determine how much the behavioral norms related to poverty would persist under changing situations. Whether or not there is a persisting and holistic culture (or a set of subcultures) among the poor should be an empirical question.

In studying behavioral norms and aspirations among the poor, the following questions are most important: does a given behavioral pattern block a potential escape from poverty, and if so, how? Conversely, are there aspirations related to this behavioral pattern, and do they diverge? If so, are they held intensively enough to provide the motivation for an escape from poverty when economic and other opportunities are available? Are there behavioral norms that encourage this escape?

In analyzing the behavior patterns that do block the escape from poverty, one must look for the social and cultural sources of that behavior. Is the behavior a situational response that would change readily with a change in situation, or is it internalized? If it is internalized, how does it become internalized (and at what age), what agents and institutions encourage the internalization, and how intensive is it? How long would a given behavioral norm persist if opportunities changed, and what are the forces that encourage its persistence?

Similar questions must be asked about aspirations: what are their sources, how are they internalized, and how intensely are they held? How responsive are they to changes in situation, and can they enable people to give up poverty-related behavior once economic opportunities are available? And what kinds of noneconomic helping agents and institutions are needed to aid poor people in implementing their aspirations?

Equally important questions must be addressed to the affluent members of society. Indeed, if the prime purpose of research is the elimination of poverty, studies of the poor are not the first order of business; they are much less important than studies of the economy that relegate many people to underemployment and unemployment and nonmembers of the labor force to welfare dependency. They are also less important than studies of the political, social, and cultural factors that enable and encourage the affluent population to permit the existence of a poverty-stricken underclass. In the final analysis, poverty exists because it has many positive functions for the affluent society: for example, by providing a labor force to do the "dirty" work of that society.

Consequently, assuming that lower-class culture is less pervasive than has been thought and that poor people are able and willing to change their behavior if economic opportunities are made available to them, one must ask what kinds of changes have to take place in the economic system, the power structure, the status order, and the behavioral norms and aspirations of the affluent members of society for them to permit the incorporation of the poor into that society? Which of the functions of poverty for the affluent population can be eliminated, which can be translated into functional alternatives that do not require the existence of poverty, and which functions absolutely require the existence of either a deprived or a despised class, or both?

In addition, one must ask questions about the affluent society's attitudes toward behavior associated with poverty. Many behavior patterns may be the result of poverty, but they do not necessarily block the escape from poverty. They do, however, violate working- and middle-class values and thus irritate and even threaten working- and middle-class people. For example, the drinking bouts and extramarital sexual adventures that have been found prevalent among lower-class people may be correlated with poverty, but they do not cause it and probably do not block the escape from poverty.

They might persist if people had secure jobs and higher incomes, or they might not, or they might take place in more private surroundings, as they do in the middle class. But since they shock the middle class, one must also ask which behavior patterns must be given up or hidden as the price of being allowed to enter the affluent society. This question must be asked of affluent people, but one would also have to determine the impact on poor people of changing or hiding the behavior. In short, one must ask: what changes are *really* required of the lower class, which ones are absolutely essential to the escape from poverty and the move into the larger society, and which are less important? [28]

These rather abstract questions can perhaps be made more concrete by applying them to a specific case: the set of behavioral norms around the female-based or "broken" family. The first question, of course, is: does this family structure block the escape from poverty? Assuming that the answer could be yes, how does it happen? Is it because a mother with several children and without a husband or a permanently available man cannot work? Or is the female-based family per se at fault? Does it create boys who do poorly in school and on the job and girls who perpetuate the family type when they reach adulthood? If so, is the matriarchal dominance to blame (perhaps by "emasculating" boys) or is it the absence of a father? Or just the absence of a male role-model? If so, could surrogate models be provided through schools, settlement houses, and other institutions? Or are there deeper, dynamic forces at work that require the presence of a stable father figure? Or is the failure of the boys due to the mother's lack of income, that is, a result of her being poor and lower class? Or does their failure stem from the feelings of dependency and apathy associated with being on welfare? Or is their failure a result of lack of education among the mothers, which makes it difficult for them to implement their aspirations for raising their children to a better life? (But lack of income and education are not restricted to the female-based family.)

Next, what are the social, economic, political—and cultural—sources and causes of the female-based family, and to what situations, past and present, does this institutional array of behavioral norms respond? Moreover, how persistent are the behavioral norms that uphold this family type, and what aspirations exist that would alter or eliminate it if conditions changed? If the female-based family is an adaptive response to frequent and continuing male unemployment or underemployment, as I suspect it is, one must then ask whether the family structure is a situational response which would disappear once jobs were available. But if the norms that underlie this family have been internalized and would persist even with full employment, one would then need to ask: Where, when, and how are these norms internalized? Do the men themselves begin to lose hope and become so used to economic insecurity that they are unable to hold a good job if it becomes available? Do the women develop norms and even aspirations for independence, so that, doubting that men can function as husbands and breadwinners, they become unable to accept these men if they are employed?

Are such attitudes transmitted to the children of female-based families, and if so, by whom, with what intensity, and at what age? Do the boys learn from their mothers that men are unreliable, or do they conclude this from the male adults they see around them? At what age does such learning take place, and how deeply is it internalized? If children learn the norm of male unreliability during the first six years of their life, would they have difficulty in shedding their beliefs under more favorable economic conditions? If they learn it when they are somewhat older, perhaps six to nine, would they be less likely to internalize it? If they learn this norm from their mothers, is it more persistent than if they learn it later from their peers and the male adults they see on the street? And at what age does the boy begin to model himself on these male adults?

It may be that the diverse norms underlying the female-based family are much less persistent than the questions in the previous paragraph assume. Whether or not they are persistent, however, one would have to go on to ask: under what conditions is it possible for people, adults and children, to give up the norms of the female-based family? Would it follow quickly after full employment, or would adults who have become accustomed to economic insecurity and female-based families pass on these norms to their children even if they achieved economic security at some time in their lives? If so, the female-based family might persist for another generation. Or are there helping institutions that could aid parents and children to give up irrelevant norms and speed up the transition to the two-parent family? And if it were impossible to help adults to change, how about eighteen-year-olds, or thirteen-year-olds, or six-year-olds?

Moreover, what aspirations exist among the poor for a two-parent family? Do lower-class black women really want a two-parent family, and are their aspirations intense enough to overcome the behavioral norms that have developed to make them matriarchs?

In addition, one must also ask what functions the female-based family performs for the affluent members of society and what obstacles the latter might put in the way of eliminating this family type. How quickly could they overcome their belief that black family life is often characterized by instability, illegitimacy, and matriarchy? Would they permit public policies to eliminate male unemployment and to provide higher and more dignified income grants to those who cannot work? And most important, would they permit the changes in the structure of rewards and in the distribution of income, status, and power that such policies entail?

If such questions were asked about every phase of life among the poor, it would be possible to begin to determine which of the behavioral norms of poor people are causally associated with poverty. I suspect that the answers to such questions would show what Hylan Lewis found among the people he studied: "The behaviors of the bulk of the low income families appear as pragmatic adjustments to external and internal stresses and deprivations experienced in the quest for essentially common values." [29]

Structuring New Opportunities

If the major aim of research is to eliminate poverty, one would also have to ask questions about how to structure new economic and noneconomic opportunities to enable poor people to accept them, so that the incentives created by these opportunities will overcome the restraints of persisting behavioral norms. Current experiments with providing job training and even jobs to the unemployed have encountered enough refusals to indicate quite clearly that giving unemployed men any kind of job training or any kind of job is not enough. Since unemployed youth do not have lower-class aspirations, but want the kinds of jobs that are considered decent, dignified, and status bearing by working- and middle-class cultures, the new opportunities must be designed accordingly.

The first policy question is: what kinds of opportunities have highest priority, economic or noneconomic opportunities? Assuming that the first priority is for economic opportunity, what is most important for whom, a job or an income grant? What type of job would actually be considered an opportunity by poor people, both unemployed and underemployed, and what type would be inferior to present methods of earning an income: for example, welfare payments, illicit employment provided by the numbers racket, or various forms of male and female hustling?

This would require an analysis both of job aspirations and of persistent behavioral norms that interfere with holding a job. What elements of a decent job are most important to poor people: the wage or salary, the security of the job, physical working conditions, the conditions, the social characteristics of the work situation, the relationship to the boss, the skills required, the opportunities for self-improvement and promotion, or the status of the job—and in what order of priority?

What behavioral norms function as incentives to holding a job? And what are the obstacles? Is it the lack of skills; the unwillingness to work every day, or an eight-hour day; the pressures to associate with the peer group; or the inability or unwillingness to adapt to the nonwork requirements of the job: for instance, in terms of dress, decorum, or submission to impersonal authority? What kinds of incentives, monetary and otherwise, can overcome these obstacles, and what kinds of training programs, job guarantees, and social groupings on the job would be necessary to "acculturate" people who have never or rarely held a full-time job in the society of workers?

Similarly, for those who cannot work, what kinds of income grants would provide the best means for a permanent escape from poverty for them and particularly their children? Is the amount of income alone important? If not, how important is the release from stigmatization and identification as poor that would be provided by a family allowance, rather than by welfare payments or a negative income-tax grant? What forms of payment will provide the least discouragement and the most encouragement to go to work among people who want to be in the labor force? Would across-the-board grants be more desirable than a set of categorical grants, such as family allowances, rent supplements, and Medicaid?

Also, what kinds of noneconomic opportunities are necessary or desirable? Would jobs and income grants replace the need for social case work, or would people be more likely to ask for help from social workers once they did not depend on them for welfare payments? And what helping milieu is most effective? Should services be provided in special institutions for the poor, or should the poor be given grants so that they can buy the same services purchased by affluent people? Would poor people go more often to a private physician whom they pay like everyone else, or would they be readier to visit a superior—or average—clinic or group practice that is set up specially for them? Which alternative would be most compatible with the behavioral norms and aspirations of different kinds of poor people—and what are the benefits and costs of grants to use private medical and other services, as compared to expenditures that would offer improved services expressly for the poor?

Finally, how long must special opportunities be made available before poor people can truly be on their own? How much security, economic and other, must be provide for how long in order for people to take the risk of grasping at new opportunities and to be able to give up present behavioral norms and associations?

Other questions must be asked of the affluent society: for example, of employers and employees who will be working alongside the newly employed poor. Yet other questions arise because many of the poor are nonwhite, and their poverty is a result of segregation. Eventually, questions must also be asked of the voters, to estimate the political feasibility of instituting the needed programs and to determine what program designs have the greatest chance of political acceptance. In the last analysis, the shape of an effective antipoverty program probably depends more on the willingness of affluent voters to accept such a program than on the economic and cultural needs of the poor.

SOME METHODOLOGICAL IMPLICATIONS: THE NEED FOR SOCIAL EXPERIMENTS

MANY OF the questions I have raised about the culture of the poor can be investigated through a combination of presently available empirical research methods, including participant observation; the mixture of ethnological techniques, participant observation, and life-history collection used by Oscar Lewis; intensive or depth interviewing; and extensive interviewing of large samples by social surveys.

Yet none of these methods are able to get at the prime question about the culture of the poor: what behavioral norms will and will not persist under changed economic and noneconomic conditions. *This question can be answered best by altering the conditions and then seeing how people respond.* Consequently, the most desirable method of antipoverty research is inducing social change and observing the results.

Researchers lack the power and the funds to undertake social change on a large scale, but they can do it on a small scale, through social experimentation. The best technique is the field experiment, which enables a sample of poor people to live under improved conditions and then measures their response: whether or not they change their behavior and implement their aspirations. Such experiments can determine what effect the provision of a variety of new opportunities has on poverty-related behavioral norms, such as family structure, mental health, physical health, work and work performance, school attendance and school performance, political participation, and the like.

A wide range of experiments is needed to determine (and compare) the response of poor people to different kinds of new opportunities, economic and noneconomic: the efficacy of secure and well-paying jobs, a guaranteed income without employment, income derived from public welfare, the negative income tax or a family allowance, superior education for the children, better housing for families, and yet others. All the alternative politics for eliminating poverty must be tested among various kinds of poor people, with control groups established wherever possible to determine how much of the impact is a result of the specific policy or policies being tested. A few such experiments have been carried out, notably by the Office of Economic Opportunity, which was asked by Congress to test the impact of the negative income tax on work incentives and other behavior patterns and attitudes. Studies evaluating a variety of new job and job-training programs can also be treated as if they were experiments.

Most experiments would have to be set up *de novo,* but others can treat existing social processes as experiments. One approach is historical: to analyze the experience of the European immigrants in America and their descendants as a field experiment, to measure, however imperfectly, the impact of stable jobs and decent incomes on the cultural patterns that they brought with them from Europe. Further useful studies could be conducted among people, white and nonwhite, who have recently been able to move out of the slums of American cities, to determine what opportunities were available to them, how they took hold of these opportunities, and what changes in behavior followed. A comparison of an experimental group that escaped from a ghetto and a control group that did not might yield some useful preliminary answers to the questions raised in this paper.[30]

In addition, it is possible to analyze the various antipoverty programs and demonstration projects now going on all over the United States as experiments, to determine how the participants reacted to the opportunities they were offered. Such studies would examine program elements, on the one hand, and the behavioral norms and aspirations of participants, on the other hand, to determine what program elements and cultural factors were responsible for successes—and failures.

The great need is for more experiments. Most such experiments can be initiated only by the government or by well-endowed private foundations, but they can be undertaken only if social scientists are willing to design them in the first place. If social science is to serve the ends of policy, and particularly to help eliminate poverty, it must place less emphasis on the study of existing conditions and more on experimentation with improved conditions. Such an approach would also be fruitful to social-science theory, for it would answer more reliably than current research methods whether there is a culture of poverty and a lower-class way of life.

· P O S T S C R I P T ·

THIS PAPER DOES not really need a postscript, in part because I would change little in it were I to rewrite it, and in part because chapter 21 is a sequel, continuing the argument against cultural analyses of poverty that blame the poor for being so. Today, *the culture of poverty* and even such less graphic terms as *lower-class culture* have been replaced by *the underclass,* but the relations among culture, class, and poverty have not changed to any great extent over the last two decades.

Actually, I already used the term *underclass* in this essay, and sufficiently in passing to suggest now that it had already become part of the vocabulary of antipoverty analyses. At that time, the only available—and still the most sensible—definition was Gunnar Myrdal's, which he proposed in 1962 to refer to a jobless population that was becoming economically marginal. As I indicate in more detail in chapter 21, Myrdal did not see the underclass as undeserving, but he did once or twice mention its lack of hope with respect to its economic future, and following Myrdal's lead, I used the term in the preceding pages to describe that part of the very poor population which had lost hope.

One part of this essay drew on what Hylan Lewis, Lee Rainwater, Hylan Rodman, and others had written about how the poor coped with the conflict between what we now call mainstream values and the values that drove their behavior in trying to survive the constant crises of their lives. My only contribution here was to distinguish between aspirations, i.e., the goals that people sought, and behavioral norms, which they had to follow in order to survive with some dignity and emotional stability.

I still think my dichotomy has the virtue of clarity, but I also think that it is overly simple. For one thing, it leaves out *expectations,* a term that covers both the goals people expect to achieve and what they expect will actually happen to them. The latter is very important for the poor who have little control over their lives as it is; but precisely for that reason, terms that deal with their aspirations, or with the norms implicit in their behavior, are not exactly what is needed.

Of course the poor have aspirations, and these are important for their hopefulness about the future and in their striving to escape poverty. What I did not discuss, and what none of us discussed in much detail in the 1960s as far as I know is when, where, and how they had a chance to pursue these aspirations, and how this related to their expectations, in both senses of the term.[31]

If I were to start afresh, I would want to question the comprehensiveness and applicability of my concept of behavioral norms, and of Rodman's value stretch and other equivalents. Further, it seems to me now that we were all overly concerned with the role of values in behavior, perhaps an inheritance from the Parsonian approach which hung over all of sociology at the time, as well as an influence from the anthropologists who were studying the values of the poor. Whether behavior is driven by behavioral norms or by expectations—and aspirations—is really an empirical question, but I suspect that what most people do most of the time is to make choices between alternatives, and that aspirations and expectations play their roles then and mainly then.

The ability to have and make choices varies inversely with class, and the poor have less choice than anyone else. There are only a limited number of ways of surviving and coping when money and power are scarce, which is one reason why lower-class cultures are fairly similar the world over.

In other words, two sets of questions, both empirical, need to be asked. One is what alternative choices people get or can wrest from the situations in which they live; the second is what alternatives they choose, and why they choose these. At this point, aspirations, expectations, and behavioral norms play their roles—and presumably these roles are positively related to class. Thus, the rich can choose more often, have more alternatives among which they can choose, and can achieve their aspirations more often than anyone else. However, even *they* live under some imposed limits, as the mass media never tire of telling us. The choices of the poor are not only few, but often they are only choices between the lesser of two evils.

From the perspective of policy, the most important part of the paper is my proposal to give poor people diverse economic and other opportunities to escape from poverty, and to study who takes advantage of these opportunities how quickly and with what effects. If enough poor people are offered such opportunities, it should be possible to understand what kinds of opportunities can be grasped quickly, and what kinds not—and also when cultural and other patterns associated with poverty become obstacles to the escape from poverty, and for whom. This requires knowledge about how long overcoming these obstacles takes, and what kind of help is needed to overcome them.

Although I omitted it in the original essay, Oscar Lewis implied that the culture of poverty was a comprehensive and unscalable obstacle to the escape from poverty, in part because of its self-perpetuating cultural power. Conversely, pure situationalists, if they existed, would argue that the opportunities themselves eliminated all possible obstacles. The truth is always somewhere in between but policy-makers need to know in detail the opportunity-obstacle-escape-from-poverty relationship so that they can react appropriately. On the one hand, they must develop programs to help poor people with the most stubborn obstacles; and on the other hand, they must counsel patience to the nonpoor, who generally expect a poorly paying dead-end job or a small welfare benefit and a few months of education, job training, or counseling to work miracles and eliminate poverty. I recall that in the 1960s, we likened the War on Poverty to a plant which impatient politicians pulled up every six months to see if it was growing. In that respect, too, nothing has changed, because they still expect fast miracles from antipoverty programs even though the Pentagon, the Department of Agriculture, and most other public agencies get years to test and improve their programs without generating much public impatience.

Since the essay was written, a good deal of evaluation research has been carried out on a large number of experimental and demonstration projects, so that it should be possible to begin to understand which opportunities to escape poverty generate what obstacles of what length. Three general lessons have surely been learned already. One is that, as I noted in chapter 13, p. 223, opportunities that function as resources or investments can aid in the escape from poverty; while those that are amenities just make life more comfortable without offering any help in the escape from poverty.[32]

A second lesson is that small inputs have small effects and are not likely to make much of a difference. This, on the whole, was the general result of the OEO income grant experiments I mentioned on p. 323; the sums involved were too small to make much of a difference, either in enhancing or hurting work incentives.

Third, so little is known about how poverty affects the poor that unintended effects should always be anticipated. For example, one of the effects of one OEO experiment was to increase the number of family breakups among the recipients of funds. Opponents of the experiment argued that this finding proved further the antisocial effects of giving poor people money, while supporters suggested that a number of women in unhappy families used the money to free themselves from bad marriages. Since the effects were unintended, however, not enough explanatory data was collected to determine which interpretation was empirically most reasonable, ideology aside.

A most graphic example of such unintended effects was reported by Harlan Padfield and Roy Williams, who studied what happened after more than two dozen previously unemployable men were trained for and given good jobs in a California airplane factory.[33] Most had no trouble with the work, but troubles there were nevertheless. One came from jealous or angry peers who were still unemployed, which led to neighborhood fights; another from the new workers' continued reluctance to buy auto licenses and insurance for the cars with which they commuted to work. Since they now used these cars more often outside the ghetto, the police also stopped them more often. The third set of troubles developed at home. Wives and girlfriends did not always appreciate their loss of household power after the men came home with sizable paychecks, and one result was increased family conflict. As an ironic result, the men's contacts with the police and arrests increased after they got the jobs.[34]

By the early 1970s, the War on Poverty was over. Instead, as economic crises beset the country, from OPEC to double-digit inflation and then double-digit unemployment, the poor began to lose more of what little they had. Thus it should not be surprising that rates of criminal behavior, and behavior that deviates from the values in the American Dream, began to rise—and one unintended effect of *that* is the dangerous label to be discussed in the next chapter.

THE DANGERS OF THE UNDERCLASS: ITS HARMFULNESS AS A PLANNING CONCEPT

S INCE THE ERA of master planning came to a close, planning has evolved into a more catholic and eclectic discipline, and as a result, it has become hospitable to concepts and terms from other disciplines and professions. At times, planners also use the buzzwords that show up in the public discourse of these disciplines and professions, as well as in the news media, official reports, and other informational material targeted at elite and college-educated Americans.

One of the concepts planning—along with other forms of public and social policy—has begun to pay attention to most recently is the *underclass*. While this word can be used as a graphic technical term for the growing number of persistently poor and jobless Americans, it is also a value-laden and increasingly pejorative term that seems to be becoming the newest buzzword for the *undeserving* poor. As such the term carries with it a number of dangers for planners, ten of which will be discussed in this chapter. Nonetheless, the term itself is less significant than the attitudes underlying it, as well as its general usage and the affects of that usage. The

A somewhat shorter version of this essay appeared as "Deconstructing the Underclass" in the Summer 1990 issue of the *Journal of the American Planning Association*. I am grateful to Michael Katz and Sharon Zukin for helpful comments on an earlier draft of this chapter.

underclass is still only a word, but at times, powerful words *are* like sticks and stones.

Buzzwords for the undeserving poor are hardly new, for in the past, the poor were described by such terms as "paupers," "rabble," "white trash," and "the dangerous classes." Today, however, America no longer uses such harsh terms in its public discourse, whatever people may say to one another in private. If possible, euphemisms are employed, and if they are from the academy, so much the better. A string of these became popular in the 1960s, the most famous of which is Oscar Lewis' anthropological concept *culture of poverty,* a term that became an earlier generation's equivalent of the underclass.[1]

Lewis invented this concept in the late 1950s to describe a minority of poor people who had so internalized the stressful processes of living in poverty that they passed these processes on to their children in the form of a near-permanent culture—although he had little evidence for the existence of such a culture.[2] Lewis believed that some poor people would get so used to poverty that they could no longer adapt to change when improved economic conditions offered the possibility of escaping poverty, so that the culture became in effect *self-perpetuating.*[3] He also made a list of about sixty-five traits which served him as indicators of the culture of poverty, and since most of the traits were behavior patterns or attitudes usually thought to be deviant or antisocial, *the culture of poverty* became a euphemism for *the undeserving poor.*

When Gunnar Myrdal revived the 19th century Swedish word for lower class in his 1962 book *Challenge to Affluence,* he used "underclass" as a purely economic concept, to describe the chronically unemployed, underemployed, and underemployables being created by what is many years later often called the post-industrial economy.[4] He was thinking of people being driven to the margins, or entirely out, of the modern economy, here and elsewhere; but his intellectual and policy concern was with reforming that economy, not with changing the people who were its victims.

Some other academics used the term with his definition, in the 1960s and 1970s, this author included.[5] Gradually, however, the term's users shifted from Myrdal's concern with unemployment to poverty so that by the late 1970s, social scientists began to identify the underclass with acute or persistent poverty rather than joblessness. However, around the same time a very different new definition of the underclass also emerged that has by now become the most widely used, but is also the one I consider dangerous.

That definition has two novel elements. First, it is quasi-racial for it currently sees the underclass as being almost entirely black and Hispanic.[6] Second, it has added a *behavioral* element to the economic one, describing a number of behavioral patterns that signify membership in the underclass —and almost always these patterns include some behavior thought to be undeserving by the definers.[7]

Different definers concentrate on somewhat different behavior patterns, but most include antisocial or otherwise *harmful* behavior, such as crime, as well as various patterns judged *deviant* or aberrant from what they consider middle-class norms, but that in fact are not necessarily harmful, like common-law marriage. Some definers even measure membership in the underclass by deviant answers to some public-opinion poll questions.

Many of the researchers initially making up or using these new definitions were actually engaged in another enterprise, to estimate the size of the underclass in the nation, and for that purpose they looked for indicators of "underclass behavior" which existed in the form of easily available and computer-accessible national data. Since the researchers could, however, choose from a fairly wide variety of data, their decision to deemphasize indicators of economic conditions and concurrently to emphasize kinds of antisocial and deviant behavior was not impelled by methodological concerns. In fact, some made it quite clear that they were seeking to identify poor people involved in actions that violated middle-class norms.[8]

Incidentally, their choices of behavior indicators generally fit the two basic categories into which the undeserving poor have nearly always been divided, the paupers (and potential paupers) on the one hand and the "dangerous classes" on the other. Today, paupers are called "welfare dependents" and potential paupers are viewed to be the high school dropouts or jobless men of working age assumed to have left the labor force partly from choice. Today's dangerous classes include criminals and those violating the dominant norms, such as unmarried mothers.[9] Even poor people who tell the pollsters that they do not plan ahead fall into this category, for they manifest a trait Oscar Lewis and like-minded analysts of the 1960s had already identified as the inability to defer gratification, a prime symptom of undeservingness among the poor.[10]

Several of the studies to estimate the size of the underclass have included attempts to isolate "underclass neighborhoods," and with dangers for planning which I will discuss below. These attempts generally demarcate such neighborhoods by census tracts—or zip codes—and define them by an unusually high amount of antisocial and deviant behavior within the tract boundaries, as if neighborhoods and their boundaries were established by such behavior.[11] Moreover, when the researchers measure only behavior patterns and say nothing about economic and other conditions in these areas, they leave the implication that the behavior is caused by norm violations on the part of area residents and not by the conditions under which they are living, or the norms and behavioral choices open to them as a result of these conditions. [12]

The search for estimates of the size of the national underclass has been funded not only by government agencies but also by foundations and other semipublic research bodies. Moreover, the research has rarely been a purely academic exercise, for presumably some funders and researchers have been trying to estimate the size of the threat to the public peace and the dominant American norms, while others were calling attention to an apparently new population that needed various public forms of help. Whatever the researchers' and funders' explicit and implicit aims and however they defined the underclass, they agreed that it had grown dramatically since the 1960s.

Since the mid-1980s, the term's various definitions have remained basically unchanged, although the defining attempt itself has occasioned a very lively, often angry, debate among scholars. Many have accepted much or all of the now-dominant behavioral definition; some have argued for a purely economic one like Myrdal's; and some—this author included—have concluded that the term has taken on so many features of undeservingness and blaming the victims of poverty that it has become hopelessly polluted in meaning, ideological overtone, and implications, and should be dropped. The issues involved and folded into the term can and should be studied with other concepts.

Basically the debate has been between positions usually associated with the Right and the Left, partisans of the former arguing that the underclass is the product of the unwillingness of the poor to adhere to the American work ethic, among other cultural deficiencies, and the latter claiming that the underclass is a consequence of the development of the postindustrial economy which no longer needs the unskilled poor.

The debate has swirled in part around William J Wilson, the University of Chicago sociologist and author of *The Truly Disadvantaged,* who is arguably the most prominent analyst of the underclass in the 1980s. [13] He focuses entirely on the black underclass and insists that it exists mainly because of large-scale and harmful changes in the labor market. He also notes its resulting spatial concentration into underclass areas as well as the isolation of such areas from the more affluent parts of the black community which, he believes, can supply the very poor with access to jobs and other kinds of help. One of his early definitions also included a reference to aberrant behavior patterns, although his most recent one as of this writing, offered in November 1989, centers on the notion of "weak attachment to the labor force," an idea that seems nearly to coincide with Myrdal's, especially since Wilson attributes that weakness to faults in the economy rather than in the jobless. [14]

Wilson's work has inspired a lot of new research, not only about the underclass but about poverty in general, and has made poverty research funding, public and private, available again after a long drought. Meanwhile, various scholars have tried to resolve or reorient the political debate, but without much luck, for eventually, the issue always boils down to whether the fault for being poor and the responsibility for change should be assigned more to the people or more to the economy and the state. Actually, a formulation in which the basic responsibility is assigned to the economy and the state but some also to those people who *can act differently when they have a choice* may be more accurate and could also offer a way out of the political dilemma.

Since the mid-1980s, journalistic use of the behavioral definition of the underclass has increased, and so much so that there is a danger of researchers being carried along by the popularity of this definition in the elite public discourse. Some researchers view both the term and the definition as journalistic, but feel they should use it nonetheless—perhaps because it attracts research funds. Concurrently, however, other scholars turn against the term altogether and drop it from their conceptual repertoire. Both tendencies may also be found among other professionals, including of course planners and policy designers.

By the end of the 1980s, the only really notable innovation in underclass definitions has been the increasing flexibility of the term and its cancerlike tendency to find more "members," so that it has been applied—mostly by journalists—to new people or groups thought to be acting in harmful or deviant ways. For example, when crack use became widespread, drug users and even drug dealers were included in the underclass. The latter were usually mentioned with the notation that they were often not poor— although in all fairness, nonpoor stock swindlers, embezzlers, and corrupt politicians should then be added to the underclass. In the last two years, I have also seen the term applied to public-housing tenants sui generis, to Russian immigrants being victimized by the lack of opportunities to learn English so they could continue their professional or other careers, and to Chinese workers demonstrating in Beijing's Tianaman Square (albeit by a government spokesman). It even came up in a news feature about Mexican iguanas, which referred to those at the bottom of the iguana pecking order as underclass iguanas.

The behavioral definition of the underclass, which in essence proposes that some very poor people are somehow to be selected for separation from the rest of society and henceforth treated as especially undeserving, harbors many dangers—for their civil liberties and everyone else's, as well as for democracy and social cohesion, for example. However, the rest of this essay will concentrate on what seem to me to be the major dangers for planners.

The first danger of the term is its unusual power as a buzzword because, sounding technical as it does, it lends itself to being employed as a euphemism, which seems inoffensively technical on the surface but hides within it all the moral opprobrium Americans have long felt toward those poor people they have judged to be undeserving. It may even be used by journalists, scholars, and others as a technical term, but, still, it carries with it the moral and other baggage noted above and the dangers discussed below.

Once planners resort to the term, they are touched by all its baggage, too—much of which, of course, has policy implications. Also, unless planners make very clear how they define it, they run the risk that their constituents, whether politicians or citizens, will define it another way. This creates yet further policy problems, especially since the planning constituency is always ideologically diverse. Planners are best off if they avoid the problems, the term, and—since they are not hired to be moral judges— the very notion of undeserving people *per se,* whether these are poor or rich.

A second, and related, danger of the term is its use as a racial codeword that subtly hides antiblack and anti-Hispanic feelings, since race need never be mentioned. Such a code word fits in with the tolerant public discourse of our time, but it also submerges and may further repress racial —and class—antagonisms that continue to exist, yet are sometimes not expressed until sociopolitical boiling points are reached. Needless to say, planners should not want to use concepts that can be interpreted by others as racial—or class—code words. [15]

A third danger of the term is its flexible character. With the freedom of definition properly available in a democracy, anyone can decide, or try to persuade others, that yet additional people should be included in the underclass. For example, it is conceivable that in a city, region (or country) with a high unemployment rate, powerless competitors for jobs, such as illegal immigrants or even legal but recently arrived workers, might be added to the list of undeserving people. The supply of potential candidates for the underclass is very large; for, as I noted earlier, Oscar Lewis had identified sixty-five traits for his culture of poverty.

The fourth danger of the term, a particularly serious one, is that it is a synthesizing notion—or what William Kornblum has more aptly called a lumping one—that covers a number of different people.[16] Like other synthesizing notions that have moved far beyond the researchers' journals, it has also become a stereotype. Stereotypes are lay generalizations that are necessary in a very diversified society, and are useful when they are more or less accurate. When they are not, however, or when they are also judgmental terms, they turn into *labels,* to be used by some people to judge, and usually to stigmatize, other people, usually those with less power or prestige.

Neither the researchers who added behavioral patterns to Myrdal's original definition nor the funding agencies that supported these researchers were trying to develop a new judgmental label or add to the stigmas already bore by the poor. Once the underclass took on the characteristics of a label, however, the researchers gave it legitimation because they were viewed as social *scientists,* and the research funders gave it further legitimation simply because their prestige as well as their money were behind the work.

Insofar as poor people keep up with the labels the rest of society sticks on them, they are aware of the latest one. We do not all know the "street-level" consequences of stigmatizing labels, but they cannot be good. One of the likely, and most dangerous, consequences of labels is that they can become self-fulfilling prophecies. People publicly described as members of the underclass may begin to feel that they *are* members of such a class and are therefore unworthy in a new way. At the least, they now have to fight against yet another threat to their self-respect, not to mention another reason for feeling that society would just as soon have them disappear.

More important perhaps, people included in the underclass are quickly treated accordingly in their relations with the private and public agencies in which, like the rest of us, they are embedded—from workplaces, welfare agencies, and schools to the police and the courts. We know from social research that teachers with negative images of their pupils do not expect them to succeed and thus make sure, often unconsciously, that they do not; likewise, boys from single-parent families who are picked up by the police are often thought to be wild and therefore guilty because they are assumed to lack male parental control.[17] We know also that areas associated with the underclass do not get the same level of services as more affluent areas.[18] These populations are not likely to protest.

Although planners may not mean to stigmatize anyone, the danger that they do so implicitly always exists, and so does the danger that their constituents may do the labeling and stigmatizing. To be sure, we are not responsible for our constituents'—and readers'—misinterpretations of what we write and say. Nonetheless, however, the use of terms that can be easily misinterpreted is professionally irresponsible, whether the users are planners, sociologists, or politicians.

The remaining dangers are more directly, and thus especially, relevant for planners, other policy researchers, and policy-makers. The most general one, and the fifth on my list, is the term's interference with planning and policy analysis as well as antipoverty policy and other kinds of planning. The underclass is a synthesizing notion, but it is a quite distinctive one insofar as it lumps together a variety of diverse people with different problems who need different kinds of help. Categorizing them all with one term, and a buzzword at that, can be disastrous, especially if the political climate should ever require planners to formulate a single "underclass policy." So far the political climate has not heated up to this level, but not long before he was forced to resign as Vice President of the United States, Spiro T. Agnew suggested that an earlier generation's undeserving poor be put away in rural new towns built far away from the cities and suburbs.[19]

Whether one thinks of the poor as having problems or making problems for others, or both, they cannot be planned for by a single policy. For example, educational policies to prevent young people from dropping out of school, especially if they happen to attend a good school, have nothing to do with housing policies to eliminate various kinds of homelessness and the lack of affordable housing. Such policies are in turn different from programs to reduce street crime, and from methods of discouraging the very poor from escaping into the addictions of drugs, alcohol, mental illness, or pentecostal religion—which has its own harmful side effects. To be sure, policies relevant to one problem may have positive overlaps for another, but no single policy works for all the problems of the different poverty-stricken populations. Experts who claim one policy can do it all, like education, are simply wrong.

This conclusion applies even to jobs and income grant policies. Although it is certain that all the problems blamed on the people assigned to the underclass would be helped considerably by policies to decimate persistent joblessness and poverty, such policies also have limits. While all poor people need economic help, such help will not alone solve other problems they have or make for others. Although the middle class does not mug, neither do *the* poor; only a small number of poor male youngsters and young adults do so. Other causal factors are also involved, and effective antipoverty planning has to be based on some understanding of these factors and how to overcome them. Lumping concepts like the underclass can only hurt this effort.

A very different lumping danger of the underclass concept emerges when it is applied to the black underclass, for then it conflates the complex issue of the roles of race and class in black poverty. To be sure, that issue precedes the invention of the underclass concept, and scholars have been arguing for a long time whether black poverty is primarily the result of unskilled poor blacks being disadvantaged by today's economy, or whether the major cause of their poverty is race and racial discrimination in the economy as well as elsewhere.

This issue is important for planners because it has major policy implications. If economic causal factors are uppermost, economic policies are the right solution; if racial factors are more significant, antidiscrimination and antisegregation policies are required. Most analysts agree that both economic and racial policies are needed, but there is no agreement yet on which type of policy is more effective.[20]

Most likely the proper answer is some mixture of both; for as Gunnar Myrdal pointed out in his *American Dilemma,* a "vicious circle" is at work in which class and race interact with each other to keep blacks in a poverty-stricken position.[21] For planners and other policy-makers, the crucial question is where best to cut into the circle, i.e., what kinds of economic and/or antidiscrimination policies work best in the short and long run. The underclass concept helps to confuse this issue, in part because it does not encourage the policy analyst to ask what kinds of economic and/or anti-discrimination policies should be applied when, how, where, and in what mix.

A sixth planning danger stems from the persuasive capacity of concepts or buzzwords, for they may therefore become so *reified* that people think that they represent actual groups or aggregates, and may also begin to believe that membership in what are in fact imaginary groups is a *cause* of the characteristics included in a buzzword's definition.

The underclass is on its way to being reified; and sometimes journalists and even scholars—especially those of a conservative bent—appear to think that becoming very poor and acting in antisocial or deviant ways is an *effect* of being in the underclass. When the underclass becomes a causal term, however—especially on a widespread basis—then planners, but also politicians and citizens, are in trouble. This is true because sooner or later, someone will argue that the only policy solution is a direct attack on the cause itself, i.e., the troubled and trouble-making people who have been described as underclass members.

Similar planning problems develop if and when the reification of a term leads to its being assigned *moral* causality. Using notions that blame victims may allow the blamers to feel better by blowing off the steam of righteous indignation, but it does not eliminate the problems very poor people have or make. Indeed, those who argue that all people are entirely responsible for what they do sidestep the morally and otherwise crucial issue of determining how much responsibility should be assigned to people who lack resources, who are therefore under unusual stress and also lack effective choices in many areas of life in which even moderate-income people can choose relatively freely.

The ideal is of course to give people as much public aid, and of the right kind, as they need to exercise the same responsibilities as nonpoor Americans. Of course, even the most persistently poor have to be law-abiding, but beyond that, what resources will maximize other forms of responsibility (and self- or group-help) has not yet been figured out. In the meantime, neither blaming the poor as undeserving nor romanticizing them as helpless victims of societal inequities is very helpful.

The seventh danger of the term, and one also particularly salient for planners, stems from the way the underclass has been analyzed. As noted before, some researchers endeavoring to count the underclass have tried to identify underclass census tracts, which they have called neighborhoods, but neighborhood is a complex and often emotion-laded term, which planners cannot use lightly.

Moreover, counting exercises are dangerous sui generis for planners, because often their decisions and plans may rest on the outcomes of such exercises, even though all counting exercises that rely on indicators or proxies for the desired but unavailable data can only produce numbers about the indicators. Thus, they are at best substitutes which cannot be taken as replacements for the desired data. Furthermore, they may include value choices and decisions made by the individuals and agencies who collected the indicator data, even if the researchers using them for their own "secondary" analyses are not necessarily aware of them. Substitute data and unknown value choices can in turn result in unwanted policy choices, for just as data help shape the subsequent analysis, so can they shape later plans.

Counting school conditions that interfere with learning produces different numbers and policies than counting high school dropouts, for example; likewise, a count of the number of poor people paying more than 30 percent of their income for rent leads to a different housing policy than one based on the number of destructive or antisocial tenants.

Planners must be especially sensitive to the concept of an underclass area or neighborhood because once such areas, i.e., the adjacent census tracts that define them, are marked with the underclass label, the politicians who make the basic land use decisions in the community might propose a variety of harmful policies, since the people in them are thought to be both undeserving and powerless. Thus, public officials might suggest moving all of a city's homeless into such areas, or declaring them ripe for urban renewal. Recall that this is how much of the federal urban renewal of the 1950s and 1906s was planned—and justified.

In addition, neighborhood policies tend to assume that people inside the boundaries of such areas are more homogeneous than they in fact are, and that they remain inside boundaries which are more often nothing but lines on a map. Since very poor people tend to suffer more from public policies than they benefit, and since they have fewer defenses than more affluent people against harmful policies, "neighborhood policies" may hurt more often than they will help.

Another danger—the eighth—stems from William J. Wilson's "concentration and isolation" hypothesis. As I suggested above, Wilson argues that the economic difficulties of the poorest blacks are compounded by the fact that, as better-off blacks move out, the poor who remain are more and more concentrated, having only other very poor people, and the few institutions that have remained to minister to them, as neighbors. Among other things, this concentration causes social isolation, Wilson suggests, because the very poor are now isolated from access to the people, job networks, role models, institutions, and other connections that might help them escape poverty.

Wilson's hypotheses, summarized all too briefly here, are already being accepted as dogma by many outside the research community. Fortunately, they are also being tested in a number of places, but until they are shown to be valid, planners should go slowly in designing action programs— especially to reduce concentration. In the minimal-vacancy housing markets in which virtually all poor blacks live, such a policy might mean having to find a new, and surely more costly, dwelling unit, or having to double up with relatives—or in some cases being driven into shelters or into the streets. Even if working- and middle-class areas would be willing to accept relocates from areas to be deconcentrated, which seems unlikely given the political effectiveness of NIMBY protests, dispersal itself has some harmful consequences for people who need neighbors in the same boat as they are. In fact, the dysfunctions of dispersal may be as bad as those of overconcentration, not because the latter has any virtues, but because until an effective jobs-and-income-grants program has gone into operation, requiring very poor people to move away from the neighborly support structures they *do* have may deprive them of one of their major resources.

Attempts to reduce isolation are worth trying, however, since there seem to be no virtues to such isolation. One form of isolation, the so-called urban-suburban mismatch between the residences of jobless urban workers and available suburban jobs, is already being attacked again, which is all to the good. Perhaps something has been learned from the failures of the 1960s to reduce the then-existing mismatches, although in too many cases the alleged mismatch is only a cover for class and racial discrimination, and the widespread unwillingness of white employers—and white workers—to have black coworkers.[22]

Likewise, we do not yet know how many of the very poor are actually isolated from job networks, role models, and other social contacts that might help them escape poverty. Many probably remain connected to extended kin networks that usually include some moderate and middle-income relatives so that these very poor people are literally not socially isolated. However, whether any of the relatives can provide access to jobs and reduce the *economic* isolation of their poorer kin is another question. Furthermore, if the institutions that have departed along with the better-off residents are abler at providing economically relevant help than the institutions that remain, the people who are left behind in these areas are *institutionally* isolated.

Although the actual nature of the isolation and its effects need still to be established empirically, Wilson's fear of the isolation of the very poor must be taken seriously. If it is shown to be reasonably accurate, planners must try to figure out what spatial and other policies can be developed to reduce especially those kinds of isolation that can hinder the escape from poverty, especially since the spatial concentration of the poorest blacks is not likely to be reduced soon.

The ninth danger is inherent in the concept of an underclass, for while the term assumes that the people assigned to it are poor, it can be used to avoid discussing their economic condition and what should be done about it. For example, conservative researchers can look at the homeless either as mainly mentally ill or as the victims of rent control, which frees them from any need to discuss the disappearance of jobs, SROs, and other low-income housing.

Indeed, to the extent that the underclass notion is turned into a synonym for the undeserving poor, the political conditions for reinstituting effective antipoverty policy are removed. If the underclass is undeserving, then the government's responsibility is limited to beefing up the courts and other punitive agencies and institutions that try to isolate the underclass and protect the rest of society from it. Conversely, the moral imperative to help the poor through the provision of jobs and income grants is reduced. Describing the poor as undeserving has long been an effective if immoral short-term approach to tax reduction.

Tenth and last, there is the danger of inventing new but unnecessary words—because no one can predict how they will be used. To be sure, it would be neither desirable nor possible to stop people from such inventing, but in the case of the underclass, the current use is in many ways diametrically opposed to what Myrdal had in mind in the early 1960s. I assume that when he coined the word, he thought there was a need for a dramatic new term that would attract more attention to and therefore more help for the poorest of the poor. I was one of several people who used the term with that strategy in mind, and with hindsight, it is clear we made a strategic mistake.

Further hindsight suggests that the term "underclass" creates far more social and other costs than benefits. While it may still turn out to have some virtues as an attention-getting metaphor for the very poor, it has so far gotten mainly the wrong attention, and its limited virtues as an *analytic* concept must be compared to its major faults as a *policy* concept.

Its use ought to be discouraged as much as possible, although eliminating the reasons for the existence of such a term would be better still. [23] Even William J Wilson's neo-Myrdalian conception of the underclass referred to above adds little, for if the main problem is joblessness, as Wilson has always insisted, then why not call the people involved the jobless—and figure out politically feasible ways of moving toward full employment. If future research should show that some of the very poor are so isolated that they are literally separated from the rest of society and could therefore be called an underclass in the analytic sense, the term would still not serve a useful policy function, since as I have suggested earlier, the very notion of underclass policy has all kinds of dangers for planners and the poor. If one of the problems of the persistently jobless *is* isolation, then policies to reduce isolation are needed in addition to full employment.

If a distinctive analytic term for some of the very or most persistently poor is really needed, then W. Lloyd Warner's *lower-lower* class could be revived.[24] Those who use the underclass as a euphemism for the undeserving poor should instead talk and write about the undeserving poor, so that their political stand is explicit. The rest of us ought to analyze joblessness and poverty—particularly the persistent varieties—and then study their causes and effects.

The cause-and-effect studies ought to include the social and emotional problems jobless and poor people *have,* while other studies ought to examine the problems they *make:* the antisocial acts, as well as the behavior patterns thought deviant by large numbers of other Americans. After all, these large numbers of other Americans have to provide political support for any future antipoverty policies. For this reason alone, they deserve to be told why some poor people have and make the troubles that upset and scare them: for example, why economic pressures and the need to feed the family may get in the way of being law-abiding, and why a mixture of despair and anger may produce deviant behavior of which the despairing and angry may themselves disapprove. Evading the fact that poor people commit most of the street crime seems as irresponsible as assigning them the label underclass, although exaggerating the proportion of antisocial acts among the very poor so as to scare the nonpoor citizenry is equally irresponsible.

Researchers ought also to try to establish how secure and decent jobs and/or income grants will enable people to leave poverty and reduce their problems and problematic behavior. We also need to know how long the process of problem reduction will take, so that impatient politicians and citizens can be persuaded not to demand immediate behavior change; how much the poor people involved can and will be able to help themselves; and what else if anything needs to be done to make sure the process of behavior change proceeds on as widespread a basis and as quickly as possible.

The greatest danger of all is not caused by the underclass concept; indeed, the concept is only yet another symptom of it. That danger is the possibility already referred to in previous chapters that we are moving toward a new form of postindustrial economy in which there may not be enough decent jobs for all.

At the start of the 1990s, America's *official* unemployment rate is higher today than most of the past half century, even though it is still lower than that of some West European welfare states. However, the way we count the jobless has worked effectively to hide the *actual* unemployment rate. Poverty researchers in the 1960s learned that this actual rate was always close to double the official one, once the discouraged, the involuntarily at-home or school-going, the totally unreachable, and the involuntary part-timers were counted. Consequently, at the start of 1990, the actual rate was over 10 percent.

Both the official and the actual rate report a sizable racial difference in unemployment, for in the United States, as in too many other countries, the people condemned to persistent joblessness and poverty are not just those already low on the class ladder and low in skills, but also those with a darker skin. None of this is automatic or natural. Even if there are not enough jobs in the society for everyone who wants to work, the people to go jobless could be children of inherited wealth, the best educated, anyone under twenty-five or over fifty-five, those who will trade their right to a job for a minimal lifetime income—or anyone else. Nonetheless, political majorities and their leaders somehow "select" minorities, and for race and class reasons, the selected have often been the darkest skinned.

The past and present do not completely determine the future, and if there is indeed a labor shortage in the 1990s, then additional workers may be drawn from the persistently jobless and poor—even if their skins are dark. Unfortunately, other scenarios are possible, including the encouragement of yet another wave of low-wage immigrants, or the reemployment of military and defense industry personnel left jobless by the end of the cold war—not to mention further computerization and the further departure of American jobs to the third world.

In that case, the underclass notion may turn out to be what I fear it is: a signal that the economy, the society, and the language are preparing to adapt to a future in which some people are going to be more or less permanently jobless. To put it baldly, we may be entering an era in which, with the general public's concurrence, those who make the decisions in the economy and the polity are beginning to establish a new class of the jobless, who, as so often before in American history, are then blamed for their own joblessness and forced to behave in ways that allow the nonpoor to describe them as undeserving and write them off. Worse still, the word *underclass* and the imagery describing those being labeled with it suggest the possibility that many of its "members" may never get out again, for economic or moral reasons. In short, the people now assigned to the underclass may be assigned to what could someday become an American *caste*.

It is of course conceivable that long before such tendencies become significant, Americans will find new sources of work, including those of a modernized New Deal. They may also begin to think seriously about ways of sharing the work, such as the work-time reduction schemes discussed in chapter 16. Nor should I exclude what has always saved the United States in the past, new forms of economic growth that cannot even be imagined now. Still, it is also conceivable that all the techniques of modern zoning will be applied in order to create and put in place physical barriers to supplement the political and economic boundaries so as to wall off the jobless caste from the rest of America. Unfortunately, such a solution is in many ways easier to implement in our political system than deliberate planning for job creation.

Obviously, an America with a jobless caste—or even a jobless stratum—would be *socially* dangerous; for crime, addiction, mental illness, as well as various forms of covert and overt protest, some of it violent, would be sure to go up sharply. In the long run, such a solution would also be *politically* dangerous, because however much the term seems to imply the opposite, the people assigned to an underclass would remain an integral part of the larger society. There has always been a relation, albeit complex, between rising joblessness and the emergences of fascist movements, of the Right or the Left. If such movements begin to appear, the source of the danger will not be the underclass but the *overclasses* (a term that curiously enough has not yet surfaced) who would permit the evolution of such a dangerous—and immoral—society.

· N O T E S ·

1. TOWARD A HUMAN ARCHITECTURE

1. The story is told and analyzed in Lily Hoffman, *The Politics of Knowledge: Activist Movements in Medicine and Planning* (Albany: S.U.N.Y. Press, 1989).

2. Robert Goodman, *After the Planners* (New York: Simon & Schuster, 1971); Brent Brolin, *The Failure of Modern Architecture* (New York: Van Nostrand & Reinhold, 1978); and John R. Short, *The Humane City* (New York: Blackwell, 1989), esp. ch. 3.

3. Herbert Gans, *Popular Culture and High Culture* (New York: Basic Books, 1974); and Pierre Bordieu, *Distinction: A Social Critique of the Judgment of Taste* (Cambridge: Harvard University Press, 1984).

4. In 1989, the overall Consumer Price Index was about 470 percent that of 1955–56. On that basis, which is conservative for housing, the architectural prototype would today cost $470,000, while Levitt houses would cost from $54,000 to $68,000. A more reasonable projection for the New York area would be 1000 percent of the mid-1950s Consumer Price Index, although no builder in the New York area in 1989 sold two-bedroom houses, or condominiums, for $115,000 to 145,000.

5. Daniel Wilner et al., *Housing Environment and Family Life* (Baltimore: Johns Hopkins University Press, 1962); and Herbert J. Gans, *The Levittowners* (2d ed.; New York: Columbia University Press, 1982).

6. Clare Cooper. *Easter Hill Village* (New York: Free Press, 1965).

7. Jon Freedman, *Crowding and Behavior* (New York: Viking, 1975) and Mark Baldassare, *Residential Crowding in Urban America* (Berkeley and Los Angeles: University of California Press, 1979). For children, the evidence is more ambiguous, although no one has yet proved that children are seriously affected by crowding. See e.g., Susan Saegert, "Environment and Children's Mental Health," in A. Baum and J Singer, eds., *Handbook of Psychology and Health,* vol. 2 (Hillsdale, N.J.: Erlbaum Associates, 1981).

8. For a good discussion of the place of users in architecture, see Roger Montgomery, "Architecture Invents New People," in Russell Ellis and Dana Cuff, eds., *Architechts' People* (New York: Oxford University Press, 1989), ch. 13. Incidentally, his is one of only three chapters out of thirteen in the book that deals at all with actual human users of buildings.

9. Robert Gutman and Barbara Westergaard, "Building Evaluation, User Satisfaction and Design," in J. Lang et al., *Designing for Human Behavior* (Stroudsberg, Pa.: Hutchinson and Ross, 1974), pp. 320–330.

10. On the division of labor in architectural firms, see Judith Blau, *Architects and Firms* (Cambridge, Mass.: MIT Press, 1984).

11. John Zeisel, *Sociology and Architectural Design* (New York: Russell Sage Foundation, 1975).

12. Cooper, *Easter Hill Village,* ch. 10.

4. URBANISM AND SUBURBANISM AS WAYS OF LIFE

1. Louis Wirth, "Urbanism as a Way of Life," *American Journal of Sociology* (July 1938), 44:1–24; reprinted in Paul Hatt and Albert J. Reiss, Jr., eds., *Cities and Society* (Glencoe, Ill.: Free Press, 1957), pp. 46–64.

2. Richard Dewey, "The Rural–Urban Continuum: Real but Relatively Unimportant," *American Journal of Sociology* (July 1960), 66:60–66.

3. I shall not attempt to summarize these studies, for this task has already been performed by Dewey, Reiss, Wilensky, and others. The studies include: Morris Axelrod, "Urban Structure and Social Participation," *American Sociological Review* (February 1956), 21:13–18; Dewey, "The Rural–Urban Continuum;" William H. Form et al., "The Compatibility of Alternative Approaches to the Delimitation of Urban Sub-areas," *American Sociological Review* (August 1954), 19:434–440; Herbert J. Gans, *The Urban Villagers* (New York: Free Press of Glencoe, 1962); Scott Greer, "Urbanism Reconsidered: A Comparative Study of Local Areas in a Metropolis," *American Sociological Review* (February 1956), 21:19–25; Scott Greer and Ella Kube, "Urbanism and Social Structure: A Los Angeles Study," in Marvin B. Sussman, ed., *Community Structure and Analysis* (New York: Crowell, 1959), pp. 93–112; Morris Janowitz, *The Community Press in an Urban Setting* (Glencoe, Ill.: Free Press, 1952); Albert J. Reiss, Jr., "An Analysis of Urban Phenomena," in Robert M. Fisher, ed., *The Metropolis in Modern Life* (Garden City, N.Y.: Doubleday, 1955), pp. 41–49; Albert J. Reiss, Jr., "Rural-Urban and Status Differences in Interpersonal Contacts," *American Journal of Sociology* (September 1959), 65:182–195; John R. Seeley, "The Slum: Its Nature, Use, and Users," *Journal of the American Institute of Planners* (February 1959), 25:7–14; Joel Smith, William Form, and Gregory Stone, "Local Intimacy in a Middle-Sized City," *American Journal of Sociology* (November 1954), 60:276–284; Gregory P. Stone, "City Shoppers and Urban Identification: Observations on the Social Psychology of City Life," *American Journal of Sociology* (July 1954), 60:36–45; William F. Whyte, *Street Corner Society* (Chicago: University of Chicago Press, 1955); Harold L. Wilensky and Charles Lebeaux, *Industrial Society and Social Welfare* (New York: Russell Sage Foundation, 1958); Michael Young and Peter Willmott, *Family and Kinship in East London* (London: Routledge and Kegan Paul, 1957).

4. Greer and Kube, "Urbanism and Social Structure," p. 112.

5. Wilensky and Lebeaux, "Industrial Society," p. 121.

6. By the *inner city* I mean the transient residential areas, the Gold Coasts and the slums that generally surround the central business district, although in some communities they may continue for miles beyond that district. The *outer city* incudes the stable residential areas that house the working- and middle-class tenant and owner. The *suburbs* I conceive as the latest and most modern ring of the outer city, distinguished from it only by yet lower densities and by the often irrelevant fact of the ring's location outside the city limits.

7. Louis Wirth, *The Ghetto* (Chicago: University of Chicago Press, 1928).

8. Arnold M. Rose, "Living Arrangements of Unattached Persons," *American Sociological Review* (August 1947), 12:429–435.

9. Gans, *Urban Villagers*.

10. Seeley, "The Slum."

11. *Ibid.* The trapped are not very visible, but I suspect that they are a significant element in what Raymond Vernon has described as the "gray areas" of the city in his *Changing Economic Function of the Central City* (New York: Committee on Economic Development, Supplementary Paper No. 1, January 1959).

12. Wirth, *The Ghetto*, p. 283.

13. If the melting pot had resulted from propinquity and high density, one would have expected second-generation Italians, Irish, Jews, Greeks, and Slavs to have

developed a single "pan-ethnic culture," consisting of a synthesis of the cultural patterns of the propinquitous national groups.

14. The corporation transients, who provide a new source of residential instability to the suburb, differ from city transients. Since they are raising families, they want to integrate themselves into neighborhood life and are usually able to do so, mainly because they tend to move into similar types of communities wherever they go. See William H. Whyte, Jr., *The Organization Man* (New York: Simon & Schuster, 1956), and Wilensky and Lebeaux, "Industrial Society."

15. The negative social consequences of overcrowding are a result of high room and floor density, not of the land coverage of population density which Wirth discussed. Park Avenue residents live under conditions of high land density, but do not seem to suffer from overcrowding.

16. Whether or not these social phenomena have the psychological consequences Wirth suggested depends on the people who live in the area. Those who are detached from the neighborhood by choice are probably immune, but those who depend on the neighborhood for their social relationships—the unattached individuals, for example—may suffer greatly from loneliness.

17. Needless to say, residential instability must ultimately be traced to the fact that, as Wirth pointed out, the city and its economy attract transient—and, depending on the sources of outmigration, heterogeneous—people. However, this is a characteristic of urban-industrial society, not of the city specifically.

18. By neighborhoods or residential districts I mean areas demarcated from others by distinctive physical boundaries or by social characteristics, some of which may be perceived only by the residents. However, these areas are not necessarily socially self-sufficient or culturally distinctive.

19. Wirth, "Urbanism as a Way of Life," p. 56.

20. For the definition of *outer city*, see note 6.

21. Wirth, "Urbanism as a Way of Life," p. 56.

22. Because neighborly relations are not quite primary and not quite secondary, they can also become *pseudo-primary*, that is, secondary ones disguised with false affect to make them appear primary. Critics have often described suburban life in this fashion, although the actual prevalence of pseudo-primary relationships has not been studied systematically in cities or suburbs.

23. Stone, "City Shoppers."

24. These neighborhoods cannot, however, be considered as urban folk societies. People go out of the area for many of their friendships, and their allegiance to the neighborhood is neither intense nor all-encompassing. Janowitz has aptly described the relationship between residents and neighborhoods as one of "limited liability." "The Community Press," ch. 7.

25. Were I not arguing that ecological concepts cannot double as sociological ones, this way of life might best be described as small-townish.

26. Arthur J. Vidich and Joseph Bensman, *Small Town in Mass Society: Class, Power and Religion in a Rural Community* (Princeton, N.J.: Princeton University Press, 1958).

27. Harold Wattel, "Levittown: A Suburban Community," in William M. Dobriner, ed., *The Suburban Community* (New York: Putnam, 1958), pp. 287–313.

28. Bennett Berger, *Working Class Suburb: A Study of Auto Workers in Suburbia* (Berkeley: University of California Press, 1960). Also Vernon, *Changing Economic Function of the Central City*.

29. Berger, *Working Class Suburb.*

30. Wattel, "Levittown." They may, of course, be significant for the welfare of the total metropolitan area.

31. Otis Dudley Duncan and Albert J. Reiss, Jr., *Social Characteristics of Rural and Urban Communities, 1950* (New York: Wiley, 1956), p. 131.

32. Donald L. Foley, "The Use of Local Facilities in a Metropolis," in Hatt and Reiss, *Cities and Societies,* pp. 237–247. Also see Christen T. Jonassen, *The Shopping Center versus Downtown* (Columbus: Bureau of Business Research, Ohio State University, 1955).

33. Jonassen, "The Shopping Center," pp. 91–92.

34. A 1958 study of New York theatergoers showed a median income of close to $10,000, and 35 percent were reported as living in the suburbs. That year, the median U.S. family income was $5087. John Enders, *Profile of the Theater Market* (New York: Playbill, undated and unpaged).

35. A. C. Spectorsky, *The Exurbanites* (Philadelphia: Lippincott, 1955).

36 I am thinking here of adults; teenagers do suffer from the lack of informal meeting places within walking or bicycling distance.

37. Herbert J. Gans, "Planning and Social Life: Friendship and Neighbor Relations in Suburban Communities," *Journal of the American Institute of Planners* (May 1961), 27:134–140.

38. These must be defined in dynamic terms. Thus, class includes also the process of social mobility; the stage in the life cycle, the processes of socialization and aging.

39. Thomas Ktsanes and Leonard Reissman, "Suburbia: New Homes for Old Values," *Social Problems* (Winter 1959–1960), 7:187–194.

40. Leonard J. Duhl, "Mental Health and Community Planning," in *Planning 1955* (Chicago: American Society of Planning Officials, 1956), pp. 31–39; Erich Fromm, *The Sane Society* (New York: Rinehart, 1955), pp. 154–162; David Riesman, "The Suburban Sadness," in Dobriner, *The Suburban Community,* pp. 375–408; W. Whyte, *The Organization Man.*

41. William M. Dobriner, "Introduction: Theory and Research in the Sociology of the Suburbs," in Dobriner, *The Suburban Community,* pp. xiii–xxviii.

42. Sylvia Fleis Fava, "Contrasts in Neighboring: New York City and a Suburban Community," in Dobriner, *The Suburban Community,* pp. 122–131.

43. This formulation may answer some of Duncan and Schnore's objections to sociopsychological and cultural explanations of community ways of life. Otis Dudley Duncan and Leo F. Schnore, "Cultural, Behavioral and Ecological Perspectives in the Study of Social Organization," *American Journal of Sociology* (September 1959), 65:132–155.

44. The ecologically oriented researchers who developed the Shevsky-Bell social-area analysis scale have worked on the assumption that "social differences between the populations of urban neighborhoods can conveniently be summarized into differences of economic level, family characteristics and ethnicity." Wendell Bell and Maryanne T. Force, "Urban Neighborhood Types and Participation in Formal Associations," *American Sociological Review* (February 1956), 21:25–34. However, they have equated "urbanization" with a concept of life-cycle stage by using family characteristics to define the index of urbanization, *Ibid.* Also see Scott Greer, "The Social Structure and Political Process of Suburbia," *American Sociological Review* (August 1960), 25:514–526, and Greer and Kube, "Urbanism and Social Structure." In fact, Bell has identified suburbanism with familism: Wendell Bell,

"Social Choice, Life Styles and Suburban Residence," in Dobriner, *The Suburban Community*, pp. 225–247.

45. Duncan and Schnore, "Cultural, Behavioral and Ecological Perspectives."

46. Dobriner, "Introduction," in Dobriner, *The Suburban Community*, p. xxii.

47. Because of the distinctiveness of the ways of life found in the inner city, some writers propose definitions that refer only to these ways, ignoring those found in the outer city. For example, popular writers sometimes identify "urban" with "urbanity," that is, "cosmopolitanism." However, such a definition ignores the other ways of life found in the inner city. Moreover, I have tried to show that these ways have few common elements and that the ecological features of the inner city have little or no influence in shaping them.

48. Even more than Wirth's they are based no data and impressions gathered in the large eastern and midwestern cities of the United States.

49. Personal discussions with European planners and sociologists suggest that many European apartment dwellers have similar preferences, although economic conditions, high building costs, and the scarcity of land make it impossible for them to achieve their desires.

5. AMERICAN URBAN THEORIES AND URBAN AREAS

Author's note: This chapter substitutes a bibliography for the notes that accompany the other chapters.

Banfield, Edward C. *The Unheavenly City* and *The Unheavenly City Revisited*. Boston: Little Brown, 1970 and 1974.

Berry, Brian J.L. and John D. Kasarda. *Contemporary Urban Ecology*. New York: Macmillan, 1977.

Bluestone, Barry and Bennett Harrison. *The Deindustrialization of America*. New York: Basic Books, 1982.

Castells, Manuel. *The Urban Question: A Marxist Approach*. Cambridge, Mass.: MIT Press, 1977.

Dear, Michael and Allen J. Scott, eds. *Urbanization and Urban Planning in Capitalist Society*. New York: Methuen, 1981.

Forrester, Jay W. *Urban Dynamics*. Cambridge, Mass.: MIT Press, 1969.

Gallup, George Jr. "Small Towns, Rural Areas Still Beckon Many Americans." Press Release, March 24, 1985.

Gans, Herbert J. *Middle American Individualism: The Future of Liberal Democracy*. New York: Free Press, 1988.

Goering, John M., ed. "Marx and the City: A Symposium." *Comparative Urban Research*, vol. 6, nos. 2–3, 1978. (entire issue).

Gottdiener, Mark. *The Social Production of Urban Space*. Austin: University of Texas Press, 1984.

Harloe, Michael, ed. *Captive Cities: Studies in the Political Economy of Cities and Regions*. New York: Wiley, 1977.

Harrison, Bennett. "The Once and Future City." *Challenge* (September–October 1973), 1:8–21.

Harvey, David. *Social Justice and the City*. Baltimore: Johns Hopkins University Press, 1973.

Herbers, John. *The New Heartland*. New York: Times Books, 1986.

Hicks, Donald. *Urban America in the Eighties: Perspectives and Prospects*. New Brunswick: Transaction Books, 1982.

Jackson, Kenneth T. *Crabgrass Frontier: The Suburbanization of the United States.* New York: Oxford University Press, 1985.

Kasarda, John D. "The Implications of Contemporary Redistribution Trends for National Urban Policy." *Social Science Quarterly* (December 1980), 61:373–400.

Katznelson, Ira *City Trenches: Urban Politics and the Patterning of Class in the United States.* New York: Pantheon Books, 1981.

Kristol, Irving. "An Urban Civilization Without Cities." *Horizon* (Autumn 1972), 14:36–41.

Logan, John R. and Harvey L. Molotch. *Urban Fortunes: The Political Economy of Place.* Berkeley: University of California Press, 1987.

Mollenkopf, John H. *The Contested City.* Princeton: Princeton University Press, 1983.

Musil, J. "The Development of Prague's Ecological Structure." In R.E. Pahl, ed., *Readings in Urban Sociology,* pp. 232–259. London: Pergamon Press, 1968.

Peterson, Paul E., ed. *The New Urban Reality.* Washington: The Brookings Institution, 1985.

Pickvance, C. G., ed. *Urban Sociology: Critical Essays.* New York: St. Martin's Press, 1976.

Saunders, Peter. *Social Theory and the Urban Question.* New York: Holmes & Meier, 1981 (2d ed. 1986).

Saunders, Peter. "The Sociology of Consumption: A Research Agenda." Unpublished paper, 1986.

Savas, E.S. *Privatizing the Public Sector.* Chatham, N.J.: Chatham House, 1982.

Starr, Roger. "Making New York Smaller." *New York Times Magazine,* November 14, 1976, pp. 32–33, 99–106.

Street, David and Associates, eds. *Handbook of Contemporary Urban Life.* San Francisco: Jossey Bass, 1978.

Szelenyi, Ivan. *Urban Inequalities Under State Socialism.* New York: Oxford University Press, 1983.

Tabb, William K. and Larry Sawers, eds., *Marxism and the Metropolis: New Perspectives in Urban Political Economy.* New York: Oxford University Press, 1978 (2d ed. 1984).

U.S. President's Commission for a National Agenda for the Eighties. "From an Urban Policy to a Social Policy: New Perspectives on Urban America." *A National Agenda for the Eighties,* pp. 64–76. Washington, D.C.: GPO, 1981.

Zukin, Sharon. "A Decade of the New Urban Sociology." *Theory and Society,* 9:575–601, 1980.

6. THE HISTORICAL COMPARISON OF CITIES

1. Incidentally, it would be interesting to compare how past and present societies have decided which settlements were to be called cities, which criteria they used to make this decision, and why these.

2. R. E. Wycherly, *How the Greek Built Cities* (New York: Anchor, 1969), p. 3.

3. *Ibid.,* p. 186. In all fairness to Wychery, others share the same biases. Thus, Donald J. Olsen's *The City as a Work of Art: London, Vienna, Paris* (New Haven: Yale University Press, 1986) devotes $7\frac{1}{2}$ of its 311 pages to working-class housing.

8. CITY PLANNING IN AMERICA, 1890–1967

1. Hans Blumenfeld, "Theory of City Form, Past and Present," *Journal of the Society of Architectural Historians* (1949), 7:7–16.

2. Arthur Mann, *Yankee Reformers in an Urban Age* (Cambridge: Belknap, 1954).

3. Roy Lubove, *The Progressives and the Slums: Tenement House Reform in New York City, 1890–1917* (Pittsburgh: University of Pittsburgh Press, 1962).

4. Joseph Lee, *How to Start a Playground* (New York: Playground and Recreation Association, 1910).

5. Daniel H. Burnham and E. H. Bennett, *Plan of Chicago* (Chicago: The Commercial Club, 1909).

6. Charles M. Haar, "The Content of the General Plan: A Glance at History," *Journal of the American Institute of Planners* (1955), 21:66–75, and "The Master Plan: An Impermanent Constitution," *Law and Contemporary Problems* (1955), 20:353–377; Allison Dunham, "City Planning: An Analysis of the Content of the Master Plan," *Journal of Law and Economics* (1958), 1:170–186; David Farbman, *A Description, Analysis and Critique of the Master Plan* (Philadelphia: Institute for Urban Studies, University of Pennsylvania, 1960—mimeographed).

7. Clarence A. Perry, "The Neighborhood Unit," in *Regional Survey of New York and Its Environs* (New York: Committee on Regional Plan of New York and Its Environs, 1929), 7:22–140; James Dahir, *The Neighborhood Unit Plan* (New York: Russell Sage Foundation, 1947).

8. Edward M. Bassett, *The Master Plan* (New York: Russell Sage Foundation, 1938); T. J. Kent, *The Urban General Plan* (San Francisco: Chandler, 1964); F. Stuart Chapin, Jr., *Urban Land Use Planning* (2d ed.; Urbana: University of Illinois Press, 1964).

9. Thomas A. Reiner, *The Place of the Ideal Community in Urban Planning* (Philadelphia: University of Pennsylvania Press, 1963).

10. Homer Hoyt, *The Structure and Growth of Residential Neighborhoods in American Cities* (Washington: Government Printing Office, 1939).

11. Martin Meyerson and Edward C. Banfield, *Politics, Planning and the Public Interest* (New York: Free Press of Glencoe, 1955); Alan Altshuler, *The City Planning Process* (Ithaca: Cornell University Press, 1965).

12. Frances F. Piven, "The Function of Research in the Formation of City Planning Policy," Ph.D. dissertation, University of Chicago Department of City Planning, 1962.

13. Reginald Isaacs, "The Neighborhood Theory: An Analysis of Its Inadequacy," *Journal of the American Institute of Planners* (1948), 14:15–23.

14. Catherine Bauer, "Social Questions in Housing and Community Planning," *Journal of Social Issues* (1951), 7:1–34.

15. Norman Beckman, "Federal Long-Range Planning: The Heritage of the National Resources Planning Board," *Journal of the American Institute of Planners* (1960), 26:89–97.

16. Robert B. Mitchell and Chester Rapkin, *Urban Traffic: A Function of Land Use* (New York: Columbia University Press, 1954).

17. Henry Fagin, "The Penn Jersey Transportation Study: The Launching of a Permanent Regional Planning Process," *Journal of the American Institute of Planners* (1963), 29:9–18.

18. Alan M. Vorhees, ed., "Land Use and Traffic Models," *Journal of the American Institute of Planners* (special issue—1959), 25:59–103; Britton Harris, "Plan or Projection: An Examination of the Use of Models in Planning," *ibid.*, (1960), 26:265–272.

19. Edward C. Banfield and Morton Grodzins, *Government and Housing in Metropolitan Areas* (New York: McGraw-Hill, 1958).

20. Scott Greer, *Metropolitics: A Study of Political Culture* (New York: Wiley, 1963).

21. John W. Dyckman, "National Planning for Urban Renewal: The Paper Moon in the Cardboard Sky," *Journal of the American Institute of Planners* (1960), 26:49–59; Bernard J. Frieden, *The Future of Old Neighborhoods* (Cambridge: Massachusetts Institute of Technology Press, 1964); Martin Anderson, *The Federal Bulldozer: A Critical Analysis of Urban Renewal 1949–1962* (Cambridge: Massachusetts Institute of Technology Press, 1964).

22. Melvin M. Webber, "The Prospects for Policies Planning," in Leonard J. Duhl, ed., *The Urban Condition* (New York: Basic Books, 1963), pp. 319–330.

23. Peter H. Rossi and Robert A. Dentler, *The Politics of Urban Renewal* (New York: Free Press of Glencoe, 1961); James Q. Wilson, "Planning and Politics: Citizen Participation in Urban Renewal," *Journal of the American Institute of Planners* (1963), 29:242–249.

24. Meyerson and Banfield, *Politics, Planning and the Public Interest.* Martin Meyerson, "Building the Middle-Range Bridge for Comprehensive Planning," *Journal of the American Institute of Planners* (1956), 22:58–64; Paul Davidoff and Thomas A. Reiner, "A Choice Theory of Planning," *ibid.*, (1962), 28:103–115; Webber, "The Prospects for Policies Planning."

25. Kevin Lynch, *The Image of the City* (Cambridge: Massachusetts Institute of Technology Press and Harvard University Press, 1960).

26. Clarence S. Stein, *Toward New Towns for America* (New York: Reinhold, 1957).

27. Edward P. Eichler and Marshall Kaplan, *The Community Builders* (Berkeley: University of California Press, 1967).

28. Harvey S. Perloff, "New Directions in Social Planning," *Journal of the American Institute of Planners.* (1965), 31:297–303.

29. Paul Davidoff, "Advocacy and Social Concern in Planning," *Journal of the American Institute of Planners* (1965), 31:331–337.

30. Edgar S. Cahn and Jean C. Cahn, "The War on Poverty: A Civilian Perspective," *Yale Law Journal* (1964), 73:1317–1352.

31. Melvin M. Webber, "Comprehensive Planning and Social Responsibility," *Journal of the American Institute of Planners* (1963), 29:232–241.

32. Frances F. Piven and Richard A. Cloward, "Desegregated Housing: Who Pays for the Reformers' Ideal," *New Republic* (December 17, 1966) 155, no. 25:17–22.

33. Nelson Foote et al., *Housing Choices and Housing Constraints* (New York: McGraw-Hill, 1961); John Lansing, Eva Mueller, and N. Barth, *Residential Location and Urban Mobility* (Ann Arbor: Survey Research Center, 1964—mimeographed).

10. PLANNING, SOCIAL PLANNING, AND POLITICS

1. Needless to say, gentrification proposals often originate other than with planners, but where planners play some role in approving or disapproving such proposals, they can raise the question of what goals are involved and whether these are desirable for the community to pursue. They can even raise such questions when they do not play such a role, but simply because they are planners whose job it is to think about community goals.

2. Originally developed as a planning concept that would help the victims of

urban renewal, it later became part of the War on Poverty, and eventually meant planning with rather than for poor people, and under Model Cities, allowing the poor to do at least some of the planning themselves.

Incidentally, social policy initially was defined primarily as helping the poor, but then was also viewed as counteracting the disadvantages of the private enterprise. In 1990, it has been used particularly in the latter sense in postrevolutionary Eastern Europe.

3. Janet S. Reiner, Everett Reimer, and Thomas Reiner, "Client Analysis and Planning of Public Programs," *Journal of the American Institute of Planners* (November 1963), pp. 270–282.

4. Incidentally, planners must also be more specific about the clients, for "the poor" is a middle-class abstraction, and people with low incomes are as heterogeneous as any other socioeconomic class or stratum.

5. This argument is presented in more detail in my commentary on John Friedmann's "The Public Interest and Community Participation," in *Journal of the American Institute of Planners* (January 1973), pp. 3, 10–12.

6. See, e.g., Frances Piven, "Comprehensive Social Planning," *Journal of the American Institute of Planners* (July 1970), pp. 227–228.

7. Paul Davidoff, "Advocacy and Pluralism in Planning," *Journal of the American Institute of Planners* (November 1965), pp. 331–337.

8. Herbert J. Gans, "From Urbanism to Policy Planning," *Journal of the American Institute of Planners* (July 1970), pp. 223–225, quote at p. 224.

11. SOCIAL SCIENCE FOR SOCIAL POLICY

1. Herbert J. Gans, "From Urbanism to Policy Planning," *Journal of the American Institute of Planners* (July 1970), 36:223–225.

2. For a more systematic analysis of the relationship between researchers and politicians, see Irving Louis Horowitz, "The Academy and the Polity: Interaction Between Social Scientists and Federal Administrators," *Journal of Applied Behavioral Science* (1969), 5, no. 3:309–335.

3. The model is described in more detail in chapter 9.

4. Herbert J. Gans, "From Urbanism to Policy Planning."

5. Henry W. Riecken, "Social Sciences and Social Problems," *Social Science Information* (February 1969), 8:101–129.

6. On the politics of the systems analysts, see Robert Boguslaw, *The New Utopians* (Englewood Cliffs, N.J.: Prentice-Hall, 1965), ch. 8. The reinventors of policy research of a generation ago were also conservatives or cold war liberals, at least by 1970s standards. Thus, Harold Lasswell and his colleagues developed the concept of the policy sciences in the late 1940s in part as a weapon in the cold war. Lasswell's introduction to a book on this subject begins by noting that "the continuing crisis of national security in which we live calls for the most efficient use of the manpower, facilities and resources of the American people," and in the second paragraph refers to "the problem of overcoming the divisive tendencies of modern life and of bringing into existence a more thorough integration of the goals and methods of public and private action." See Harold Lasswell, "The Policy Orientation," in D. Lerner and H. Lasswell et al., eds., *The Policy Sciences* (Stanford University Press, 1951), p. 3.

7. Sociologists have of course devoted much attention to values, but largely to values implicit in behavior rather than to aspirations.

8. For a more detailed analysis of these points, see chapter 20.

9. Amitai Etzioni, *The Active Society* (New York: Free Press, 1968).

10. Conversely, if and when policy research becomes established, it will undoubtedly provide a fertile source for new theories and findings in basic research, for one can often understand human behavior best when it is encouraged or forced to change.

12. THE HUMAN IMPLICATIONS OF SLUM CLEARANCE AND RELOCATION

1. Among the principal publications are Marc Fried and Peggy Gleicher, "Some Sources of Residential Satisfaction in an Urban 'Slum,' " *Journal of the American Institute of Planners* (November 1961), 27:305–315; Marc Fried, "Grieving for a Lost Home," in Leonard J. Duhl, ed., *The Urban Condition* (New York: Basic Books, 1963), pp. 151–171; Chester Hartman, "The Limitations of Public Housing: Relocation Choices in a Working Class Community," *Journal of the American Institute of Planners* (November 1963), 29:283–296; Chester Hartman, "The Housing of Relocated Families," *ibid.* (November 1964), 30:266–286; and Marc Fried, "Transitional Functions of Working Class Communities: Implications for Forced Relocation," in Mildred B. Kantor, ed., *Mobility and Mental Health* (Springfield, Ill.: Charles C Thomas, 1965), pp. 123–165.

2. Hartman, "The Housing of Relocated Families."

3. The terms *West End* and *project area* will hereafter be used interchangeably.

4. The eastern boundary of the project area fronts on Massachusetts General Hospital and the back of Beacon Hill; the northern, on the Charles River; the southern, on a number of blocks much like the West End, although in poorer condition, and on Scollay Square. This is one of Boston's major skid-row areas, soon to be redeveloped as a government center. The western boundary faces a major railroad station and a wholesaling-industrial area which separates the West End from the North End.

5. "Buildings now cover 72 per cent of the net land area in the West End, excluding streets and vacant lots. Of the total of 48 blocks, 11 have building coverages of over 90 per cent." Boston Housing Authority, "West End Project Report" (Boston: 1953), p. 5. This refers to the 72-acre study area. An unpublished Housing Authority report indicated that according to the 1950 census, the ground density was in excess of 152 dwelling units per net residential acre. "Supporting Documentation to the Redevelopment Plan" (Boston: September 1955), p. 7.

6. This paper is based largely on conditions at the time of the taking; the figures are from a survey made by the Boston Redevelopment Authority just prior to the taking.

7. For an analysis of the kinds of people who live in slums and the ways in which they deviate from the rest of the urban population, see John Seeley, "The Slum: Its Nature, Use, and Users," *Journal of the American Institute of Planners* (February 1959), 25, no 1:7–14.

8. Consequently, the planning reports that are written to justify redevelopment dwell as much on social as on physical criteria and are filled with data intended to show the prevalence of antisocial or pathological behavior in the area. The implication is that the area itself causes such behavior and should therefore be redeveloped (see, for example, Boston Housing Authority, "West End Project Report").

9. Actually, a considerable number of West End families had moved into the area from the North End during the 1930s and 1940s, since West End apartments were more spacious and modern and had their own, rather than shared, bathrooms.

10. The latter point is developed further in the author's unpublished paper, "Some Notes on the Definition of Mental Health: An Attempt from the Perspective of the Community Planner," 1957.

11. Planners like to describe such housing as "obsolescent." However, it is obsolescent only in relation to their own middle-class standards and, more important, their incomes. The term is never used when alley dwellings of technologically similar vintage are rehabilitated for high rentals, as in Georgetown, Washington, D.C.

12. A number of West End mothers want to isolate their children from the culture of "the street." Since peers are a strong influence on older children and teenagers, the conflict between the norms of home and street within the child may be resolved in favor of the latter. Only systematic research can determine whether or not such neighborhood characteristics as high density and the mixture of "respectable" and "rough" working-class residents are responsible for any subsequent delinquency. I suspect that relations within the family, and the external socioeconomic and cultural factors creating them, are probably more important.

13. Because of the high land coverage, the first- and second-floor apartments of many buildings received less air and sunlight than desirable, although there is no evidence that this had deleterious effects. This may be owing in part to the fact that many West Enders spent much time outside, since the street is a major location for neighborhood sociability. I would not defend such apartments as desirable, but I can understand the preferences of low-income West End residents for these dwellings at rentals of $30 a month over those with more air and sunlight at $75.

14. The eight-year interim period was taken up by the usual technical and political problems that make up the "natural history" of a redevelopment project. However, owing to poor newspaper coverage and the West Enders' inability as well as unwillingness to understand the complex administrative process, many of the residents were convinced until the last minute that what they called "the steal" of their neighborhood would never go through. The less sanguine suffered greatly from the uncertainty as to whether the project would or would not go through, as did the landlords and the businessmen, who lost tenants and customers during this period. This is one of the hidden costs of redevelopment paid by the West Enders.

15. The stereotype of the "greedy" slum landlords who fail to maintain their buildings applied mainly to the absentee owners. The resident owners with one or two buildings generally kept up their buildings until the land taking. Most of the vacancies in the area were in absentee-owned buildings; the resident owners had been able to hold their tenants, partly because many of them were friends or relatives.

16. Visitors were often surprised that West End apartments differed little from those in lower-middle-class neighborhoods and could not easily reconcile this with the stereotype of slum housing.

17. Because most of the residents are of Italian or Polish descent, some aspects of life in the West End resembled that of the European villages from which they or their parents came. The extended family plays an important role, since relatives often reside in adjacent apartments. People here live within an intricate social network and a multitude of informal groups which are crucial to the functioning of people in a culture in which the individualism of the middle-class professional is unknown. Despite published statistics, antisocial behavior among permanent West End residents was low, in part because of the strict (though decreasing) parental

control over children and of the persuasive sanctions against any kind of nonconformity.

18. Some of the people who left the West End after 1950 were young people who participated in the suburban boom. They were replaced by people of lower incomes and more transitional living habits, single transients, gypsies, and families with obvious pathological characteristics. Such people found a home in the West End because landlords with vacant units could no longer afford to reject what they defined as "undesirable tenants." The arrival of the new kinds of tenants also helped to convince the community at large that the West End was a slum. Despite this self-fulfilled prophecy, the majority of the West Enders who lived there before 1950 remained until the time of the land taking. Many had lived in the area for from twenty to forty years.

19. The Redevelopment Authority claimed that delinquency statistics in the area were among the highest in the city, but these figures were questioned by local sources, including the police. The disparity is due in part to the fact that youngsters from other neighborhoods perpetrated their antisocial acts in the West End, just as some West End teenagers, true to the code of protecting the in-group and hurting only the stranger, were delinquents in other neighborhoods.

20. For the past few years, politicians and other community leaders have used West End redevelopment as a major symbol of Boston's emergence from its economic doldrums. This may be a false hope, since the apartments to be built in the area will probably draw tenants primarily from other parts of Boston and there is little indication that the project represents any significant amount of new growth.

21. Many of these people were being subsidized by low rentals. However, the proportion of their total income paid for rent was not lower than that of the average high-income Bostonian.

22. Evidence of both types of discrimination came to my attention even before relocation had formally begun.

23. Thus the businessmen who are economically strong enough to relocate will receive funds for the move, but those who are most in need of aid will receive nothing. Redevelopment officials justify this by the argument that the small stores are already marginal and are being driven out by economic processes, not by redevelopment policies. However, these stores are less marginal in their present neighborhoods; and in addition, they serve a variety of social and communication functions. There are also a number of small businessmen and semiprofessionals in the area who were able to escape from factory jobs by being able to rely on low residential rentals. These will also be forced out of business when their rent bills go up.

24. Several deaths among older residents at the time that West Enders realized the area would be cleared were attributed by informants to the shock of this recognition.

25. The other beneficiaries will be the absentee landlords, who were losing money on partly or totally vacant buildings and will now be able to sell their buildings to the city. Since they have the funds for legal fees and the political know-how to choose the right lawyers, they can go to court and may be able to get higher prices for their buildings than can the small resident owners.

26. This is owing in part to the animus against authority and middle-class bureaucracy in Italian-American working-class culture. West Enders are particularly opposed to the review of income and to the raising of rents with increases in earnings.

27. The West Enders I talked with were willing to accept units in the small projects in or near middle-class districts, but were violently opposed to the large "institutional" projects built in recent years. Since the former already have long waiting lists, the Housing Authority plan was to move West End people into vacancies in the latter.

28. The Authority based its estimate on newspaper rentals, without knowing whether or not these were eligible to be used for relocation. Federal provisions require that relocatees must be moved into decent, safe, and sanitary (that is, standard) housing.

29. The more West Enders go into public housing, the more competition there will be among those leaving public housing and the remaining West Enders for the limited supply of private low-rent or low-cost housing.

30. Since the relocation will take several years, the trickling-down process may throw some low-cost units on the regional housing market and thus reduce somewhat the discrepancy between supply and demand for relocation housing.

31. One of the reasons families like to live in the West End is its central location with respect to other Italian neighborhoods in the Boston area, so that family members scattered over them can be visited easily.

32. At the start of relocation, officials indicated that they would be more liberal than the law requires in allowing West Enders to reject apartments offered to them.

33. Thus, many West Enders were convinced that the redevelopment was just another instance of government action to benefit those with greater economic resources and political influence. Since a member of the redeveloper firm had managed the mayor's election in 1950 and had subsequently served in his office, they believed that the redevelopment project was set up to pay off a political debt and also to fatten the mayor's purse before he left office. Such beliefs can arise in Boston more easily than in other cities, since the city government has been unusually inefficient and in recent years more attentive to the demands of the business interests than to those of the rest of the population.

34. Although one of the city's nine councilors came from the West End, and another from the North End, there were not enough voters in the West End to make it politically possible for these representatives to support the West End at the expense of other districts.

35. The Boston press was of little aid to the West Enders, since it was very much in favor of the redevelopment and also seemed to assume that West Enders do not read the papers.

36. There were other reasons. First, many working-class people rarely think in community-wide terms, since they believe that the community is exploiting them. Second, they are not inclined to, or skilled in, the middle-class pattern of community participation; and they expect their political representatives to take care of this function. Finally, the protest organization was led by a Beacon Hill resident and a small group of West Enders of middle-class background, who were not "natural leaders" by the standards of most of the residents of Italian and Polish descent.

37. However, many residents were not planning ahead. Since they have traditionally suffered from economic uncertainty, they have adjusted to this by a flexible and fatalistic day-to-day philosophy of living. The kind of planning familiar to middle-class households would have raised too many false hopes and left them psychologically unprepared to accept sudden job losses and the like.

38. Kindly relocation officials attempted to soften the hurt by allowing owners to postpone their rent payments until they had been reimbursed for their buildings.

39. Needless to say, more farsighted and analytically oriented officials might have ameliorated the process to some extent. Moreover, if there had been some criticism of the program on the part of planners (commissioners as well as professionals), some changes might now be under way. However, some planners seem to feel that relocation is not their responsibility, even though it is a direct consequence of their plans.

40. For example, objectives such as attracting middle- and upper-income citizens back from the suburbs, contributing potential shoppers to a declining central retail area, creating symbols of "community revival," or providing more statusful surroundings (and parking lots) for powerful community institutions.

41. This statement is based on a comment made by Ruth Glass, the British planner, after her observations of American renewal. She described it as primarily for the benefit of the redeveloper and his tenants, whereas British renewal tries to aid mainly the present residents of the slum area.

42. Studies made by redevelopment agencies rarely concern themselves with the characteristics and needs of the project area residents or the ways in which they live. Instead, they try to prove, on the one hand, how undesirable the area is in order to persuade the federal and local agencies to provide funds for renewal and, on the other, how desirable the area is for potential redevelopers. Thus, they judge the area from the narrowly class-determined values of their clients and ignore the neighborhood's positive functions. The previously cited West End Project Report is a particularly blatant example. The fault here lies not so much with the local agency that writes such a report as with the federal procedures which permit no real alternative.

43. This is defined as any relocation proposal that requires the rehousing of more people than is possible, given the existing low-rent housing supply of the community.

44. "Proper" should be defined by the standards of the residents who are to live in the relocation units as well as by those of the housing and planning officials.

45. Current rehabilitation frequently takes low-rent apartments and transforms them into dwellings that fit the demands, tastes, and pocketbooks of middle- and upper-class people, but not those of their present residents.

46. For example, where the reuse is luxury housing, clearance of existing housing should be scheduled so that if the market for high-rent units suddenly shrinks, the remaining stock of existing housing can be rehabilitated for low- or middle-income tenants or redeveloped for them if necessary.

47. The relocation office in the West End has done some pioneering work in this respect. The relocation staff should also call on resource persons in those areas to which site residents are moving and employ them to facilitate the adjustment of the relocatees in their new neighborhoods.

48. Thus, the redeveloper could be asked to include some proportion of relocation expenses in his costs and pass them on to his tenants as their share of the renewal charges. Alternatively, the city could bear relocation costs initially and require the redeveloper to repay part of them if his project shows more than an agreed-upon reasonable profit. In either case, the lower the rentals of the redevelopment housing, the lower should be the share of relocation costs to be paid by the redeveloper.

49. Many of the conclusions and recommendations described here were reached also by a thorough Philadelphia study, "Relocation in Philadelphia" (Philadelphia

Housing Association, November 1958), which was published after this article had been written.

13. FROM THE BULLDOZER TO HOMELESSNESS

1. The 1959 article that is chapter 12 of this book supplied empirical evidence to support the critiques of slum clearance by such influential housers as Robert C. Weaver and the late Charles Abrams, but my ideas probably received the widest attention as a result of my "The Failure of Urban Renewal: A Critique and Some Proposals," *Commentary* (April 1965), 39:29–37. (*Commentary* was then widely read by liberal professionals and policymakers.) Nevertheless, professional opinion was undoubtedly most affected by Jane Jacobs' now-classic *The Death and Life of Great American Cities*, even though she was less concerned with urban renewal than with the kind of planning that results in high-rise housing projects.

2. In the mid-1980s, New York City began such a small-area project on one Forty-second Street block in Times Square which will, among other things, eliminate about a half dozen movie theaters that cater largely to low-income patrons, thus "displacing" many thousands of movie-goers who will not likely find other theaters to supply them with double-feature films. However, the primary victims are a small number of very poor people, as well as some prostitutes, petty criminals, and others who make their living in the area but are probably not far above the poverty level either. In other respects, the project is typical, for once more the poor are being displaced, at public expense, to make room for the affluent. In this case, the plan calls for a set of private office buildings which, in good economic times, some experts insist, would most likely be built by private enterprise without the significant subsidies and abatements now called for. In bad economic times, which New York is experiencing at this writing, they will either flood an already overbuilt office market further, or will be put off until prosperity returns.

3. Chester W. Hartman et al., *Yerba Buena: Land Grab and Community Resistance in San Francisco* (San Francisco: Glide Publications, 1974).

4. Firm trends and even overall totals are hard to establish, since the federal housing agency has changed the data base several times, sometimes because of changes in housing law, sometimes because of orders from the Office of Management and Budget. Until 1964, data were provided only on relocated but not displaced families; from 1964 to 1971, on the number of families and individuals displaced as well as relocated. In 1972 the local agencies were asked to guess; in 1973 and 1974 data were collected on paid moving claims for households; and since then, displaced households have again been tabulated.

5. This estimate is based on the 1972 HUD *Statistical Yearbook* figure of "total cumulative displacement" of about 334,000 families and 170,000 individuals since the beginning of slum clearance, a guesstimate of 30,000 households for 1972, and the sum of HUD figures for 1973 to 1980. I have probably added a few apples and oranges, but so, I imagine, have federal and local agencies. For 1973 to 1980 figures, I am indebted to HUD, but I am responsible for all guesses and estimates.

6. More accurate displacement figures are available from local studies, but from only a small number of communities. For reviews of these studies, see the references cited in notes 23 and 24 below.

7. Office of Policy Development and Research, "Displacement Report," Washington: HUD, February 1979.

8. Richard LeGates and Chester Hartman, "Displacement," Berkeley: National Housing Law Project, February 1981, p. 38.

9. Chester Hartman, personal communication, February 1990.

10. "Displacement Report," p. 20.

11. Robert W. Burchell and David Listokin, *The Adaptive Reuse Handbook* (New Brunswick: Center for Urban Policy Research, 1981), computed from Addendum 1, pp. 35–38. (The list excludes some growing cities with abandoned housing, notably southern, but including them would not significantly change the result. Robert Burchell, personal communication.) A number of the officials surveyed guessed at, and may therefore have underestimated, the amount of abandonment in their communities.

12. Following his extensive study of New York City's rental housing supply, Marcuse developed an estimate of 125,000 to 175,000 abandoned units in that city. (Personal communication.) New York contains about one-sixth of the country's urban rental units, but, in order to exclude newer cities unlikely to have as many abandoned rental units, I multiplied Marcuse's New York figure by 5. Burchell's New York City survey was limited to the Bronx, Brooklyn, and Manhattan, and reported 55,000 abandoned units. Burchell and Listokin, *The Adaptive Reuse Handbook*, p. 35.

13. Peter Marcuse, "Abandonment, Gentrification and Displacement: the Linkages in New York City," in Neil Smith and Peter Williams, eds., *Gentrification of the City* (Boston: Unwin Hyman, 1986), p. 172.

14. U.S. Department of Housing and Urban Development, "Whither or Whether Urban Distress," Washington, D.C.: GPO, March 1979.

15. Marcuse, "Abandonment, Gentrification and Displacement," p. 163.

16. Strictly speaking, tenants can refuse to rent vacant apartments but only landlords can abandon buildings, while an aggregate of landlords and city government can abandon neighborhoods. However, if tenants set fire to or otherwise destroy their apartments, landlords may have considerable incentive to abandon a building. Even so, most arson in areas undergoing abandonment appears to be instigated by landlords.

17. George Sternlieb and Robert W. Burchell, *Residential Abandonment: The Tenement Landlord Revisited* (New Brunswick: Center for Urban Policy Research, Rutgers University, 1973).

18. Although some writers blame abandonment on rent control, charging therefore that it is initiated more by governments than by landlords, widespread abandonment has taken place in cities without rent control. Conversely, a number of cities with rent control do not have abandoned buildings. Peter Marcuse, "Housing Abandonment: Does Rent Control Make a Difference?", Washington, D.C.: Conference on Alternative State and Local Policies, June 1981.

19. However, the area's emptying out was also caused by the building of the huge Coop City project in the North Bronx, which pulled thousands of South Bronx residents out of the area in a very short time.

20. Some abandonment had taken place in the West End once the plan to tear down the neighborhood was announced. By the time I arrived, the built-up alleys and cul-de-sacs were entirely abandoned, but buildings fronting on streets remained occupied. However, landlords had trouble renting fifth and sixth floors, which then remained vacant. Still, the landlords were able to hold on to their buildings because they obtained enough rent to pay the bills or because they were hoping to make a profit by selling the buildings to the Boston Development Authority.

21. Originally, public housing was also a housing improvement program, requiring the demolition of a slum unit for every new unit of public housing, but it appears

as if just about all the public housing projects built since the 1949 Housing Act were net additions to the housing supply.

22. Data are available only for the "235" and "236" programs, but according to the HUD *Statistical Yearbooks,* in 1970, when the poverty line was $3,968 for the prototypical family of four, only 5 percent of new "235" units and 24 percent of "236" units went to households earning less than $4,000. By 1979, data were available only for the "236" program, and about 60 percent of the tenants then being certified for occupancy were earning less than the poverty line figure.

23. Peter Dreier and J. David Hulchanski, "Affordable Housing: Lessons from Canada," *The American Prospect* (Spring 1990), 1:123.

24. See e.g., Peter H. Rossi, *Down and Out in America: The Origins of Homelessness* (Chicago: University of Chicago Press, 1989), ch. 3.

25. Martha R. Burt and Barbara E. Cohen, *America's Homeless: Numbers, Characteristics and Programs that Serve Them* (Washington, D.C.: The Urban Institute Press, July 1989).

26. Michael Stegman, *Rental Housing in New York City* (New York City Department of Housing Preservation and Development, 1988).

27. While some readers considered *The Urban Villagers* an appeal for the retention of urban villages with ethnic ways of life, my opposition to slum clearance and relocation was always first and foremost economic and political, with emphasis on the financial and other costs the West Enders were paying and the unfairness of destroying their community for a luxury housing project. Although I liked the West End, urban villages or ethnic enclaves have advantages and disadvantages like all other neighborhood types. None can be proved to be entirely beneficial or harmful. More important, people have a right to choose how and where they want to live, except when they deprive others of that same right, so that the debate over whether urban villages are better or worse than suburbs or new towns or high-rise housing projects has always struck me as essentially irrelevant. The real issues are how to resolve the conflicts inherent in choices that deprive others of the right to choose; and how to establish freedom of choice for people who are now unable to choose for reasons of poverty, racial segregation, and the like.

28. See for example Daniel Wilner et al., *Housing Environment and Family Life* (Baltimore: Johns Hopkins University Press, 1962); and Clare Cooper, *Easter Hill Village: Some Social Implications of Design* (New York: Free Press, 1975).

29. For a dramatic illustration see Cooper, *Easter Hill Village,* a study of a very thoughtfully designed and prize-winning public housing project. See also Oscar Newman, *Defensible Space* (New York: Macmillan, 1977); and *Community of Interest* (Garden City: Doubleday, 1980).

30. S. M. Miller and Pamela Roby, *The Future of Inequality* (New York: Basic Books, 1970), p. 86. Housing is an investment if and when improvements in health and morale as effects of housing increase people's ability to obtain jobs, get better jobs, or lose less time and wages due to illness. Housing would be a *resource*—my addition to the Miller-Roby dichotomy—if the poor were able to live rent free or if they were given a dwelling unit that they could sell for a large sum on the open market, but such policies have not been tried in America.

31. Lee Rainwater, "Fear and the House-as-Haven in the Lower Class," *Journal of the American Institute of Planners* (January 1966), 32:23–30.

14. THE ROLE OF EDUCATION IN THE ESCAPE FROM POVERTY

1. See, for example, Ivar Berg, *Education and Jobs: The Great Training Robbery* (New York: Praeger, 1970); Christopher Jencks et al., *Inequality.* New York: Basic Books, 1972; and Bennett Harrison, *Education, Training and the Urban Ghetto.* Baltimore: Johns Hopkins University Press, 1972.

2. For a summary statement, see Colin Greer, *The Great School Legend* (New York: Basic Books, 1970); see also Sam Bowles, "Getting Nowwhere: Programmed Class Stagnation," *Society,* (June 1972), 6:42–49.

3. A good analysis of the two labor markets is in Peter Doeringer and Michael Piore, "Unemployment and the 'Dual Labor Market,'" *The Public Interest* (Winter 1975), no. 38: 67–79. For a poignant sociological analysis of life in the secondary labor market, see Elliott Liebow, *Tally's Corner* (Boston: Little, Brown, 1967).

4. John Ogbu, *Minority Education and Caste* (New York: Academic Press, 1978).

5. For fragmentary evidence that most Jewish immigrants did not escape poverty through education, see Thomas Kessner, *The Golden Door: Italian and Jewish Immigrant Mobility in New York City, 1880–1915* (New York: Oxford University Press, 1976); and Sherry Gorelick, *City College and the Jewish Poor* (New Brunswick, N.J.: Rutgers University Press, 1981)—both of which I read earlier as dissertations.

6. These observations reflect my questions about the meaning of the term *urban,* and about the nature of the city itself. See chapters 4 and 6 above.

7. See, for example, Stephen Thernstrom, *Poverty and Progress* (Cambridge: Harvard University Press, 1964).

8. Stephen Thernstrom, *The Other Bostonians* (Cambridge: Harvard University Press, 1973).

9. See Robert Schrank and Sol Stein, "Yearning, Learning and Status," in Sar Levitan, ed., *Blue Collar Workers* (New York: McGraw-Hill, 1971), pp. 318–341; and Herbert J. Gans. *Urban Villagers* (New York: Free Press, 1982), ch. 10.

10. Greer, *The Great School Legend,* p. 85.

11. Herbert J. Gans, *More Equality* (New York: Vintage, 1975).

12. See, e.g., Peter Rose, "Asian Americans: From Pariahs to Paragons," in Nathan Glazer, ed., *Clamor at the Gates: the New American Immigration* (San Francisco: Institute for Contemporary Studies, 1984).

13. Ill Soo Kim, *New Urban Immigrants: The Korean Community in New York* (Princeton: Princeton University Press, 1981).

15. PLANNING FOR A LABOR-INTENSIVE ECONOMY

1. Likewise weapons that put an end to individual wars with only a small loss of life would by this token be superior to more primitive ones in which many have to die before the war can be declared over.

2. However, private enterprise is not very good because far more new products fail the market test every year than succeed.

3. Here I am thinking particularly of Paul and Percival Goodman, the former a poet and social critic, the latter an architect and artist, who were world famous for their imaginative planning. See particularly their *Communitas: Ways of Life, Means of Livelihood* (New York: Random House, 1947) and the most recent edition, Columbia University Press, 1990. For a not especially poetic but very innovative

approach to job creation, see Philip Harvey, *Securing the Right to Employment: Social Welfare Policy and the Unemployed in the United States* (Princeton: Princeton University Press, 1989).

4. Some or many of them will also need help to get back into the labor force.

5. Herbert J. Gans, *Middle American Individualism: The Future of Liberal Democracy* (New York: Free Press, 1988), ch. 6.

16. TOWARD THE THIRTY-TWO-HOUR WORKWEEK: AN ANALYSIS OF WORKSHARING

1. My research on worksharing was supported by a fellowship from the German Marshall Fund of the United States. A longer analysis appears in my "Planning for Worksharing: Toward Egalitarian Worktime Reduction," in Kai Erikson and Steven P. Varnas, *The Nature of Work: Sociological Perspectives* (New Haven: Yale University Press, 1990).

2. Worksharing differs from jobsharing in that the latter is generally a personal arrangement, often between spouses or otherwise related people, to divide up the same full-time job, whereas worksharing is a universal society-wide arrangement to reduce work time so as to create new jobs. If jobsharing took place on a very widespread basis, it would turn into worksharing as well. This is not likely, however, because jobsharing essentially creates two half-time jobs, and these have to be very well paid for jobsharing to spread beyond the professional jobs where it is currently most prevalent.

3. For a comprehensive analysis of worksharing, see Fred C. Best, *Worksharing: Issues, Policy Options, and Prospects.* Kalamazoo, Mich.: Upjohn Institute for Employment Research, 1981.

4. The long history of U.S. worktime reduction proposals is reported in Marion Cahill, *Shorter Hours* (New York: Columbia University Press, 1932) and in Irving Bernstein, *The Lean Years: A History of the American Worker, 1920–1933,* and *The Turbulent Years: A History of the American Worker, 1933–1941* (Boston: Houghton Mifflin, 1960 and 1970). On the 1960s revival, see Sar A. Levitan, *Reducing Worktime as a Means to Combat Unemployment* (Kalamazoo, Mich.: Upjohn Institute for Employment Research, 1964).

5. For an empirical study showing these results in England, see Michael White and Abby Ghobadian, *Shorter Working Hours in Practice* (London: Policy Studies Institute, September 1984).

6. Worksharing is actually an ideological chameleon, its spots changing with what happens to worker income. Probably the most radical option, not discussed here, involves the workers sharing the profits as well as the work, but one can also imagine a conservative worksharing scheme in which only one breadwinner per household is permitted. For a discussion of the Hoover administration's version of worksharing, see Irving Bernstein, *The Lean Years,* pp. 476–480. For a more favorable assessment of the Hoover administration's efforts, see Martin Nemirow, "Work-sharing Approaches: Past and Present," *Monthly Labor Review* (September 1984), pp. 34–39.

7. See U.S. Department of Labor. *Exchanging Earnings for Leisure* (Washington: U.S. Government Printing Office, 1980). The study was written by Fred Best. The report of a German study can be found in Uwe Engler et al., "Arbeitszeitsituation und Arbeitszeitverkuerzung in der Sicht der Beschaeftigten," *Mitteilungen aus der Arbeitsmarkt- und Berufsforschung* (1983), 16(2):981–1005.

8. Irving Bernstein, *The Turbulent Years,* p. 22–31. The Black-Connery bill

actually called for a six-hour day and five-day week, a formula first proposed by the United Mine Workers in the 1920s.

9. See, for example, David Macarov's argument for separating work and income and finding other ways of providing income and economic security, in *Work and Welfare: The Unholy Alliance* (Beverly Hills, Calif.: Sage Publications, 1980).

10. The possibilities and problems of short-term worksharing, as well as various existing U.S., Canadian, and European versions of it, are reported in Ramelle MaCoy and Martin J. Morand, eds., *Short-Time Compensation* (New York: Pergamon Press, 1984). For a more detailed analysis, see Fred C. Best, *Reducing Workweeks to Prevent Layoffs: The Economic Impacts of Unemployment Insurance Supported Work Sharing* (Philadelphia: Temple University Press, 1988).

17. THE USES OF POVERTY

1. Robert K. Merton, "Manifest and Latent Functions," in his *Social Theory and Social Structure* (Glencoe, Ill.: Free Press, 1949), p. 71.

2. For an earlier analysis in the same vein as mine, see Arland D. Weeks, "A Conservative's View of Poverty," *American Journal of Sociology* (1917), 22: 779–800. My article was meant to be deadly serious and an example of the usefulness of functionalism for radical analyses, but Weeks, who does not seem to have been a conservative, was thought to have written in a satirical vein. Even so, many of the points he made half a century before me are similar to mine.

3. I shall henceforth abbreviate positive functions as functions and negative functions as dysfunctions. I shall also describe functions and dysfunctions at times in the planning and policy terminology of benefits and costs.

4. A longer version of the original article appeared as "The Positive Functions of Poverty," *American Journal of Sociology* (September 1972), 78:275–289.

19. THE BLACK FAMILY: REFLECTIONS ON THE "MOYNIHAN REPORT"

1. "Crucible of Identity: The Negro Lower Class Family," in Talcott Parsons and Kenneth B. Clark, eds., *The Negro American* (New York: Houghton Mifflin, 1966).

2. That wage is equal to $4.75 in December 1989 dollars. However, the minimum wage stood at $3.35 for most of the 1980s and was raised to $4.25 as of April 1991.

3. Thomas S. Langner and Stanley T. Michaels, *Life Stress and Mental Health* (New York: The Free Press of Glencoe, 1963), ch. 8.

4. These data are taken from U.S. Bureau of the Census, *Statistical Abstract of the United States 1989* (109th Edition) (Washington D.C.: 1989, tables 72, 67, 93 and 44 respectively.

5. William J. Wilson, *The Truly Disadvantaged* (Chicago: University of Chicago Press, 1987) table 2-8.

6. Moynihan's analysis, which suggested that slavery incapacitated black men and was a major cause of the female-headed black family, reflected the historical consensus at the time his report was written. Later, however, Herbert Gutman and others pointed out that slaves married whenever they were permitted to do so, and that the high rates of single-parent family formation were largely the result of urban living and especially the urban labor market of the twentieth century.

However, there is also evidence that black men became marginal in the urban economy much earlier, having a much harder time getting relatively secure and stable jobs than women, who could always find work as domestics, although that did not necessarily interfere with men and women getting married. Still, in 1850 and 1880 Philadelphia, black families were headed by women twice as often as white families, even when wealth, perhaps a better indicator of class than income, was held constant. Many of the missing men may have been dead already, but some must have been economically so marginal as to leave the women heading the family. Frank F. Furstenberg, Jr., Theodore Hershberg, and John Modell, "The Origin of the Female-Headed Black Family," in Theodore Hershberg, ed., *Philadelphia: Work, Space, Family and Group Experience in the 19th Century* (New York: Oxford University Press, 1981), pp. 435–454, tables 3 and 6.

7. Poor women also learn—and want to protect themselves from the fact— that jobless young men sometimes take their economic despair out on their mates and children with physical abuse.

8. As I will suggest in more detail in chapter 21, today's elite public discourse is given to more polite—and euphemistic—terminology than that which prevailed in the 1960s. This may help to explain why the single-parent family has replaced the broken one. Also, the broken family implies a damaged one; the single-parent one does not have the same pathological connotation.

9. Furstenberg also supplies data indicating that occupational and wealth differences among blacks and whites were already great during the nineteenth century, which helped to explain the higher rates of black single-parent family formation at that time. Furstenberg et al., "The Origin," tables 5, 7.

10. Although I believe that most of the differences in family structure between poor whites and poor blacks is due to the fact that the black economic condition is worse than that of the whites, this can only be shown persuasively if and when more sophisticated measurements of income, income stability, wealth, quality of school attended etc. are available. Still, the best test of whether the patterns of sexual activity and family formation among the poor is a function of poverty or of race—and in what mixtures—is more comparison between poor and middle-class families, white and black.

20. CULTURE AND CLASS IN THE STUDY OF POVERTY

1. Lee Rainwater, "Neutralizing the Poor and Disinherited: Some Psychological Aspects of Understanding the Poor," in Vernon L. Allen, ed., *Psychological Factors in Poverty* (Chicago: Markham, 1970), pp. 9–27, at p. 10.

2. *Ibid., passim.*

3. See for example, David Matza, "The Disreputable Poor," in Reinhard Bendix and Seymour Martin Lipset, eds., *Class, Status and Power* (2d ed.; New York: Free Press of Glencoe, 1966), pp. 289–303.

4. For a useful review of these writings, see Robert H. Bremner, *From the Depths* (New York: New York University Press, 1956).

5. See for example, Barbara Solomon, *Ancestors and Immigrants* (Cambridge: Harvard University Press, 1956).

6. William F. Whyte, Jr., *Street Corner Society* (2d ed.; Chicago: University of Chicago Press, 1955); Michael Young and Peter Willmott, *Family and Kinship in East London* (London: Routledge and Kegan Paul, 1957); Walter Miller, "Lower Class Culture as a Generating Milieu of Gang Delinquency," *Journal of Social Issues* (1958), 14:5–19; Oscar Lewis, *The Children of Sanchez* (New York: Random House, 1961), and *La Vida* (New York: Random House, 1966); Herbert J. Gans, *The Urban Villagers* (New York: The Free Press of Glencoe, 1962); Hylan Lewis,

Culture, Class and Poverty (Washington: Cross-Tell, 1967); Elliott Liebow, *Tally's Corner* (Boston: Little, Brown, 1967); and Lee Rainwater, "The Problem of Lower-Class Culture and Poverty-War Strategy," in Daniel P. Moynihan. ed., *On Understanding Poverty* (New York: Basic Books, 1969), pp. 229–259.

7. Rainwater, "The Problem of Lower-Class Culture."

8. Bernard Beck, "Bedbugs, Stench, Dampness and Immorality: A Review Essay on Recent Literature about Poverty," *Social Problems* (Summer 1967), 15:101–114.

9. Some writers have even resurrected Karl Marx's pejorative *Lumpenproletariat* to describe participants in the rebellions, ironically forgetting that Marx applied the term to people who did not share his revolutionary aims. Still, it is interesting that Marx, who apotheosized the working class, nevertheless felt the poor were undeserving, although his pejorative refers to political rather than moral lapses. Conversely, nineteenth-century American observers felt the poor were politically immoral for the opposite reason, because they were drawn to socialist and Communist movements.

10. See, for example, Jerome Carlin, *Lawyer's Ethics* (New York: Russell Sage Foundation, 1966).

11. See, for example, Louis Kriesberg, "The Relationship between Socio-Economic Rank and Behavior," *Social Problems* (Spring 1963), 10:334–353.

12. Hylan Lewis, *Culture, Class and Poverty*, pp. 17–18.

13. Miller, "Lower Class Culture," p. 7.

14. *Ibid.*, p. 19.

15. *Ibid.*, p. 7.

16. Hyman Rodman, "The Lower Class Value Stretch," *Social Forces* (December 1963), 42:205–215; Rainwater, "The Problem of Lower-Class Culture."

17. Hylan Lewis, *Culture, Class and Poverty*, pp. 38–39.

18. See Robert A. Nisbet, *The Sociological Tradition* (New York: Basic Books, 1967).

19. For more extreme examples of the use of the term *culture* see Hylan Lewis, *Culture, Class and Poverty*, pp. 14–15. See also Jack L. Roach and Orville R. Gurselin, "An Evaluation of the 'Culture of Poverty' Thesis," *Social Forces* (March 1967), 45:383–392.

20. For a persuasive illustration, see Margaret Mead, *New Lives for Old* (New York: Morrow, 1956).

21. For some illustrations of the policy implications of conceptual conservatism, see Frederick S. Jaffe, "Family Planning and Public Policy: Is the 'Culture of Poverty' Concept the New Cop-Out?" Paper presented to the 1967 meeting of the American Sociological Association.

22. Miller, "Lower Class Culture," p. 18 (emphasis added).

23. Oscar Lewis, *La Vida*, p. xliv.

24. *Ibid.*, p. xlviii.

25. See, for example, Kriesberg, "The Relationship between Socio-Economic Rank and Behavior."

26. For excellent discussions of this point, see S. M. Miller, "The American Lower Classes: A Typological Approach," and S. M. Miller and Frank Riessman, "The Working Class Subculture: A New View," in Arthur B. Shostak and William Gomberg, eds., *Blue-Collar World* (Englewood Cliffs, N.J.: Prentice-Hall, 1964), pp. 9–23, 24–35.

27. Lee Rainwater, "The Problem of Lower-Class Culture," p. 241.

28. See here S. M. Miller, "The American Lower Classes," p. 20.

29. Hylan Lewis, *Culture, Class and Poverty*, p. 38.

30. Zahava Blum has suggested studies of American Indians who received large cash payments from the government for their reservations, to determine how they spent these funds and what successes and failures they encountered in escaping from the poverty of reservation life.

31. This is not entirely true, for some studies were carried out on the educational aspirations of black parents for their children, but no attempt was made to determine systematically what happened to these aspirations if and when children did not perform accordingly in school.

32. See here my earlier reference to these concepts in chapter 13, and note 30.

33. Harlan Padfield and Roy Williams, *Stay Where you Were* (Philadelphia: Lippincott, 1973).

34. The job program was planned to be long-term and eventually most of the men, their friends, and their mates would have learned to cope with their new economic condition. Unfortunately, however, the program was canceled after a year so that this fascinating and virtually unknown study could only demonstrate the short-term unintended effects that can stem from an otherwise well-designed job program.

21. THE DANGERS OF THE UNDERCLASS: ITS HARMFULNESS AS A PLANNING CONCEPT

1. Oscar Lewis, "The Culture of Poverty," in Daniel P. Moynihan, ed., *On Understanding Poverty* (New York: Basic Books, 1969), pp. 187–192.

2. Susan M. Rigdon. *The Culture Facade: Art, Science and Politics in the Work of Oscar Lewis* (Champaign: University of Illinois Press, 1988).

3. The "Moynihan Report" (discussed in chapter 19) sometimes suggested that the female-headed black family was self-perpetuating, which created the political brouhaha that followed the publication of the report in 1965.

4. Gunner Myrdal, *Challenge to Affluence* (New York: Pantheon Books, 1962). The book was published several years before Oscar Lewis' concept and the Moynihan Report became part of the public discourse, but somehow neither it nor its now well-known concept caused a stir. Indeed, many people writing about the underclass do not know that the term is originally Myrdal's.

5. See my postscript to chapter 20.

6. The authors who have applied the underclass term solely or mainly to blacks include William J. Wilson, *The Declining Significance of Race* (Chicago: University of Chicago Press, 1978); Douglas G. Glasgow, *The Black Underclass* (San Francisco: Jossey Bass, 1980); Ken Auletta, *The Underclass* (New York: Random House, 1982); and William J. Wilson again in *The Truly Disadvantaged* (Chicago: University of Chicago Press, 1987).

7. For a survey of these definitions, see Robert Aponte, "Definitions of the Underclass: A Critical Analysis," in Herbert J. Gans, ed., *Sociology in America* (Newbury Park, Calif.: Sage Publications, 1990), ch. 8.

8. The best and most graphic statement is by Isabel V. Sawhill, "The Underclass: An Overview," *The Public Interest* (Summer 1989), no. 96:3–15.

9. Unmarried mothers, and others violating family and sexual norms are thought dangerous because they are questioning the officially dominant sexual morality. On

this aspect of the traditional American conception of undeservingness, see Michael Katz, *The Undeserving Poor: From the War on Poverty to the War on Welfare* (New York: Pantheon Books, 1989), p. 185.

10. Edward Banfield's critique of the urban poor, *The Unheavenly City* (Boston: Little, Brown 1970), was dominated by his charge that they were "present-oriented."

11. The classic analysis is Erol R. Ricketts and Isabel V. Sawhill, "Defining and Measuring the Underclass," Washington: The Urban Institute, December 1986 (Revised).

12. For a thoughtful critique, see David T. Ellwood. *Poor Support: Poverty in the American Family* (New York: Basic Books, 1988), pp. 192–193.

13. As pointed out in note 6, Wilson already wrote about the underclass in his *Declining Significance of Race* but it became controversial for other reasons, and the argument about the underclass has swirled around his second book.

14. William J. Wilson, "Social Research and the Underclass Debate," paper given at the SSRC conference on the Truly Disadvantaged, Evanston, Ill., October 1989. After this book went to press, Wilson suggested that he may abandon use of the term "underclass" altogether. In his presidential address to the American Sociological Association, entitled "Social Theory and Public Agenda Research," and given on August 12, 1990, he replaced "underclass" with "ghetto poverty."

15. Some black scholars favor using the term nevertheless, largely because they feel it calls attention to the high amount of persistent poverty among blacks.

16. William Kornblum, "Lumping the Poor: What *Is* the Underclass?" *Dissent* (September 1984), pp. 295–302.

17. Karen Wilkinson, "The Broken Family and Juvenile Delinquency," *Social Problems* (June 1974), 21:726–739.

18. Robert L. Lineberry. *Equality and Urban Policy: The Distribution of Municipal Services* (Beverly Hills, Calif.: Sage Publications, 1977).

19. Agnew's proposal was quickly rejected, but the United States has a tradition of using the countryside to banish, punish, and also rehabilitate various kinds of people who carry out antisocial and deviant acts.

20. William J. Wilson is a strong supporter of economic, "race-blind," policies. See *Declining Significance of Race*. For an equally fervent advocacy of "racial" policies, see Stephen Steinberg, "The Underclass: A Case of Color Blindness," *Politics* (New Series) (Summer 1989), 2:42–60.

21. Gunner Myrdal, et al., *An American Dilemma: The Negro Problem and Modern Democracy* (New York: Harper & Row, 1944), p. 78.

22. See, e.g., Joleen Kirschenman and Kathryn Neckerman, "We'd Love to Hire Them, But . . . : The Meaning of Race for Employers," in Christopher Jencks and Paul Peterson, eds., *The Urban Underclass* (Washington, D.C.: Brookings Institution, 1991); and Bruce Williams, *Black Workers in an Industrial Suburb* (New Brunswick, N.J.: Rutgers University Press, 1987). For a defense of the hypothesis, see John D. Kasarda, "Jobs, Migration, and Emerging Urban Mismatches," in Michael G. H. McGeary and Laurence E. Lynn, Jr., eds., *Urban Change and Poverty* (Washington D.C.: National Academy Press, 1988), pp. 148–198. A more general critique of the mismatch notion is by Norman Fainstein, "The Underclass/Mismatch Hypothesis as an Explanation for Black Economic Deprivation," *Politics and Society* (1986), 5, 6:403–451.

23. For some other recent analyses that reject the underclass concept see Katz, *The Undeserving Poor*, ch. 5; Thomas D. Cook and Thomas R. Curtin, "The

Mainstream and the Underclass: Why Are the Differences So Salient and the Similarities So Unobtrusive," in J. C. Masters and W. P. Smith, *Social Comparison, Social Justice, and Relative Deprivation* (Hillsdale, N.J.: Erlbaum Associates, 1987), pp. 218–263; and Richard McGahey, "The Underclass Label and Social Policy," *USA Today,* September 1983, pp. 22–24.

24. W. Lloyd Warner and Paul S. Lunt, *The Social Life of a Modern Community* (New Haven: Yale University Press, 1941), pp. 447–450 and passim.

· I N D E X ·

Abandonment, of inexpensive housing, 214-17, 360*n*20
Abortion, 295, 296
Academic research, policy design and, 173-86; *see also* Social sciences
Acculturation, 53, 55, 309, 321
Activism, and planning, xii, 10, 21, 148, 168
Advocate planning, 139
Aesthetics, 9, 13, 14; *see also* High culture
Affordable housing, 217, 224
African-American, as ethnic concept, x; 275; *see also* Blacks; Race
Agnew, Spiro T., 335
Agriculture, 250, 267
Ancient cities, 99, 105
Anthropology, and antipoverty research, 301, 304, 306, 307
Antipoverty policy: affluent society and, 321-22; antipoverty research and, 320-23; black family structure and, 292-93; city planning and, 135; ecology and, 84; economic and race-specific policies compared, 273-74; edu-

cation and, 190, 225-43; equality and, 294, 303; functional analysis, 268-70; homelessness and, 223; housing quality and, 24; job creation and, 242; job policy and, 232-33; judging the poor and, 302-3; planner-client relationships, 137; planning failures, 40-41; private enterprise and, 40-41, 43; slum clearance and, 148; underclass and, 333, 335-43; urban design and, 4; *see also* Escaping from poverty; Poverty; War on Poverty
Antipoverty research: antipoverty policy and, 320-23; black family and, 293, 298; culture and, 310-14; escaping from poverty and, 320-22; history of, 300; proposals for, 216-17, 341; researchers, class and, 299; single parent family and, 318-20; social experiments for, 322-23; underclass neighborhoods and, 337-38; William J. Wilson and, 331-32
Architecture: class and, 18; educational implications, 22; ethnicity and, 10; functionalism in, 13, 14, 23; high cul-